THE **!**

UNION AND
REVOLUTIONARY
WARFARE

—

THE **SOVIET UNION** AND **REVOLUTIONARY WARFARE**

—

PRINCIPLES, PRACTICES, AND REGIONAL COMPARISONS

Richard H. Shultz, Jr.

HOOVER INSTITUTION PRESS

Stanford University   Stanford, California

Hoover Press Publication 371

First printing, 1988
Manufactured in the United States of America
94 93 92 91 90 89 88   9 8 7 6 5 4 3 2 1

Library of Congress Cataloging in Publication Data
Shultz, Richard, H., 1947–
    The Soviet Union and revolutionary warfare : principles,
practices, and regional comparisons / Richard H. Shultz, Jr.
        p.   cm.   —   (Hoover Press publication ; 371)
    Bibliography: p.
    Includes index.
    ISBN 0-8179-8711-8.   ISBN 0-8179-8712-6 (pbk.)
    1. Soviet Union—Military policy. 2. Revolutions—History—
20th century. 3. Military history, Modern—20th century. I. title.
UA770.S514 1988   88-4536
355'.02184'0947—dc19   CIP

Contents

Foreword

Sun Tzu identified the fundamentals of protracted revolutionary war about 500 B.C. His basic precepts were elusiveness and unpredictability, which, skillfully applied, permit inferior forces to prevail against superior foes that specialize in set-piece battles. When strong, seem weak, he advised. Feign weariness when refreshed. Concentrate power against opponents when least expected where they are least prepared and allow little surcease until fatigue and frustration cause them to collapse.

Mao Zedong put those ancient theories into practice on a grand scale in China, his home territory, 24 centuries later. He synthesized Sun Tzu in four slogans that stand the test of time:

— When adversaries advance, retreat
— When they halt, harass
— When they are hurt, advance
— When they retreat, pursue

A few years later Soviet strategists turned revolutionary war into an art form in foreign countries. They launched relatively low cost, low risk, potentially high payoff operations that minimize direct Soviet participation by employing proxies. This survey by Richard H. Shultz, Jr. traces trends since World War II that show how Soviet-sponsored and/or -supported insurgencies have integrated political, economic, military, social, and psychological instruments into strategies and tactics. Four case studies of Soviet involvement with revolutionary movements in Vietnam, the Middle East, Angola/Namibia, and Central America reveal a spotty track record, replete with strengths and weaknesses, successes and failures, similarities and differences. Shultz illuminates lessons learned, predicts probable courses of future Soviet action in this fertile field, and postulates consequent problems for U.S. defense planners.

The product is particularly timely because most authorities agree that low-intensity conflicts, mainly revolutionary wars, will pose the most serious threats to U.S. national security into the twenty-first century. Assorted tendencies support their contention; population explosions in the Third World, where poverty already is endemic, are among those most often mentioned. Gaps almost surely will widen between popular expectations and the ability of governments to feed, clothe, house, educate, and gainfully employ impatient teenagers, who are about to become a majority in many afflicted states. The climate is ripe for revolution that cynical outsiders could maliciously exploit.

Secretary of State George P. Shultz (no relation to Richard) warned the World Affairs Council of Washington in that regard on December 4, 1987. His words are worth remembering:

> Wars in the Third World are being fought with increasing sophistication and firepower. The spread of modern technical skill coincides with the modern resurgence of age-old ethnic, religious, and communal conflict. [Instances include] fighting in Sri Lanka, ethnic conflict in Fiji, the devastation of Lebanon . . . the New Caledonia and Cyprus disputes, the continuing Arab-Israeli conflict.
>
> . . . Violence itself is undergoing a qualitative change, as terrorists and narcotics traffickers spread new forms of destruction around the world. We now recognize the long, tough battle we are fighting with these modern-day barbarians, equipped with effective weaponry and uninhibited by traditional norms of civilized conduct.

Dr. Shultz's qualifications to write a comparative analysis of *The Soviet Union and Revolutionary Warfare* are unquestioned. He is a widely recognized writer on that subject, installed as the only non–Department of Defense member of the Pentagon's Special Operations Advisory Group. The remainder are retired generals, most with three or four stars. Thorough research, thoughtful assessments, and extensive documentation make this book valuable to policymakers, practitioners, news commentators, members of the academic community, and concerned citizens everywhere.

John M. Collins
Senior Defense Specialist
Library of Congress

Preface

During 1984 I had the opportunity to participate in the Soviet Strategy Project of the Hoover Institution on War, Revolution and Peace. A major focus of the project is to examine whether, and if so to what extent, the Soviet Union employs the military and nonmilitary capabilities of allies and surrogates to achieve its foreign policy and national security objectives. I wish to thank Paul Seabury both for bringing my interest in the subject to the attention of Dennis Bark, the director of the Hoover project, as well as for nominating me to take part in the project's ongoing work. Out of this experience and with the encouragement of Dr. Bark, I proposed and received a research fellowship from the Hoover Institution to undertake a study of Soviet policy, strategy, and capability for assisting revolutionary insurgent movements in various parts of the developing world since the late 1960s. This book is the result of that research and analysis. I am most grateful to Dr. Bark for all his advice and support. Additionally, once the manuscript was in draft form, Richard F. Staar of Hoover reviewed the study and helped move it to the publication stage.

I would like to express my deep appreciation to those colleagues and associates who either provided advice during the research phase of the project or commented on the entire manuscript or different parts of it. A special and warm note of appreciation is due to Uri Ra'anan, who strongly encouraged me to undertake the study and then freely gave help and advice along the way. I would also like to express my appreciation to John Collins, John Dziak, Roy Godson, Igor Lukes, and Robert L. Pfaltzgraff, Jr. During the research and writing of the manuscript I had the good fortune to have the aid of a number of talented graduate student assistants, including Steve Adragna, Andy Burton, Walter Levin, Mike Metcalf, Randy Scheunemann, John Springer, and Yaacov Tygiel, all of whom contributed in ways too varied to enumerate. I am also extremely indebted to Freda Kilgallen, administrative assistant of the International Security Studies Program of the Fletcher School of Law and Diplomacy, for her help and patience. Finally, Ann Wood of the Hoover Institution Press provided outstanding editorial advice and assistance.

Conditions of Revolutionary Warfare

FOCUS AND APPROACH

Over the last four decades the developing world has been the scene of extensive turbulence and instability, including revolutionary warfare, insurgency, rebellion, coup d'état, and state-to-state confrontations. The pressures and challenges underlying this violence have been the result of crises of legitimacy, sectarian disputes, redistribution of power, secessionist pressures, regional conflicts, and East-West competition. An early study of conflict in the Third World by Harry Eckstein categorized many of these forms of violence under the rubric of "internal war." This included "revolution, civil war, revolt, rebellion, uprising, guerrilla warfare, mutiny, jacquerie, coup d'état and insurrection."[1] Thus, for Eckstein, internal war "stands for the genus of which the others are species."[2] Over the past twenty years other students of these conflicts have referred to them as irregular or unconventional warfare.[3] They are currently being characterized, in the lexicon of the U.S. national security community, as low-intensity conflicts.[4] There is, however, no agreement over the parameters of low-intensity conflict or the degree to which its various forms threaten U.S. interests in the Third World. We will return to the latter issue and its policy implications in the concluding chapter of this study.

Although internal war, or low-intensity conflict, involves a host of different types of political-military strife, perhaps its most complex and often misunderstood manifestation is that of revolutionary warfare, or what the Soviet Union terms "wars of national liberation." This will be the subject of the following study.

The Post–World War II Experience

The American national security community has frequently misunderstood the concept of revolutionary warfare. This was true in the 1960s as the United States ensconced itself in the Vietnam War, and it remains the case in the 1980s.[5] Revolutionary warfare has often been equated with irregular military tactics, which may be elements of this protracted strategy but are not synonymous with it. Consequently, guerrilla warfare and revolutionary warfare are used interchangeably. This reveals the degree to which misunderstanding has occurred.

Guerrilla tactics have been employed throughout history. The roots of this form of combat can be traced to ancient times. A number of studies have documented these developments, including the comprehensive work by Robert Asprey, *War in the Shadows: The Guerrilla in History*.[6] In the first volume of this two-volume tour de force, Asprey describes how guerrillas hindered Alexander the Great during his campaign in Persia. He likewise notes the degree to which guerrillas plagued both Hannibal during his epic march from Spain to northern Italy and the Roman army in its pacification of Spain. In each of these instances, irregular and predominantly indigenous forces carried out paramilitary operations in enemy-held or hostile territory. None of these efforts, however, can be characterized as equivalent to revolutionary warfare.

The military history of the United States also is dotted with involvement in guerrilla conflicts. This was true during the War of Independence as well as in the Civil War. Additionally, throughout most of the nineteenth century, the U.S. Army conducted counterguerrilla operations against various Native American tribes. At the turn of the century it faced guerrilla challenges in the Philippines and Mexico. In World War II, guerrilla forces were organized in the Philippines and provided General MacArthur with invaluable assistance in the retaking of the island. Similarly, in 1943 the Office of Strategic Services trained and organized the Kachin tribe of northern Burma into guerrilla units, and U.S. officers led them in operations against the Japanese. After World War II, U.S. advisers assisted the Greek army in defeating a communist guerrilla movement. Finally, during the Korean War special operations forces were employed and gained permanent status within the U.S. military. These historical and contemporary U.S. experiences with irregular combat are not analogous with revolutionary warfare.

This raises the question of why guerrilla warfare, or the related concepts of jungle, irregular, partisan, and unconventional warfare, is not synonymous with revolutionary warfare. The answer lies outside of the military tactics adopted. Revolutionary warfare strategy employs ancient military tactics in conjunction with political and psychological techniques to transfer governmental power as a prelude to the transformation of the social structure. The objective is to impose a new regime on the society through a protracted conflict strategy. Herein lies the difference between revolutionary warfare and other forms of irregular or guerrilla combat.

Revolutionary warfare strategists combine unconventional military tactics with political and psychological operations to establish a competing political and ideological structure. This form of protracted conflict is principally a post–World War II phenomenon, the roots of which can be traced to the strategy developed by the Chinese communists during the 1930s.[7] Its practitioners frequently refer to it as "People's War."[8]

In the West, the French were among the first to grasp the meaning of revolutionary warfare and to articulate a counterstrategy. Many of the French originators of this counterstrategy had served in Indochina where, according to Bernard Fall, "they learned their Mao Tse-tung the hard way."[9] His remarks are contained in the preface to Roger Trinquier's *Modern Warfare*, perhaps the most succinct statement by a French officer about this form of conflict.[10] Another French military analyst, Colonel Georges Bonnet, advanced the following equation to describe revolutionary warfare:[11]

$$RW = G + P$$

(Revolutionary Warfare) (Guerrilla Tactics) (Political and Psychological Activities)

Bonnet and other French officers concluded that in revolutionary warfare the military tactics of the guerrilla are secondary to the central strategic objectives that are achieved through political and psychological means.[12] The principal goal is to destroy the legitimacy of the target government through the establishment of a counterideology and counterinstitutions. Thus, for the French officers, it was the objectives sought, and the central importance placed on political warfare and psychological operations in achieving them, that differentiated revolutionary warfare from other forms of irregular combat.

The British specialist, Sir Robert Thompson, drew conclusions quite similar to his French counterparts. He observed that "in revolutionary war the aim is always political . . .[T]he revolutionary party seeks to gain control over the population first before it can defeat the opposing military forces."[13] Thompson is perhaps the best known of a number of British specialists who understood the strategy of revolutionary warfare as it was employed during the years immediately following World War II.[14] There were also a handful of U.S. specialists who drew similar conclusions, most notably George Tanham, Edward Lansdale, Douglas Pike, Bernard Fall, William Yarborough, and Richard Stilwell.[15]

Drawing on theoretical literature and on the practical application of revolutionary warfare, we can identify a number of general tenets that underlie this strategy. Although differences exist among both theorists and practitioners, the generalizations described below constitute, in my judgment, the central characteristics of this form of protracted conflict.

Revolutionary warfare involves the use of an illegal political organization and, until its final stages, irregular military forces. It is a protracted political-military activity. The instruments of revolutionary warfare include propaganda, psychological operations, political mobilization, establishment of a shadow government or infrastructure organization, guerrilla tactics, terrorism, and mobile conventional combat.

The doctrinal literature, as well as the post–World War II experience, discloses the critical role assigned to political and psychological measures. These instruments of revolutionary warfare are aimed at both the indigenous population and the groups, states, and organizations in the international arena. As a result of the imbalance of forces during the initial stage of an insurgency, stress is placed on the primacy of propaganda, psychological warfare, and political action. Through these activities the insurgent leadership hopes to advance to a point where it may seriously challenge state power. In light of this requirement, the vanguard party concentrates on the formation of a competing or counter-ideology. This does not call for the redressing of particular problems but instead challenges the regime's basic legitimacy and right to govern. Ideology contains guidance and justification for revolutionary war.

Although the leaders of movements employing this strategy have generally followed a variation of Marxism-Leninism, the ideology they have formulated has blended the idealistic elements of communism with attention to the resolution of indigenous economic, social, and political inequalities. In communicating this ideology, the insurgents and those states that support them will focus their propaganda and political action tactics on both indigenous targets and actors in regional and international arenas.

A second and related element of revolutionary warfare strategy is mass mobilization. To accomplish this, insurgent movements and their state patrons employ a host of programs and communications techniques. For example, within the vanguard party structure, one of its major committees has responsibility for proselytizing. The objectives are threefold: attract elements of the population, attack the enemy through psychological warfare, and utilize indoctrination measures to maintain allegiance. A related set of objectives are sought in the international arena.

The practitioners of revolutionary warfare stress the importance of what might be termed positive psychological operations to mobilize indigenous support (described above), but they also employ negative incentives. For example, if that portion of the population inclined to support the government can be intimidated into remaining neutral, this is a victory for the insurgents. To accomplish this, various tactics may be utilized, ranging from threats to the use of terrorism. These techniques are part of the psychological weaponry employed by many insurgents in protracted revolutionary war.

The instruments described above are part of a larger objective: the establishment of a political-military infrastructure or organization. The classical statement on this can be found in Lenin's 1902 pamphlet, *What Is to Be Done?*. The adaptation of Lenin to the strategy of revolutionary warfare resulted in an expansion of the size of the overall revolutionary organization. This is especially true of the hierarchy of mass organizations controlled by a vanguard party. The hierarchy becomes part of a political structure, controlled by the vanguard party, that serves as a shadow government. In the regional and international arenas, this shadow government seeks to become recognized as the legitimate alternative to the existing regime. Many of the themes and political messages of the insurgent psychological operations advanced internally are likewise amplified internationally by this organization and its state supporters.

In sum, ideological thrust, organizational form, and programmatic content are all part of political and psychological operations that have as their objective the creation of an image or perception, both internally and internationally, of the insurgent movement as the legitimate alternative to the regime in power. It should be noted that the relationship between the reforms and political freedoms articulated in the insurgent ideology before assuming power and what takes place during the postrevolutionary consolidation of control is a tenuous one. Frequently, the programmatic aspects of insurgent ideology are not implemented once state power is seized.[16]

The final two general characteristics of this strategy include military-paramilitary tactics and the acquisition of external assistance. For the former, insurgents rely on the hit-and-run operations of guerrilla warfare. As suggested above, terrorist tactics may also be directed against government officials and those elements of the population inclined to support them. Other forms of irregular combat (including sabotage and kidnapping) are also utilized during the initial stages of the conflict. Larger unit conventional tactics are added to these irregular actions as the insurgency grows.

The question of whether and to what degree foreign or external support constitutes an important factor in the development of an insurgent movement has been a controversial issue. Those who have utilized this strategy downplay its significance. However, a review of the last two decades reveals that outside support and assistance to revolutionary insurgent movements have increasingly become of more consequence. Further, as the next section will demonstrate, the issue of outside assistance and the degree to which it contributes to the growth of an insurgency have not been adequately addressed in the relevant scholarly and analytic literature.

Internal-External Nexus

Over the past 25 years, the volume of literature analyzing internal conflict in different regions of the Third World has grown to immense proportions. Generally, this can be divided into two categories: studies of the various forms of internal political violence and/or war, and research focused on the process of modernization and development (and the instability and violence that frequently ensues). This study is concerned with the literature on internal political violence.

The subject has been approached on two levels: first, an analysis of the causes of internal war, and second, an examination of the strategy and tactics employed by various factions and movements involved in these protracted conflicts. In the case of the former, one recent comprehensive examination of research conducted over the past two decades has concluded that "the literature provides many theoretical suggestions as to the causes of revolutions yet hardly a body of systematically derived theory." The author goes on to note that "nevertheless, on the basis of theoretical analyses some vague 'uniformities' were found."[17] The conclusions of another recent assessment are even less certain: "[D]espite a voluminous literature . . . the explanatory power of the postulated theories remains low and the predictive power virtually nonexistent."[18]

The inability to develop a more rigorous theory that explains the causes of internal war is a serious, albeit understandable (in light of the complexity and regional ideosyncracies of these conflicts), social science problem; however, there are additional flaws in the literature. Specifically, over the past two decades, studies purporting to identify the causes of internal political violence in the Third World have emphasized the importance of indigenous factors. Although certain external causes are identified, as I will note below, what tends to be overlooked is the degree to which other states can contribute to the growth and expansion of an insurgent movement. A brief review of the literature will document the lack of attention to, and understanding of, the role of outside or external forces (mainly states) in promoting and facilitating the growth of revolutionary insurgent movements.

According to one student of revolution, this form of internal war "does not occur haphazardly or purely spontaneously." Its conditions or causes "consist of an array of observable economic, political-social, and psychological changes or occurrences."[19] Attempts to identify and elaborate these causes or conditions have been undertaken by many scholars and policy analysts. As we shall see below, the result has been a diversity of explanations and findings.

Growing interest in the study of revolution and insurgency began during the 1960s. Many of those who undertook this research sought to develop explicit causal explanations of why, when, and how such situations unfold. These studies relied heavily on a large body of social behavior theory drawn from economics, political science, psychology, and sociology.[20] One can divide this analysis into somewhat discrete categories, depending on the theoretical assumptions tested.[21]

For example, Ted Robert Gurr, James Davies, and Ivo and Rosalind Feierabend, to name the most prominent, based their analyses on the cognitive psychological theory of frustration-aggression. Gurr extends this hypothesis to the realm of political conflict to answer the question "why do men rebel?" He asserts that in the realm of internal war, a relationship exists between relative deprivation and political violence. He defines the former as a perception of a discrepancy between value expectations (or aspirations) and capabilities (or achievements). Revolution is a state of mind that grows out of an increase in frustration.[22]

Those scholars who adopt the frustration-aggression thesis differ over the source of frustration or relative deprivation. The Feierabends, for instance, argue that internal political violence results from the modernization process. They postulate that the peak discrepancy between systemic goals and their satisfaction comes somewhere in the middle of the transition phase between traditional society and the achievement of modernity. It is in this middle stage that awareness of modernity should be complete but achievement levels still lag behind.[23]

Raymond Tanter and Manus Midlarsky, in contrast, focus on the economic variables. Internal political violence is most likely to occur when a prolonged period of economic prosperity is followed by a period of sharp reversal. This results, according to their analysis, in the creation of an unacceptable gap between aspirations and actual achievements. "The higher the rate of increase of GNP preceding the revolution and the sharper the reversal immediately prior to the revolution, the greater the duration and violence of the revolution."[24] This holds true for Asian and Middle Eastern countries, but they find a different development in Latin America. There the economic presence of the United States has an impact on the degree of economic development which, in turn, influences the likelihood of revolution.[25] In many ways, the work of Davies parallels that of Tanter and Midlarsky.[26]

Finally, Gurr presents a more complicated theory in which the underlying causes of internal war—the systematic closure of political and/or economic opportunities—are mediated by a number of intervening factors.[27] In sum, for this group of specialists the causes of revolution result generally from widespread frustration with the internal political-economic milieu. Of course, external forces can affect this milieu. However, these principally involve the same external forces identified by Tanter and Midlarsky.

A second group of specialists associate the causes of internal war with pluralist and interest-group conflict theory. For instance, Samuel Huntington argues that "it is most likely to occur in societies . . . where the processes of political modernization and political development have lagged behind the processes of social and economic change."[28] Thus, although the process of mobilization may lead to the entrance of new groups into the political arena, the existing political structure may not allow for the realization of their goals or aspirations. There-fore, revolution is treated as an extreme form of political competition, one in which normal forms of conflict resolution prove ineffective. In a similar manner, Charles Tilly asserts that revolution depends on "four proximate conditions: (1) the emergence of coalitions of contenders making exclusive alternative claims to control of the government; (2) the expansion of commitment to those claims by members of the population; (3) the formation of coalitions between members of the polity and members of the revolutionary bloc; (4) repressive incapacity of the government's agents."[29]

Taking a somewhat different although related approach to Huntington and Tilly, Bard O'Neill attempts to use the general concept of legitimacy to explain internal violence and war. Legitimacy "refers to whether or not existing aspects of politics are considered moral or immoral . . . by the population or selected elements therein."[30] The extent to which this occurs will, in turn, shape the degree of political violence directed against the regime. Note that those employ-ing interest-group conflict theory generally focus on internal causes.

The explanations above focus on one or a few variables. Other students of revolution base their assessment on the broader sociological theory of structural-functionalism. They approach society as a system whose proper functioning re-quires the maintenance of an equilibrium in the flow of demands and resources between the system and its environment and between the various subsystems that make up the social system. These subsystems include politics, culture, and economy. Disruption in the equilibrium between demands and resources leaves a society open for internal political violence. The most prominent scholars who have adopted this approach include Chalmers Johnson, Neil Smelser, Robert Jessop and Mark Hagopian.[31] Although they agree on the basic thesis stated above, they disagree about the causes of disequilibrium. Hagopian presents per-haps the most comprehensive range of causes. He suggests that disequilibrium "is produced by a multiplicity of interdependent causes," which may be placed in the "well-established formula" of long-term causes (conditions occurring be-tween a decade and century before the revolution, including economic growth, scientific advance, secularization, and nationalism), middle-term causes (con-ditions emerging in the decade prior to internal war, including economic depres-sion, alienation, ruler ineptness, and war), and precipitant causes (planned or accidental events resulting in an immediate drastic reaction, including riots, strikes, assassinations, and attempted coups).[32] While emphasizing internal fac-tors, Hagopian asserts that disequilibrium between the social system and international environment, principally resulting from war and economic crisis, may also be a cause of internal political violence.

Although each category of specialists identified above suggests that a range of societal groups or factions may become involved in revolutionary violence, a great deal of attention has been focused on the structure of peasant communities. However, disagreement exists over how to define a peasant and which portion of the peasantry is more likely to revolt. Eric Wolf's theoretical outline is among the most prominent.[33] He argues that "there are only two components of the peasantry which possess sufficient internal leverage to enter into sustained rebellion. These are (a) a landowning 'middle peasantry' or (b) a peasantry located in a peripheral area outside the domains of landlord control."[34] For middle peasants to revolt a number of conditions must be met. One is the impact of modernization, the other is the strength of existing traditional ties and organizations. Jeffrey Paige proposes a more complicated theory of agrarian revolution that rests on a number of highly complicated interaction terms. These include the size and type of income various classes receive, which depend on the agricultural products raised, and the social and political organization of the sphere of production.[35] In addition to peasants, other analysts have focused on workers, students, intellectuals, or a combination of these social forces.[36]

The objective of this brief review has been to demonstrate that, although there exists a rich and diverse body of literature seeking to explain the preconditions of internal political conflict in the Third World, much of this analysis has focused on indigenous factors. Thus, from a causal point of view the presence or absence of this form of conflict is seen as the result of forces and developments that lie within the society and not outside of it. This does not mean that the literature reviewed above ignores the role of outside forces. As I noted, some scholars do recognize the possible intrusion of international political and economic pressures on regimes undergoing a revolutionary crisis. They argue that as states are increasingly drawn into international economic and military competition (including war), this may have a negative impact on domestic politics, contributing to the outbreak of internal violence.[37] However, the impact of external support as a precondition for the growth and expansion of revolutionary forces is not seriously contemplated.

When we move from preconditions or causes to the strategies of insurgency and revolutionary warfare, O'Neill, among others, views external support as a tactical element that insurgents may or may not incorporate into their overall strategy. Although it may play an ancillary role in a successful insurgency, external support is not seen as a condition that might serve to promote and facilitate the process itself.[38] Others who have focused on the relationship between preconditions and insurgent strategy, including Mostafa Rejai and Thomas Greene, come to similar conclusions.[39]

To summarize, it would seem appropriate to conclude that, although students of revolution and internal war see the underlying causes of this form of conflict as resulting from internal and external factors (with much greater emphasis placed on the former), one specific kind of external influence—the contribution of states in promoting and facilitating the growth of such conflict—has been overlooked. To borrow from Hagopian, the external support by foreign governments of revolutionary insurgent movements has not been viewed or understood as a middle-term cause or precondition. One of the central assertions of this study is that over the past fifteen years, while the basic or initial causes of internal war remain predominantly due to indigenous developments, an important factor contributing to the growth of insurgent movements is the presence and activities of external forces. A closer look at the strategy and policies of the USSR and its allies and surrogates over the past decade will bear this out. Since the early 1970s, as the ensuing chapters of this study will demonstrate, the Soviet Union has significantly accelerated its involvement in revolutionary warfare or, in their terminology, wars of national liberation in the Third World. This has had an important impact on the ability of revolutionary insurgent movements, who have been recipients of this assistance, to attain legitimacy and carry out operations.

Attempting to identify the reasons for this oversight in the literature on revolution and internal war is, in many respects, more difficult than documenting the growing importance of external support and assistance for movements and factions conducting revolutionary warfare. Nevertheless, there are at least two explanations. First, it has only been since the late 1960s and early 1970s that the contribution of outside forces (principally the USSR and its allies and surrogates) began to be of greater significance, although by the end of the 1970s this contribution was more apparent. However, it is not unusual for a scholarly discipline to adopt paradigms that are not easily revised.[40] This may be the case here and may also be true, to a somewhat lesser degree, of more traditional area specialists. Like those who approach the study of internal war and revolution in a more generalized and analytic manner, as noted above, area or regional specialists have been inclined to view this form of conflict as a result of indigenous developments.

A second reason for the lack of attention to external forces may be a reaction to the inclination of U.S. policymakers during the 1950s and 1960s to overemphasize the role of the communist bloc in Third World conflict. Thus more current analysis may be, in part, an overreaction to this earlier assessment. Consequently, as Soviet-bloc involvement in Third World internal wars grew in the 1970s, analyses of the causes of this conflict have emphasized the importance of indigenous factors. In reality, as the cases examined in this study will demonstrate, in most instances neither internal nor external factors should be overlooked.

Focus and Approach

The focus of this study will be on the evolution of Soviet support for revolutionary warfare, or what they term wars of national liberation in the Third World. Although theoretically a part of Soviet foreign policy since the early years of the Communist Party of the Soviet Union (CPSU) rule, it was only in the late 1960s and early 1970s that the Kremlin leadership began to increase its involvement significantly in these conflicts. This has continued into the 1980s. Various studies have surveyed Soviet policy in the Third World during the period, including involvement in revolutionary warfare, but none have attempted to assess analytically and comparatively how the USSR integrates and employs various political and military instruments as part of its strategy to affect the course of insurgent conflicts.

Specifically, this study will employ a comparative case-study approach to address the following set of questions: How does the USSR determine whether, and to what extent, to support a national liberation movement? Once a decision is made to increase support, what instruments of statecraft are adopted to assist these movements? How do the capabilities of allies and surrogates augment Moscow's involvement in these conflicts? Does the USSR approach each situation in a uniform way or do situational and regional factors modify its strategy? What comparative generalizations can be drawn about the Soviet policy of supporting revolutionary movements in the Third World? Finally, on the basis of the answers to these questions, what course will the USSR follow in the future and what will the implications of this be for U.S. foreign and national security policy?

The evolution of Soviet policy as it concerns revolutionary insurgent movements is reviewed in Chapter 2, with particular attention to the years surrounding the Twenty-fourth CPSU Congress in 1971. Soviet political and military commentary from that period is examined to assess how the USSR viewed revolutionary warfare and the degree to which Moscow was willing to provide assistance to movements and factions employing this strategy. The rationale and underlying international political and military developments that influenced this new course in Soviet Third World policy are likewise addressed. The chapter concludes with an identification of the political and military instruments of policy employed by Moscow to assist revolutionary insurgent movements. This includes the related capabilities of Soviet allies and surrogates.

Chapter 2 thus sets the course for a comparative analysis of how the USSR implemented this political-military strategy in support of its policy in four specific regional cases since the early 1970s. The comparative approach adopted to conduct this assessment is that which Alexander George and Richard Smoke have termed "focused comparison."[41] This method examines multiple cases to establish results by making comparisons among them. It proceeds by addressing a select number of questions or hypotheses, all of which are interrelated. Each case is investigated in depth and, by addressing the same questions or hypotheses, comparability is ensured. Thus, this methodological approach allows the investigator to identify, in a systematic and analytic manner, both generalizations and differences in the cases examined. Analysis of differences, as well as common patterns, allows us to determine the complexity and flexibility of those aspects of Soviet policy and strategy examined in this study.

The cases examined include movements that have adopted revolutionary warfare strategies in Southeast Asia, the Middle East, southern Africa, and Central America (Chapters 3–6, respectively). In each instance the objective will be to identify trends and patterns in Soviet policy and strategy, including the use of the capabilities of allies and surrogates. An additional objective will be to determine the extent to which these political and military techniques coincide in terms of coordination and implementation. Does an increase in one or more signal an increase in others?

In Chapter 7, comparative generalizations and differences from the four case studies will be identified. The objective will be to specify trends in strategy, tactics, and methods as well as policy objectives. This will be followed by an estimation of future trends in this and related aspects of Soviet policy in the Third World. Finally, the implications of these developments for U.S. foreign and national security policy will be addressed in the final chapter of the study.

The Evolution of Soviet Policy, Strategy, and Organization

Since the second half of the 1950s, Soviet involvement in the Third World has been the subject of considerable research and commentary.[1] What emerges from a review of this literature is the conclusion that, in a broad sense, there has been no consistent or one-dimensional policy and program. For example, a recent major study on the subject—prepared by the Congressional Research Service for the Committee on Foreign Relations of the U.S. House of Representatives—states

> Beyond the most generalized declarations (e.g., support for national liberation movements), Soviet policy-makers have not developed a single uniform policy toward the less developed countries (LDCs). Rather, they have continued increasingly to diversify their policies and actions . . . The invasion of Afghanistan added a new dimension to Soviet policy, contributing still further to its diversity.[2]

The lack of a uniform Soviet policy has been the case even though Moscow's interest in Third World states—both as potential revolutionary allies and as places in which to extend Soviet state interest—dates back to the early years of CPSU rule. Alvin Rubinstein argues that, although the LDCs "have long occupied an important place in Soviet ideological formulations and long-term projections," Moscow's pursuit of these objectives intensified only with its "emergence . . . as a superpower." This was "marked by a shift from a continental-based strategy to a global one."[3] It was during the 1960s, according to Rubinstein, that this change took place. Stephen Hosmer and Thomas Wolfe, in their study of Soviet involvement in Third World conflicts, likewise detect different policies and approaches during the post–World War II period.[4] Perhaps Daniel Papp most accurately sums up these developments in the following terms:

> [T]he evolution of Soviet perceptions of the developing world to 1980 has amply illustrated [that] even the constraints imposed by the Soviet version of Marxist-Leninist orthodoxy have permitted diverse and competing outlooks of the developing world to exist in the past . . . Soviet perceptions of the developing world during the 1980s are, thus, the end products, at least for now, of a continuing process.[5]

If a consensus exists over general trends in Soviet–Third World relations, disagreement persists over both the objectives pursued and the degree of success or failure. Although most analysts would agree that these objectives include ideological, political, geostrategic, and economic dimensions, there is divergence over the degree to which each influences policy.[6] Nevertheless, a composite of these factors appears to have contributed to a policy of globalism since the 1960s.[7]

In pursuit of these objectives, the Soviet Union has conducted a dual foreign policy in the Third World. On the one hand, it has sought normalized relations with the LDCs. On the other hand, Moscow has been involved in the promotion of conflict and revolution.[8] Each of these consists, in turn, of specific variations. For example, the way in which the Soviets have defined the nature of a specific state has influenced the parameters of their relations with it. During the 1960s, a country referred to as a revolutionary democracy was considered more eligible for assistance than other developing countries. The reason for this was the belief that such regimes were in a period of transition in which far-reaching social change would create the preconditions for socialism. Additionally, these states frequently maintained close economic and cultural ties with the Soviet bloc and pursued a pro-Moscow foreign policy. Aid to Egypt, Algeria, and Ghana was justified on these grounds. When the number of revolutionary democracies increased as the 1960s turned into the 1970s, special importance was attached to Afghanistan, Angola, Ethiopia, Mozambique, and South Yemen. These states, which were offered Soviet friendship treaties, established one-party systems modeled on Marxism-Leninism and committed themselves to build a society based on scientific socialism. Distinctions between revolutionary democracies have affected the contours of Soviet policy. As we shall see in later chapters, the Soviets did, at one point in the late 1960s and early 1970s, differentiate among military regimes in the Third World. Those designated as progressive were candidates for Soviet economic and military assistance.

In addition to conducting relations with ruling groups on a state-to-state basis, the Kremlin has promoted various forms of conflict and revolution in the Third World. Although this has varied depending on time period and region of the world (as will be demonstrated in later chapters), three specific types of conflict can be identified. First is the direct or indirect Soviet-bloc involvement in Third World civil wars or state-to-state confrontations. In Bruce Porter's study, *The USSR in Third World Conflicts,* he reviews five such cases: the Yemeni civil war, Nigerian civil war, Yom Kippur war, Angolan civil war, and Ogaden war.[9] A second type is Soviet policy toward and involvement in coups in Third World countries. Over the years the USSR has both gained and lost ground as a result of these developments. A recent study by Steven David has begun to shed light on this much-neglected aspect of Soviet policy.[10] Third, the USSR has been involved in promoting and assisting national liberation movements that seek to overthrow existing governments. This will be the topic under examination in this study.

In the Soviet lexicon, national liberation movements are composed of classes and social strata that are fighting against either foreign domination and/or what they refer to as local reaction. This distinction was intially made at the Twenty-second CPSU Congress in 1961. According to the program, "a powerful wave of national liberation revolutions is sweeping away the colonial system and undermining the foundations of imperialism."[11] However, having gained independence from colonial domination did not necessarily guarantee that autonomy was inviolate. Consequently, the CPSU program went on to observe that "formally independent countries" may come to be ruled by "reactionary pro-imperialist regimes." Therefore, even after independence the national liberation "struggle is not over."[12] As I shall discuss below, support for national liberation movements predates the 1961 program. Since the establishment of the Soviet state, the CPSU leadership has assigned to itself a role and responsibility in these conflicts.

In the West a number of scholars focusing on this form of conflict have sought more neutral terminology to describe wars of national liberation.[13] "Insurgency" or "revolutionary warfare" seems to come closest to achieving this requirement. Each term defines this form of conflict by the political objectives sought and by the strategy and tactics employed. Revolutionary insurgent warfare is an attempt by an organized group or movement to overthrow an existing government through the use of a combination of political, psychological, and paramilitary measures. These movements are composed of both a political infrastructure or organization and guerrilla units. Using an ideology as a basis, revolutionary insurgent movements generally rely on a protracted strategy to wear down and undermine a government. A host of political and psychological tactics are utilized to build support, mobilize elements of the population, and isolate the existing regime. In conjunction with these, paramilitary measures including subversion, sabotage, ambushes, guerrilla operations, and terrorism are employed.

Throughout its history the USSR has declared that it has a duty to support national liberation movements or revolutionary insurgency. What follows is a brief overview of these historical developments and an analysis of the relationship between theoretical precepts and actual policy.

Soviet Policy and
National Liberation Movements

From the inception of the Soviet regime, the CPSU leadership has identified an almost symbiotic relationship between itself and national liberation movements in the Third World. According to Rubinstein, this policy has been predicated on both ideological and practical factors.[14] On the one hand, the USSR has consistently portrayed itself as the champion of the liberation of all peoples under colonial or neocolonial rule. On the other hand, practical political considerations have influenced the degree to which the USSR has been willing to provide direct or even indirect support. The amount of assistance has varied throughout the history of the Soviet Union. During the late 1960s and early 1970s, a number of national liberation and insurgent movements began to receive significantly more help from Moscow. By the mid-1980s, yet another new turn in policy had become apparent.

Historical Evolution

In the period between the 1905 and the 1917 Russian revolutions, Lenin wrote several articles that addressed developments in the colonial world. In 1915 he referred to national liberation movements for the first time.[15] Perhaps his most complete statement on these issues can be found in his pamphlet, "Imperialism—The Highest Stage of Capitalism."[16] Following the Bolshevik seizure of power, Lenin argued that revolution was quite likely in the colonial world, which he described as capitalism's weakest link. He further asserted that the national bourgeoisie of colonial countries should be seen as temporary allies of national liberation movements. The CPSU leadership anticipated the establishment of other communist regimes as proof that the revolution in Russia was the harbinger of a worldwide revolutionary movement.

Practical political considerations also entered into Lenin's calculations. Rubinstein notes that "Lenin shrewdly perceived that the East could be used to improve Russia's military and political situation. Accordingly, he assigned colonial areas a more significant place in Soviet strategy."[17] These theoretical and practical political considerations were drawn together at the second congress of the Comintern in 1920. Lenin asserted that revolution in the colonial world would pass through two stages. The national bourgeoisie would lead the first stage of national independence, and the second stage of the revolution would be directed by communists. The latter would be a socialist revolution, culminating in proletarian dictatorship.[18] The Comintern was the general staff of the world revolution and, because it was headquartered in Moscow and its Executive Committee dominated by CPSU members or agents, an extension of Soviet foreign policy. Lenin directed the Comintern to help facilitate world revolutionary developments. Adam Ulam describes this mission as follows:

> The new International would break away from the fatal tradition of the Second. It would bring true revolutionary socialism to the leading industrial countries of the world. It would light the flame of revolution in the backward colonial areas, thus dealing an indirect but eventually fatal blow to the hateful capitalists . . . It would really be the beginning of a new world of which the communist experiment in Russia, with all its imperfections resulting from the backwardness of the country and the lack of culture among its masses, would be but the first and by no means the most exciting development.[19]

Not all members of the Comintern agreed with Lenin. The Indian communist, M. N. Roy, believed that the national bourgeoisie was not able to carry out the first stage specified by Lenin. Roy argued they were too dependent on the colonial powers and assigned responsibility for both stages to the communists.[20] Lenin's incapacitation and eventual death in 1924 limited the implementation of this policy of support for national liberation movements.

Stalin's accession to power led to a new course. Papp notes that "Soviet interest and involvement in the colonial world occupied, at best, third place in Soviet priorities, behind building socialism in one country and coping with the threat presented by capitalist encirclement."[21] The first priority was, in part, an outgrowth of the celebrated debate between Stalin and Trotsky. The controversy was over the degree to which the embryonic Bolshevik regime should concentrate on building socialism in the USSR or strive to promote world revolution in other countries. Stalin stressed the former and Trotsky the latter. In the aftermath of Stalin's victory over Trotsky in the succession struggle, building socialism in the USSR was given priority. According to Ulam, the result was that "whenever an unusually promising situation would arise in a foreign country, the Comintern would lend its resources toward a revolutionary push, but day-to-day policy had to be one of normalization of relations with the capitalist countries."[22] The latter became an increasingly compelling goal with Hitler's coming to power.

Another reason Soviet involvement in the colonial world received a low priority was due to the fact that, when Stalin did venture into the colonial world, he was stung with a defeat. Soviet support of the Kuomintang (KMT)–Chinese Communist Party (CCP) alliance in the mid-1920s failed when Chiang Kai-shek nearly annihilated the CCP.[23] By following the tactics laid down by Stalin—a KMT-CCP united-front alliance—the Chinese communists met with disaster in 1927 when Soviet policy collapsed. Stalin's stated plan had been to manipulate the KMT and Chiang Kai-shek until they were "utilized to the end, squeezed out like a lemon, and then thrown away." However, in April 1927 Chiang struck first and massacred the local CCP in Shanghai. Stalin countered by directing the CCP to revolt against the KMT, but the rebellion was suppressed and by 1928 Soviet policy in China was a disaster. The containment of communism in Asia during the latter half of the 1920s and the emerging fascist threat in Europe resulted in much less Soviet attention to national liberation in the colonial world.

At the sixth congress of the Comintern in 1928, new principles were enunciated to guide all foreign communist parties (ruling and nonruling) and movements. These included recognition of the Soviet Union as the citadel of world revolution, preservation of the USSR as the primary concern of all communist parties, and complete allegiance of these parties to Moscow. These principles, bearing the imprimatur of Stalin, were to be a source of dissension that would beset the communist world following World War II.

During the 1930s, Soviet foreign policy increasingly concentrated on Europe and the rapid growth of Nazi power on the continent. The colonial world faded quickly from Stalin's agenda. With the Nazi attack on June 22, 1941, and the Soviet alliance with the capitalist powers, Stalin formally disbanded the Comintern in 1943, officially ending any Soviet commitment to world revolution and the liberation of those under colonial rule.

Even after World War II, Stalin minimized Soviet involvement in the Third World. Two primary factors appear to explain this decision. First, Soviet foreign policy was preoccupied with Eastern Europe. According to Rajan Menon, for "Stalin no task abroad was more important than that of consolidating Soviet hegemony over this area. This involved manipulating noncommunist political parties into oblivion, establishing Soviet-style governments, excommunicating the rebellious Tito, and, in the late 1940s, launching a series of purges to root out those communists in Eastern Europe who were thought capable of emulating his defiant example."[24] Second, Stalin distrusted nationalist leaders like Jawaharlal Nehru and appears to have misunderstood the implications of rapidly emerging Third World nationalism. Consequently, while the post–World War II disintegration of the colonial empires presented the possibility of reigniting the world revolution against the international capitalist system, Soviet foreign policy paid only secondary attention to these possibilities. For Stalin, newly independent states not under the control of pro-Soviet communist parties were seen not as an opportunity but as a threat to be contained.

This is not to say that Moscow completely ignored the Third World. For instance, at the 1947 founding of the Cominform, Andry Zhdanov observed that the Vietminh struggle against the French constituted "a powerful movement for national liberation in the colonies."[25] This resulted, in turn, in some propaganda encouragement and minor material assistance.[26] At that time Soviet military-aid programs were largely confined to the East European states, the People's Republic of China, and North Korea. Elsewhere in Asia, local communist parties in Malaya, the Philippines, Burma, and Indonesia were encouraged to carry out armed insurrection in accordance with the line set forth at the Cominform meeting. This line rejected cooperation between local communist parties, bourgeoisie-nationalist groups, and elites seeking independence from colonialism.[27] In effect, as Hosmer and Wolfe note, "by pursuing the dogmatic line that 'the solution of colonial slavery is impossible without a proletariat revolution,' and by asserting that nationalist leaders of the period such as Gandhi, Nehru, and Sukarno were merely imperialist 'lackeys,' the USSR left itself little room for effective courtship of potential anti-Western allies in the formerly colonial states."[28]

"The dramatic changes in postwar international politics, Stalin's death in 1953 and the ensuing succession struggle contributed," according to the author of one recent study, "to a rethinking of the international environment in which the Third World would acquire increasing significance."[29] Khrushchev re-initiated the Leninist view of the Third World to advance Soviet interests in these regions. When Stalin died, the USSR had few diplomatic or economic ties with the developing world. As Khrushchev gradually consolidated his position within the Politburo, he promoted discussion within the party to re-examine perceptions of the developing areas. He believed that some of the newly independent states and their leaders, having strong nationalistic and anti-Western perspectives, presented opportunities for Soviet inroads. Examples included Egypt, Iraq, Ghana, Guinea, Mali, and Indonesia. This constituted a reversal of the Cominform line of 1947.

Consequently, Khrushchev, who did not hold Stalin's view of the developing world and was aware of emerging foreign policy opportunities, undertook to reorient Soviet policy. At the Twentieth CPSU Congress in 1956, he proclaimed that a "zone of peace" including socialist and nonsocialist states had arisen in Europe, Africa, and Asia. Thus, Khrushchev allied the socialist camp with the national bourgeoisie in the developing world.[30] According to Papp, "to Khrushchev and his supporters . . . the national bourgeoisie with their national democratic states did have sufficiently revolutionary credentials and, therefore, could move toward socialism."[31]

Whereas the related issues of national bourgeoisie, national democratic states in the developing world, and Soviet support were addressed at the Twentieth CPSU Congress, the subject of national liberation movements challenging a colonial power or a government closely linked to a former colonial power was left to the Twenty-second CPSU Congress in 1961. The resulting program stated that "Socialist countries are sincere and true friends of peoples fighting for their liberation and of those that have freed themselves from imperialist tyranny and render them all-around support."[32]

During Khrushchev's tenure, Soviet policy followed the dual approach of normalized state-to-state relations with national democracies and of assistance to liberation movements. However, in reality, Moscow directed a greater degree of attention to the former.[33] Support for national liberation movements was, from Moscow's perspective, complicated by two factors. One was the ongoing Sino-Soviet confrontation, which spilled over into competition in the developing world. The second was concern that a national liberation war could escalate from a local to a regional conflict and, possibly, to a world war. These factors affected both the amount and the kinds of assistance that could be offered to a revolutionary insurgency.

The period 1961–1964 saw Soviet military-aid agreements with Third World countries grow to an estimated $2.5 billion.[34] The number of recipients expanded from eleven to sixteen, with the major expenditures going to Egypt, Indonesia, India, Iraq, Syria, Afghanistan, and Algeria.[35] Other countries receiving assistance were Somalia, Ghana, Mali, Tanzania, and Morocco.[36] Ben Bella of Algeria, Sekou Toure of Ghana, Achmed Sukarno of Indonesia, and Modibo Keita of Mali, among others, regularly received praise from the Kremlin. There was significant enthusiasm for this new type of Third World leader because it was predicted that they could transcend class background and lead their countries along state-oriented paths of development.[37] Support for national liberation movements, however, was much more constrained for the reasons noted above. "The risk of confrontation with the United States and other Western countries," according to Hosmer and Wolfe, limited Soviet aid to movements in the Middle East, Asia, and Latin America. "The fact that this risk appeared to be smaller in Africa" resulted in this region being seen by Moscow "as an especially promising national-liberation arena."[38]

Khrushchev's policy was marked by both successes and failures. However, his oversimplified and overoptimistic approach had an impact on the policy adopted by the post-Khrushchev leadership. Additionally, shortly after his ouster, Soviet Third World policy suffered two important setbacks. In June 1965, Houari Boumédienne overthrew Ben Bella in Algeria. In the same year an abortive communist coup and successful countercoup by the Indonesian military brought about the fall of Sukarno. In the years immediately following, two other Third World revolutionary democrats—Keita in Mali and Kwame Nkrumah in Ghana—were removed through military coups. These setbacks, in conjunction with Moscow's desire to avoid confrontation with the United States, resulted in a Third World policy of caution and constraint in the years following Khrushchev's removal.

Whelan and Dixon have observed that "in contrast to Khrushchev, the approach of the Brezhnev successor regime . . . was highly rationalistic, realistic, pragmatic, and, until Angola in the mid-1970s, cautious."[39] The new policy concentrated on countries that fell within the national liberation zone, a Soviet euphemism for states contiguous to the USSR or, as in the case of India, that constituted a counterweight to China.[40] Within these areas, the USSR continued to follow, in a more restrained manner, Khrushchev's dual approach of diplomatic normalization with newly independent governments deemed friendly and of promotion of national liberation movements.

In addition to the aforementioned setbacks in Africa and Asia, the Soviets were expelled from Egypt in 1972. However, the Brezhnev leadership had some successes in the period between 1964 and the early 1970s. For instance, Soviet power was introduced in the Mediterranean and in the Persian Gulf, and the leadership extended its influence into the northern tier of Turkey and Iran as well as into Southeast Asia. Nevertheless, there was a question of how far the USSR could go in supporting the national bourgeoisie leaders of Third World states.[41]

By the early 1970s the Soviets had undertaken a policy shift toward greater interest in Marxist parties and other left-wing revolutionary groups. The roots of this change lay in developments that took place in the second half of the 1960s. For instance, during that time Moscow rapidly expanded its support for the North Vietnamese and Viet Cong. Likewise, a shift in Soviet attitude toward the Palestinian guerrilla movements followed the Arab-Israeli war of 1967. The USSR also began to provide a degree of paramilitary assistance to other Middle Eastern–North African insurgency movements, including the Popular Front for the Liberation of Oman and the Sahara Liberation Movement. During the first half of the 1970s, a number of sub-Sahara African insurgent movements were also granted Soviet-bloc aid, and by the end of the decade this was extended into Latin America.

The Twenty-fourth CPSU Congress and Wars of National Liberation

It is unclear precisely when the USSR decided to undertake the change in policy discussed in the previous section, but the change was set forth officially in Brezhnev's report to the Twenty-fourth CPSU Congress in March 1971. According to the CPSU general secretary, "Lenin's prediction that the peoples of the colonies and dependent countries, starting with a struggle for national liberation, would go on to fight against the very foundations of the exploitative system is coming true. Success in the struggle largely depends on the cohesion of the anti-imperialist forces, above all the world communist movement, their vanguard." Brezhnev then pledged the USSR to "give undeviating support to the people's struggle for democracy, national liberation and socialism," and "further to invigorate the worldwide anti-imperialist struggle."[42] This official pronouncement gave authoritative endorsement to a policy already being implemented in the field. Following the Twenty-fourth Congress, considerable official commentary was devoted to the subject. In addition to frequent declarations by top party leaders and other official pronouncements, this change in policy was discussed in great detail by leading CPSU foreign-policy experts as well as in the professional military literature.

Examination of this material suggests that the following factors are likely to have contributed to Moscow's decision. By the early 1970s the USSR's investment in defense had altered the military correlation of forces. As they reached parity with the West in both strategic and conventional terms, the leadership appeared less constrained in proclaiming its right to project power into Third World conflicts. Furthermore, the growth of certain military capabilities, including the capacity to rapidly transport large amounts of men and arms by sea and air, enhanced the Soviet's capacity to project force. Andrey Gromyko's assertion at the Twenty-fourth Congress illustrates this. Commenting on the current power balance in world politics, the former foreign minister stated that "there is no question of any significance which can be decided without the Soviet Union or in opposition to it."[43]

It is important to note, as Vernon Aspaturian points out, that nonmilitary factors also contribute to changes in the overall correlation of forces.[44] Included are a wide range of what Moscow terms "active measures," such as propaganda, agents of influence, activities of international fronts, disinformation, deception, and similar instruments of political and psychological warfare. At the time of the Twenty-fourth Congress, the Committee for State Security (KGB), the International Department of the CPSU, and other parts of the apparatus and Central Committee responsible for conducting active measures were in the midst of major increases in these activities following the decision in 1959 to enter a new phase in political warfare operations. It seems reasonable to assume that these developments contributed to Moscow's perception during the early 1970s that the correlation of forces was shifting in its favor.[45]

A lack of resolve and splits in the Western alliance also contributed, according to Soviet commentary, to the new power equation. Consequently, the declining willingness of the United States to maintain commitments, exemplified by the withdrawal from Vietnam, as well as reduced defense spending and dissension in NATO are likely to have been factored into the Kremlin's new assessment of the East-West balance of power.[46]

These developments and their relationship to expanding Soviet support for national liberation movements have been articulated by leading foreign-policy specialists from the Central Committee's International Department (ID). During the past decade there has been considerable disagreement over whether the Ministry of Foreign Affairs or the ID plays the major role in foreign policy. This has been debated by both Western specialists and former Soviet officials. On the basis of a number of factors discussed by Leonard Schapiro and Elizabeth Teague, the ID appears to have a more decisive influence, subject to Politburo approval.[47] This is especially true with respect to national liberation movements. It is not surprising, therefore, that the underlying rationale for this new policy has been authoritatively recounted in the publications of senior members of the ID.

The ID's major theoretician is its recently retired chief, Boris Ponomarev. Considered the elder statesman of Soviet foreign policy, Ponomarev's publications over the years have established him as the leading official voice on theoretical issues related to Soviet international relations doctrine, including national liberation movements. His pronouncements on revolutionary insurgent conflicts and Soviet policy accelerated during the 1970s. Among the most important are *Some Problems of the Revolutionary Movement* and *Lenin and the World Revolutionary Process,* both of which mirror those factors previously identified as underlying Moscow's decision to escalate support for insurgent or national liberation movements.[48] In the November 1977 *Kommunist,* Ponomarev asserted that the worldwide "national liberation movement has entered a qualitatively new stage." While noting that "imperialism and the local oligarchy were able to deal major blows at the liberation movements in Chile, Uruguay, Brazil and some other countries . . . the liberation movement was not extinguished."[49] In 1980 the head of the ID pronounced the 1970s the decade of significant "progress of the world revolutionary process," as a result of the "merciless objective laws of social development."[50]

> The 1970s witnessed a new considerable progress of the anti-imperialist movement in many parts of the world. This included the victory of the Vietnamese people and unification of Vietnam, the strengthening of the people's system in Laos, and the elimination of the Pol Pot regime in Kampuchea. Ethiopia, Angola, and Mozambique freed themselves from the chains of imperialism. Their peoples . . . are bridgeheads for socialist orientation in Africa. In this respect South Yemen is playing an important role. The dictatorial regime in Nicaragua was overthrown. The revolution in Afghanistan, the overthrow of the monarchy of the Shah in Iran, and the victory of the Zimbabwe patriots were blows struck at imperialism.[51]

The theme of declining U.S. influence in the world also permeated Ponomarev's reflections: "American imperialism has always been and continues to be the chief bulwark of tyrannical and mercenary regimes. Today, under the onslaught of the liberation forces, which are rapidly increasing both on a national and international scale, American imperialism is no longer capable of protecting its protégés and puppets against being overthrown."[52]

In sum, Ponomarev makes clear that the overthrow of colonial or pro-Western Third World governments by revolutionary insurgent movements contributes to the overall and inevitable shift in the global correlation of forces from the West to the East. While stressing that radical indigenous elements—not the "hand of Moscow"—must advance the protracted revolutionary struggle, the former head of the ID has stated that the USSR offers both its solidarity and its support: "Whenever such forces exist and fight, they can rightfully count on our solidarity and support. Those who raise the banner of struggle . . . are considered by us to be representatives of a just cause."[53]

In light of the importance of the ID, Ponomarev's statements have both theoretical and operational implications. In addition to serving as the leading official voice on issues related to conflict in the Third World, during 1978–1980 he met personally with many of the leaders of the national liberation movements supported by the USSR.[54] For example, during November 1979 Ponomarev and Foreign Minister Gromyko met with a Palestine Liberation Organization (PLO) delegation headed by Yasser Arafat and including representatives from Sa'iqa, Popular Front for the Liberation of Palestine (PFLP), PFLP–General Command, Democratic Front for the Liberation of Palestine, and Arab Liberation Front.[55] In sum, as the head of the ID, Ponomarev had principal responsibility for formulating, coordinating, and conducting Soviet political warfare operations, including those in support of national liberation movements.

In addition to Ponomarev, three of the deputy chiefs of the ID—Rostislav Ulyanovsky, Karen Brutents, and Petr Manchka—are considered leading specialists on national liberation movements. Ulyanovsky appears to be the senior expert of the three, specializing in Afro-Asian movements. A former deputy director of the Institute of Oriental Studies, he has authored numerous essays on the subject, including *National Liberation*, an examination of liberation struggles in Africa and Asia.[56] Brutents supervises the activities of the Middle Eastern and Latin American sections of the ID, and it appears that he is the CPSU's second-ranked specialist on national liberation movements. In his best-known work, the two-volume study entitled *National Liberation Revolutions Today*, Brutents outlines how the focus of Soviet policy has changed from its earlier defensive approach toward revolutionary insurgency:

> In accordance with the whole course of the world revolutionary process, the question of alliance with the national liberation movement . . . has now acquired both objectively and subjectively—in the light of the struggle between the two social systems—a largely different

meaning than it had, say, in the early period of the Soviet state. At that time, it was largely a matter of defense of the first socialist revolution against imperialism and world capitalism as a whole to do away with them.[57]

Manchka, who specializes in African affairs, takes a similar approach in his book *In the Vanguard of the Revolutionary Struggle in Africa.*[58]

By the mid-1970s, Soviet military professionals had begun to assert that the armed forces of the USSR also would play an active role in this policy of supporting insurgencies. According to leading Western experts Harriet Scott and William Scott, "1974 marked a doctrinal shift" in Moscow's view of the role of military force as an instrument of statecraft:

> Soviet leaders announced that the responsibilities of the Soviet Armed Forces were no longer restricted to defense of the fatherland and other Socialist states. Henceforth imperialist aggression would be repulsed wherever found. This was called a new "external" role for the Armed Forces. In the early 1980s it is receiving more and more attention . . . Since they first began to emphasize "external" functions on the power projection role, Soviet spokesmen have stated that the Armed Forces must be prepared to resist imperialist aggression wherever it may appear.[59]

Beginning in the mid-1970s, both the senior leadership of the Soviet armed forces and the professional military literature reiterated this point. In actuality, this assertion first appeared in the third edition of Marshal V. D. Sokolovskiy's *Soviet Military Strategy*, which was originally published in 1968.[60] Apparently, the new military role was to include both direct support to insurgent movements and assistance to newly established Marxist-Leninist regimes seeking to consolidate power.

In 1974, Marshal A. A. Grechko, then minister of defense, described this new role in the following terms: "At the present stage the historic function of the Soviet armed forces is not restricted merely to their function of defending our Motherland . . . In its foreign policy activity the Soviet state actively and purposefully opposes the export of counterrevolution . . . supports the national liberation struggle, and resolutely resists imperialist aggression in whatever distant region it may appear."[61] Along the same lines, Marshal N. V. Ogarkov, the former chief of the General Staff, stated in an essay contained in the *Soviet Military Encyclopedia*: "Soviet military strategy takes into account the possibility of local wars rising . . . according to the classic positions and Leninist theses on just and unjust wars. While supporting national liberation wars, the Soviet Union decisively opposes the unleashing by imperialists of local wars."[62]

This new emphasis on external power projection was also the subject of frequent discussions in Soviet military periodicals. For example, in the second of a two-part essay entitled "Documents and Materials: Long-Range Subjects for Military-Historical Research in 1981–1990," the following subjects were listed under the heading "Developing Countries":

1. Strategy and tactics of counterinsurgency actions of American imperialism in Indochina (1960–1975).
2. The art of war of warring nations and their armies in modern national liberation rebellions and wars.
3. Unique features of military development in countries assuming the path of revolutionary transformation of society.
4. Pressing problems in organization of the armed defense of people's liberation revolutions.[63]

This list reflects a dual concern of the Kremlin leadership. On the one hand, the USSR seeks to assist certain insurgent factions in seizing power through protracted revolutionary warfare. On the other hand, Moscow provides military and security support to newly established pro-Soviet, Marxist-Leninist regimes threatened by noncommunist insurgent movements. In the case of the former, the policy objective is the seizure of power, while the latter concentrates on the consolidation and institutionalization of control. These two themes run simultaneously through Soviet military literature of this period.[64] Mark Katz summarized these developments in Soviet military policy during the 1970s in the following manner. At first, in the late 1950s and early 1960s, Soviet military thinkers said nothing specific about the role of the USSR in local conflicts. In the middle and late 1960s, they discussed arms transfers, and in the early 1970s, the role of Cuban armed forces and treaties of friendship and cooperation. Even some hints of the use of Soviet armed forces were given, although no formal statement advocating this as a general policy has yet been made. Thus, in these statements there has occurred a progression over time toward increasing Soviet involvement in Third World conflict.[65]

In sum, what was authorized by Brezhnev at the Twenty-fourth CPSU Congress and explicitly reaffirmed at the Twenty-fifth Congress—a new policy of power projection to influence the course of Third World conflicts—has been the subject of extensive commentary by key CPSU foreign-affairs specialists and military professionals. Finally, it should be noted that Moscow saw no contradiction between détente/peaceful coexistence and expanding involvement in Third World conflicts. Détente did not alter the USSR's understanding of war and politics in international relations. Soviet writers stated that peaceful coexistence and support for national liberation struggles were not incompatible.[66] In fact, the conditions of détente created an atmosphere in which these struggles could flourish. If we return once again to the Twenty-fourth CPSU Congress, we find Brezhnev and other leading CPSU officials declaring that peaceful co-existence with the West was not incompatible with Soviet assistance to "progressive forces in wars of national and social liberation." Détente certified that the USSR had reached the stature of an "equal" with the United States, which had important ramifications for the normalization of relations. These developments, however, did not alter and should not affect the favorable historical course of events in the Third World and the Soviet role in them. These themes run concurrently in Soviet pronouncements following the Twenty-fourth CPSU Congress.

An Overview of Developments in the 1970s

During the early 1970s, Soviet involvement in Third World conflicts was marked by an expansion in form and focus. The national liberation zone was extended well beyond areas contiguous to the USSR into southern Africa, the southern part of the Arabian Peninsula, and Central and South America. Within these regions the USSR increased its efforts to encourage various kinds of violence and instability. Here I will briefly summarize these developments, leaving more extensive documentation, analysis, and assessment for the case-study chapters that follow.

In retrospect it would appear that underlying increased Soviet assistance to revolutionary insurgent movements was the objective of exploiting opportunities that might emerge from these conflicts. Consequently, during the early 1970s, support for promising guerrilla movements in the Middle East and sub-Sahara Africa began to increase. In the Middle East, the principal recipient was the PLO. In sub-Sahara Africa a number of movements received assistance. These included the African National Congress (ANC), the Front for the Liberation of Mozambique (Frelimo), the Popular Movement for the Liberation of Angola (MPLA), the South-West Africa People's Organization (SWAPO), the Zimbabwe African National Union (ZANU), and the Zimbabwe African People's Union (ZAPU). During the early 1970s, Moscow also began to recognize the "anti-imperialist and national liberation" potential in Latin America. However, unlike other parts of the Third World, the road to social change in Latin America was not to be through revolution. This was due, in large part, to Salvador Allende's electoral victory in Chile and to the Soviet view of new military regimes in Peru and Bolivia as progressively leftist in orientation. Consequently, in Latin America it was through means other than wars of national liberation that social change could be fostered.

During the latter half of the 1970s, Soviet policy continued to expand as Moscow displayed increasing readiness to assist Third World clients, particularly Marxist-oriented regimes and a variety of guerrilla movements. This policy was evident in Angola and Ethiopia, where the Soviets combined large-scale military-logistic support with Cuban surrogate troops. The Kremlin success in Angola furnished fresh momentum to expand support to other guerrilla groups in southern Africa. In conjunction with these developments, pro-Moscow communist parties came to power in six other nations (in addition to Angola): Afghanistan, Ethiopia, South Yemen, North Vietnam, Laos, and Cambodia. These and other developments during the latter half of the 1970s paralleled a shift in Soviet policy to target support to Moscow-oriented, Marxist-Leninist regimes and movements. These were seen as potentially more reliable and lessened the possibility of suffering the kinds of setbacks the Soviets experienced in earlier dealings with non-Marxist regimes and movements. According to one analyst, this shift in Soviet policy was due to the following considerations:

- Moscow's dissatisfaction with simple nonalignment or even pro-Soviet neutralism among its Third World clients, wanting active collaboration instead.

- Soviet awareness that influence without political control may be inadequate to permit Soviet manipulation of local politics . . . hence, greater Soviet willingness to interfere in the internal affairs of client states to achieve political control.

- Appreciation by the Soviet leadership of the USSR's growing capabilities for power projection in the Third World, permitting the USSR to supplement the sometimes ineffective bartering of arms for influence with the application of direct military pressure.

- Soviet recognition that an effective international infrastructure for Soviet military intervention in critical Third World areas requires mutual support and cooperation of the kind best assured among states led by Soviet-dominated communist regimes.[67]

In summary, support for insurgency movements, a facet of Soviet Third World policy since the inception of the regime, received considerably more emphasis during the 1970s, particularly in the latter half of the decade. This continued into the 1980s. The main thrust of this policy has focused on Africa and the Middle East. Since the mid-1970s, this has included assistance to guerrilla forces in Zimbabwe until the new state was established, to SWAPO in Namibia, and to the ANC of South Africa. Moscow also assisted the PLO, the PFLO, and the Polisario front. By the end of the decade, the Soviet bloc and Cuba were assisting insurgent groups in Central and South America.

The Twenty-sixth and Twenty-seventh CPSU Congresses: Continuity and Caution

As with the Twenty-fifth Congress, Brezhnev reconfirmed at the Twenty-sixth meeting Soviet commitment to continue to support national liberation movements.[68] His address to the 1981 session reiterated the forward strategy of globalism initiated by Khrushchev. The national liberation zone remained a fertile area for Soviet influence and involvement, and specific movements could expect Soviet support and assistance.

Nevertheless, it appears that the tone and enthusiasm of the general secretary had undergone a change. As was noted above, his speeches at the Twenty-fourth and Twenty-fifth Congresses were confident and assertive. This was particularly true of the Twenty-fifth session in February 1976. At that time he noted that profound changes were taking place in the developing areas as the class struggle intensified. Victories by national liberation movements had opened up "new horizons" for similar elements in the regions of the Third World. The "class struggle," according to Brezhnev, was "gaining strength" and, consequently, so was the "worldwide revolutionary process." In conjunction with this, the highest authority of the CPSU pledged the full support of the USSR.[69]

It could be argued that Brezhnev had reason to be assertive. The war in Indochina had culminated in Marxist-Leninist regimes coming to power in Vietnam, Cambodia, and Laos. There were important gains in Africa, most notably in Angola. Additionally, Ethiopia was about to come under Soviet influence, and a 1978 coup in South Yemen would bring a more staunchly pro-Soviet leadership to power. A number of other insurgent movements were also growing in strength and expanding their activities. Moreover, the United States was fully ensconced in what has been termed the "Vietnam syndrome." Following withdrawal from Vietnam, the United States appeared to resolve never again to become directly engaged in a revolutionary war in the Third World. This was codified into law by the U.S. Senate on December 19, 1975, with the passage of the Clark Amendment, which cut off aid to the forces of the National Front for the Liberation of Angola and the National Union for the Total Independence of Angola. With the assistance of Havana and Moscow, the result was the consolidation of control by the MPLA for the remainder of the 1970s.

Brezhnev's report to the Twenty-sixth Congress did not contain this kind of enthusiasm. Important developments contributed to this somewhat new outlook, including the "burden of empire," described in a recent study by Charles Wolf and his colleagues at the Rand Corporation. The Soviet empire includes internal territory (multinational peoples of the USSR), contiguous states (hegemony over Eastern Europe and efforts to establish control over Afghanistan), and nations abroad (control and/or degrees of influence in Cuba, Vietnam, Angola, South

Yemen, Ethiopia, Mozambique, Libya, Syria, and Nicaragua).[70] What are the costs of maintaining this expansion? Wolf utilizes a complex economic model in an attempt to estimate this in U.S. dollars. Although admitting that such an approach suffers from "enormous data problems," he summarizes the costs as follows: "In constant 1981 dollars, using official exchange rates, costs of the Soviet empire rose from about $18 billion in 1971 to $24 billion in 1976 and about $41 billion in 1981."[71]

There are obvious problems in determining the degree to which this burden is bearable or unbearable for Moscow; nevertheless, it is apparent that it has complicated Soviet policy in the Third World. As noted previously, the USSR has traditionally been the promoter of insurgency and related forms of conflict in developing areas. However, the advances of the 1970s required the Kremlin to provide the means to help defend these gains in the 1980s. This has involved the Soviets in counterinsurgency and other internal security activities. In Afghanistan the result has been a major deployment of Soviet armed forces. Additionally, Cuban troops have been utilized in Angola and Ethiopia against resistance forces. Security and military assistance and advisory support from the Soviets and their surrogates have likewise been provided to Nicaragua, South Yemen, Libya, and Syria to help these regimes counter internal security and/or insurgent challenges. In Nicaragua, Afghanistan, and Angola, these problems have been further intensified by the Reagan administration's support of anticommunist insurgent forces.

Of course, there are burdens that accompany expansion, but there also are political and strategic benefits. Has the game been worth the candle? Brezhnev's address to the Twenty-sixth CPSU Congress, although not as sanguine as his commentary in the 1970s, does not suggest disillusionment to the point of withdrawal from these commitments. What it appears to imply is a realization by Moscow that power projection and expansion in the Third World carry both costs and burdens as well as political and strategic advantages. In the early 1980s, the advantages seem to continue to outweigh the disadvantages in the Soviet calculus.

Will this remain the case in the years to come? We will speculate on this in the concluding part of this study. The Twenty-seventh CPSU Congress, held from February 25 to March 6, 1986, unfortunately did not provide conclusive answers.[72] Third World issues received less attention than they had at the three previous congresses, and the evidence suggests that Soviet interest in retrenchment may result in reduced support for revolutionary insurgency in developing areas. Some Western specialists have speculated that the new Soviet leadership has signaled an interest in shifting its policy in the Third World to entail both less reliance on military instruments and a reduction in direct or indirect involvement in protracted conflicts.[73] Others argue that they detect "no lessening of the commitment," especially in assisting pro-Soviet, Marxist-Leninist regimes to consolidate control.[74] Thus, what appears to be withdrawal may more accurately be described as a reordering of priorities. Consequently, less assistance for national liberation movements in the 1980s, compared with the 1970s, may have resulted from the need to shift resources to assist Third World allies threatened by anticommunist insurgent movements and other internal security challenges.

Soviet Policy Instruments and Organizational Apparatus

The instruments of power and influence utilized by the Kremlin leadership to promote and support revolutionary insurgent movements range from propaganda and various political influence techniques to paramilitary assistance. More specifically, these may be grouped under the Soviet concept of active measures. These include political measures (foreign propaganda, international front organizations, and political activities within international and regional organizations) and paramilitary measures (arms and logistical support, political-military training, advisory assistance, and deployment of forces).

Since the late 1950s and early 1960s the Soviets have apparently used the term "active measures" to describe many political and paramilitary techniques for influencing events and behavior in and actions of foreign countries. In supporting insurgent movements, both political and paramilitary measures are important for achieving policy objectives. Political measures are utilized to champion the cause and objectives of the insurgents in the international arena. International acceptance of the "just cause" of the insurgency and of the "repressive immoral" character of the incumbent regime can play an important role at each stage of insurgent development. Paramilitary assistance, in contrast, seeks to improve the political-military proficiency of the insurgents to conduct operations against the target government. I will now briefly examine each of these instruments, identify those parts of the Soviet apparatus charged with planning and implementing them, and then describe how Soviet allies and surrogates augment the capabilities and assets of the USSR.

Political Measures

An important Soviet political technique for promoting the cause of insurgent movements in the international arena is *foreign propaganda*. Since the period before the Russian Revolution in 1917, propaganda has been an essential policy instrument. According to one leading authority, "Lenin established a tradition within which Bolshevik professional revolutionaries and, later, specially trained functionaries of the Soviet state . . . have systematically employed modern communications techniques."[75] Propaganda remains an important instrument for conducting political warfare.

Escalation in propaganda coverage of an insurgent movement often indicates that it has become a more consequential policy issue for Moscow. It also triggers the initiation of a broader political warfare campaign in which other political and paramilitary instruments are brought into play (for example, the activation of international front organizations). In the case of SWAPO, Soviet overt propaganda set the thematic pattern for the other political warfare instruments and signaled the amplification of the international campaign (I will examine this more closely in Chapter 5).

The Soviet message is transmitted through a vast and coordinated array of propaganda channels, including international broadcasts, numerous publications with worldwide circulation, and two major news services.[76] An examination of this output reveals the degree to which Moscow can mobilize and integrate specific propaganda campaigns, which are characterized by the Soviet technique of *kombinatsia,* "combining and integrating multiple issues in support of a specific policy." In the Soviet propaganda campaign to support SWAPO, six specific themes (with multiple subthemes) were integrated and combined into a broadly targeted international effort. Other general features included intensity and concentration, flexibility and adaptivity, deception and manipulation, and centralized control and coordination.[77]

Because these campaigns are conducted on an international basis, they can be expected to be broad in scope. This is partly because multiple audiences are targeted. The Soviet campaign in support of the North Vietnamese and Viet Cong sent a message to Third World states that Moscow was aligned with and actively supporting the cause of national liberation. The Kremlin also sought to present the United States as the new neocolonial power and to characterize it to the Europeans as warlike, recklessly aggressive, and capable of plunging Europe into war over Vietnam. The call for international opposition to U.S. policy was part of a long-term post–World War II campaign to characterize the United States as the greatest threat to world peace. In light of these multiple objectives, it is not surprising that propaganda campaigns in support of specific insurgent movements are broadly cast.

What is interesting about the Vietnam case, as well as a number of subsequent ones examined in this volume, is the extent to which the United States is characterized as a major cause of the conflict. The degree or even absence of U.S. involvement appears to have no apparent impact on the way in which Soviet propaganda covers the subject. Consequently, Vietnam, Namibia, Nicaragua (before the Sandinista victory), or El Salvador—four very different cases in terms of U.S. involvement—show little variance in their Soviet propaganda pattern.

Within the Soviet apparatus, the International Information Department (IID) of the CPSU Central Committee was established in 1978 to improve the coordination of what was already an impressive program of foreign propaganda activities. In an organizational change that is difficult to assess, the CPSU abolished the IID in the spring of 1986. Not a great deal is known about the IID, and there are conflicting opinions regarding its purpose and scope of responsibilities. Available evidence, however, suggests that it neither set the propaganda line nor had the responsibility for programmatic guidance. These appear to be the duty of the International Department (ID) of the CPSU Central Committee (under Politburo direction).[78] The IID, in contrast, concentrated on improving the coordination of the various overt propaganda channels. How this will be handled in its absence is unclear.

A second political technique for promoting the cause of insurgent movements internationally is through the activities of Soviet-directed *international front organizations*. As with many other aspects of Soviet policy and organization, the use of international fronts can be traced back to the early days of the regime. Lenin saw the importance of advancing Soviet foreign-policy objectives through broad organizations that, because of their ostensibly idealistic objectives, would attract greater support than openly communist parties.[79] The Comintern was assigned responsibility for organizing and directing the fronts, and during the 1920s and 1930s a number came into existence.[80]

Overt Soviet propaganda themes in support of insurgent movements are promoted and enhanced through the Kremlin's major international fronts, whose techniques include propaganda and international conference diplomacy.[81] The latter is the more action-oriented and can take the following forms:

- *Meetings of the front organizations.* The fronts use their own deliberations as international forums to promote the cause of different insurgent movements. Once the meeting is over, a communiqué is released and final report published (both are used for propaganda). The representatives of the national-level affiliates of the fronts are then expected to promote the themes of the meeting back home.

- *International and regional conferences sponsored by one or more fronts.* The fronts use international and regional conferences, which are attended by both front and nonfront individuals and organizations, to promote insurgent causes. These may be regionally or internationally focused and, on occasion, run on an annual basis.

- *International conferences involving the U.N. or regional organizations.* The major fronts attempt to link themselves to different U.N. committees and organizations, which includes participating in and even cosponsoring U.N. international and regional conference activity. They also will carry out similar activities in other nongovernmental and regional organizations, including the Nonaligned Movement and the Organization of African Unity.

The purpose of each of these techniques is to reach a much larger audience than the Soviets could hope to influence on their own. The case study of SWAPO demonstrates how two of Moscow's major international fronts—the World Peace Council (WPC) and the Afro-Asian People's Solidarity Organization (AAPSO)—utilized all three conference diplomacy techniques. The escalation in these activities by the WPC and AAPSO coincided with the activation of other Soviet political warfare tactics. The use of fronts in the campaign to mobilize support for the guerrillas in El Salvador (described in Chapter 6) reveals a different pattern. Rather than one or two fronts having primary responsibility, a broader and more decentralized campaign has been waged in which a number of fronts are employed. No one organization appears to have responsibility for conducting the majority of operations.

Through their various publications, the fronts conduct propaganda campaigns in support of insurgent movements. In almost every respect their general thematic pattern mirrors Soviet commentary. However, some differences can be detected. For example, as the case study of Central America shows, the number of themes covered by the fronts was fewer and the treatment of issues was more simplistic in approach and vitriolic in tone than those found in Soviet overt propaganda. This front campaign focused on audiences in the Latin American region and carried a basically simple message that was played back through international and regional conference activities. The principal theme concentrated on U.S. policy in Central America in general and El Salvador in particular.

The ID of the CPSU Central Committee is responsible for directing the front organizations and conducting relations with nonruling communist parties. However, as noted earlier and as John Dziak points out below, its duties extend far beyond those publicly identified, and its lineage can be traced back to the Comintern:

> For the formulation of political strategy (including foreign policy) one must look to the Central Committee [of the CPSU] rather than the Ministry of Foreign Affairs. The critical department here is the Central Committee's International Department, headed since the 1950s by Boris Ponomarev. This department, under various names, dates back to 1943, the year the Comintern was dissolved. Ponomarev was a high official in the latter body, which is viewed by some observers as the lineal predecessor to the International Department.[82]

Schapiro likewise argues that the ID is more important than the Ministry of Foreign Affairs.[83] In addition to planning, and coordinating, and implementing active measures through more than a dozen major international fronts and several nonruling communist parties, Dziak notes that the ID "has its own representatives in a number of Soviet embassies under special Central Committee tasking." These include "such sensitive areas as relations with the United States, the Middle East, and West Europe, among others."[84] This has been substantiated by former Soviet officials. For example, Vladimir Sakharov has noted that Ponomarev's cadre plays a major policy implementation role in certain Soviet embassies, orchestrating active measures through Soviet diplomats, the Chief Intelligence Directorate of the General Staff (GRU), trade and aid personnel, and even the KGB residencies.[85] Likewise, former KGB officer Stanislav Levchenko, who specialized in active measures operations, supports this view of the central importance of the ID.[86]

A third technique increasingly utilized by Moscow since the early 1970s is *political action* within the U.N. and other international and regional organizations. The Kremlin has sought to align itself and its allies and surrogates with radical and anti-Western Afro-Asian states in these organizations to promote revolutionary alternatives in the Third World.[87] Rubinstein notes that in 1960, when "seventeen new nations—sixteen of them African—became independent and members of the U.N.," Moscow "seized the moment to propose a declaration . . . embodying the most radical denunciation of colonialism in all its aspects and calling for the independence of all colonial countries and peoples."[88]

By the early 1970s, Soviet cooperation and support for the radical Afro-Asian bloc within the U.N. appears to have paid dividends with respect to the PLO, SWAPO, MPLA, ANC, and other insurgency movements. The increasingly militant Afro-Asian bloc has pressed the initiative in the U.N. to support and assist these movements, with the encouragement and direct involvement of the Soviet Union and its surrogates. One important result—among many—has been the granting of permanent observer status to SWAPO, the PLO, and other such groups, recognizing them as the sole legitimate representatives of the people for whom they claim to be fighting. Additionally, Soviet access to and support from Third World states and movements has been enhanced. According to Rubinstein, the Soviet Union approaches the U.N. and other international and regional organizations as arenas of political warfare:

> Conflict, not cooperation, is the dynamic that impels Soviet behavior in international organizations . . . [T]he USSR has taken to bloc politics in the U.N. with a vengeance, exploiting voting majorities to weaken the West and advance Soviet proposals and preferred resolutions. International organizations are battlefields for competing ideas and approaches to concrete issues, and Moscow has decided the game is worth the effort.[89]

This appears to be true of Soviet promotion of SWAPO, the PLO, and similar movements. Moscow approaches the U.N. as a forum to promote an insurgent cause and thereby enhance its reputation and credibility.

Of the three political warfare instruments examined in this study, political action within the U.N. and other international and regional organizations seems to be the most difficult for the Soviets to employ. In large part, this is due to the environments in which Moscow and its surrogates must operate. These are not controlled situations, which affects the degree to which the Kremlin can successfully employ political influence techniques. For example, during the latter half of the 1960s, before the U.N. power balance shifted to the anti-Western stance of the 1970s, Moscow sought to maneuver the General Assembly to take up the question of U.S. involvement in Vietnam. As the next chapter demonstrates, it was unsuccessful in this effort because, in addition to the unfavorable power balance that existed at that time, there was no specialized committee concerned with Vietnam through which Moscow could lay the foundation for such action within the General Assembly.

By the 1970s, Soviet fortunes in the U.N. changed. Consequently, the USSR was able to be more effective in promoting certain insurgent movements. Specialized U.N. committees had come into existence, and Moscow and its surrogates were actively involved in their deliberations.[90] As these committees became increasingly militant, U.N. support and assistance to SWAPO and the PLO increased significantly. Through an alliance with like-minded Afro-Asian states, the Soviets and their surrogates have been increasingly able to promote the cause of national liberation or insurgent movements in the U.N.

In the case of Central America, the U.N. appears to be of secondary importance. This is probably because no specialized committee structure exists to promote the cause of guerrilla movements in this region. As a result, it appears that in 1979 Moscow began to use its Cuban surrogate to maneuver the Nonaligned Movement and the Socialist International to more actively support insurgent movements in Central America. Soviet strategy seeks to take advantage of all avenues for building international support for movements conducting revolutionary warfare. As the head of the Nonaligned Movement in 1979, Cuba was instrumental in focusing the nonaligned nations on this subject.

Although specific components of the organizational apparatus involved in conducting active measures have been identified above, others are more difficult to ascertain, which is also true of political action within international organizations. Existing evidence, however, points to a large KGB and bloc intelligence role in the U.N.[91] In 1983, R. Jean Gray, head of the FBI's New York section, estimated that there were 1,100 communist-bloc officials in New York, including 150 Soviets in the U.N. Mission and about 180 in the Secretariat.[92] Arkadi Shevchenko, a former Soviet Ministry of Foreign Affairs official who served as under secretary general of the U.N. during 1973–1978, estimates that 30 percent of

Soviet U.N. employees, including Mission and Secretariat, are KGB officers.[93] Others believe that 40 or 50 percent of all Soviet-bloc officials in the U.N. are intelligence officers. They further suggest that half of these are what the Soviets term line-PR, political intelligence officers. These officers have responsibility for political matters, including overt and covert collection of information and active measures (each is responsible for one to five agents of influence).[94] If we use Gray's figure of 1,100 Soviet-bloc officials in New York, we can estimate that 50 percent, or 550, are intelligence officers. Half of these would be line-PR, conducting active measures in the U.N. and elsewhere. In Moscow, Service A, located within the KGB's First Chief Directorate, has responsibility for planning and overseeing these covert active measures.[95]

The ID is also involved in political active measures in the U.N. Several Soviet-controlled international front groups (for example, the WPC) are officially recognized as nongoverning organizations and take part in U.N. deliberations. Because the fronts are under the direction of the ID, these organizations can be employed for influence operations. Whether the ID has officials in the Soviet U.N. mission, similar to its representatives in key embassies in the United States and Western Europe, is uncertain. Some believe that, given the importance of the active measures effort in the U.N., the ID is likely to have its own representatives in place. Others suggest that the ID plans and coordinates active measures but that their officials are not operationally involved at the U.N.

Paramilitary Measures

Whereas international propaganda and political action aim to establish insurgent legitimacy in the world arena, the objective of Soviet paramilitary assistance is to improve insurgent operational effectiveness in the field. Since the early 1970s, significant growth in this form of assistance has coincided with the expansion of the political instruments described above. The principal kinds of paramilitary assistance include arms and logistical support, political-military training of insurgent cadres, and advisory assistance.

The military establishment and the KGB are among the key elements of the Soviet apparatus for implementing these activities. With respect to the military, since the early 1970s authoritative sources have identified a much greater external role for the Soviet armed forces. As noted earlier in this chapter, in 1968 Marshal Sokolovskiy stated that the USSR "will render, when it is necessary, military support" to "national liberation" movements.[96] The paramilitary techniques identified above are implemented through specific directorates of the Soviet military's General Staff and the KGB.

Arms and logistical support are essential to the growth and development of insurgent movements.[97] A detailed analysis of the various insurgent movements receiving arms and of the different channels through which the Soviets transfer them is not possible, relying solely on open sources. In certain cases, however, there is little doubt where and how the arms arrive, while in other instances the evidence is quite fragmentary. Moscow, seeking to maintain a policy of non-attribution, uses covert and indirect channels, especially those of surrogates and Third World states. An example is the case of SWAPO, where, since the latter half of the 1970s, arms have been transferred through the front-line states. According to one source, this military assistance included "T-34 and T-54 tanks, 122-millimeter rocket launchers, armored personnel carriers, and large quantities of small arms. Much of the equipment was landed in Dar es Salaam, Tanzania, and Maputo and Beira, Mozambique."[98] More recently, Soviet-bloc military equipment has been transmitted to SWAPO through Angola.

A similar pattern can be observed in Central America. During preparation for the Sandanista Front of National Liberation offensive in Nicaragua in the fall of 1978, arms from Bulgaria, East Germany, Hungary, and Czechoslovakia were shipped to Cuba, flown from Cuba to Panama, transshipped to Costa Rica on small planes, and supplied to guerrillas based in northern Costa Rica. An analogous situation exists with respect to the Salvadoran insurgents. Cuba, though providing few of its own weapons, plays an important role in coordinating the acquisition and delivery of arms from Vietnam, Ethiopia, and Eastern Europe through Nicaragua. The arms flow continues through a clandestine air and surface network that involves Havana.

The Military Assistance Directorate of the General Staff appears to have principal responsibility for directing Soviet and surrogate arms transfers and other forms of logistical support. In addition to the transport of equipment, personnel from the Military Assistance Directorate play a supportive role in Third World states contiguous to the location of the insurgency conflict.[99] The GRU utilizes the military assistance staffs in Third World countries for cover, which allows them to conduct in-country espionage and penetration operations and to provide assistance to insurgent groups.

Beyond arms and logistical support, Moscow and its surrogates provide political-military training for insurgent cadres. There are, however, important analytic distinctions. First, training is not confined to military tactics but includes political-ideological techniques, for example, instruction in establishing an insurgent infrastructure. Second, political-military training can take place within the USSR, in its surrogate states, or in base areas contiguous to the actual location of internal conflict. Training will vary according to whether the insurgency is in an initial or more advanced stage. Finally, the level of support depends on the degree to which the Kremlin believes the insurgency can contribute to its foreign-policy objectives.

In the USSR a network of facilities has been established for basic and advanced training of insurgent leadership and cadres. Each facility provides instruction in organizational, political warfare, and military tactics. The leadership of an insurgent movement is likely to receive instruction in the organizational, ideological, and mobilization aspects of establishing and directing a clandestine apparatus at the Institute of Social Sciences of the CPSU Central Committee. Michael Voslensky, who taught a course on the strategy and tactics of the world communist movement at the Institute of Social Sciences and was also a member of the faculty of Patrice Lumumba University, described the former as the CPSU school for communists from nonruling parties. The curriculum included, according to Voslensky, a course of studies in what he described as illegal methods for underground parties and movements. The objective was to provide instruction in the various operational skills for the illegal seizure of power. Voslensky speculated that the instructors for this part of the curriculum were drawn either from the KGB or the GRU. There were also courses of instruction in Marxism-Leninism, legal party building, strategy and tactics of the world communist movement (which constituted the basic or core element of the curriculum), and political economy.[100]

Specialized facilities for advanced paramilitary and military training include those at Simferopol in the Crimea and those near Odessa, Tashkent, and Baku.[101] In the *KGB Today*, John Barron identifies a special KGB complex near Moscow known as Balashikha, which is under the supervision of Directorate S (Department 8) of the KGB's First Chief Directorate. Barron explains that "a school in one area of the grounds provides training in terrorism to students imported directly from Third World countries or from Patrice Lumumba University in Moscow."[102] Additionally, more specialized training may take place at the military and higher military schools and academies of the Soviet armed forces.[103] This may be true particularly of schools for *spetsnaznachenie* or *spetsnaz* "special designation" units. These troops are charged by the CPSU with missions too sensitive for the regular military. The border guard schools at Alma-Ata (named for Feliks Dzerzhinski), Golitsyno (named for Kliment Voroshilov), and Moscow (named for Mossoviet) are all possibilities. Ministry of Internal Affairs schools also may be used for advanced training.[104]

Insurgents and terrorists can also be trained in Soviet-bloc and surrogate facilities. For instance, during 1980 Cuba helped Salvadoran guerrillas prepare to mount a major offensive against the Salvadoran military.

Information on specific parts of the apparatus involved in training insurgents both in the USSR and in surrogate facilities is sketchy, but it appears that elements from the GRU and the KGB play key roles. These elements fall within the *spetsnaz* category noted above.

Paramilitary training in irregular or special tactics is not a new phenomenon for the USSR. The origins of this facet of active measures and its political dimensions can be traced back to the early days of party rule.[105] During World War

II, the Central Committee of the CPSU established a Central Staff of the Partisan Movement, which conducted guerrilla operations behind German lines. According to Dziak,

> Apparently three groups exercised strong influence over the partisan movement: the General Staff's Chief Intelligence Directorate (GRU), the Fourth Directorate of the NKGB, and the Armed Forces Counterintelligence Directorate (GUKR, NKO, or SMERSH) headed by General Abakumov, an NKGB officer. The two former of these three were part of the state security apparatus. SMERSH, though nominally subordinate to the Commissariat for Defense, was in fact directly answerable to Stalin.[106]

Dziak goes on to observe that "the Partisan experience had a profound impact on subsequent Soviet planning and organization for special operations." After World War II "*spetsnaz* units gradually took on external roles," including training insurgent and terrorist cadres.[107]

As noted above, within the KGB's First Chief Directorate, Department 8 of Directorate S is involved in insurgent and terrorist training. It also is likely that it maintains links with training facilities in Third World countries.[108] Additionally, the Cubans, East Germans, Bulgarians, and other surrogates are also involved in guerrilla training under KGB guidance.[109] Other KGB elements that might be involved in insurgent and terrorist training are the Eleventh Department of the First Chief Directorate (which conducts liaison with and penetrates the intelligence services of Soviet satellite states), the border guards, and the troops of the Ninth Directorate.[110] However, links between these *spetsnaz* forces and training facilities both inside and outside of the USSR are difficult to establish.

KGB officers are complemented by their GRU counterparts, who provide expertise in guerrilla, diversionary, and intelligence training to Third World insurgents and terrorists. As with the KGB, specific elements within the GRU play roles through both its intelligence training and its insurgency branches. Finally, military-aid personnel from the General Staff's Military Assistance Directorate, whose presence in large numbers throughout the developing world is well documented, are likely to assist KGB and GRU officials in conducting training.

In sum, Dziak explains that the Soviets (and their surrogates) maintain large numbers of elite or quasi-elite forces tasked with missions that are clearly political-military in nature. This includes the use of KGB, GRU, and General Staff elements to train insurgent cadres both inside and outside the USSR.[111]

For analytic purposes, we have separated training from advisory support. In terms of the Soviet apparatus, this distinction may not be meaningful, as many of the military and security organs involved in training also provide advisory support. However, important distinctions can be drawn in terms of function and location. Advisory assistance generally appears to take place in areas contiguous to the location of the insurgency. For example, within sub-Sahara Africa, Soviet and surrogate officials provide advisory support to SWAPO guerrillas in base areas in Angola and Zambia. Functionally, this includes tactical intelligence, irregular combat direction, and other forms of field paramilitary advisory support.

Surrogate Assets

Imperial regimes have frequently used others to project power and gain influence beyond their borders. In early times, for instance, the Romans employed such forces to fight various enemies. More recently, the British used Gurkhas in Malaya, and the French rely on the Foreign Legion. The Soviet use of surrogates, however, differs in many respects from these examples: the missions are more specialized, Soviet control appears to vary markedly, and proxies play a political-military role in peace as well as in twilight war.[112]

Specialists have written much about Soviet proxies, but confusion persists over both the nature of the patron-client relationship and the mission specialization of the surrogates. With regard to the former, it would seem inaccurate to categorize these relationships as uniform because Moscow's control and influence appear to vary. For certain clients, there is little divergence of opinion about the nature of the relationship, but in other cases there is significant disagreement.

The Soviet–East European–bloc association is the least contentious for Western specialists. The patron has the power and expects the client to follow its direction in all missions. Trong Gilberg has characterized these states as "faithful agents" who consider "themselves as representatives of the Soviet Union in the Third World." Their activities are "designed to enhance the stature of the Kremlin and its power and influence . . . in ideological, political, and military-strategic terms." The East Germans, Czechs, and Bulgarians belong in this category.[113] In the case of Poland and Hungary, Gilberg perceives a difference, for although they remain "true to the principle of solidarity with the Soviet Union," he detects "less enthusiasm than [is] the case among the 'faithful agents.'"[114] This is an interesting thesis in light of the fact that the Soviets rely on East Germany, Czechoslovakia, and Bulgaria, but Gilberg does not document his assertion concerning Poland and Hungary.

Perhaps the most debated patron-client relationship is the one between Moscow and Havana.[115] On the one hand, there are those who believe that Havana is not performing as a Soviet proxy in Africa or elsewhere but is following a foreign policy linked directly to the early days of revolutionary rule in Cuba. According to Edward Gonzalez, Cuban policy is the result of the wranglings between three elite factions—pragmatists (technocrats and managers), *fidelista* (revolutionary anti-imperialists), and military professionals (advocates of an offensive military role in support of foreign-policy objectives).[116] Cuba's policy in Africa is the result of the victory of the latter two factions. Thus, although Cuban and Soviet policies converge, Havana is self-motivated and not following Moscow's direction.

Gavriel Ra'anan, on the other hand, marshals evidence pointing to Cuba playing a surrogate role on behalf of the Soviet Union: "To guarantee Cuba's economic, and perhaps military, viability and to insure implementation . . . of the 'Brezhnev Doctrine,' Castro would have to cooperate and even closely collaborate, with the USSR, not only in terms of trade, but also ideologically."[117] However, Ra'anan goes on to observe that in addition to much-needed economic assistance, playing a surrogate role provides Castro with "an opportunity to reassert the regime's virility . . . Consequently, the Cuban venture in Africa, starting in Angola, constituted the natural confluence and culmination of three factors": ideological predilections, Castro's need to bolster the fading image of the regime, and the phenomenon of increased Soviet-Cuban cooperation based on complementary needs and capabilities.[118] Beyond economic dependence, which is considerable, other analysts believe that Moscow maintains influence over Havana through penetration of Cuban security services, particularly the General Directorate of Intelligence (DGI).[119]

Between these two perspectives emerges W. Raymond Duncan's description of Cuba as a "preferred client." On the one hand, he notes that Havana has a very strong interest in cooperation and in policies that serve Soviet aims. On the other hand, despite nearly total economic dependence on the USSR, Duncan asserts that Castro makes his own decisions.[120]

In sum, Cuba is a difficult case. Walter Laqueur frames the dilemma as a question: Is Cuba's role that of a paladin or a surrogate? In light of the evidence, it seems highly unlikely that Cuba is acting independently. I concur with Laqueur that "despite outward appearances, Cuba no more has a specific African policy than Bulgaria does."[121]

Whereas Soviet-Cuban relations have been the subject of extensive Western scrutiny, other communist surrogate states have received little attention. For example, what kind of influence does Moscow maintain over the North Koreans and the Vietnamese, and can we expect them to play an increased surrogate role in the future? Similar questions should be raised about Marxist-Leninist governments in Angola, Ethiopia, Nicaragua, and South Yemen, and what about Libya and Syria? Clearly, they have helped promote the aims of Soviet foreign policy (for example, assistance to PLO factions and to guerrillas in Central America and elsewhere). However, it seems inappropriate to place Libya and Syria in the same category as the East European bloc and Cuba. The PLO is another difficult case to differentiate because of its factional composition and its changing power base.

To discover more about the nature of Soviet-surrogate power relations and how Moscow influences and/or controls its proxies, we should direct our analytic efforts toward a clearer understanding of the functional tasks or specialization of Soviet surrogates. For example, in southern Africa the East Germans and Cubans serve various functions. Chester Crocker, assistant secretary of state for African affairs, has characterized this as a "communist division of labor."[122] According to two specialists, "the security mission of the East Germans in Africa has been broadly defined . . . there are about 2,500 East Germans training the Angolan army and the Namibian insurgents, the South-West Africa People's Organization (SWAPO)." They note that East German troops stationed in Angola also have "participated in search and destroy missions against the UNITA insurgents and challenged the spearhead of South African columns deep inside Angola in November 1981."[123] In addition to training, advising, and supporting limited combat, the East Germans provided sophisticated knowledge of the military and intelligence sciences during the postinsurgency period of power consolidation. In Angola, a corps of advisers have been involved in training the regime's intelligence and security services.[124]

Cuba also plays multiple roles in southern Africa and elsewhere in the developing world. In Africa this has involved political-military training of both insurgent and government forces as well as actual combat operations. Because of Cuba's Third World credentials, it has a great deal of credibility among states and movements in these regions. As a result, Havana has the potential to achieve long-term penetration, leverage, and control on behalf of its Soviet patron.

In terms of political techniques, Cuban and East German personnel are active in Soviet front organizations and promote insurgent movements through political action in the U.N. and other international organizations (for example, the Cuban role in the Nonaligned Movement). Their overt propaganda is also targeted to support these efforts. Other Soviet clients play similar roles in supplementing Moscow's propaganda and political action efforts in support of insurgent movements.

In addition to Cuba and East Germany, we can observe the involvement of other Soviet surrogates in southern Africa. For example, the Bulgarians have provided military assistance to African liberation movements, including the MPLA in Angola, SWAPO in Namibia, and the Patriotic Front in Zimbabwe.[125] Similarly, accounts of the weaponry used by Third World insurgent movements reveal that Czech arms constitute an important part of their arsenal.[126]

In sum, a wide range of surrogate political and military assets appears to supplement and enhance Soviet capabilities for assisting insurgent movements both internationally and in the field. Here I have focused on surrogate involvement in southern Africa. This pattern has been repeated in Central America and elsewhere and appears to benefit Moscow in a number of ways. Surrogate assets expand and enhance the array of Soviet capabilities, which allows the Kremlin to acquire more flexible means for implementing policy. The use of surrogates also permits plausible denial in those situations in which Moscow does not wish to reveal its role.

Coordination and Integration

During the past ten to fifteen years, Soviet strategy for assisting revolutionary insurgent movements appears to have evolved not only in terms of the range of political-military instruments employed but also with regard to their coordination and integration. This is reflected, for example, in Soviet support of SWAPO. In the aftermath of the MPLA victory in Angola, Moscow escalated its assistance to SWAPO. This new policy (described in Chapter 5) was officially set forth by the Kremlin in 1978 with the publication of a "Manifesto for the Freedom, Independence, National Revival, and Social Progress of the Peoples of Tropical and Southern Africa."[127]

However, increased support actually began in 1976–1977. Political-military instruments described above were activated and integrated. Thus, as Soviet overt propaganda increased to promote the cause of SWAPO, the same themes were advanced by the Kremlin's major international front organizations. Through propaganda and conference diplomacy, the WPC and AAPSO intensified their efforts. Similarly, in the U.N. and other international organizations, Moscow and its surrogates and fronts stepped up their political activities to bolster and legitimize SWAPO.

Political techniques are part of an integrated Soviet political-military strategy. Consequently, the paramilitary elements of active measures were increased concurrently with propaganda and other political influence techniques to assist SWAPO operationally in the field. This coordination of multiple Soviet instruments was augmented by surrogate assets. A similar pattern will be evidenced in the other case studies contained in this volume.

Conclusion

This chapter has examined both the evolution of Soviet foreign policy as it relates to revolutionary insurgent movements and the political-military instruments and organizations utilized to promote and assist these groups and factions. Soviet involvement in this aspect of international relations is not new but dates back to the early days of CPSU rule in Russia. At that time they were not called active measures; nevertheless, the various political-military techniques described above were employed by Lenin and those who followed him to pursue foreign-policy objectives.

I have hypothesized, however, that, beginning in the late 1960s and early

1970s as Soviet policy shifted to one of increasing activism in the Third World, these political and paramilitary techniques were sharpened, integrated, and orchestrated in a more sophisticated fashion to promote and assist revolutionary insurgent movements. The remainder of this volume will examine four specific cases to test these propositions.

THREE

Soviet Involvement in the Vietnam Conflict

The origins and historical development of the Vietminh and the National Liberation Front (NLF), or Viet Cong (VC), have been described in numerous books as well as in *The Pentagon Papers*. Therefore, it is not necessary to reiterate these developments here.[1] I will focus instead on the evolution of Soviet support for the Democratic Republic of Vietnam (DRVN) and the NLF (VC) within the context of a fluid military situation in South Vietnam during 1964–1965. It now appears that Soviet involvement in the Vietnam conflict came to serve as the prototype for the Soviet strategy of assistance and support for insurgent movements in the 1970s and 1980s. Although there are differences between this case and Soviet assistance for movements since the early 1970s, significant parallels exist and will become evident in the chapters that follow.

Although the roots of the Vietnamese insurgency predate World War II, Soviet interest in Southeast Asia before the war was marginal. World War II was a watershed period in several Southeast Asian countries because it provided nationalist and communist leaders with the opportunity to mobilize the population against Japanese intervention. During the immediate postwar period, the revolutionary potential of these new forces was overlooked by Moscow, as Stalin was preoccupied with advancing Soviet objectives in Europe. Additionally, Stalin had suffered a major setback in China during the late 1920s and early 1930s, and this is said to have given him "reason to discount Asian communist parties as important vehicles for pursuing his goals."[2] With respect to the Vietminh,

Stalin may also have underestimated their strength (as he had done with the Chinese communists).[3]

The Korean War began to alter Soviet attitudes toward Asia. According to Adam Ulam, "the continuation of hostilities in the Far East was viewed in Moscow with mixed feelings."[4] On the positive side, U.S. forces would be tied down in Korea and resources would be diverted from NATO. As the war continued, it also must have become apparent to the Soviet Union that contention within the United States over the conflict could have a residual impact on its broader foreign policy.[5] The war might also make the People's Republic of China (PRC) increasingly dependent on the USSR. However, as Ulam observes, "these 'positive' aspects had their corresponding dangers."[6] The war could lead to an increased U.S. defense commitment that would strengthen NATO. This might include going "full speed ahead in arming Germany."[7] With respect to the PRC, the war would allow Mao to solidify Chinese Communist Party control over China. In light of these contradictions, Moscow appears to have preferred protracted war and extended negotiations. Following Stalin's death in March 1953, the Soviet leaders appear to have concluded that the risks of stringing out the conflict were greater than those of bringing it to an end.

Moscow also exerted pressure on Ho Chi Minh to accept the partition of Vietnam, which became the basis for the Geneva Accords in 1954.[8] In *Vietnam: A Political History*, Joseph Buttinger notes that the Vietminh were "unhappy about the prospects of a negotiated peace" by 1954, as they "now were looking toward total victory."[9] Nevertheless, the settlement was agreed to and Vietnam was partitioned. The Hanoi regime was also disappointed over the Soviet Union's unwillingness to protest to the U.N. when the 1956 elections in Vietnam were canceled. Apparently, these were viewed as necessary concessions by the DRVN, who hoped to convince the USSR to become its primary source of assistance.[10] This hope was not realized, however, and between 1955 and 1965, aid from the USSR was kept to a minimum and Soviet–North Vietnamese relations deteriorated. Various reasons have been advanced to explain Soviet reluctance. For example, William Zimmerman attributes it to fear of increasing involvement in the war:

> Khrushchev's position was that Soviet nuclear might was sufficient to deter the export of counterrevolution and that revolution in individual countries could therefore proceed apace without interference from the outside. Fearful of the risk of escalation, Khrushchev put forth a plausible and attractive rationalization for a policy that did not involve large amounts of military aid, much less large deployments of Soviet troops abroad, to foreign communists engaged in waging national liberation wars—namely, the Vietnamese.[11]

Ulam likewise stresses fear of increasing involvement: "The Soviets had every reason to avoid their own overcommitment in Indochina. Khrushchev . . . was after a bigger game."[12] Therefore, to keep up appearances, especially as the PRC increased its interest in encouraging wars of national liberation, the Soviets remained involved in the affairs of Indochina. In fact, Khrushchev's 1961 assertion of the Soviet duty to support wars of national liberation may have been aimed as much at China as at the United States. It allowed him to counter PRC charges that Moscow was not living up to its responsibility.

Changing Soviet–North Vietnamese Relations: 1960–1965

In December 1960, the Kremlin intervened in Laos on behalf of the Vietminh-dominated Pathet Lao Party. At that time, Soviet aircraft, providing military assistance, flew 184 missions into Laos.[13] In the spring of 1961, Soviet military supplies began to be transported to the VC via eastern Laos.[14] However, as one analyst noted, this did not serve as the impetus for a major increase in Soviet aid. In fact, the opposite occurred, and the USSR rejected a direct request from Hanoi in December 1962 for increased military assistance. The denial was delivered by CPSU Secretary Yuri Andropov during his January 1963 visit to North Vietnam.[15]

As a result of these developments, relations between Moscow and Hanoi declined further during 1963–1964, and Ho Chi Minh began to look increasingly to the PRC for help. According to Donald Zagoria, "by 1964 . . . Hanoi had moved so close to Peking—a position from which it subsequently withdrew—that Khrushchev no longer believed the game was worth the candle. Soviet aid to Ho Chi Minh's government dwindled significantly in the last two years of Khrushchev's rule."[16] Zagoria goes on to note that by June 1964, Khrushchev was "prepared to resign Soviet cochairmanship of the permanent body of the International Control Commission (for Laos) and to disengage from all of Indochina."[17]

While Hanoi was suffering a setback in its attempt to persuade Moscow to increase assistance, the military situation in South Vietnam was approaching a crisis point for the United States and the Government of Vietnam (GVN). In the fifteen months following the military coup against the Ngo Dinh Diem government, Lyndon Johnson's administration faced a rapidly deteriorating political and military situation. The North Vietnamese and the VC were quick to exploit these developments. In the weeks following the Diem coup, the VC expanded their control in the countryside of South Vietnam. With assistance and support from Hanoi, the insurgents launched a major political and military offensive at the end of 1963. The VC infiltrated strategic hamlets and initiated a record number of military attacks against the Army of Vietnam (ARVN); major towns and highways in the delta region experienced a significant reduction in government control, and the guerrillas attacked a U.S. Special Forces training camp.[18]

By the end of January 1964, a group of army officers led by General Nguyen Khanh carried out a coup against the junta that had removed Diem. The situation described above was becoming worse as Khanh assumed power. The strategic hamlet program and ARVN military operations had come almost to a complete standstill, and GVN authority in many parts of the countryside had vanished.[19] The war, according to U.S. intelligence, was approaching the final stages for the GVN. Unless it dealt immediately and effectively with its problems, South Vietnam had, "at best, an even chance of withstanding the insurgency menace during the next few weeks or months."[20]

The Khanh government, with U.S. assistance, developed ambitious plans for reform but produced meager results during the spring and summer months. The ARVN remained in a state of flux as a result of increasing desertions and poor leadership. The government itself was split, and a coup was attempted against Khanh in July 1964. Maxwell Taylor, the U.S. ambassador in Saigon, assessed the situation in the following terms:

> Khanh has not succeeded in building any substantial body of active popular support in the countryside . . . The most important and most intractable internal problem of South Vietnam in meeting the Viet Cong threat is the political structure at the national level. The best thing that can be said about the Khanh government is that it has lasted six months and has about a 50-50 chance of lasting out the year.[21]

By the fall of 1964, political turmoil in South Vietnam intensified as politicians and generals jockeyed for power. In November, the VC attacked the U.S. air base at Bien-hoa, killing four Americans and destroying five aircraft. By the end of the year, the administration realized that an escalation in U.S. involvement was required. The majority of Johnson advisers endorsed some form of air war against North Vietnam.

It is beyond the scope of this chapter to review the debate over the feasibility of the bombing option and over how to employ air power, but by the end of January 1965, the compelling arguments against bombing and increased air power were rejected.[22] The ensuing sustained air offensive against the North Vietnamese was soon coupled with the rapid introduction of U.S. ground forces in the south to stem the tide against the VC. By July 1965, the Johnson administration was committed to a major military effort in Vietnam. These developments blocked what must have appeared to Hanoi to be the impending successful culmination of the war for which it had provided the covert support and assistance necessary to allow the VC to accelerate the internal breakdown and collapse of the GVN. U.S. intervention denied Hanoi and the VC the chance of victory in 1965.

Soviet policy significantly changed during this period. The Gulf of Tonkin incident of August 1964 and the events described above resulted in efforts by Hanoi to strengthen its relations with Moscow. In the aftermath of Khrushchev's ouster and with the growing U.S. involvement in the conflict, the new Soviet leadership signaled its intentions to increase military and economic assistance to North Vietnam. An examination of a chronology of public statements by Moscow between 1955 and 1971 discloses that not until 1965 did the theme of Soviet assistance begin to receive significant commentary.[23] Before this, Soviet remarks were minimal, reflecting limited commitment to the DRVN and the VC. Zimmerman has observed that the decision on the part of the USSR to increase its role in Vietnam can be demarcated by examining "Soviet media utterances" on the subject:

> Moscow was intent on convincing external and domestic audiences that the Soviet Union would match the United States step for step, though Soviet leaders preferred to climb shorter steps. In 1964 Moscow's themes had been that "it would not remain indifferent" and that it would take "necessary measures" (unspecified). In 1965–1967 it stated that it was taking practical measures . . . to strengthen the security and build up the defense capabilities of the DRV or, in Brezhnev's words, to provide "real support." Such phrases were generally coupled with declarations that the USSR would compete with the United States by matching U.S. escalation. "The Soviet Union is prepared to give the Democratic Republic of Vietnam whatever assistance it needs . . . The Soviet Union has given and will continue to give fraternal Vietnam its full political support and the necessary economic and military assistance.[24]

During mid-1965, as the U.S. bombing of North Vietnam and the introduction of 100,000 troops transformed the conflict into a new phase, Moscow faced an important decision. Ulam notes that "Vietnam now became the testing ground not only for the Americans' theories of how to cope with wars of liberation but also for the Soviet readiness and ability to protect a Communist regime from the superior power of the United States . . . [T]he bombing of the North was in the eyes of the Communist world a challenge."[25] Following harsh Chinese communist criticism that the Soviet failure to react quickly to the bombing signaled its unwillingness to lead the communist world, Moscow began to make good on its promise to increase assistance. This change in policy toward Hanoi appears, in retrospect, to have been part of a broader transformation in Soviet doctrine toward conflict in the Third World, including a greater readiness to employ political and military means to influence the course of events in these conflicts.

Evidence of this new policy began to appear in Soviet doctrinal and declaratory statements. Among the signals was the addition of military assistance to other kinds of support the Soviets asserted they had a duty to provide to national liberation movements in the Third World. As discussed in Chapter 2, statements to this effect appeared in the 1968 edition of Marshal V. D. Sokolovskiy's *Soviet Military Strategy*. His commentary not only signaled a more general change in Soviet policy—"the USSR will render, when it is necessary, military support as well to people subject to imperialist aggression"—but also specified that Vietnam was the most likely candidate for this assistance.[26] According to Sokolovskiy, "U.S. imperialism today plays the role of world gendarme, coming out against democratic, revolutionary transformation . . . The clearest example of this is the barbaric war of the USA in Vietnam."[27] It is the duty of the USSR to assist the Vietnamese and other liberation movements "in their struggle with imperialism not only ideologically and politically but materially as well."[28] Although Sokolovskiy's revised edition appeared in 1968, as early as 1966 we can find statements suggesting this change in policy.[29]

The post-Khrushchev leadership began in 1966 to assert publicly that the USSR would come to the aid of the Vietnamese at this time. For instance, Aleksey Kosygin let it be known during a visit to Cairo that the USSR had offered to send military volunteers to North Vietnam but that Hanoi had declined the offer.[30] These and other public declarations of support were underlined by the USSR's exercise of its power projection capabilities. It now seems evident that Moscow's political, military, and economic assistance between 1965 and 1972 played an important part in Hanoi's successful prosecution of the war.

In 1965, in conjunction with the acceleration of military assistance to North Vietnam, the Soviets increased the use of propaganda and other political warfare activities in the international arena to promote the cause of the DRVN-VC, while attempting to discredit U.S. involvement with and support of its GVN ally. According to a number of Soviet specialists, this was a significant about-face for Moscow. For instance, as noted earlier, Zagoria asserted that by 1964, Soviet–North Vietnam relations had become strained to the point that the game was no longer worth the candle. Evidence in support of this is that "Soviet economic aid to Ho Chi Minh's government dwindled significantly."[31] The beginning of 1965 saw changes in the Soviet position. However, in both Peking and Hanoi's view, the degree of the USSR's commitment was still too limited. In February 1965, Kosygin apparently suggested to Mao a plan for dealing with the crisis through diplomatic negotiation. According to the Chinese, Kosygin "stressed the need to help the United States 'find a way out of Vietnam.'"[32]

By the end of 1965, Soviet reluctance had changed to large-scale material and diplomatic support for the DRVN-VC. To revise Zagoria's phraseology, now the game was worth the candle. The reasons for this appear to be threefold. First, Moscow wished to demonstrate to the world communist movement that it was committed to assist the DRVN-VC achieve victory. Second, through the supply of more sophisticated equipment (in larger amounts), the Soviet Union hoped to increase its influence over Hanoi and draw it away from the PRC. The first objective was also related to Peking's claim of leadership of the world communist movement. Moscow hoped to wean not only the DRVN-VC but the entire communist movement away from the PRC. Third, through a low-cost and low-risk policy the Soviets sought to provide Hanoi with the means of ensnaring the United States in the Vietnam quagmire and of eventually defeating it through protracted conflict.

Soviet Political-Military Support of North Vietnam and the Viet Cong

During 1966–1972 the USSR focused its international propaganda and political warfare capabilities on U.S. involvement in the Vietnam War. The United States had been the principal target of these activities since the end of World War II, with the major themes being U.S. aggressiveness and militarism centering on nuclear weapons and the arms race. During the latter half of the 1960s and early 1970s, however, no theme received more coverage than the Vietnam policy of the United States.[33] As I will demonstrate below, this involved a number of subthemes and was linked to Washington's problems at home and abroad. Additionally, the Soviet propaganda and political action campaign was designed to promote the cause and legitimacy of the DRVN-VC, while isolating the GVN. In conjunction with these activities, the USSR significantly increased its military equipment and support.

Soviet Foreign Propaganda

Before 1966 the Vietnam conflict and U.S. involvement were not primary targets of Soviet international propaganda. This changed as Washington's role expanded. The major themes propagated in 1966 set the focus for the 1966–1972 period. Thus, although events like the peace talks on the 1968 Tet offensive might alter these trends somewhat, in general the following topics were reiterated in Soviet propaganda: the United States is the aggressor in Vietnam, U.S. military strategy is genocidal and its diplomatic policy duplicitous, victory for the DRVN-VC and defeat for the United States–GVN is inevitable, and international and U.S. domestic public opinion has mobilized to oppose U.S. policy and to support the DRVN-VC. The objective was to promote and enhance the cause of Hanoi and the VC, while censuring and discrediting U.S. policy.

The characterization of U.S. policy in Vietnam as aggressive and imperial is a generic charge found in Soviet propaganda throughout the post–World War

II period. Consequently, U.S. "imperialist aggressiveness" in Southeast Asia, according to Moscow, "has its roots in its own nature."[34] Economic concerns, especially those of the arms merchants, were a part of this. "American lads are perishing by the thousands in the South Vietnamese jungles . . . in the interests of the U.S. monopolies . . . enriching the very merchants of death."[35] Spending on arms was also a means by which Washington hoped to avoid an economic depression.[36]

U.S. military strategy was characterized as extremely brutal and "thousands of Vietnamese" were said to have "fallen to toxic gases, poisonous chemicals, and phosphorous and napalm bombs . . . Vietnam has been turned into a military testing ground for 50 types of chemical and bacteriological weapons."[37] The chemical warfare charge was not a new one. Soviet and front-group propaganda levied similar accusations against the United States during the Korean War.[38] In Vietnam chemical warfare was part of a general strategy of "waging a war of annihilation against [the Vietnamese] people. The Americans have . . . slaughtered old men, women, and children and have been torturing the civilian population."[39]

Washington was also said to have employed diplomatic maneuvers and deception to manipulate its allies, domestic public opinion, and the international community to support its Vietnam policy. For example, the United States was charged with attempting to draw the U.N. into the Vietnam conflict "to mediate" as a way of sidestepping the Geneva Accords.[40] These military and diplomatic tactics were unsuccessful, resulting instead in a policy of escalation. According to the Soviet news agency TASS, "the Pentagon leaders themselves now have to scratch their earlier-voiced high hopes for an early military victory in Vietnam."[41] As a result, they have no choice but to "allocate another 15 billion dollars for the war" and take "steps to spread the flame to Laos, Cambodia, and Thailand."[42]

If U.S. actions were guided by malevolent forces, the DRVN and the VC were described as fighting for a completely just cause. This distinction, according to Moscow, explained the failure of U.S. policy. *Radio Moscow* asserted that "the Pentagon strategists fail to consider two factors: first, their troops are up against well-organized resistance from the broad masses . . . resolved to continue fighting for their freedom; and second, the moral and particularly the material aid to the Vietnamese from the Socialist countries."[43] *Red Star* observed that "it is impossible to defeat a people . . . who are fighting for a just cause."[44] The South Vietnamese government, in contrast, represented "no one but a small group of generals and they would certainly lose any election."[45] This is why the government refused to hold the elections that had been promised.[46]

Opposition to U.S. policy, both domestic and international, was the subject of extensive Soviet propaganda. Within the United States this included members of Congress:

Senator Curtis of Nebraska has said that the nation does not like the war at all. Congressman Udall of Arizona believes that the Vietnam war has bred a very alarming mood among conservatives. Senators Mansfield, Fulbright, and many others have expressed concern over the possibility that the war may spread because of America's escalation efforts.[47]

On March 18, 1966, TASS noted that Senators Robert Kennedy, Wayne Morse, William Fulbright, and Abraham Ribicoff urged President Johnson to negotiate with the NLF to bring an end to the war. Furthermore, Morse was reported to have charged that the "U.S. represents the greatest threat to world peace" and that "we are imposing a course of action on Southeast Asia although we have neither a legal foundation nor moral justification."[48] Criticism outside of congressional circles was also covered, with the apparent objective of portraying a broad and divergent opposition to the Vietnam War within U.S. society (well before anything resembling this existed).[49]

Opposition within the international arena, particularly among West European allies, was an equally important aspect of this theme. For instance, Bertrand Russell's War Crimes Tribunal to Investigate U.S. Activities in Vietnam was presented as indicative of growing international opposition to Washington policy.[50]

Finally, the Soviets characterized their own role in the conflict as one of complete commitment to the DRVN-VC and to the principle of proletarian internationalism. Accordingly, *Radio Moscow* stated on January 20, 1966, that "the Soviet Union itself is doing everything it can to help the Vietnamese . . . our aid embraces all spheres—defense, political, and economic. We exert every effort to deliver modern weapons as quickly as possible to the freedom fighters in Vietnam."[51] Furthermore, the Soviets promised that should the United States escalate, the USSR would step up its assistance to the DRVN-VC.[52]

Although the propaganda themes identified above were reiterated throughout 1966–1972, at specific points critical events received particular attention. The Tet offensive and the initiation of peace talks during 1968 were two such examples. According to Moscow, these events marked 1968 as a pivotal year in the conflict (which it was).

The Tet offensive reaffirmed the Soviet assertion that the United States could not succeed in Vietnam. "[T]here is no military solution for Washington . . . The latest events [Tet] make it plainer than ever."[53] According to the Kremlin, the war had entered a new and final phase. "The patriots are pursuing their partisan operations . . . but at the same time they are waging a conventional war, using regular army tactics."[54] Within the Johnson administration, Moscow claimed, Tet created panic. Faced with defeat "U.S. ruling circles are openly threatening to use atomic weapons in Vietnam."[55] In fact, the assertion that the

Tet offensive was a catastrophic defeat for the Johnson administration constituted a major psychological operation mounted against the United States during the Vietnam War. Its impact on the Johnson administration remains an issue of debate; however, there is little doubt that this perception of Tet had an important effect in the United States.[56]

A second issue that received considerable attention in 1968 and thereafter was the Paris peace talks. The United States was charged with procrastination and with using the talks as a tactic or as camouflage, while escalating the bombing.[57] For instance, on August 1, 1968, *Radio Moscow* stated that the "fifteenth official talk between representatives of the DRVN and the United States . . . like its fourteen predecessors . . . ended without results. The course of the talks has given rise to the serious fear [that] the United States is bent upon preventing a result."[58] On December 4, 1968, Moscow asserted that "while American diplomats . . . are trying every possible way to drag out the negotiations, the Pentagon is extending its aggression."[59]

Escalating the war was doomed because of the indomitable spirit of the DRVN-VC,[60] the quality and quantity of Soviet bloc aid,[61] the corruptness of the Saigon regime,[62] and the poor showing of the ARVN and U.S. forces.[63] During 1968, Soviet propaganda increasingly focused on the effects of the Vietnam conflict on domestic U.S. politics. This coverage centered on the antiwar movement and on racial tensions.[64]

During the final years of U.S. involvement in Vietnam, Soviet propaganda continued to follow the themes identified above, but the intensity of the campaign heightened. A main issue was the U.S. policy of Vietnamization, described as a deception that sought to prolong the conflict, while making the U.S. role less visible. According to *Izvestiya,* Vietnamization did not reverse "former President Johnson's Asian doctrine . . . this doctrine proclaimed the United States' intention of establishing its dominance in Asia." However, Vietnamization sought to "strangle Asian national liberation movements with the hands of the reactionary forces in the Asian countries themselves."[65] Even in the final stages of U.S. troop withdrawal, Moscow reported that "Vietnamization does in no way mean a de-Americanization of the war."[66]

In addition to Vietnamization, the U.S. employment of air power received harsh criticism during 1970–1972. According to Soviet propaganda, the United States was guilty of the kinds of atrocities for which the Nazis were tried and convicted at Nuremberg.[67] TASS of July 2, 1972, characterized U.S. actions as "nothing but genocide, a war of extermination . . . The American brass unleashed an air war against the Democratic Republic of Vietnam . . . on an unprecedented scale." Washington was charged with the "criminal bombing of the system of dykes along all major rivers in the DRVN."[68] The objective was to "turn Vietnam into an area of scorched earth."[69]

With respect to the peace talks, even as the final settlement approached, the

Soviets continued to assert that the United States followed a strategy of delay and manipulation. Washington had no intention of agreeing to a settlement of the conflict. For instance, on October 26, 1972, TASS charged that objections raised by President Nguyen Van Thieu were "issued by the USA as a pretext for postponing the implementation of the agreements reached."[70] Soviet propaganda also noted that "the White House's delaying tactics . . . only lead to more destruction and victims . . . this policy is being condemned throughout the world."[71] The strategy of Vietnamization likewise caused "a storm of anger and indignation" both internationally and within the United States.[72]

To summarize, the themes identified above constitute the parameters of Soviet propaganda directed against U.S. policy in Vietnam during 1966–1972. They were set within the context of the general or paradigmatic theme of U.S. imperialism versus national liberation and served as the basis for other Soviet political warfare activities.

International Front Activities

In addition to their own international propaganda, the Soviet political warfare campaign against the Vietnam policy of the United States was conducted through the Kremlin's major international front organizations. The USSR utilizes both overt and covert instruments to promote foreign-policy objectives. Soviet propaganda and political actions directed against U.S. policy in Vietnam did not veer from this pattern.

The methods of Soviet-directed international front organizations include the use of propaganda and international conference diplomacy. The international front utilized by the Soviet Union in this instance was the World Peace Council (WPC). As *the* major Soviet front organization, the WPC generally takes the lead in all important campaigns. This was the case with respect to U.S. policy in Vietnam. As noted above, during the second half of the 1960s, Soviet propaganda focused on U.S. involvement in the conflict. The WPC's concern with the issue paralleled these developments. To carry this out, the WPC utilized its major propaganda publications, including the *World Peace Council Bulletin (WPC Bulletin), New Perspectives* (originally, *Perspectives*), *Bulletin of Peace,* and *Peace Courier.* These materials, as well as related booklets and pamphlets, were circulated on a worldwide basis. Additionally, WPC propaganda activities were augmented and amplified through its sponsorship of major international conferences, primarily in Western Europe.

International front propaganda. Following the Soviet propaganda campaign in terms of both themes and time sequence, WPC commentary began to grow during 1965. The WPC devoted a special issue of the *Bulletin of Peace* to the Vietnam issue, which, in retrospect, appears to have set the focus for sub-

sequent front propaganda campaigns. The issue condemned "the highly dangerous action of the United States in ordering aerial bombing raids on the Democratic Republic of Vietnam" and asserted that these actions "should be
condemned by world public opinion and by the United Nations." The *Bulletin of
Peace* demanded immediate "withdrawal of U.S. Forces."[73]

In the years that followed, the WPC and other fronts expanded their propaganda efforts. Although these fronts condemned U.S. policy and actions as criminal and praised those of the DRVN and the VC, the major topic of discussion
was the rapidly growing opposition to the role of the United States in Vietnam
both at home and worldwide. Consequently, WPC propaganda paid close attention to the antiwar movement in the United States, using WPC publications to
significantly expand the coverage of the movement's growing influence on the
U.S. political scene. In the early spring of 1966, for instance, *Perspectives* carried an interview with Madeleine Duckles, a U.S. antiwar movement activist
and leader of Women Strike For Peace. She stated that "women, students, intellectuals and businessmen have joined the movement . . . to arouse the con-
science of our people." This opposition would continue to expand, according to
Duckles, because "there are hundreds of thousands of children in Vietnam who
are burned beyond recognition . . . this crime is the primary responsibility of
the American people."[74] The WPC publications also carried appeals by various
domestic groups opposing Johnson administration policy, including the American Friends Service Committee.[75]

Similar attention was devoted to individuals and groups in the West European anti–Vietnam War movement. The fall 1967 issue of *Perspectives* reported
on the activities of fourteen Vienna churches that sent aid to North and South
Vietnam, while other issues focused on demonstrations and related action-
oriented programs.

> The day of 21 October 1967 will go down in the history of the world
> peace movement as one of its greatest days. First launched by the
> U.S. National Mobilization Committee to End the War in Vietnam
> . . . the call to demonstrate on this day with American peace friends
> was taken up across the world . . . The response exceeded all expec-
> tations. In almost every corner of the world massive demonstrations
> and protests of every kind were held . . . At many rallies and dem-
> onstrations there were direct link-ups with American demonstrations
> and with protesters in other parts of the world.[76]

The technique of reporting worldwide opposition linked to its domestic U.S.
counterparts sought to create the perception of a broadly coordinated movement
opposed to U.S. policy.

This propaganda method was employed principally through the *WPC Bul-*

letin. A more action-oriented instrument than other WPC publications, the *WPC Bulletin* appears to have been employed for organizing and coordinating purposes. During the latter half of the 1960s, its main functions appear to have been both reporting past demonstrations and serving as a channel through which to coordinate future ones. It sought to convey the impression of a massive and rapidly expanding worldwide movement. The June 1967 issue was characteristic. Entitled "Action for Peace in Vietnam," it called for the coordination of demonstrations planned for the fall months. Additionally, demonstrations that had taken place during the spring in Britain, Czechoslovakia, Portugal, France, East Germany, Spain, Argentina, and elsewhere were described as part of worldwide opposition to U.S. policy.[77] This pattern was repeated in each issue of the *WPC Bulletin* during the latter half of the 1960s; these issues included information on how to contact various peace and antiwar groups and suggested ways of integrating activities.

The WPC also used its various propaganda channels to report on its own international conferences and other anti–Vietnam War organizing activities, including extensive coverage of its major activity in Western Europe, the Stockholm Conference on Vietnam. First held in 1967, the Stockholm conference convened annually until the DRVN consolidated power in Vietnam in 1975. During 1967–1972 the Stockholm conference and its national-level spin-offs became the vehicles through which the WPC sought to play a role in coordinating and organizing West European and U.S. opposition to the war. Even after the final U.S. withdrawal and Paris peace agreement, the annual conference continued to be held. Ostensibly, the reason was to ensure that the United States did not reintervene.

WPC propaganda organs treated these meetings as integral to the expanding worldwide movement against U.S. policy.[78] For example, *Perspectives* stated that Stockholm was the spark that "has given such a big push forward to the campaign all over the world in solidarity with the Vietnamese people in their heroic struggle to end the U.S. aggression." According to Romesh Chandra, head of the WPC, "cooperation among the different international peace organizations . . . took its first halting steps during the Stockholm Conference." The conference established a Continuing Committee to coordinate the activities of "all organizations national and international, which agree with the aims of the Stockholm Conference and agreed to affiliate themselves with the Conference."[79] The Stockholm conference became the central element of international front conference activities directed against U.S. policy in Vietnam.

The thematic patterns of front propaganda established during 1965 and 1966 remained basically the same until the 1973 U.S. withdrawal from Vietnam. These themes included condemnation of U.S. policy as criminal, acclamation of the DRVN and the NLF, and promotion of the anti–Vietnam War movement. Additionally, important developments like the Tet offensive and the Paris peace talks received special attention. In almost every respect international front propaganda patterns paralleled those of the USSR. The principal difference was the degree to which the fronts focused on and promoted international opposition to U.S. policy. In light of the international political activities of the fronts, the WPC emphasis on the opposition theme is not surprising.

A brief review of WPC propaganda during 1970–1972 shows the continuity with its earlier commentary. In terms of U.S. policy, the focus continued to be on alleged criminal behavior and deception. The latter was attributed to the strategy of Vietnamization and the Paris peace talks. The charge of criminal behavior became particularly vitriolic by the 1970s. For example, a special issue of *New Perspectives* focusing on "Indochina: The Criminal War" contained a number of articles charging the United States with criminal behavior, including one by the highly respected Swedish scholar Gunnar Myrdal, entitled "To Bring the Atrocities into the Open." According to Myrdal, "it is not enough that the United States stop its war of aggression . . . the American nation must live through an intellectual and moral catharsis." This involved being "made to understand, acknowledge, and recognize the atrocious crimes committed."[80] Other front publication articles were even harsher. The following passage is from a *New Perspectives* article of 1972 entitled "Ecocide, Biocide, and Genocide in Vietnam," which states, "The Nixon Administration . . . has resorted to chemical war, the automatic warfare of electronics, meterological or climate warfare, craterization of the landscape, carpet bombing, destroying dikes and dams, creating more and more floods by seeding artificial rain and so on."[81] All of these tactics were directed, as Myrdal asserted, "against the people of Indochina and against humanity."[82] According to the WPC, the United States sought to "exterminate groups of people" and to attack the "life-supporting environment."[83]

A standard tactic of the fronts is to present their commentary as a reflection and a part of the mainstream of world public opinion. One way of achieving this is to carry reports about and by other individuals and groups opposed to U.S. policy. The charge of war crimes illustrates this tactic. The previous example of Professor Myrdal, along with those that follow, demonstrates how this was carried out. During the summer of 1971, *New Perspectives* reported on the Winter Soldier Investigation. Held during January–February, the inquiry was organized and jointly sponsored by the National Committee of Vietnam Veterans Against the War and by the Citizens Enquiry Commission. Carrying excerpts of the testimony of "ex-Vietnam GIs . . . about atrocities they witnessed or themselves committed," the editors of *New Perspectives* lead the reader to understand that most Vietnam veterans are of the same opinion and that the evidence cited in the article is only a glimpse of the prevailing U.S. behavior in Vietnam.[84] The WPC also reported on the findings of the International Commission of Inquiry into U.S. Crimes in Indochina, held in Oslo in June 1971. Headed by Professor Myrdal, the commission is reported to have substantiated the "indiscriminate killing and systematic torturing inflicted by the U.S. imperialists."[85] Finally, *New Perspectives* carried purported interviews with U.S. prisoners in North Vietnam who "freely" provided confirmation of the "barbarism of the U.S. imperialists and their Saigon puppets."[86]

In addition to the charge of criminal behavior, front propaganda presented the U.S. troop reduction and the Paris peace negotiations as subterfuges. Troop withdrawals did not de-escalate the war and therefore were a hoax. The United States simply changed its approach to utilize other means, especially "electronic death."[87] The Vietnamization policy simply shifted responsibility for "suppressing the liberation struggle to the South Vietnamese." Direction of the war, as well as financial support for conducting it, still came from Washington. The Nixon administration had no intention of withdrawing from Vietnam.[88]

During 1970–1972 the fronts devoted considerable attention to the "expanding and worldwide antiwar movement."[89] This theme was frequently reiterated in *Peace Courier,* which replaced the *WPC Bulletin* as the WPC's more action-oriented, organizing publication. It served (and continues to serve) the dual function of propagandizing and mobilizing.

International conference diplomacy.   A second major technique employed by the Soviet fronts is what this study has termed international conference diplomacy. The conferences and meetings dealing with U.S. policy in Vietnam that the WPC and other fronts either sponsored or took part in during 1966–1972 were numerous. Front publications and reports provide a means by which to observe these activities. Of the three categories of international conference activities—front organization meetings, front-sponsored international and regional conferences, and conferences sponsored by an international organization in which fronts actively participate—the WPC centered its activities around the Stockholm Conference on Vietnam, which it organized and directed.

An examination of the documents and reports of the Stockholm conference for 1967–1972 serves as a case study of how the fronts combine words and actions in support of Soviet policy. A large and ongoing operation like this is generally focused on multiple audiences. In the case of Stockholm, West European and U.S. anti–Vietnam War groups appear to have been the first priority. Opposition in Western Europe was also a potential means of affecting the NATO alliance. Finally, fostering opposition in the Third World appears to have been the third and more ancillary goal.

The objectives of the Stockholm conference on Vietnam were set forth by the head of the WPC, Romesh Chandra, following the initial session in 1967. He observed that the meeting had resulted in "cooperation among the different international peace organizations." To expand this, the participants in the 1967 meeting established "some machinery for cooperation, for coordination of actions, for liaison and consultation among different organizations working to end the war in Vietnam."[90] To accomplish this, the Continuing Committee and an International Liaison Committee of the Stockholm conference were established. They were responsible for coordination of the various members during the interim between annual conferences. A monthly bulletin and less-frequent information letter were established to assist in coordinating the activities of "all organizations, national and international, which agree with the aims of the Stockholm conference."[91] During 1967, for instance, the Continuing Committee planned and coordinated the following activities:

- *Human Rights Day.* Held on December 19, 1967, to focus international attention and activities on U.S. war crimes in Vietnam.

- *Anniversary of the National Liberation Front.* Held on December 20, 1967, to focus attention and activities on the NLF and its cause.

The Stockholm conference of July 6–9, 1967, set the operational pattern for a six-year international campaign of action directed against U.S. policy in Vietnam. The ultimate objective was U.S. withdrawal from the conflict. The initial meeting was sponsored by the WPC, the Swedish Peace and Arbitration Society, the International Conference for Disarmament and Peace, the War Resisters' International, the International Fellowship of Reconciliation, and the Christian Peace Conference. According to the conference documents, "450 delegates and observers from 62 countries and 22 international organizations" participated. However, in addition to representatives from the various Soviet fronts, the DRVN, and the VC, the conference was attended by individuals not generally associated with international front activities, including academics of international reputation: Gunnar Myrdal (Sweden), D. F. Fleming, (United States) Philippe Devillers (France), and Lelio Basso (Italy). Other internationally recognized individuals included Jean Lacouture (France) and Benjamin Spock (United States). By attracting these and similar personalities, the Stockholm conference, a Soviet front organized and influenced activity, acquired an image of cooperation among politically diverse individuals and groups who shared a common concern.[92]

The 1967 conference established eight commissions and working groups to investigate a number of issues including U.S. violations of international law, U.S. criminal behavior, the NLF struggle for independence, peace initiatives, the growing isolation of the United States in the world arena, and coordination of activities to oppose U.S. policy in Vietnam. The final report of each of these commissions generally followed the arguments, findings, and objections found in WPC propaganda as outlined above. For example, the commission concerned with international law found U.S. actions in Vietnam to be in violation of all international law, the U.N. charter, and its pledges at the Geneva Conference of 1954.[93]

Reports from these commissions and working groups, along with the conference's "Appeal to the World for Vietnam" (which condemned U.S. policy as "nothing less than genocide"), were published and distributed worldwide through the machinery of the Stockholm conference and groups participating in it. Additionally, the 1967 conference assigned the Continuing Committee and the International Liaison Committee the following responsibilities: unify those organizations pursuing objectives similar to the conference, exchange information and plans with these groups, expand the campaign into new areas and attract new groups, and raise funds to support the work of the conference.[94]

Between the annual meetings, the activities of the Stockholm conference, including the organizing functions of the International Liaison Committee and the Continuing Committee, can be observed through a review of its bulletin and information letter. For example, information letter no. 2 of 1968 reported on the June 18–19 meeting in Rome of the International Liaison Committee. It contained documents issued at the meeting and stressed the "importance of the intensification of the campaign for the Stockholm Appeal for the stopping of the bombing." The letter went on to explain that the "Appeal has been extremely successful in many countries. The deadlock in Paris makes it a duty for us to intensify this campaign so as to show the strength of the international movement for peace in Vietnam."[95] To this end, the liaison committee called "for further actions, aimed at enlarging and widening the movement and drawing into it political and other forces, which have not yet taken part." The proposed actions were to include signature campaigns, actions directed toward governments and parliaments, national and international demonstrations, approaches to heads of states and governments, and approaches to mass organizations, political parties, and publications.[96]

The information letter no. 1 of 1969, in most respects, followed the same pattern. It called for international mobilization during 1969 "to give the strongest possible support to the Vietnamese people in their struggle . . . to help end the U.S. war in Vietnam." The letter proposed political arguments to be articulated and identified specific actions to be carried out, including planning for demonstrations during Easter that would promote the following themes: recognize the NLF as an equal and independent participant at the Paris Peace Conference, support the positions taken by the DRVN at Paris, and demand the immediate withdrawal of the United States from Vietnam.[97] Finally, this information letter announced plans to hold a world meeting to prepare for new actions.

Held on May 16–18, 1969, the Emergency Action Conference on Vietnam was the annual Stockholm conference under a new title and with some important new developments. While the conference "Appeal" and "Report of the Working Group on Action" followed the earlier pattern, the size of this meeting was much larger and included an even broader array of antiwar groups, principally from Western Europe and the United States. Among these were Amnesty International, the Bertrand Russell Peace Foundation, and the International Student Movement for the United States. The conference was attended by many national-level anti–Vietnam War groups. Among those from the United States were the Student Nonviolent Coordinating Committee, Women Strike For Peace, American Friends Service Committee, National Committee for a Sane Nuclear Policy, Clergy and Laymen Concerned About Vietnam, and the National Lawyers' Guild.[98]

During the late 1960s and early 1970s, the WPC, through the Stockholm conference, had direct contact with the New Mobilization Committee to End the War in Vietnam and its successor, the People's Coalition for Peace and Justice (PCPJ). These were two of the major antiwar factions in the United States at that time.[99] According to congressional hearings, the "interrelationship between the American Peace Movement (specifically PCPJ) and the Stockholm Conference (WPC) is quite significant."[100] Evidence was presented in support of this claim. In addition to U.S. antiwar activists, the documents from the 1969 conference also list representatives from a number of antiwar groups and factions in Denmark, Finland, France, West Germany, Britain, Italy, the Netherlands, and Sweden.

This pattern remained unchanged during the 1969–1972 meetings of the Stockholm conference, as the conferences continued to draw numerous individuals and groups—from both Western Europe and the United States—generally not associated with Soviet fronts.[101] This, in turn, contributed to the further legitimization of the DRVN-VC and to the opposite for the United States and its allies. The themes promoted at the conferences and through the committees followed WPC propaganda as described above. These conferences also sought to continue to organize and mobilize international opposition to U.S. policy. To this end, the conferences and activities of the committees established a calendar of action for each year. An examination of the Calendar of the Fall Offensive for 1969 is a case in point. The liaison committee urged "all organizations to support this campaign as it signifies the biggest move so far to oppose the war." The dates for worldwide actions were identical to similar events in the United States:

- October 8–11—Bring the War Home
- October 15—Vietnam Moratorium
- October 25—Demonstrations in Support of the Chicago Eight trial
- November 8–15—Week of anti–Vietnam War activity

The information letter explained the importance of each of these actions and concluded with the call to "start preparation for November 15 *NOW* . . . the Day of International Mobilization against the War in Vietnam."[102] The goal of "full cooperation" between the Stockholm conference and the "U.S. movement" was set out in a special communique from the liaison committee to "Our U.S. Friends."[103] This pattern continued during 1970–1972, as other documents from the Stockholm conference disclose.

In summary, the Stockholm conference served as the major WPC international activity directed toward organizing international public opinion against U.S. policy in Vietnam, while building support for the DRVN and the VC. The International Liaison Committee, which had responsibility for the conferences and other political activities, was under the leadership of the WPC and those aligned with it. Among its members were Romesh Chandra, Alexander Berkov (Soviet Peace Committee), and Irving Sarnoff (a member of the U.S. New Mobilization Committee to End the War in Vietnam and a CPSU official).

The WPC and other fronts sponsored, cosponsored, or participated in other international actions focused on U.S. policy in Vietnam, but during 1967–1972 the Stockholm conference was, by far, the major, ongoing activity. Its importance was indirectly referred to some years later by Boris Ponomarev, the former chief of the International Department of the CPSU. In a 1979 meeting with Yasser Arafat, Ponomarev discussed the importance of an international solidarity committee the USSR had recently established to promote the PLO cause. During the Vietnam War, Ponomarev noted, "a similar solidarity committee had been established. Vietnam, as you know, later won and we hope that this time victory will be achieved too."[104]

Political Activities Within the U.N.

We observed previously that during the late 1950s and early 1960s the Soviet Union changed its view of international organizations, particularly the U.N. Before this, the USSR followed a defensive strategy, offsetting a Western numerical advantage by the use of its Security Council veto. However, once the Kremlin recognized that with the influx of many new Third World states Western ascendance could be reversed, it changed its strategy. Moscow sought to position itself in U.N. deliberations on the side of the emerging anticolonial Third World majority. As this new movement became increasingly radical and anti-Western, the USSR maneuvered to remain aligned with it. In effect, the Soviet approach to the U.N. changed as the organization evolved. Moscow had always viewed the U.N. as an arena for political struggle or political warfare, but as power shifted in the organization, Soviet strategy likewise changed.

In the chapters that follow, I will show that by the mid-1970s, alignment with the radical Third World bloc contributed favorably to Soviet foreign policy. This has especially been the case with respect to Third World insurgency movements. Through an alliance between the Soviet bloc and the radical Afro-Asian states, Moscow has sought to use the U.N. as a forum to promote the causes and enhance the reputation and credibility of such movements. These developments, however, have only occurred since the mid-1970s. In the latter half of the 1960s, the USSR was not successful when it came to U.S. involvement in Vietnam.

Moscow, in conjunction with its change in policy toward the DRVN and the VC during 1965 and with the initiation of its propaganda and international front campaign, sought to maneuver the U.N. to critically review the issue of U.S. involvement in the conflict. However, in the mid-1960s, the power balance in the U.N. had not yet shifted to the anti-Western stance of the 1970s and 1980s. Furthermore, there was no specialized committee in the U.N. through which the Soviets could lay the foundation for the pursuance of this policy in the General Assembly. In the case of the PLO and SWAPO, the Soviets worked through specialized committees (see Chapters 4 and 5). No such mechanism existed to address the Vietnam question, for it had been dealt with in a different forum for adjudication—the Geneva Accords of 1954. Moreover, "neither North Vietnam nor South Vietnam was a member of the United Nations" and, according to the secretary general, "parties directly interested in the conflict had openly voiced the view that the United Nations as such had no place in the search for a solution to the problem." However, the secretary also noted that this "could not prevent the United Nations from discussing the problem." Nevertheless, "it did mitigate against the organization being able to play a constructive role at the present time."[105]

During 1965 the Soviets sought to move the U.N. from discussing the Vietnam issue to acting on it. At their request the Twentieth Session of the General Assembly (1965) was asked to consider the question of "the inadmissibility of intervention in domestic affairs of states and the protection of their independence and sovereignty." In an explanatory memorandum sent with its request, the USSR declared that "international tension had increased of late, certain powers had been seeking to impede the advance of history by aggressive acts and open intervention in the domestic affairs of States and peoples fighting against colonial domination, for their national liberation and for their independent sovereign existence."[106] The Soviet draft declaration proposed that the General Assembly had the responsibility and duty to take the following steps:

- Reaffirm that every sovereign state and every people had an inalienable right to freedom and independence and to defend its sovereignty.
- Urge all member states to fulfill their charter obligations.
- Demand that acts constituting armed or any other type of intervention in the domestic affairs of states, as well as those against the just struggle of peoples for national independence and freedom, should be halted forthwith and not permitted in the future.
- Call on all states to abide by the principle of mutual respect and non-intervention in domestic affairs for any reason whatsoever.[107]

The United States and other Western states viewed this as a pretext for an attack on U.S. policy in Vietnam, which appears, in retrospect, to have been the case. The representatives of the USSR, Bulgaria, Hungary, Poland, Mongolia, and the Byelorussian Soviet Socialist Republic, during the debate over the declaration, argued that "certain Western powers," by intervening in the domestic affairs of states, were seeking to undermine the political independence of Asian, African, and Latin American states. Events in Vietnam, Laos, Cambodia, the Congo, and the Dominican Republic were cited as examples of armed aggression carried out by "certain states" against the peoples of Asia, Africa, and Latin America.[108]

Because the U.N. had not yet moved to the anti-Western position that would characterize it in the 1970s, the United States was able to block the Soviet resolution. Consequently, the attempt to maneuver the U.N. to openly criticize U.S. policy in Vietnam backfired on Moscow. Eventually, a much-diluted resolution on the subject was passed by the General Assembly. Some of the Western states expressed certain reservations about the declaration on the grounds that it was vague, imprecise, and more political than legal; nevertheless, the resolution was quite different from the initial Soviet draft. It was adopted by a roll-call vote.

Following these developments the Soviets did not advance a new initiative to mobilize the General Assembly against U.S. policy in Vietnam. Although the U.N. reserved for itself the right to discuss the Vietnam question in the General Assembly, it did not choose to do so formally. The conflict in Vietnam had repercussions on the members of the U.N., but the organization was not organizationally prepared to play an active role. Furthermore, the rather awkward efforts of the Soviets described above worked against a change in this situation. The Johnson administration, with the exception of Adlai Stevenson, wanted to keep the Vietnam issue out of the U.N. This was apparent in Johnson's coolness towards U Thant's attempt to arrange ambassadorial-level negotiations between Washington and Hanoi. Although a meeting did take place in Rangoon, Washington declined to hold bilateral talks on the grounds that the Saigon government would fall and that Hanoi was really not serious about the talks.[109]

Where did this leave the Soviets in terms of the Vietnam issue and the U.N.? Although there was no specialized committee from which to build a basis for support and although the General Assembly proved unreceptive as a body, Moscow was still free to use the U.N. as a forum for criticizing U.S. policy. From 1965 to 1972, it did just that. Either before the Security Council or the General Assembly, on numerous occasions each year, the Soviets or one of their allies would address these bodies about the dangers of U.S. policy and action in Vietnam.

As we might expect, this criticism paralleled the Soviet propaganda campaign described above. A review of the annual record of the U.N. bears this out. In its formal U.N. statements on the Vietnam War in 1971, Soviet commentary varied little from the earlier years. Moscow condemned the United States for "new criminal acts . . . in gross violation of the accepted standards and principles of international laws." The "policy of Vietnamization" was characterized as "cynical" and did not signal American de-escalation of its involvement in the war. No matter what course the United States followed, the will of the DRVN-VC could not be broken. The USSR would continue to provide all necessary assistance to North Vietnam. Finally, the U.S. stance in the peace talks was characterized as duplicitous and not serious about the deliberations. Similar arguments were presented by the Bulgarian, Czechoslovakian, and Mongolian delegations in the U.N.[110]

Arms Transfers

The initiation of the political warfare campaign appears to have coincided with a significant increase in Soviet-bloc military and economic assistance to the DRVN and the VC. Begun during 1965, this assistance continued unabated through the U.S. withdrawal in 1972. Economic assistance from the Soviet bloc and China grew from $100 million in 1964 to $275 million in 1966. Military aid was $270 million in 1965 but increased to approximately $455 million one year later.[111] During the 1965–1973 period, the Soviet Union provided the DRVN-VC with approximately $4 billion in various kinds of military equipment, which accounted for approximately 70 percent of North Vietnam's external arms support. For the same period the Chinese furnished between $1 and $2 billion.[112]

The immediate impact of this assistance can be seen in various 1966 Central Intelligence Agency reports. For example, one assessment summed up matters by concluding that outside assistance—economic and military—was an essential factor in sustaining the enemy's ability to prosecute the war.[113] During 1967 the Jason Division of the Institute for Defense Analysis, under the auspices of the office of the secretary of defense, completed a study of the effectiveness of U.S. bombing and various alternatives that might produce better results. The report noted that during 1965–1967, Hanoi had "built up the strength of its armed forces at home and acquired sufficient confidence in its supply and logistical organization to equip VC-NVA forces in South Vietnam with a modern family of imported weapons which require externally supplied ammunition." Furthermore, it estimated that the North Vietnamese had "the potential to continue building the size of its armed forces, to increase the yearly total of infiltration of individual soldiers and combat units, and to equip and supply even larger forces in South Vietnam for substantially higher rates of combat."[114] The Jason study left little doubt of the important contribution outside assistance made to these developments:

NVN [DRVN] has transmitted many of the material costs imposed by
the bombing back to its allies. Since the bombing began, NVN's allies have provided almost $600 million in economic aid and another
$1 billion in military aid—more than four times what NVN has lost
in bombing damage . . . NVN is now a stronger military power than
before the bombing and its remaining economy is more able to with-
stand bombing. The USSR could furnish NVN with much more sophisticated weapons systems.[115]

In his annual testimony before Congress on February 1, 1968, Secretary of
Defense Robert McNamara reviewed the events in Vietnam during the previous
year. In this assessment, the secretary noted that "preliminary estimates indicate
that total aid [for North Vietnam] for 1967 may have reached $1 billion ($660
million military and $340 million economic)." He also observed that "Soviet
military aid since 1965 has been concentrated on air defense material—SAMs,
AAA guns and ammo, radar, and fighter aircraft."[116]

An examination of North Vietnamese military capabilities reveals a dramatic growth in weapons and logistical support. In 1964 their air defense capabilities included approximately 700 antiaircraft artillery (AAA) guns, 20 early-
warning radars with limited tracking ability, and 34 MiG-15 and MiG-17 fighter
aircraft.[117] During 1965 the USSR began to deploy what would become a thor-
oughly integrated combination of radars, AAA guns, surface-to-air missiles
(SAMs), and MiGs. Although systematic attacks during 1965, when the entire
system was in an embryonic state, might have destroyed it, bombing restrictions
prevented this.[118] During 1966 the North Vietnamese air defense system expanded to "some 50 surface-to-air missile sites for SA-2 Guideline missiles."
Each site included four to six launchers.[119] The accompanying radars included
"three major ground control sites: Bac Mai, Phuc Yen, and Kep." Once completed there were "about 200 radars in the North Vietnamese air defense system."[120] The number of AAA also grew significantly, although disagreement
exists over to what extent. The Institute for Strategic Studies' annual publication, *The Military Balance, 1966–1967,* estimated that there were "some 3,000
antiaircraft guns, including 37 mm, 57 mm, 85 mm, and 100 mm; about half of
these are radar-controlled."[121] The U.S. Air Force's *Corona Harvest Report,* an
assessment of air operations in Southeast Asia during U.S. involvement, estimated that by the summer of 1966 there were some 7,000 AAA guns of all
calibers in North Vietnam.[122] The North Vietnamese Air Force now included 66
MiG-15/17s and 15 MiG-21 fighters.[123]

The Military Balance, 1968–1969 reflected the ongoing expansion of these
capabilities. Interceptors and fighters included 100 MiG-15/17s and 20 MiG-21s
(with Atoll air-to-air missiles).[124] Others estimate MiG-21 strength at between
40 to 50 by mid-1967.[125] *The Military Balance* doubled its figure on AAA guns

to 6,000, including 37 mm, 57 mm, 85 mm, and 100 mm, and "thousands of air defense machine guns." It continued to report that North Vietnam maintained 50 SAM sites for SA-2 Guideline missiles.[126] By this time, the Air Force put the number of sites at 200,[127] while "U.S. intelligence had identified approximately 170 SAM sites in North Vietnam."[128]

By 1972 the North Vietnamese Air Force contained 60 MiG-21s, 30 MiG-19s, and 130 MiG-15/17 fighters.[129] In addition to the SA-2, the shoulder-fired SA-7 Strela SAM appeared in the North Vietnamese arsenal.[130] With respect to SA-2s, the number of sites remained the same, and it is estimated that during April–July 1972, 1,600 SAMs were fired at U.S. aircraft.[131] The AAA weapons now included KS-12 85-mm and KS-19 100-mm guns and ZSU-67-2 self-propelled antiaircraft (AASP) guns.[132]

The air defense system just described, once fully integrated, was considered a major contribution to the North Vietnamese war effort. Its importance was noted in a Joint Chiefs of Staff (JCS) memorandum of May 20, 1967. The JCS expressed serious concern over the introduction by the Soviet Union into North Vietnam of new weapons that included upgraded AAA guns, SAMs, guided-missile patrol boats, surface-to-surface missiles, and a variety of artillery and direct-fire weapons. These capabilities not only improved North Vietnamese air and coastal defenses, but added to their offensive power projection ability.[133]

Retrospective studies of the North Vietnamese air defense network, which was Soviet in design and operation, suggest that the system made a major contribution to Hanoi's war effort.[134] As I noted above, the system was based on a web of 200 radar systems with three major ground-control intercept (GCI) sites. The redundancy in the system, according to William Momyer, made it "impossible to jam all of them" and "provide[d] good GCI during an engagement regardless of our countermeasures."[135] In addition to radar, the AAA defenses, once in place, were considered formidable. There were more than 7,000 guns of all calibers, most of them located either along the primary air routes used by the United States or in the Hanoi and Haiphong areas. These guns were considered capable of producing the heaviest flak in the history of air warfare up to that time. Momyer notes that "the point defenses around the Doumer bridge, Hanoi Railcar Repair Shop, Thai Nguyen steel mill, Viet Tri thermal power plant . . . were as tough as one could possibly imagine."[136] In fact, in Vietnam the United States suffered more aircraft losses to AAA fire than to SAMs, even though the latter received more media attention.

Nevertheless, the SAM component expanded rapidly and was an important aspect of the North Vietnamese air defense. During 1966, Paul Burbage and his coauthors note that while "the SAM threat became more definite, it was not as bad as it could have been due to the following factors: poor missile quality, inadequately trained missile crews, and the evasive tactics and effective electronic countermeasures used by the USAF aircrews." He goes on to explain that "even though the aircraft loss rate to SAMs was not high, the avoidance tactics combined with the enemy threat, reduced U.S. target strike effectiveness."[137] After 1967 the number of SAM systems remained fairly constant. However, because the SAM systems were mobile, the North Vietnamese could change their locations, thereby reducing their vulnerability to attack.

The expansion of the SAM component of the North Vietnamese air defense can also be determined by the number of missiles fired. During 1965, 180 SAMs were fired, downing eleven aircraft. The eleven-day campaign of December 1972 saw the North Vietnamese employ more than 1,000 SAMs, resulting in the loss of fifteen B-52s and other aircraft.[138] However, the 1972 Christmas bombing also demonstrated that the Soviet supply line was not unlimited, evidenced by the decreased firing rate of Hanoi about halfway into the eleven-day campaign. Coupled with good weather and the deployment of a highly sophisticated U.S. strike formation, Henry Kissinger and others have asserted that air power was the decisive factor leading to the DRVN signing the peace agreement of January 15, 1973.[139] A number of senior military officials have argued that a similar application of concentrated air power in the summer of 1967 would have forced Hanoi to negotiate a settlement at that time. They believed the DRVN was on the verge of making this decision, and by pressing the attack and striking at the heart, with virtually no restraints on military targets, Hanoi would have been compelled to negotiate.[140]

Finally, as with AAA guns, SAMs, and radar, the MiG component was also upgraded by the USSR during 1966–1972. This was noted above in terms of numbers, but it was also true with respect to quality. For instance, the armaments of the MiG-21 were improved during 1966, including the addition of Atoll heat-seeking missiles (similar to the U.S. Sidewinders). By the 1970s the MiG-21 carried four of these weapons. With a top speed of about Mach 2, this aircraft was of great concern to the U.S. Air Force.

Soviet arms transfers were also important to the development of the North Vietnamese Army (NVA). To begin with, Soviet and Chinese military aid allowed for the re-equipping of the NVA and the VC with standardized bloc weapons. It is difficult to estimate exactly how extensive this was, but one source observed that by 1968 North Vietnamese infantry regiments had "Chinese or Soviet bloc light arms, and the artillery regiments mostly Soviet equipment." The same source put the strength of the NVA at 440,000 regulars (including at least 85,000 in South Vietnam and 40,000 in Laos), with an additional regionally organized armed militia of about 300,000.[141] The size of the VC force has been a controversial issue both during the war and since the U.S. withdrawal. The debate continues, but an estimate of approximately 250,000 VC regulars during the latter half of the 1960s does not appear to be unreasonable. Arming and equipping this NVA-VC force required significant amounts of light arms and supporting supplies.

The Soviet bloc also provided Hanoi with the necessary mobile, heavier weapons and ammunition stocks necessary to mount a general conventional offensive. The transfer of this assistance during the latter part of the 1960s culminated in the emergence of the NVA as a conventional force capable of initiating the March 1972 invasion of South Vietnam. In 1966 the size of the NVA was 240,000 regulars, "thought to have 100 miscellaneous armored vehicles." These included "some Soviet PT-76 tanks" and the previously discussed air defense capabilities. Beyond this, the NVA had "no heavy equipment, and meager transport and logistic support."[142] By 1968, the North Vietnamese were said to have obtained T-34 medium tanks and PT-76 reconnaissance tanks. Improvements in artillery and related heavy weaponry also had taken place.[143]

By the early 1970s the modernization of the NVA and its development as a conventional force had been achieved. Composed of fifteen infantry divisions, one artillery division (ten regiments), twenty independent infantry regiments, and a number of related units, the NVA now numbered more than 500,000 regulars. Heavy equipment included 20 T-34, 75 T-54, and 100 PT-76 tanks; BTR-40 armored personnel carriers; SU-76 and INS-122 self-propelled guns; 75-mm, 105-mm, 122-mm, 130-mm, and 152-mm guns; 57-mm, 75-mm, 82-mm, and 107-mm recoilless rifles; 82-mm, 100-mm, 107-mm, 122-mm, and 140-mm rocket launchers; the Sagger antitank guided weapon; and the shoulder-fired SA-7 Strela SAM.[144] Also included were the previously mentioned AAA guns and SA-2 sites. By the time of the Easter offensive of 1972, the quantities of these weapons appear to have been even higher. This was especially true of tanks and related mobile weapons.

On March 30, 1972, the North Vietnamese launched a conventional invasion of South Vietnam. As a result of a disengagement schedule that began in 1971, the United States had 95,000 in-country forces, only 6,000 of which were combat troops.[145] Hanoi's objectives appear to have been threefold: achieve a psychological effect in the United States (equivalent to the Tet offensive of 1968) and produce irresistible pressures during the presidential campaign for an immediate peace settlement, discredit the Vietnamization strategy by engaging and defeating as many Government of Vietnam regular forces as possible, and assist the VC in resuming offensive actions in the rural areas. However, once under way the DRVN came to believe that the "whole thing could be won." This was apparent when on May 1, 1972, they rejected a new cease-fire proposal by the United States that included a willingness to permit NVA forces to remain in South Vietnam. Confident of victory—Hue and Kontum were on the verge of falling—Hanoi flatly rejected the offer.[146]

The NVA offensive in I Corps (northern section of South Vietnam) was spearheaded by 40,000 regulars, supported by artillery and rocket regiments, 400 armored vehicles, and SA-7s and SA-2s.[147] In addition to troops crossing the demilitarized zone (DMZ), other NVA forces struck in the Central Highlands and came across the Cambodian border northwest of Saigon. It is estimated that more than 120,000 regulars were deployed in the initial phase of the offensive. This was the first time Hanoi utilized large numbers of tanks in the south. It is estimated that 267 tanks were destroyed during the offensive, many by U.S. air power.[148] The North Vietnamese supported their armored and infantry attack across the DMZ with long-range artillery (122-mm and 130-mm guns). On April 30, Quang Tri fell and Hue and Kontum appeared to be next. The pattern of the attack followed the same tactics, with tanks and heavy shelling taking place before the infantry assault. The third prong of the North Vietnamese offensive came from across the Cambodian border and was initiated at An Loc. The attack began on April 9 with 25 tanks leading the way. Support was provided by large amounts of artillery, AAA guns, and SA-7s. If the North Vietnamese objectives in I and II Corps were to capture the northern provinces and from Kontum push south to Pleiku and then east along Highway 19 to the port city of Qui Nhon, cutting the Republic of Vietnam (South Vietnam) in half, the attack on An Loc was a stepping-off point leading to a move against Saigon.

The previous description leaves little doubt that by the early 1970s, the NVA deployed in South Vietnam was a formidable conventional force. Armed mainly with Soviet-bloc weapons, it initiated a swift and large-scale offensive in March 1972 that caught Washington by surprise. It seems likely that had the Nixon administration not suspended the peace talks and undertaken the most extensive escalation of the war since 1968 (including a naval blockade and massive, sustained bombing), Hanoi might have achieved victory. However, such a large conventional army assault requires vast quantities of fuel, ammunition, and related logistical support. The U.S. air power pummeled NVA supply lines in the south and, in conjunction with the intensive bombing attacks and blockade in the north, made resupply difficult. Additionally, air power played a decisive role against exposed NVA forces conducting the attack. With the vital assistance of U.S. air power, the ARVN forces were able to stabilize the situation and even mount a small counterattack.

Nevertheless, the Easter offensive unveiled a North Vietnamese force that was large, mobile, and armed with heavy weapons. It was no longer a guerrilla or irregular army. The general offensive of March 1972 was carried out by a regular conventional force. In 1975 this same force, with even more conventional capabilities and facing an ARVN without U.S. support, achieved the objective denied Hanoi by the Nixon administration's strategic use of air power in 1972.

Training and Advisory Support

Unlike many insurgent movements supported by the USSR in the 1970s and 1980s, the DRVN-VC forces did not require basic training and advisory assistance. Additionally, in terms of an insurgent political-military infrastructure and political cadre, the DRVN-VC were in a very advanced stage. In fact, over the last three decades no other movement has achieved this degree of organizational complexity, integration, and sheer magnitude.[149] Consequently, training and advisory support by the Soviet bloc were concentrated on the North Vietnamese learning to operate the air defense system and employ the MiG aircraft.

The number of Soviet military advisers and technicians in Vietnam was estimated at approximately 3,000.[150] During 1965–1966 some of these personnel exercised operational control over the DRVN's SAM sites. It was reported in October 1966 that Russian voices had been heard on the radio networks that tied Hanoi's air defense system together. These radio intercepts apparently contained conversations in which Soviet advisers were coordinating operations directed against U.S. pilots.[151] This substantiated what had been reported as early as the summer of 1965.[152] However, the primary objective of these advisers was to install the air defense network and train the North Vietnamese to operate it. Zimmerman notes that they also may have played a deterrent role, preventing greater U.S. escalation: [T]he Pentagon Papers . . . are replete with evidence that concern about the possible Soviet response to U.S. escalatory steps affected American calculations and resulted in options being precluded and forces being deployed in less than optimal ways."[153]

The Soviet Union also trained Vietnamese pilots to fly the MiG-21s, and during the summer of 1966 Moscow publicized this fact.[154] However, unlike the Koreans, Soviet pilots are not reported to have flown combat missions on behalf of the North Vietnamese. The Chinese also helped train DRVN pilots, and it has been reported that North Korean pilots flew MiG-17 missions to "defend North Vietnamese airfields and patrol at low altitudes along our [U.S.] approach and departure routes."[155]

The Soviet advisory effort could have been larger but apparently was restrained. Earlier we noted that Soviet combat personnel were made available when Brezhnev floated the possibility of Soviet volunteers going to Vietnam— "our central agencies are receiving many declarations from the Soviet people expressing readiness to take part in the Vietnamese people's struggle for freedom and independence."[156] However, Hanoi appears to have seen this as unnecessary. Others speculate that the Chinese prevented the USSR from undertaking a larger advisory effort by denying them an air corridor and bases.[157] The People's Republic of China did permit the transport of Soviet-bloc military equipment and other aid across China to Vietnam.

Although it is possible that the USSR may have contemplated stationing a larger advisory mission in North Vietnam, those eventually deployed served an important function. The air defense network over North Vietnam was an important contribution to the DRVN war effort. The Soviet Union not only supplied it but operated the system until it could train North Vietnamese to do so. Officials in the United States said this greatly assisted the DRVN to sustain its efforts during the U.S. escalation of 1965–1968.

Conclusion

During 1965 the Soviet Union reversed its policy of marginal support for the North Vietnamese and the VC. This marked the beginning of a greater readiness on the part of Moscow to support and promote the cause of insurgency in the Third World. It appears that, in part as a result of its role in Vietnam, Soviet support for insurgent movements grew during the 1970s and early 1980s.

Apparently, once the decision was made to reverse its policy, Moscow employed both political and paramilitary measures to assist the DRVN-VC. Once committed, Moscow adamantly refused, during the course of the war, to cut back its support in return for Washington's offer to improve U.S.-Soviet relations. This was stated to Kissinger by Anatoly Dobrynin in the following terms: "The Soviet Union would never threaten to cut off supplies to their allies in North Vietnam."[158] In terms of political tactics, the overt Soviet propaganda campaign signaled the initiation of a broader political warfare campaign, as well as outlined the subjects and targets to be addressed. The escalation of Soviet propaganda coincided with and provided direction for the other instruments of political warfare.

The major focus of Soviet propaganda was U.S. policy and actions in Vietnam. The propaganda themes condemning the United States took a number of forms, all of which were interrelated. On balance, these themes received more coverage than the cause of the DRVN-VC (although this was an important subject). We need not recite and summarize these themes here, but why did this pattern occur? In part, Moscow saw U.S. involvement as an opportunity to amplify the charges of imperialism and militarism that have dominated the Soviet foreign propaganda since World War II. However, it may also be that Moscow saw the potential of the antiwar movement both in Western Europe and in the United States and sought to champion its opposition to U.S. policy. Although it is not always easy to identify the specific target audiences of Soviet international propaganda, in this case the emphasis on U.S. imperialism, war crimes, continuing policy failures, and growing opposition to U.S. policy at home and in Europe point in this direction.

The focus of the propaganda and political action campaign of the international fronts substantiates this argument. The scope and duration of the six-year Stockholm program concentrated on these targets. This is a good example of the degree to which Soviet political warfare techniques support and reinforce each other. The WPC Stockholm effort sought to organize and mobilize the opposition against U.S. policy. The Soviet effort in the U.N., although not successful, was geared toward the same objectives. The goal was to discredit the U.S. policy in Vietnam and maneuver the U.N. to condemn this policy as a cynical violation of the principles of international law and morality.

The initiation and escalation of the political warfare campaign coincided closely with the growth in Soviet arms transfers, logistical assistance, and advisory support to the DRVN-VC. These important contributions to the war effort included installing a sophisticated air defense network, arming the NVA-VC with standardized Soviet-bloc light weapons, and providing the heavy weaponry to allow the NVA to make the transition to a larger, mobile conventional army.

Soviet policy in Vietnam was an integrated strategy of political and paramilitary assistance. The objectives were to promote the legitimacy of the DRVN-VC's cause in the international arena and improve their military ability in the field. The success of this effort apparently contributed to the decision to expand Soviet assistance to national liberation movements in the 1970s and 1980s. The following chapters support this assertion.

FOUR

Soviet Support for the Palestine Liberation Organization

From the late 1960s to the mid-1980s, the relationship between the USSR and the Palestine Liberation Organization (PLO), although not one of mutual admiration or identical views, has, nevertheless, become increasingly close. The PLO suffered serious setbacks in Lebanon in the 1980s at the hands of Syria, the principal Soviet ally in the region; nonetheless, its relations with Moscow over the last fifteen years have been marked by a steady intensification of cooperation. Documents captured in Lebanon by Israel in 1982 support this assertion. For instance, included in this material are recorded accounts of top-level meetings between leading personalities at which issues of tactical and operational importance were discussed. In 1979, one such meeting took place between Yasser Arafat, Andrey Gromyko, and Boris Ponomarev in Moscow. A similar strategy session between Gromyko and Farouk Kaddoumi (the foreign minister of the PLO) occurred in November 1983. The minutes from this session reveal the degree of Soviet-PLO involvement. In fact, Gromyko goes so far as to strongly intimate that the PLO align itself with and defer to Syria.[1]

During this period of evolution there have been a number of important developments. As the relationship unfolded, Soviet political and paramilitary assistance increased. Additional support came from Soviet allies and surrogates in Eastern Europe, Latin America, and Asia as well as from the Middle East. Thus, the PLO became both a recipient and a supplier of this assistance. It acts, in effect, as a middleman and is often at the center of an international support apparatus that assists a number of insurgent and terrorist organizations.

In light of these developments, what role does the PLO play in Soviet strategic and regional policy? Support for the PLO contributes to Moscow's twofold objective of exacerbating the Arab-Israeli conflict and at the same time strengthening its relations with the Arab states. The Soviet-PLO-Arab (states) triangle can potentially weaken and limit U.S. influence in the region. This triangle can also be used to divide NATO, given the clash of views between a number of West European states and the United States over the Palestinian issue. The PLO also serves as a conduit for transferring various forms of assistance to terrorist and insurgent factions from the Caribbean, Latin America, Western Europe, and Africa. Finally, support of the PLO strengthens Moscow's bilateral relations with many Third World states and improves its position within international and regional organizations, where the representatives of the developing world have become increasingly influential.

Although the USSR and the PLO share various regional and international concerns, there are limits to the Soviet commitment. Moscow appears to draw a distinction between its support of certain Arab states and the PLO. This distinction was apparent during the Beirut siege when the USSR did very little to alleviate the Palestinians' position. The Soviets also have been less than helpful during the post-Beirut rift between Arafat's faction and Syria, although there are indications that Moscow may have pressured President Hafiz al-Assad to make some accommodation with Arafat.

Does this mean that the PLO has changed its attitude and moved away from the Soviet Union? Apparently not. Although the PLO may constitute a secondary element of Soviet policy in the Middle East, the USSR is a very important ally for the PLO. As will be seen below, the Soviet Union and its surrogates provide an array of vital political and paramilitary assistance, and although the Kremlin's commitment has its limitations, time is not one of them. The Soviet-PLO connection does not stem from a temporary policy or tactical shift but is the long-term outgrowth of shared interests. Consequently, even after Beirut and the rift with Syria, one finds Arafat visiting Moscow in March 1985, preceded by visits of representatives of Fatah and other PLO factions to Eastern-bloc states during the latter months of 1984.[2] Perhaps Abu Iyad, Arafat's second deputy, summed up the essence of this unequal relationship in his 1981 statement: "[I]f we had the capacity to sign a treaty with the Soviet Union, we would have signed 1,000 treaties, and if we controlled land we would have allowed the Soviets 1,000 bases, because we are dealing with a foe stronger than Israel, the United States."[3]

The Evolution of
Soviet-PLO Relations

Before the 1967 war there were supposedly no "official" contacts between the USSR and the PLO. For instance, Aryeh Yodfat and Yuval Arnon-Ohanna in their study *PLO Strategy and Tactics* assert that following the official founding of the PLO at the Arab Summit Conference of January 1964 and before the Six-Day War of 1967, "the USSR preferred at that time not to express a clear opinion about the status of the rights of Palestinian Arabs and what they said (and very little was in fact said about it) could be interpreted in more than one way. The Soviet aim was to attract Arab Nationalism [and] . . . Palestinian organizations which declared themselves to be struggling for the rights of the Palestinian people and a Palestinian state in place of Israel met initially with Soviet reservations."[4]

This generally appears to be the case during this period, although Moscow did have indirect contacts with the newly established Palestinian organization. In May 1966 there was a meeting between the foreign minister of the USSR, Andrey Gromyko, and Ahmad Shuquairy, the first leader of the PLO. Little is known about the session, but the fact that such a senior Soviet official met with this infant organization suggests that Moscow had some interest in it. Additionally, before 1967, PLO members, under the auspices of the General Union of Palestinian Students (a PLO affiliate), began to travel to Bulgaria, Czechoslovakia, and East Germany for education.[5] This has been corroborated by General Jan Sejna, former secretary of the Czech Defense Council. According to Sejna, in 1964 the USSR convened a meeting of East European–bloc intelligence services. The subject of the conference was "terrorism, production of special equipment, training of foreign agents in sabotage and terrorism." At the meeting "each satellite was given its area of responsibility and a list of prospects." As a result of the assignment to Czechoslovakia of partial responsibility for these operations in the Middle East, "some of those recruited [were] taken to Czechoslovakia for education and training . . . If they [were] to be trained as a group for terrorist operations they [went] to Doupov, near Karlovy Vary . . . There was also a training camp in Boletice, near Krumlov."[6] The specific composition of the elements coming from the Middle East at that time remains unclear.

The USSR also used the Afro-Asian People's Solidarity Organization (AAPSO) during this period to approach the PLO. A major Soviet international front organization, AAPSO was established in 1957 and adopted its formal constitution at the second Afro-Asian Solidarity Conference at Conakry, Guinea, in April 1960. The creation of AAPSO was one of the steps taken by Moscow to expand its influence in the Third World after its exclusion from the Bandung Conference of 1955. In 1966 a Palestinian delegation attended an AAPSO meeting held in Moscow. The use of these indirect channels reveals the Kremlin's limitations on how far it would go in its relations with the PLO. According to Roberta Goren, the Soviets refused a request by the PLO to open an office in Moscow in 1966 and would not agree, at least officially, to train Palestinians in the USSR.[7]

Following the 1967 war, Soviet-PLO relations took an important turn. The war, of course, was a disaster for the Arab states. Their armies emerged from the conflict in defeat and disarray. The magnitude of this defeat led PLO leaders to reject conventional combat in favor of armed struggle using unconventional techniques. The PLO quickly commenced guerrilla attacks against Israel. By conducting a "protracted popular war of national liberation" the Palestinians asserted that they could succeed where the Arab armies had failed.[8] This position was consistent both with Soviet statements suggesting that the Arabs adopt the Algerian model of protracted guerrilla warfare[9] and with the evolving Soviet policy of more actively assisting national liberation movements.

Subsequently, Soviet publications began to refer favorably to the Palestinian resistance movement and to employ the term *partisans* to legitimize their actions.[10] For instance, the Soviet ambassador to the U.N., Yacov Malik, characterized the Fedayeen as "patriotic partisans."[11] At this same time Arafat, following Fatah's assumption of the leadership of the PLO, secretly visited Moscow to establish relations with the Kremlin, as well as to arrange for arms. Following these developments, according to Vladimir Sakharov, a former Soviet Ministry of Foreign Affairs official who worked clandestinely with the KGB in the Middle East from 1967 to 1971, Soviet embassies were used to process PLO cadres for training in the USSR or Eastern Europe.[12] Following Arafat's visit, which had been arranged by Gamal Nasser, it has been reported that the Soviet ambassador in Cairo informed Nasser that the PLO would receive $500,000 worth of arms.[13] Although this did not constitute recognition (Moscow's official commentary criticized the Palestinians' lack of unity and their proclaimed objective of liquidating Israel), it marked the beginning of the Soviet-PLO connection.

By the end of the decade Moscow referred to the "Palestinian struggle," in the words of Premier Aleksey Kosygin, "as a national liberation and imperialist struggle."[14] The new terminology represented an important change in Soviet policy toward the PLO, and the guerrilla organization's new status produced the following developments. Kosygin's designation of the PLO as a national liberation movement was reiterated and amplified by other Soviet spokesmen. In 1970 the leading Soviet Middle East specialist and later director of the Institute of Oriental Studies of the Academy of Science, Yevgeny Primakov, justified PLO use of extreme violence on the grounds that it was employed in the service of "the general popular struggle . . . for the liberation of occupied territory."[15] A delegation of representatives of various Palestinian organizations, led by Arafat, was invited to Moscow in February 1970. Although considered unofficial because the visit was arranged and hosted by the Soviet Afro-Asian Solidarity Committee (Moscow's branch of AAPSO), it signaled the beginning of de facto acknowledgment. Apparently, the Kremlin began to see the Palestinians as a new force that might have an impact on Middle East developments. Therefore, preliminary steps were taken to draw them into the Soviet orbit. Finally, as Sakharov notes, arms were then provided by the USSR and the East European bloc through the Arab states.[16]

During the early 1970s the PLO suffered important setbacks. First, as Bard O'Neill has observed, the upsurge of guerrilla warfare along the borders, especially Jordan's, and terrorism within Israel and the occupied territories proved ineffective. "As things turned out, a combination of factors—sound Israeli counterinsurgency practices, a poor physical environment, insurgent disunity, organizational deficiencies, and differences with the Arab states—undermined what success the Fedayeen had enjoyed in 1968–1969."[17] This was followed by the Fedayeen's expulsion from Jordan during the latter part of 1970, a crushing blow to the PLO's operational capacity.

Moscow remained neutral during the Jordanian conflict and the internecine battles between Fatah, the Popular Front for the Liberation of Palestine, and the Democratic Front for the Liberation of Palestine that led up to it.[18] However, following the PLO expulsion from Jordan, Moscow increased support to the PLO. According to Yodfat and Arnon-Ohanna:

> The USSR provided the PLO with limited quantities of arms, some military training in the Soviet Union (that could be used by the USSR for political indoctrination) and political support. As a first step the USSR agreed to compensate Palestinians for most of the arms that they had lost in the fighting in Jordan.[19]

During 1971 and 1972, delegations headed by Arafat visited the USSR, again under the auspices of the Soviet Afro-Asian Solidarity Committee. Soviet official commentary continued to refer to the PLO as a legitimate national liberation movement. In December 1970, Ponomarev, then head of the International Department of the CPSU Central Committee (which has responsibility for Soviet-supported insurgent movements), pledged "every assistance . . . in the future" to the "Palestinian liberation movement."[20] At the Twenty-fourth CPSU Congress in April 1971, this support was given authoritative codification. The CPSU officially recognized "the legitimate rights and interests of . . . the Arab people of Palestine" and pledged to support "their efforts directed at restoring their flouted rights . . . and in defense of these lawful rights."[21]

During 1971–1972 official Soviet commentary began to defend certain PLO actions, while disavowing its more extreme terrorist acts. This marked the beginning of Soviet political and propaganda efforts to promote the legitimacy of the PLO in the international arena. Perhaps the most significant early example of this shift was the Munich Massacre of 1972, in which Moscow sought to separate the Black September Organization (BSO) from the PLO.[22] (BSO has been identified as a subgroup of Fatah, the dominant faction of the PLO.) During the 1970s, BSO conducted a number of terrorist operations for which Fatah did not wish to take official responsibility.[23]

The turning point in Soviet-PLO relations is frequently attributed to the 1972 expulsion of USSR personnel from Egypt. According to Goren, the split in the "relationship took place in the summer of 1972, as President Sadat was evicting Soviet military advisers from the country. During a visit to Moscow in July, Arafat finally obtained the long-sought Soviet agreement to provide the PLO with direct arms deliveries, which began arriving in Syria in September 1972."[24] Evidence marshaled by Uri Ra'anan, however, raises doubts about one part of this conclusion. Following the "expulsion" he points out that "an investigation of 'hard' data—in other words, the flow of weapons from the Soviet Union to the Egyptian armed forces"—demonstrates that "to the extent there really [had] been such a conflict, it [was] not reflected very much in the military field." On the contrary, the 1972–1973 period was marked by a "fairly significant Soviet military reinforcement of Egypt, both quantitatively and qualitatively."[25] Ra'anan goes on to catalog, in great detail, weapons transferred during that time and to link this to the strategic deception conducted by Anwar Sadat before the 1973 war.

A more plausible alternative explanation is that, rather than a shift from an emphasis on state-to-state relations, Moscow's escalation of support for the PLO was another step in the growing elevation of its policy toward national liberation movements. Thus, during the 1970s the latter began to approach a more equal status with Moscow's state-to-state policy, although the latter was still first priority.

The Soviet-PLO connection reached a new plateau following the Yom Kippur War of 1973. Moscow continued to defend PLO actions by drawing a distinction between terrorism and violence in the struggle for national liberation. The Soviets also transferred more arms to the PLO. The most important new elements in the relationship, however, were in the areas of political recognition and promotion of the Palestinian cause in the international arena.

An Arafat-led delegation visited the USSR from July 30 to August 4, 1974, but this time not as guests of the Soviet Afro-Asian Solidarity Committee. The delegation met officially with representatives of the CPSU and the USSR government. In the Ponomarev-Arafat communiqué following the meeting, Moscow designated "the PLO as the sole legitimate representative of the Arab people of Palestine."[26] In effect, the USSR adopted the line taken at the Algiers Arab Summit Conference of 1973. In October 1974 Brezhnev himself referred to the PLO as one of the partners in the Middle East peace negotiations.[27] The Soviets, however, did not go so far as to openly adopt the PLO's aim, as stated in the Palestine National Covenant, of the elimination of Zionism in Palestine (Article 15) and the elimination of Israel as the instrument of the Zionist movement (Article 22).[28]

This was followed, as we will see later in this chapter, by increased Soviet support for the PLO within the U.N. At this time the U.N. General Assembly invited the PLO to participate in its discussions on Palestine, provided it with observer status, and established two committees—the Committee on the Exercise of the Inalienable Rights of the Palestinian People (hereafter referred to as the Inalienable Rights Committee) and the Special Unit on Palestinian Rights— to oversee the Palestinian issue. The Soviet Union and its surrogates played an important part in the coalition of U.N. members that fostered these developments. Beyond the U.N., Soviet international media commentary referred to the PLO in exclusive terms and cajoled the United States to recognize its legitimacy. In effect, Moscow's growing emphasis on legitimacy suggests that it now saw the PLO as a government in exile and not merely as a national liberation movement. These developments culminated in the August 1974 Kremlin decision to grant the PLO permission to open an office in Moscow. Consequently, official ties were finally established.

If the USSR's propaganda portrayed the PLO as a government in exile, support of its actions in Lebanon suggest that the Soviets sought to assist the PLO to become a state within a state. The development of base camps in Lebanon for paramilitary training, political proselytizing and mobilization, and arms stockpiling actually predates the defeat in Jordan. The Syrians played a considerable role in this activity, apparently seizing an opportunity to bring Lebanon under their influence by using the PLO as a surrogate force. As events transpired Syria found that domination of Fatah was difficult to achieve.

Following the Black September of 1970 in Jordan, the PLO accelerated its activity in Lebanon to secure and expand its political, military, and logistic assets. Syria initially backed these steps until the Lebanese government, unable to prevent a PLO military takeover of the south, resigned itself to the situation. At the same time the PLO launched numerous commando operations against Israel from these sanctuaries.

With its expansion of power and influence, the PLO became an increasingly important alternative political instrument for the Kremlin. It received considerably more assistance as Moscow sought to strengthen ties with the organization to foster dependence and solidify an evolving patron-client relationship. The PLO was seen as a revolutionary force contributing to regional and international instability. It could help to both undermine U.S. interests in the Middle East and bring about the downfall of existing regimes friendly to the West. Growing Soviet-PLO cooperation occurred in conjunction with the solidification of state-to-state relations between Moscow and Damascus.

The situation took another turn during the summer of 1976, when Syria apparently decided to strengthen its position by bringing Lebanon under de facto protectorate status. Fearing a PLO-leftist coalition that could chart an independent course, Syria sent troops to gain control of the major cities and roads. By the end of the summer Syria held the northern and eastern two-thirds of Lebanon, and Christian forces controlled East Beirut and a portion of the north. A PLO-Muslim coalition dominated West Beirut, Tripoli, and southern Lebanon. In the fall of 1976, Syrian and Christian forces launched an offensive in the southern region, bringing the PLO to the brink of a military collapse.

During the 1976 war in Lebanon, the USSR increased its international political support for the PLO, while refusing to aid it in the field in its battle against Syria. Expanded international political support actually began in the spring of 1976 at the Twenty-fifth CPSU Congress. The Kremlin leadership stressed its support for a number of specific national liberation movements during the Congress, with special attention to Soviet-PLO relations. Brezhnev's report to the Twenty-fifth Congress included the PLO in a list of Arab countries friendly to the USSR and referred to the need to strengthen Soviet ties with it.[29] In June 1976 the PLO finally opened its office in Moscow, originally agreed to in 1974. Among other duties, the office handles Palestinians coming to the USSR for education and training. Internationally, Moscow continued to insist on both PLO inclusion in the Geneva talks and Palestinian statehood.

Nevertheless, during the 1976 crisis the USSR refused to jeopardize its relations with Syria by providing direct assistance to the PLO. As noted earlier, Moscow's first priority is state-to-state relations. Given the choice between Syria (its main ally in the region) and the PLO, it opted for the former, while encouraging both parties to find an accommodation with one another.

At the October 1976 Arab summit conferences convened in Riyadh and Cairo, a new cease-fire was reached and the situation was restored to its earlier status. Soviet-PLO relations likewise were put back on course, and Arafat met with Brezhnev during April 1977, which further enhanced the PLO's image and solidified its connection with the USSR. This "official" tightening of the connection may, in part, have been a direct response to Egyptian-Israeli negotiations and the subsequent Camp David agreement that Moscow sharply criticized. According to Yodfat and Arnon-Ohanna, "in contrast to past practice . . . the Soviets gave to the PLO and to the Palestinian problem in general a central role which they had not given them earlier."[30]

Following the cease-fire the PLO was able to reinforce its bases in southern Lebanon without incurring the risk of intervention by the Lebanese army. In conjunction with this action, Moscow and its surrogates escalated arms transfers and advisory support. The PLO, in turn, took on the additional responsibility of serving as a supplier to other international terrorist and guerrilla organizations. With the buildup in southern Lebanon, PLO activities against Israel continued to widen, typified by the interception of an Israeli civilian bus by Palestinian terrorists and the killing of most of its passengers. In response, Israel sent its army into Lebanon to strike at the PLO support network and bases from which such attacks originated. Israel withdrew under the guarantee that the U.N. forces in Lebanon would prevent the PLO from re-escalating its terrorist campaign; however, the U.N. forces were unable to do so. In 1979 the Israelis adopted a policy of renewed counterattacks against PLO bases and of strengthening local Lebanese militia forces headed by Sa'ad Haddad. (A former officer in the Lebanese army, Haddad was a Melkite, a Greek Catholic. His militia was composed of former regular Lebanese army soldiers and recruits, both Christian and Muslim.)

Earlier in the chapter I observed that, from the late 1960s on, the PLO-Soviet relationship has become increasingly close, with a steady intensification of cooperation and operational coordination. By the end of the 1970s this trend was demonstrated, in part, by the top level at which such official coordination of policies and actions took place. Specifically, in November 1979 Arafat met with Soviet foreign minister Gromyko and International Department chief Ponomarev in Moscow. At the meeting the Soviets provided strategic and tactical guidance on a number of issues including policymaking in the U.N., thwarting U.S. diplomatic initiatives in the Middle East, furthering PLO contacts with Cuba, and escalating the Kremlin's international propaganda and political warfare efforts to promote the cause and legitimacy of the Palestinian organization.[31]

Soviet endeavors to elevate the international image of the PLO continued to intensify in the early 1980s as the Arafat-led organization joined in the diplomatic offensive. The employment of political means to attain a Palestinian state, in conjunction with a protracted "armed struggle," reflect the "stages" strategy adopted at the thirteenth Palestine National Council of 1977.[32] Although not all PLO factions accepted this strategy, the dominant group headed by Arafat did pursue this approach, which was supported by the Soviet Union. The objective was for the PLO to present itself politically as a moderate force in turbulent Middle East politics, while clandestinely continuing to carry out terrorist strikes. This tactic dates back to the previously discussed Fatah-inspired-and-directed Black September Organization activities of the early 1970s.

In southern Lebanon the PLO stepped up attacks against Israel. It sent its elite Ein-Jalut Brigade south and introduced the use of a number of heavy weapons, including T-34 tanks, artillery, and Katyusha rockets. As the violence increased in the late spring of 1982, Israel mounted air raids against PLO bases. The PLO replied with artillery, tank, mortar fire, and cross-border attacks, as well as terrorist strikes in Western Europe (for example, the shooting of the Israeli ambassador in London). In response, Israel launched Operation Peace for Galilee on June 6, 1982.

The PLO suffered a harsh setback with the loss of West Beirut and southern

Lebanon, a loss that seriously affected its strategy and tactics. It had developed an independent political and military base that was frequently referred to as a state within a state. The destruction of this independent sanctuary caused very serious problems for the Fatah-dominated PLO. No Arab state would allow the PLO to redeploy on its territory, let alone re-establish the political-military independence the organization enjoyed in Lebanon. The physical separation of the PLO leadership, with Fatah in Tunis and the Popular Front for the Liberation of Palestine (PFLP), PFLP–General Command, Democratic Front for the Liberation of Palestine (DFLP), and Sai'qa headquartered in Damascus, further complicated existing political and organizational cleavages.

On the one hand, the Israeli intervention reminded the PLO of the extent to which it could rely on Soviet and Arab patrons. On the other hand, it left them even more dependent on these patrons. The Soviet response initially was marked by studied inaction. Perhaps, from the Kremlin's perspective, little could be done in that, after only a few days into the war, it was apparent that the Palestinian and Syrian forces had lost militarily. Soviet weapons in the hands of the PLO and Syria were no match for the highly trained and well-equipped Israeli army. Sending more arms would not have turned the tide, and Moscow was unwilling to consider any escalation of its support beyond what it had already supplied. Furthermore, the aid needed by the PLO—Soviet naval forces to threaten the Israeli blockade, an airlift of arms and equipment, and the threat and/or introduction of military advisers and troops—has never been provided to a national liberation movement. The PLO's disappointment with its Soviet allies during the war was expressed by senior officials during the sixteenth Palestine National Council held in February 1983 in Algiers. Some members argued that the USSR could have played a more symbolic and materially active role during the crisis.[33]

These limits became even more clear to the Fatah-dominated PLO in the subsequent conflict with Syria. By the end of 1983 the Soviets, greatly expanding their relationship with Syria, committed more than $2 billion in new sophisticated weapons and aircraft and deployed more than 7,000 military technicians.[34] The amount and advanced nature of the weaponry, aimed at easing Syrian anger over Soviet inaction during the Israeli intervention in Lebanon, is the first case, since Egypt in the early 1970s, of such involvement with a nonperipheral Middle East state. (The Soviet focus up to this time had been in Afghanistan, Ethiopia, South Yemen, and Libya.[35]) The arms included T-72 tanks, air-to-air missiles (with a 60-mile range), surface-to-air missile systems (including 2, 5, 6, 8, and 11s), improved MiG-23s (which approach the performance of the most advanced MiG-27 fighter planes), and a much more advanced C^3I (command, control, communication, and intelligence) system.[36] These and other advanced weapons were introduced as a result of the Treaty of Friendship, Cooperation, and Mutual Trust signed by the USSR and Syria in 1980. In light of the quality and quantity of weapons and advisers deployed under the agreement, it appears that Moscow had come to view Syria as a crucial part of its regional and, possibly, global policy.

Syrian cooperation with the USSR in the region has included extensive ties between Damascus and the Soviet-supported Popular Front for the Liberation of Oman, the Democratic Front for the Liberation of Somali, and the Tamil United Liberation Front. Syria also has aligned with pro-Soviet regimes in Afghanistan, Ethiopia, South Yemen, and Libya and with radical factions in the Sudan and Jordan. With respect to Soviet strategic goals and power projection, Syria apparently gave Moscow the option to use the port facilities of Latakia and Tartūs, as well as two air bases. Both port facilities have been improved by the Soviet Union. In conjunction with this activity, there has been accelerated military cooperation between Damascus and members of the Soviet bloc, including Syrian naval participation in Warsaw Pact maneuvers, something that suggests the strategic importance of Moscow's ally.

Consequently, when factions within the PLO challenged Arafat's control and, with Syrian military support, attacked Fatah forces, Moscow did not intervene on the side of the PLO. On the contrary, in the previously mentioned November 23, 1983, meeting between Gromyko and Kaddoumi (one of Arafat's chief lieutenants), the former Soviet foreign minister advised that the PLO might align itself with Syria.[37]

Did this signal, as some Western observers asserted, a shattering of the Soviet-PLO connection? The answer appears to be, not at all. First, although Moscow (and all of the Arab states) failed to do anything to alleviate the PLO's perilous military situation in Lebanon, the Soviets continued to actively promote the organization in the international arena. Moscow exhibited stronger-than-ever public commitment to PLO participation in any peace talks, to the need for an independent Palestinian state, and to recognition of the PLO as the appropriate political authority to rule such a state. Ironically, Arafat's Fatah emerged from the debacle in Lebanon with more international prestige, which opened up new opportunities both at the U.N. and in Western Europe. In the case of the former, the USSR and its surrogates played an important role; in the latter, a number of states became more respectful of the PLO, most notably Austria and Italy.

Second, as in 1976, when faced with a confrontation between their Syrian and PLO allies, the Soviets placed greater importance on their commitment to the former, with some qualifications, including concern about Syrian domination of the PLO. To begin with, Syrian control would eliminate Moscow's own channels into the organization and would be opposed in other parts of the Arab world. Nevertheless, Damascus was and is Moscow's only strategic foothold in the Middle East, and Syrian opposition to Fatah control of the PLO over the rejectionist elements it backed could not be easily opposed. The strategic ties between the Soviet Union and Syria limited the pressure the former could bring on the latter to end the fighting in Lebanon against Arafat's Fatah forces. Still, there is evidence that the Kremlin did try to use its influence to persuade Syria to end the bloodshed in Tripoli. Galia Golan reports that Gromyko, during the November 1983 visit of the Syrian foreign minister to Moscow, "warned against the continued conflict [in Lebanon] and pressed the Syrians to end the bloodshed."[38] Publicly, the USSR assumed a position of neutrality, calling for unity within the ranks of the PLO and for PLO-Syrian solidarity. Following Arafat's evacuation from Tripoli, the Soviets reportedly exerted more pressure on Syria during 1984.[39]

In 1984 Moscow also increased its support for a unified PLO under the leadership of Fatah, following the visit of a Fatah delegation to the Soviet Union. Additionally, the July accord between Fatah and the Democratic Alliance (DFLP/PFLP/Palestine Communist Party/Palestine Liberation Front) was received warmly by the Kremlin. Tensions continued, however, between Arafat and Moscow throughout the remainder of the year.[40]

The Fatah-led PLO has always understood and seemed to pragmatically accept Moscow's order of priorities, which places relations with certain Arab countries at a higher level than it does those with the PLO. Moscow has always believed the PLO to be of secondary importance in its Middle East policy. For the PLO, however, the USSR remains an indispensable backer. Thus, while Moscow's Syrian ally was assisting other PLO factions to drive Fatah out of Lebanon, the Arafat-dominated PLO continued to play an important part in Soviet-supported low-intensity conflicts. The geographic scope of the Soviet-PLO connection extends well beyond the Middle East to other regions of the world.

The maintenance of this relationship in the latter half of the 1980s seems highly likely. As we shall see below, the Kremlin has committed significant assets over the years—both political and military—to promote and assist the Fatah-dominated PLO. Consequently, even though the Soviets have been genuinely concerned over certain of Arafat's political maneuvers—flirtation with the West, position on Israel, opposition to a two-state solution, unity within the PLO—they have continued to back his control of the organization and opposed attempts to replace him. For Arafat, this continuation was climaxed by his aforementioned March 13, 1985, arrival in Moscow.

Soviet Political-Military Support for the PLO Since 1973

Previously I noted that in the aftermath of the 1973 Yom Kippur War Soviet-PLO relations reached a new plateau, resulting in enhanced cooperation and support in a number of related areas. What follows is a detailed examination of how this new policy toward the PLO was translated into actual political and paramilitary assistance. In conjunction with these developments,

the PLO began to expand its role of assisting other insurgent and terrorist organizations. Thus, within the network of state-sponsored and state-supported international terrorism, the PLO became both a recipient and a supplier.

Foreign Propaganda

Before 1973, the PLO was a secondary issue in Soviet international propaganda.
As Kremlin policy changed, however, so did its international propaganda casting
the PLO within the context of its broader propaganda themes. These themes
included an examination of the roots of regional tension, a prescription for peace
in the Middle East, and a defense of Soviet policy.

With respect to the causes of conflict, the Middle East was included in the
global struggle between imperial and progressive forces. Israel was described as
seeking to expand its dominion over Arab territory through both military power
and promotion of Arab disunity. The United States was said to be in full concur-
rence with this policy. According to *Radio Moscow* of November 5, 1974, "Tel
Aviv and its patrons hope to foil the solution of the key problems of the Middle
East settlement by threatening some Arab countries and enticing others with the
prospect of the so-called separate talks." The Soviet solution to the problem was
twofold: convening a Geneva peace conference; recognizing the PLO and including it at the peace talks.[41]

From this point forward Moscow firmly and consistently supported the
"PLO as the sole organization expressing the will of the Palestinian Arab people
and reviving their national aspirations."[42] Although Soviet propaganda called for
unity among all Palestinian factions, Arafat's Fatah was characterized as the
mainstream of the PLO. Consequently, Arafat's speech at the U.N. and the
granting of permanent observer status to the PLO were hailed by the USSR.[43]
When the PFLP broke with Arafat, Beirut's *As-Safir* reported that "Moscow
decided to freeze its relations with the Popular Front for the Liberation of Palestine."[44] However, covert military assistance does not appear to have been cut
off. As noted previously, support for the PLO was not unqualified. Soviet statements called for a Palestinian state composed of the occupied territories rather
than one replacing the state of Israel.[45] This ran counter to the PLO position.

Soviet propaganda, not surprisingly, sought to portray the USSR as a loyal
and long-standing ally of the Arab states and the Palestinians. Moscow's *Radio
Peace and Progress* framed Soviet policy in terms of an ideological commitment
to the struggle against imperialism.[46] In sum, Soviet propaganda in 1974 reflected important changes in Kremlin Middle East policy.

During 1975 the main current of Soviet propaganda concentrated on criticizing Egyptian diplomatic activity, disassociating the PLO from terrorism, reporting on the crisis in Lebanon, isolating Israel internationally, and promoting
the charge that Zionism is a form of racism. Sadat's "lean to the West" was

heatedly attacked as "opening the doors for foreign monopoly capitalists."[47] Furthermore, the disengagement agreement signed by Egypt and Israel in September 1975 was frequently criticized throughout the remainder of the year as a sellout of the Palestinian people.[48] Additionally, Soviet commentary often reiterated the long-standing Soviet demand for a comprehensive settlement. In conjunction with this demand, the USSR began to praise Syria for its "firm stand which rejects compromise on the Middle East issue."[49] At this time Syria moved to the forefront as Moscow's principal surrogate in the region.

Growing Soviet international promotion of the PLO during 1975 included trying to deflect worldwide criticism of PLO terrorism. To accomplish this, Moscow made a distinction between PLO moderates, led by Arafat, and fanatic Palestinian splinter groups. In fact, Moscow praised the PLO for its willingness to take steps to combat terrorism:

> [T]he PLO is prepared to sign an international agreement to combat terrorism . . . It should be said that the PLO's attitude is not of a propaganda nature because the PLO command recently took decisive measures to combat terrorism. Before a Palestinian court . . . it tried those who participated in hijacking . . . and passed various terms of imprisonment . . . The PLO proceeds, in its just struggle, from a position of maturity and reality. It is well known that terrorist actions in no way belong to the means of revolutionary struggle; rather they greatly harm such a struggle.[50]

Escalating terrorism and violence in the Middle East was attributed to Zionist Israel.[51] This and related issues were part of the general propaganda assault against Israel, but the Soviets paid particular attention to the November 1975 U.N. resolution condemning Zionism as a form of racism. "The policy of Israel toward the Arab countries [is] based on this doctrine. This is a policy of expansion . . . The racist nature of Zionism was noted at the beginning of the century by Vladimir Lenin."[52]

As 1975 came to a close, the situation in Lebanon began to deteriorate rapidly. Clashes between Christian Phalange forces and PLO units threatened to destroy the Lebanese political balance. As noted previously, following its expulsion from Jordan, the PLO embarked on a policy of establishing a state within a state in Lebanon. Phalange military activity, in conjunction with Israeli strikes against guerrilla bases, jeopardized this. As long as the crisis continued along these lines, Soviet commentary was straightforward. However, Syrian intervention on the side of the Christian forces complicated matters.

Although Soviet propaganda did not reverse its expanding support for the PLO, Moscow refused to openly criticize Syrian involvement. The Soviet news agency TASS expressed regret over the "differences between Arab capitals" that had resulted in "the striving of some countries to impose a settlement of the Lebanon crisis that would be beneficial for them," but Syria was not specifically identified.[53] If Moscow secretly expressed concern to Syria over its actions, as *Le Monde* speculated, it did so in very conciliatory terms.

> It is as friends that we express ourselves with complete frankness. And who else could speak to you in the same way? It is our duty to think of the future, both near and distant. If Syria persists in the course which it has taken, it will give the imperialists and their collaborators the opportunity to gain control of the Arab nations and progressive movements as well as the Arab states with progressive regimes . . . We exhort the Syrian leaders to take all possible measures to end the military operations conducted against the resistance.[54]

Egypt's signing of a second-stage Sinai disengagement agreement, its abrogation of the 1971 Treaty of Friendship with the USSR, and the offer of U.S. military and economic assistance most likely contributed to Moscow's position. In terms of policy priorities the Kremlin places state-to-state relations above support for national liberation movements, and Syria was rapidly becoming its main regional ally.

Nevertheless, Soviet propaganda did praise the bravery of the Palestinian fighters as a means of reinforcing the Soviet commitment. In a major commentary in *Izvestiya,* the PLO was described as the "sole legitimate representative of the Arab people of Palestine" and "in the vanguard of the Arab peoples' anti-imperialist struggle." A settlement of the Middle East crisis could not be achieved "without participation of representatives of the Arab people of Palestine in the form of the PLO."[55]

Criticism of Israel became more acerbic in 1976, and we find frequent references to the torture of Arab prisoners, the fascist character of Zionism, and Israeli terrorism.[56] U.S. complicity in all this is also the subject of considerable commentary.[57] During 1977, the election of Jimmy Carter resulted in a shift in this theme. Initially, U.S. unwillingness to either endorse a Palestinian state or reduce arms deliveries to Israel was cited as proof of the new administration's hypocrisy in its support of a Palestinian homeland.[58] Such criticism moderated, however, after the joint Soviet-U.S. communiqué on the Middle East, which was apparently perceived as a victory in Moscow in that Kissinger's shuttle diplomacy was abandoned, Geneva would be reconvened with Soviet involvement, and the participation of representatives of the Palestinian people at the conference was recognized.

Leonard Schapiro asserted that the lack of reference to the PLO as the Palestinian representative was a setback for the organization. He based his argument not only on the communiqué but also on the lack of reference to the PLO in

Brezhnev's March speech to the Congress of Trade Unions.[59] It may be, however, that the Carter policy was seen by the Kremlin as an opportunity to disrupt U.S. support for Israel as well as to exacerbate Washington–Tel Aviv relations. Whereas previously an identity of interests had been assumed, now the Soviets explained that Israeli intransigence had undermined Carter administration credibility with the Arab world.[60] This explanation was part of a larger Soviet propaganda effort to assert that Carter administration "realists" were locked in a struggle with hawks from the Pentagon and the military-industrial complex. The latter sought to wreck the Strategic Arms Limitation Talks and détente.[61] Sadat's forthcoming initiative would alter this temporary pattern.[62]

Contrary to Schapiro's assertion, Soviet international propaganda support for the PLO continued unabated. During an April visit to Moscow, Arafat met with Brezhnev for the first time. This visit was followed by numerous highly supportive commentaries about the Palestinians in general and the PLO in particular.[63] This intensification of Soviet support continued throughout the remainder of the 1970s and into the 1980s.

In a number of articles and commentaries, the Soviets made it clear that the PLO is a de facto government. Arafat's meetings with Austrian Chancellor Bruno Kreisky, King Juan Carlos of Spain, and other West European political leaders were cited as proof of the growing international prestige of the PLO.[64] As we have seen, Moscow promoted a related theme through its touting of PLO participation at the U.N., and references to the PLO as the "sole legitimate representative" of the Palestinian people continued to appear in *Pravda* and other prestigious publications. Arafat's 50th birthday in 1979 was marked by special adulation as Brezhnev himself sent greetings and proclaimed that "your courageous struggle at the head of the PLO . . . has won you the Soviet people's sincere sympathies and support."[65] An article in *Pravda* stated that Arafat's "entire life is inseparably linked with the heroic struggle of the Arab people of Palestine . . . During this struggle [he] became . . . the recognized leader of the Palestinian resistance movement."[66] On the fifteenth anniversary of the PLO, *Radio Moscow* described Arafat's Fatah organization as the "pioneer Palestinian resistance movement."[67]

By the early 1980s, the degree of Soviet support for the PLO was reflected in the granting of full diplomatic status to the organization. In an interview with Arafat on *Radio Moscow*, his offices in the USSR were referred to as the "PLO embassy."[68] His visits to the Soviet Union and meetings with Brezhnev were widely reported, further contributing to the image of Arafat as a head of state. The coverage of Israel during this time also intensified in terms of both the tone and the number of items covered. Israel's attempt to find a Palestinian alternative to the PLO was denounced as a ruse "to create the impression among critics of Israel abroad that Tel Aviv . . . sensed the winds of change."[69] Israeli-Egyptian talks on Palestinian autonomy were described in similar terms. Soviet rhetoric was particularly heated on questions of Israeli policy toward the Palestinians in Israel, and we find repeated references to Israeli genocide and terrorism: "[T]he Tel Aviv rulers have overtly embarked on the road of terror both toward the Palestinian leaders and toward peaceful Palestinian refugees in southern Lebanon . . . These are linked in one and the same policy of genocide."[70] The United States was described as the "direct accomplice" and "inspirer" of these purported Israeli actions.[71] According to TASS of June 9, 1981, "Tel Aviv openly carries out an aggressive act of terrorism on the level of state policy while Washington supplies it with arms and provides it with political cover."[72] This criticism was leveled at the Carter administration in the aftermath of Andrew Young's political demise and depicts the shift toward Carter's policy noted above. By 1979, TASS asserted that "Washington connives with the incessant raids of the Israeli Air Force on the south of Lebanon, construction of Israeli militarized settlements on the captured Arab lands, thus actually supporting Tel Aviv's annexationist policy."[73] In the case of Ronald Reagan's administration, there was no question that it unconditionally backed Israel.[74]

Since 1982, Soviet commentary has focused on events in Lebanon, including the Israeli intervention and factional strife within the PLO. In the case of the latter, Moscow found itself between two quarreling allies—Syria and the PLO. As a result, the reporting of the dispute has been extremely cautious, seeking to avoid alienating either side. Press reports expressed continual concern with PLO factionalism, asserting that "weakening the unity of the Palestinian revolution . . . is in the interest of the enemies of the Palestinians. Yitzhak Shamir, Israeli minister of foreign affairs, announced recently that any rift and any internal problems within the PLO are good news for Israel."[75] The rebellion against Arafat, however, reflected not only disagreement over political and military tactics by PLO factions but also Syria's attempt to take advantage of these differences. The latter development complicated matters for Moscow, and its commentary on it was guarded. This caution can be seen, for instance, during Arafat's so-called last stand in Tripoli during the fall of 1983, when Syrian-supported Palestinian forces cornered the remnants of Arafat's Fatah fighters in the Doddawi camp near Tripoli.

Soviet propaganda frequently appealed for an end to the fighting to prevent the annihilation of the remainder of Arafat's forces. For example, quoting and concurring with the Democratic Front for the Liberation of Palestine's secretary general, Nayef Hawatimah, TASS called for "the warring factions in Fatah to cease the fighting . . . it benefited only the enemies of the Palestinian people."[76] However, the Soviets never swung entirely over to Arafat's side in the dispute. It appears that they sought a return to the status quo ante, with the PLO remaining under Arafat's leadership but cooperating with Syria. *Pravda* on November 19, 1983, stressed the importance in the "struggle against U.S.-Israeli expansion" of the "role which is played . . . by the Palestinian resistance movement and its political vanguard—the PLO—and by solidarity with Syria, which now is the most important force in countering the aggressive plans of the United States and Israel."[77]

Whereas the Arab press contained references to Soviet diplomatic moves to mediate the dispute,[78] we see in the evidence cited above a Soviet unwillingness to criticize its Syrian ally. However, during 1984 the Soviet press did express concern that Arafat might repeat Sadat's defection and seek a separate deal with Israel, either alone or with Jordan or Egypt. Arafat's visit to Cairo following his expulsion from Lebanon was, consequently, met by Kremlin displeasure. His signing in February 1985 of a "framework for joint action" with Jordan's King Hussein I also prompted a harsh response from the USSR.[79] Arafat's early March meeting with President Muhammad Mubarak over the possibility of U.S.-sponsored Israeli-Jordanian talks on the future of the Palestinians received severe criticism.[80]

Despite these rebukes, the Soviets never abandoned Arafat in their overt propaganda. Thus, *Izvestiya's* January 1, 1984, commemoration of the origins of Palestinian resistance observed that Arafat's Fatah launched the first "daring military operations against the Israeli occupiers in the Sinai Peninsula." It also appealed for an end to disunity "regardless of the reasons which gave rise to these disagreements."[81] At the same time *Radio Moscow* reported Arafat's meeting with the Soviet ambassador to Tunisia in the following terms:

> The [Soviet] ambassador praised the struggle of the Palestinian people on all fronts and also the wisdom and courage of Yasser Arafat. He also praised the role and attitude of the Palestinian people, represented by their support for their legitimate leadership.[82]

In sum, although critical at times, Soviet propaganda continued to support Arafat and defend Fatah-PLO orthodoxy against any deviations. This criticism never approached an open rejection of a Fatah-dominated PLO as the legitimate leader of the Palestinian people.[83] Soviet treatment of Israel and its U.S. "patron" during the 1980s deserves only passing mention because Moscow's propaganda themes did not change from the late 1970s. Israel was depicted in vituperative rhetoric by the Soviet press, including frequent comparisons of fascism with Zionism.[84]

International Front Organizations

In coordination with its foreign propaganda campaign, the USSR mobilized several of its international front organizations following the 1973 war to advance the cause of the PLO and its leader, Yasser Arafat. However, an examination of front operations following the war discloses that approximately one year elapsed before any major efforts were undertaken. Thus, front propaganda and conference diplomacy picked up somewhat during 1974, but these tactics did not expand dramatically until 1975.

In light of the strategic importance of the Middle East, it is not surprising that the World Peace Council (WPC) appears to have been assigned responsibility for directing and coordinating these front operations, including the formation of the International Commission of Inquiry into Israeli Crimes Against the Lebanese and Palestinian Peoples and the International Committee of Solidarity with the Palestinian People. Beginning in the latter half of the 1970s, the WPC included under its International Commission on Human Rights a subsection to inquire into Israeli violations of human rights in the occupied Arab territories. A number of other fronts were also mobilized as part of this effort, including the International Organization of Journalists, Afro-Asian People's Solidarity Organization, and the World Federation of Trade Unions.[85]

International front propaganda. The WPC-directed propaganda campaigns on behalf of the PLO generally followed Soviet thematic trends but were more narrowly focused. Of particular interest is the continuity in front commentary directed toward Israel. In 1975 the WPC's *New Perspectives* began to produce articles accusing Israel of committing atrocities and genocide against the Palestinians. "The Israelis are treating the civilian population in the occupied Arab territories with the inhumanity and cruelty which the Jews experienced in Nazi Germany before and during World War II."[86] Soviet commentary also employed such defamatory language, but this theme was much more frequently reiterated by the fronts. Additionally, Israel was accused of mass deportation of Palestinians on a scale that led the WPC to assert that its "rulers must be brought to trial, on the pattern of Nuremberg, for committing inhuman tortures and abominable crimes."[87]

Front propaganda also linked the above to the issue of Israeli human rights violations and the U.N. As noted below, the WPC actively sought to coordinate its activities with the U.N. This coordination actually began in 1975 when the WPC issued its first detailed report on human rights violations to the U.N. Commission on Human Rights, which identified Israel as the greatest violator.[88] In addition to the "occupied territories," Soviet front group propaganda alleged that Israel was responsible for similar acts in southern Lebanon during the late 1970s.[89]

A second major theme of international front propaganda after the 1973 war was U.S. complicity in Israeli human rights violations. For instance, in discussing Lebanon in 1977 the WPC stated that "the fascist and reactionary forces [Israel] were given the green light to use weapons to liquidate their opponents, weapons which the 'Holy Alliance' of U.S. imperialists, Israeli expansionists and Arab reaction were providing."[90] The same assertions can be found in the Resolution on the Middle East Crisis contained in documents from the September 1977 WPC's Presidential Committee Bureau.[91] Apparently, the brief spate of conciliatory language that marked Soviet commentary during the early period of the Carter administration was not reflected in international front propaganda.

The theme of U.S.-Israeli collusion and conspiracy was also echoed in the fronts' interpretation of Camp David. According to *New Perspectives,* "[T]he Middle East region has recently become the main arena for the activities of U.S. imperialism and world Zionism and their surrogate Israel. The Camp David conspiracy and its aggressive designs are a basic part of U.S. imperialism's total strategy."[92] This theme was further amplified during the Israeli intervention in Lebanon during 1982: "[W]ithout heeding the calls of reason and warnings, the Begin government, moved by its military madness, received the green light from the White House in Washington during the Sharon visit."[93] This charge was reiterated during the WPC-sponsored International Conference against Israeli Occupation of Lebanon, held in Vienna in September 1982. The conference "accused the U.S. of being a culprit through its constant support of and all-round help to Israel." Furthermore, "[T]he invasion of Lebanon was part of the Camp David process and the U.S.-Israeli plan for the dismemberment of the Middle East region."[94]

A third recurring theme found in international front propaganda focused on the PLO and its leader, Yasser Arafat. Beginning in 1974, the PLO was referred to as the only legitimate leader of the Palestinian people.[95] Likewise, Arafat was frequently identified as the top leader of the Palestinians. For instance, in 1980 the WPC presented Arafat with the Ho Chi Minh Award for his outstanding leadership.[96] Furthermore, Arafat statements frequently appeared in front publications.[97] The only time this pattern was interrupted was during the initial period of the PLO-Syrian conflict in Lebanon in 1983. However, by 1984 the fronts again began praising Arafat.[98]

International conference diplomacy. The WPC and other Soviet fronts generated a great deal of printed propaganda to advance the objectives of the PLO, but even more noteworthy are the large number of regional and international conferences organized by the fronts since the mid-1970s. Available evidence discloses that although the WPC played a central role in orchestrating these meetings, a number of other fronts were also quite active. The following is an analysis of the various conference tactics employed by the fronts to mobilize regional and international public opinion on behalf of the PLO. As we shall see, the focus of these actions follows the themes described above.

During 1975 the international fronts, particularly the WPC, began to plan and hold various international events on behalf of the PLO. Specifically, during

March 10–17 the WPC played an important role in the events surrounding the Week of Solidarity with the Palestinian People. The key aim of the statements, meetings, and signature drive that took place was to promote two objectives: immediate implementation of the resolution of the Twenty-ninth Session of the U.N. General Assembly on Palestinian rights and recognition by all governments that the PLO is the sole legitimate representative of the Palestinian people. During the Week of Solidarity the WPC directed its national-level affiliates to reiterate these demands. Thus, we find in Switzerland, for instance, the Basel Peace Committee extending an invitation to the PLO to send a delegation to the country to explain the Palestinian cause. In a number of other countries similar activities were organized.[99]

During May 1975 the WPC's Continuing Liaison Council of the World Congress of Peace Forces convened an International Conference for a Just and Peaceful Solution to the Middle East Problem in Paris. Attended by 115 delegates from eighteen international and national organizations in 30 countries, the conference rejected Kissinger's "step-by-step" approach and called for convening a Geneva conference with PLO participation.[100] At the World Conference of Peace Forces held in Vienna November 27–30 by the WPC, an International Campaign Committee for a Just Peace in the Middle East was established. The PLO took part in the meeting, which promoted the same objectives as those of earlier conferences. In addition to these examples, a number of related events occurred during 1975:

- International Organization of Journalists appealed to journalists to protest Israeli attacks on Palestinian refugee camps.

- International Union of Students held a meeting to promote support of Arab liberation movements including the PLO.

- Christian Peace Conference, in a message to the PLO, reaffirmed its support for its recognition.

- WPC urged all national-level peace councils to support an immediate convocation of the Geneva conference with full PLO participation.

- WPC's Commission of the Inquiry into the Israeli Violations of Human Rights in the Occupied Arab Territories charged Israel with "violating every single article of the U.N. Declaration of Human Rights."

- WPC issued three new booklets—*The United Nations and the National Rights of the Palestinian People, Israeli Violation of Human Rights in the Occupied Arab Territories,* and *Geneva Conference: Way to Peace and Justice in the Middle East.*

- World Federation of Trade Unions' secretariat of the International Trade Union Committee of Solidarity with the People and Workers of Palestine held its second international conference in support of the PLO.

- WPC presented Yasser Arafat with its highest award—the Joliot-Curie Medal—at a ceremony in the U.N. Educational, Scientific, and Cultural Organization Hall in Beirut.

This pattern of international conferences and meetings, of the issuance of messages and appeals, and of the publication of special booklets by the Soviet fronts continued through the remainder of the 1970s. Space does not permit a year-by-year analysis of this escalating campaign, but a review of activities in 1979 is illustrative. During May 1979 the WPC, PLO, and Swiss Peace Movement organized an International Conference of Solidarity with the Palestinian People in which 200 delegates represented 60 countries and seventeen international nongovernmental organizations. The latter included participation by high U.N. officials, including the deputy director of the U.N. office in Geneva and the rapporteur of the U.N. Committee on the Exercise of the Inalienable Rights of the Palestinian People. WPC cooperation with committees and representatives of the U.N. was an important aspect of international front actions during the late 1970s and part of a larger Soviet effort, as described in the next section, to promote the cause and legitimacy of the PLO in the U.N. The themes of the conference included the legitimacy of the PLO as the representative of the Palestinian people, condemnation of the Camp David accords, charges of gross Israeli violation of human rights in the occupied Arab territories, and reaffirmation of the U.N. resolutions for the solution of the Palestine question.[101] The conference report was then published by the WPC under the title of *Rights of the Palestinian People—Key to Peace in the Middle East*. The delegates then called for a permanent organization to continue these efforts. This body was formally established at a follow-up meeting held by the WPC in Basel on February 22, 1980.[102] Arafat was informed of the Soviet decision to establish the International Committee of Solidarity with the Palestinian People in a November 13, 1979, meeting in Moscow with Foreign Minister Gromyko and International Department head Ponomarev. The latter pointed out to the PLO chief that "when the Vietnamese people struggled with the U.S.A. we established a similar committee of solidarity with it. Vietnam, as we know, won later, and we hope that this time victory will be achieved too."[103]

The WPC was also actively involved with the U.N. on the human rights issue. It participated in the General Assembly's anniversary of the Universal Declaration of Human Rights and issued a statement charging Israel with carrying out "acts of terror against the peoples of Lebanon and Palestine."[104] During the spring it submitted a special report to the U.N. Human Rights Commission making similar charges.[105] The International Association of Democratic Lawyers (IADL) also participated in the human rights aspect of the front offensive by sponsoring an international colloquium on the Israel-Egypt treaty. Attended by lawyers from more than 30 countries, the colloquium concluded that the treaty was invalid because the signatories were not empowered to dispose of the rights of the Palestinians. It also condemned Israel for its colonizing policy in the occupied territories. The work of the IADL resulted in October 1982 in the establishment of the Permanent International Legal Commission on the Middle East.[106]

The International Organization of Journalists (IOJ) also held an international conference on Palestine in Sofia during October 1979. The IOJ urged all professionally minded journalists to mobilize public opinion in defense of the Palestinian people and their sole legitimate representative, the PLO.[107] These were some of the major front activities during 1979, but a number of related actions also took place, including

- WPC International Conference of Solidarity with the Arab People
- WPC publication, *Palestinians and Human Rights*
- WPC-sponsored International Day of Solidarity with Lebanon
- WPC/Afro-American People's Solidarity Organization (AAPSO) seminar on the imperialist policy of destabilization

The Israeli intervention into Lebanon on June 6, 1982, initiated an immediate flurry of international front condemnation. What is interesting is not the predictable accusations but the rapidity with which the fronts mobilized their response. Almost immediately a number of statements and messages were issued, including a WPC/World Federation of Trade Unions/World Federation of Democratic Youth/International Union of Students/Women's International Democratic Federation/AAPSO joint appeal to the U.N. Security Council calling on it to condemn the "genocidal war" in Lebanon. This appeal claimed that the United States bore special responsibility for the situation in Lebanon because of its policy of supplying sophisticated weapons to Israel. Additionally, a number of the same fronts issued separate messages and appeals. During August the WPC sponsored an International Commission on Israeli Crimes, which met in Nicosia. The commission, which reviewed a report from a WPC delegation that had been sent to Lebanon, demanded an immediate and unconditional Israeli withdrawal.[108] During the same month the IADL announced plans to produce a "white book" on the Israeli invasion, and the previously mentioned Permanent International Legal Commission on the Middle East was officially formed.

By September 1982 the WPC had organized an international conference on Lebanon, which was held in Vienna. With delegates from more than 50 countries and fifteen international organizations, the meeting issued a report that condemned Israeli atrocities, charged the United States with culpability, and called for October 18 to be observed as an international day of solidarity with the Lebanese people. During the conference the WPC also declared Beirut a Hero City in which the "Joint Forces of the Palestine Revolution and Lebanese National Movement courageously endured a total siege."[109] During September the Christian Peace Conference and the International Union of Students used their secretariat meetings as international forums to condemn Israeli aggression and to pledge support to the PLO and other patriotic forces in Lebanon.

The intensification of the Syrian-PLO rift in 1983, which complicated matters for Soviet policy, was reflected in a decline in front actions in support of the PLO. Not all activities were brought to a halt, but there was a noticeable decline in 1983 compared with 1975–1982. Arafat, however, did take part in the WPC's major international conference in 1983—the World Assembly for Peace and Life, whereas the WPC also sponsored an International Day of Solidarity with the Syrian People. Among the slogans for the Day was the call for a "convening of an international conference under the auspices of the U.N. and with the participation of Syria, the PLO, the USSR, the USA, and all other parties concerned on an equal footing [as] the only appropriate instrument to realize peace in the Middle East."[110] Here we can see how closely the fronts follow the Soviet position on the Syrian-PLO issue. The coordination and immediate amplification of these policy themes by the fronts are also quite impressive.

By the latter half of 1984, Moscow's international fronts began to return to the pattern that existed before the Syrian-PLO crisis of 1983–1984. However, a review of front international political operations on behalf of the PLO suggests that the degree of activism has not reached that of the 1975–1982 period. Whether this upswing will continue is uncertain.

Among the more important programs initiated by the WPC during the second half of 1984 was the August 20–22 meeting of nongovernmental organizations (NGOs). The session was the result of a December 1983 U.N. recommendation that the NGO members of the U.N. evaluate the action program of the world conference on Palestine and recommend steps to be followed in the future. The WPC, which is recognized as an NGO by the U.N., called for an international diplomatic conference on Palestine under U.N. auspices with the full participation of the Arafat-led PLO. In support of this initiative, many of the NGOs in attendance agreed to start a signature campaign on November 29, the U.N.'s Day of Solidarity with Palestine. A further NGO conference on Palestine was planned for 1985.[111] Earlier in the summer the WPC used its executive committee meeting to give Arafat a forum to assert his leadership. His message to the meeting not only reiterated the PLO stand against Israeli and U.S. imperialism but also supported the Soviet propaganda campaign against the European missile and arms race.[112]

Political Activities Within the U.N.

The increasingly close relationship between the USSR and the PLO since the latter half of the 1970s can also be seen in the U.N., where the PLO counts on Soviet backing for those resolutions and actions that concern it. Over the years the PLO has achieved an ever-widening base of international support, both in bilateral contacts with individual states and in the U.N. and other transnational groupings. The latter includes the Nonaligned Movement and the Organization of African Unity (OAU). (The PLO is the only non-African national liberation movement to enjoy observer status in the OAU.)

Within the U.N. a coalition of states supporting the PLO and its program played a central role in the October 1974 General Assembly decision to invite the PLO to participate in the deliberations over Palestine. This invitation led to Yasser Arafat's appearance before the General Assembly the following month. The Soviet Union and its surrogates were an important element of the coalition of states that made Arafat's visit possible. He addressed the General Assembly and Security Council as the de facto head of a sovereign state.[113] On November 22, 1974, the PLO was admitted to observer status in the U.N. by General Assembly Resolution 3237. This resolution was preceded by Resolution 3236, which, according to Helena Cobban, has "been used by the PLO as a benchmark definition of Palestinian rights throughout the years which followed."[114] The resolution, in effect, reiterates the PLO's own program.

A year after these developments, the U.N. took a further dramatic step in support of the PLO with the passage of Resolution 3379, condemning Zionism as a form of racism. The measure carried by 72 to 35 with 32 abstentions. The maneuvering surrounding this development, according to Daniel Patrick Moynihan, reveals the active role played by the USSR and its surrogates in U.N. coalition politics. In this instance, as in related ones examined in later chapters, the political maneuvers were orchestrated by a combination of nonaligned nations (led by the Arab states) and the USSR and its surrogates. On the basis of his vantage point as U.S. permanent representative to the U.N., Moynihan was able to observe and chronicle this successful political stratagem.[115]

The General Assembly is not the only part of the U.N. structure in which this coalition of states seeks to promote and legitimize the PLO. Such activity also has taken place at the Security Council level, where the PLO has been invited to participate in its deliberations on Palestine. Members of the Security Council also use the council as a forum for criticizing Israel in very harsh terms. In 1983, for example, the representative from South Yemen referred to Israel as "the state of Zionist gangs." The PLO representative to the U.N. also referred to Israel during a Security Council meeting as being governed by "Judeo Nazis and the Judeo Nazi Junta . . . who collaborated with Hitler's hordes."[116]

These developments were followed in the mid-1970s by the creation of two important U.N. bodies concerned with Palestinian-related issues. In 1975 the General Assembly established the Inalienable Rights Committee. As we shall see below, the committee interprets its mandate—to study and propose to the General Assembly and Security Council solutions to the question of Palestine—in a manner that consistently echoes the program of the PLO.

In 1977, on the recommendation of the Inalienable Rights Committee, the Special Unit on Palestinian Rights was established under the auspices of the secretariat (Resolution 32/40B). Its mandate, in effect, instructed the special unit to organize international seminars, produce publications, and undertake related activities to bring the Palestinian issue into the purview of international public opinion. As we shall see, the activities of the special unit are heavily influenced by the PLO and its supporters.

The importance the Kremlin leadership placed in the political maneuvers and developments outlined above as well as in Soviet-PLO coordination is seen in the minutes of a 1979 meeting in Moscow between Soviet foreign minister Gromyko, International Department chief Ponomarev, and a PLO delegation headed by Arafat. In discussing an upcoming debate on the "Palestinian problem" Ponomarev explained: "You raised the subject of consultations on this matter [of the U.N. debate]. We always asked you to consult us on this subject. It is very important in the U.N. so that we can exploit the U.N. stage by exposing aggressive actions which Israel conducts in southern Lebanon."[117]

Committee on the Exercise of the Inalienable Rights of the Palestinian People. The Inalienable Rights Committee issues an annual report on its activities during the previous year. A review of the period 1976–1983 discloses the effective continuation of the work of the coalition of nonaligned and Soviet-bloc states discussed above. Since its inception the committee has been an unwavering supporter of the PLO, and although the committee asserts impartiality, a review of its actions reveals no such evenhandedness. PLO documents make clear that Arafat views the activities of this and other U.N. bodies as important. The political platform adopted by the fourth Fatah conference in May 1980 established the following operating principle for the PLO: "to act so as to turn the U.N. resolutions regarding Zionism . . . into practical measures against the Zionist imperialist colonial base in Palestine."[118]

An examination of the composition of the committee, listed in its annual report, helps explain why it has been consistently pro-PLO and anti-Israel, with little or no attempt to temper its approach to the issues.[119] By 1980 the 23 committee members included Afghanistan, Cuba, East Germany, Hungary, Laos,

Romania, the Ukrainian Soviet Socialist Republic, and Yugoslavia. Other states in the coalition within the committee are Guinea, Guyana, India, Madagascar, Mali, Senegal, Sierra Leone, and Tunisia. Additionally, since its inception the committee has invited "those State Members of the United Nations and Permanent Observers to the United Nations which wished to participate in the work of the Committee." Over the years this has included Algeria, Egypt, Iraq, Libya, Syria, Vietnam, the Arab League, and the PLO.[120] During 1982 two additional interested parties—Czechoslovakia and Nicaragua—were invited to participate.

The elected officers during the period under examination included Senegal (chairman), Cuba (vice-chairman), and Afghanistan (vice-chairman). To conduct its day-to-day deliberations, the committee established a working group (task force). According to the 1980 annual report, in addition to the elected officers, the working group included Malta, Guinea, Guyana, India, Tunisia, East Germany, and the PLO.[121] Two years later the representative from the Ukrainian Soviet Socialist Republic was added.[122] What is most notable about this list of official and unofficial members is the absence of Western or Latin American (excluding Cuba and Nicaragua) states. Furthermore, while the PLO was invited to participate in the deliberations of the committee and to serve as a member of its working group, Israel apparently has received no similar offer. The working group is directed to address the following tasks:

1. Monitor daily events related to the work of the committee and draft appropriate letters and legislation to be sent by the chairman to the secretary-general, the president of the Security Council, or the president of the General Assembly.

2. Organize and run seminars concerned with the Palestinian issues, as well as participate in similar functions sponsored by other NGOs.

3. Review, reproduce, and arrange for the distribution of studies and films sponsored by the committee. Organize the Day of Solidarity with the Palestinian People.

The committee's recommendations and actions over the years have been most one-sided. Although space does not permit a review of these activities on a year-by-year basis, an examination of 1980 is representative of what has taken place annually since 1976. During 1980 the committee focused a major portion of its efforts on the Security Council. General Assembly Resolution 34/65A urged the Security Council to adopt recommendations of the committee that it had endorsed. These included the following points:

- The question of Palestine is at the heart of the problem of the Middle East, and no solution can be envisaged without taking into account the inalienable rights of the Palestinian people.

- The "final solution . . . to the crisis" can only take place when the Palestinians return to their homes and property and exercise self-determination and national sovereignty.

- The participation of the PLO on an equal footing with all other parties is indispensable.

- The acquisition of territory by force is inadmissible, and Israel is obligated to withdraw completely from all occupied territory.[123]

Although the committee initiated various actions to press the case, the Security Council failed to adopt a draft resolution based on the above recommendations because of "the negative vote of a permanent member."[124] In the aftermath of this setback, the committee was instrumental in the decision taken by the Seventh Emergency Special Session of the General Assembly to consider the question of Palestine. The results of the session were considered quite successful by the committee:

> The General Assembly adopted a draft resolution prepared by the committee. By that resolution the General Assembly once more endorsed the committee's recommendations and fixed the date of 15 November 1980 as a deadline for withdrawal by Israel from the occupied Arab territories. Of special satisfaction to the committee was the fact that on this occasion several Western European member states had in their interventions censured Israel's settlement policy and its attempts to make Jerusalem its permanent capital; and they had also pointed out that the Palestine Liberation Organization should participate in any negotiations . . . the committee expresses its satisfaction with the results of the emergency special session of the General Assembly and considers it to have been most useful in highlighting the isolation of Israel.[125]

In addition to its own actions the committee "followed with the greatest interest action taken during the year by other organizations on questions relevant to [its own] work." In a number of instances the committee sent delegations to the international conferences and meetings of these organizations. For instance, in 1979 and 1980 these included the following:

- Finnish-Arab Friendship Society in Helsinki in January 1979
- Conference organized by the WPC Presidential Committee in Prague in April 1979
- Meeting of the heads of the nonaligned states in Havana in August–September 1979

- Meeting of the Islamic Conference in Islamabad in May 1980
- Participation at the Week of Solidarity with the Palestinian People organized by the Solidarity Committee of the German Democratic Republic in East Berlin in June 1980
- World Parliament of Peoples for Peace organized by the WPC in Sofia in September 1980.[126]

It was the view of the committee that such "attendance was of extreme importance in furthering [its] aims and objectives . . . and fulfilling its mandate."[127] The list of organizations demonstrates how the committee, in coordination with members of the communist states coalition, integrates its international political actions with like-minded groups. In the previous list one can observe how the Soviets utilized part of their front apparatus—the WPC—for this purpose. Note, however, that other fronts have been involved with the committee, including the Afro-Asian People's Solidarity Organization and the International Association of Democratic Lawyers.

The committee, on the basis of paragraph 1 of Resolution 32/40B, has been authorized by the General Assembly to "provide necessary guidelines to the Special Unit on Palestinian Rights in preparing its publications."[128] These guidelines include suggestions of themes for pamphlets and films as well as assistance to ensure that these materials receive the widest distribution.

During the 1980s the activities of the committee closely followed the pattern described above, with its one-sided approach continuing unabated. Thus, in its 1983 report the committee considered the "final documents of the International Conference on the Question of Palestine" to represent the only basis for a "just and lasting political settlement."[129] These documents reflect the continuity in outlook and mission of the committee. The international conference, held at the U.N. offices in Geneva from August 29 to September 7, 1983, under the guidance of the committee, was attended by 117 representatives from various U.N. committees and specialized agencies, numerous NGOs (including the WPC and other Soviet fronts), and three national liberation movements. The PLO was a full participant in the conference and played a central role, as reflected in the final documents. The international conference issued a three-part Programme of Action that contained 48 specific recommendations. The following selected excerpts reflect the continuity in the U.N.'s approach to the issue:

- Consider the continued presence of Israel in occupied Palestinian and Arab territories, including Jerusalem, as exacerbating instability in the region and endangering international peace.
- Oppose and reject . . . the expansionist policies pursued by Israel.

- Refrain from providing Israel with assistance . . . to continue its agression.

- Consider ways and means of meeting the threat that Israel poses to the regional security in Africa in view of Israel's . . . close collaboration with the *apartheid* regime in the economic, military, and nuclear fields.

- Express concern that the Palestinians and other Arabs in the occupied territories are . . . victims of repressive legislation, involving mass arrests, acts of torture . . . and acts which constitute flagrant violations of human rights.[130]

Nowhere in these documents is there a single criticism of the PLO or its strategy and tactics.

Special Unit on Palestinian Rights.   During 1977 the Inalienable Rights Committee was instrumental in the General Assembly's decision to establish, under the auspices of the secretariat, the Special Unit on Palestinian Rights. Its mandate directs it to carry out three principal activities: producing publications, initiating an ongoing series of regional seminars, and convening the annual International Solidarity Day with the Palestinian People. Each of these activities is, in reality, under the direction of the Inalienable Rights Committee. The special unit is widely known for its strongly pro-PLO perspective, probably because of the many PLO officials within the secretariat.[131]

The special unit's primary publication is the sometimes monthly, sometimes bimonthly *Division for Palestinian Rights,* which reports on all U.N. and international activities concerned with Palestinian-related matters. A random sample of the publication reveals a pattern of consistent and unswerving commitment to the goals and strategy of the PLO. In addition to the *Division for Palestinian Rights,* the special unit sponsors and prepares studies on historical and contemporary issues related to questions of Palestinian rights. The controversial nature of a number of these studies has been pointed out in Julius Stone's *Israel and Palestine: Assault on the Law of Nations.* Specifically, Stone critiques a series of studies on the Arab-Israel conflict prepared under the auspices of the Inalienable Rights Committee and the special unit and published and distributed by the U.N. Stone marshals weighty evidence to support the conclusion that these studies "present rather consistently anti-Israel positions on the central issues of the Arab-Israel conflict," but "even more serious are the questions they raise of the confrontation between the United Nations and the law of nations as hitherto understood, and the implications of this . . . for the stability of the international community."[132]

The publications and studies of the special unit are important aspects of the international political campaign, guided by the Inalienable Rights Committee, to advance the PLO cause. The materials are circulated on a worldwide basis by the U.N.'s Department of Public Information (DPI), which plays a significant part in the campaign to legitimize the PLO and isolate Israel. Arkadi Shevchenko, a former senior Soviet official at the U.N., maintains that the DPI has a crucial role in Soviet active measures campaigns, including efforts to promote national liberation movements. Shevchenko points out that key DPI officials from the USSR are, in reality, KGB officials.[133] The extensive KGB presence in the U.N. Secretariat has been documented in a 1985 special report by the Senate Select Committee on Intelligence.[134]

The message conveyed through regional seminars sponsored by the special unit mirrors its publications and studies, which is apparent from an examination of the proceedings from these meetings. For example, the report of the seventh U.N. seminar on the question of Palestine, which was held in Senegal in August 1982, asserted the following:

- Serious questions were raised concerning the special relationship of the United States with Israel and its responsibility and complicity in Israel's continuing aggression in Lebanon.
- Israeli intransigence and aggressiveness were encouraged by U.S. material, political, and moral support.
- To put an end to Israeli's genocidal operation in Lebanon, the Security Council was strongly urged to consider the imposition of sanctions.
- The participants of the seminar expressed their admiration for the bravery of the PLO and extended to it their wholehearted support.[135]

Of course, the purpose of the seminars is not simply to reiterate the same messages but to mobilize world public opinion in support and active promotion of these themes.

Perhaps the most important mobilization activity carried out by the Inalienable Rights Committee and the special unit is the annual International Day of Solidarity with the Palestinian People. The report on the 1981 commemoration discloses an integrated series of events that included activities not only at U.N. headquarters in New York and Geneva but in several capitals around the world. These events were publicized in press releases and radio and visual coverage by the DPI.[136]

Although costs of many of the activities undertaken by these two U.N. bodies are not easily determined, the evidence suggests that it is substantial. For instance, the cost of the August 1983 special unit seminar was nearly $6 million.[137] One can easily imagine that the annual cost of the various seminars, conferences, regular publications, special studies, the day of solidarity, and DPI distribution, as well as the day-to-day expenses of the Inalienable Rights Committee and the special unit, is quite significant. Of course, these are not the only U.N. bodies involved with the Palestinian issue and the PLO. Others include the U.N. Relief and Works Agency and the U.N. Educational, Scientific, and Cultural Organization.[138]

Arms Transfers

It is generally believed that Soviet and Eastern-bloc arms were initially made available to the PLO, on a clandestine and limited scale, during the latter half of the 1960s. According to Goren,

> The first conclusive evidence of some Eastern-bloc support for the terrorist organization was reported by Muhammed Jabih, president of the Palestinian Students' Association . . . In April 1968, upon his return to Cairo from a trip to Eastern Europe, he reported the promise made by the USSR, Bulgaria, Czechoslovakia, Hungary and Yugoslavia to supply light equipment . . . Radio Cairo had reported a year earlier that East Germany had offered to supply arms to the PLO.[139]

Yodfat and Arnon-Ohanna concur that, following the 1967 war, the PLO was not receiving direct substantial military assistance from the USSR. They qualify this, however, with the observation that the "PLO or Al Fatah received abundant [military] aid from Arab governments—much of it in the form of Soviet-made arms."[140] This pattern of limited and indirect arms transfers continued until 1972 when, according to Schapiro, Soviet arms supplies, while still limited and confined to light weapons, were transferred directly to the PLO.[141] Transferring arms directly was part of the policy of legitimizing the Palestinian movement.

Following the 1973 war, Soviet arms transfers underwent still another change, as Moscow followed the lead of the Rabat Arab summit conference and recognized the PLO as the sole legitimate representative of the Palestinian people. This development, in conjunction with the U.S. political position following the war, had an immediate impact on the flow of arms. Also during the mid-1970s, the PLO began to develop and expand its base in Lebanon, which would eventually necessitate a much larger and more sophisticated stock of military capabilities. The process of a PLO arms buildup in Lebanon was, nevertheless, graduated in scale. In 1975, for instance, it was reported that the PLO began to receive Soviet RPG-7 handheld rocket launchers and AK-47 and SKS carbines.[142]

During the latter half of the 1970s, the kinds of Soviet and Eastern-bloc weapons appearing in Lebanon changed considerably. New weapons included sophisticated antiaircraft and antitank missile systems. Consignments of antitank shells, mortars, and 160-mm, 130-mm, and 82-mm artillery were delivered overland and by sea. Soviet T-34 and T-62 tanks also were reportedly supplied to the PLO via Eastern-bloc sources. Of course, the flow of small arms likewise escalated. The exact quantity of Soviet and Eastern-bloc military assistance to the PLO by the end of the decade is not easily determined.

During the early 1980s Soviet-bloc arms transfers to the PLO in Lebanon reached their most active point. The kinds of arms provided reflects the decision to prepare the PLO in the strategy and tactics of conventional operations. This decision required the heavy weaponry applicable to this level of conflict. These supplies arrived in Lebanon during 1981–1982 by land, sea, and air routes and included T-54, T-55, T-34, and T-62 Soviet battle tanks; BM-21 rocket launchers (Katyushas, equipped with 40 barrels apiece); and ZSU-4 radar-guided antiaircraft cannons mounted on armored personnel carriers.[143]

As a result of Operation Peace for Galilee—the June 6, 1982, Israeli intervention into Lebanon—the actual quantity and quality of Soviet-bloc arms were clarified. According to information provided by the Israeli Defense Force (IDF), the military equipment seized in weapons depots in southern Lebanon and West Beirut was enough to equip several artillery units and infantry brigades. Jillian Becker, in a first-hand account of PLO arms caches, presents the following description:

> The PLO units were massively overarmed with light and heavy weapons. Their Soviet tanks were not the newest or the best, but they were not in short supply. They also had long-range artillery pieces, rocket launchers, antiaircraft guns, shoulder-fired missiles, and antitank guns . . . The rocket launchers were both fixed and mounted in trucks; machine-guns and antiaircraft guns were mounted on, or towed by, trucks and jeeps. PLO bases were defended with trenches and gun emplacements, many on top of schools and hospitals, and in the midst of houses. Underground arms-stores and shelters for the fighters were spacious, well lit and air-conditioned.[144]

Although the Israelis have not released a comprehensive accounting of the weapons captured, the IDF reported that a partial load filled 4,300 trucks.[145] Part of this inventory included the following:

- 1,320 armed combat vehicles including several hundred T-34, T-55, and T-62 tanks
- 1,352 antitank weapons, including missile launchers and antitank guns
- 62 Katyusha rocket launchers
- 82 field artillery pieces (122 mm, 130 mm, and 155 mm)
- 196 antiaircraft weapons

- 215 mortars
- 5,630 tons of ammunition.[146]

In light of the fact that many of these weapons are not commonly associated with terrorist and insurgent tactics, it seems plausible that Moscow sought to assist the PLO in developing a conventional military capability. It may also be, as Ray Cline and Yonah Alexander argue, that these weapons were earmarked for use "ultimately by Syria or even the Soviet Union in any major regional conflict that developed out of PLO destabilizing actions. Perhaps this is the reason Moscow continue[d] to bolster the PLO arsenal."[147]

Training PLO Forces

As with arms transfers, Soviet and surrogate military and paramilitary training of PLO forces can be traced back to the latter half of the 1960s. "The earliest link," according to Goren, "started in 1966 and came to light in August 1968, at the time of an Al-Fatah demand for the release of one of its colleagues held in an Israeli prison. The demand noted in passing that the man had been trained by the Viet Cong in 1966."[148] The Cuban-PLO connection also dates back to 1966, the year Castro hosted the Tri-Continental Conference. The meeting brought together 500 delegates from radical leftist organizations all over the world to plan a "global revolutionary strategy to encounter . . . American imperialism."[149] Following the conference, the training of terrorist and guerrilla cadres in Cuba, including the PLO, escalated as a cluster of new facilities was established.[150]

The exact date on which the USSR began to provide paramilitary training to PLO cadres has not been documented. According to one source, International Department chief Ponomarev first offered Soviet facilities for training Palestinian guerrillas in 1968.[151] Interestingly, unlike Soviet propaganda and political support, which concentrated on Fatah, paramilitary training was offered to several PLO factions. In 1970, George Habash, head of the Popular Front for the Liberation of Palestine, confirmed this fact in an interview with Italian journalist Oriana Fallaci.[152] Apparently, the initial Soviet assistance was restricted, but as the 1970s unfolded, a network of Soviet and surrogate facilities was opened to PLO members.

In the USSR, training facilities for paramilitary and military preparations were made available in Baku, Tashkent, Odessa, and Simferopol in the Crimean Oblast. A special school for training PLO cadres was reportedly established in Prague, with a six-week course taught by Soviet and East German security officers. The trainees were then transferred to other Czech facilities in Košice, Karlovy Vary, Doupov, and Ostrava for an additional five months of instruction.[153]

Similar facilities exist in Varna in Bulgaria, Lake Balaton in Hungary, and Pankov and Finsterwalde in East Germany. Outside the Warsaw Pact, Cuba increased its involvement with the PLO, opening more than a dozen training camps to PLO representatives. According to Claire Sterling, these facilities were under the direction of Colonel Vakim Kotchergive of the KGB, and it was at one of these locations that Carlos the Jackal was schooled in urban terrorist tactics.[154] It has been reported that North Korea, South Yemen, Libya, and Algeria have also been involved in providing training to Palestinians, which was subsequently documented in PLO records captured in Lebanon.[155]

By the end of the decade, according to various sources, an extensive infrastructure of some 40 training facilities existed within the USSR, staffed by KGB, Chief Intelligence Directorate of the General Staff, and Red Army specialists.[156] The facilities in the other Eastern-bloc countries likewise expanded. In addition to basic training, many PLO representatives received advanced military education during the second part of the 1970s. For instance, the advanced course of study at the Soviet Academy for Military Training base at Simferopol includes military field exercises, communications techniques, and lectures in strategy and tactics as well as preparation in the use of range weapons and munitions.

By the early 1980s the PLO forces in Lebanon consisted of more than 10,000 men that were armed and trained for both conventional and unconventional war. The Warsaw Pact and other Soviet surrogate contributions to the development of these forces were confirmed in a 1979 interview with Zehdi Labib Terezi, the PLO's representative at the U.N. In a broadcast over the U.S. Public Broadcasting Station television network, he stated that "the Soviet Union, and all of the socialist countries . . . open their military academies to our freedom fighters . . . there is no secret about that . . . this is sometimes done in the open."[158]

In addition to military education, PLO cadres also receive training in the techniques of propaganda and psychological and political warfare. This training includes instruction at the Lenin Institute and elsewhere in the methods of international political activities. In many instances, these methods parallel the kinds of Soviet political active measures described earlier in this chapter, including propaganda, international conference activities, cultivation of relations with governments, involvement in the U.N., and related activities. The theory and practice of psychological warfare as it relates to terrorist and guerrilla operations are also part of this training. The importance of the symbiotic linkage between these elements of protracted struggle is captured in the following quote from the book *Mind Conditioning* by Edward Rosental:

> To pile on the agony, so to speak, and to drive your audience into a
> panic which guarantees that they will accept any recipe and formula

that the propagandists may care to offer. Not only will they accept it, they will be grateful.[158]

Primary documents discovered in Lebanon during 1982 provide corroborating evidence of Soviet and surrogate training of PLO personnel. Specifically, the documentation discloses aid for the PLO coming directly from the USSR as well as from surrogates and allies in Eastern Europe, the Caribbean, Central America, and Asia. For instance, one item is the account of an April 1982 meeting between the Palestinians and senior-level East German officials (the chief of staff and deputy defense minister) at which arrangements were made for military assistance and training.[159] Other documents concerned with training disclose the change in PLO tactics to prepare for war on a conventional level. Many certificates of Palestinians trained in Warsaw Pact states were for noncommissioned officers and officers in infantry, reconnaissance, armor, defense engineering, and staff courses. This training occurred at the platoon, company, and battalion levels.[160]

In addition to military and paramilitary training, there is also evidence of the USSR and its surrogates providing advisory support to PLO military forces. Cline and Alexander, for instance, cite several examples of Soviet-PLO cooperation in the intelligence area. They observe, however, that "the operational and intelligence-gathering activities for the PLO are carefully delegated by Moscow to East European countries. They supply intelligence information to the PLO and serve as a launching area for various terrorist operations."[161] Additionally, Warsaw Pact and Cuban personnel assigned to PLO training camps in Lebanon also provide military advisory support. For example, as early as mid-1976 a small group of Cuban officers were reported to be advising PLO military formations in southern Lebanon.[162]

The PLO's International Linkages

The PLO, as an emerging Soviet ally, became a supplier as well as a recipient of the kinds of assistance previously described. The PLO often acts as a middleman or subcontractor and can be found at the center of an international support system for terrorist and insurgent movements. Its support has taken the form of training, arms transfers, and operational assistance. Since the late 1970s it has been reported that thousands of guerrillas and terrorists from many parts of the globe received training in PLO bases throughout the Middle East. Cline and Alexander assert that during 1980–1981 approximately "2,250 foreign terrorists from 28 countries in Europe, Latin America, Asia, and Africa participated in courses of one to four month's duration."[163] Goren, however, traces these linkages back well before 1980–1981 to the latter half of the 1960s.[164]

In addition to paramilitary training, the PLO has served as a channel for arms to insurgents and terrorists, including the transfer of weapons to guerrillas in Central America and Africa. There are also instances as far back as 1970 of members of the PLO taking part in joint operations with their counterparts from other movements.

As the PLO established itself, Lebanon became the principal center for the training and provision of arms to like-minded organizations. The PLO's control of territory, in conjunction with resources, facilities, and expertise, permitted it to make the transition from recipient to supplier. During the 1970s international terrorists entered Lebanon either through Syria or directly by air through the Beirut airport. These terrorists were from factions in West Germany, Italy, Northern Ireland, Spain, Holland, France, Turkey, Greece, Cyprus, Japan, Argentina, Eritrea, the United States, Chile, Nicaragua, and southern Africa. Among the main training camps were Chatila, Burj al-Barajneh, and Damour.[165] In addition to PLO cadres, training and advisory support was provided by security personnel from different Warsaw Pact members, most notably East Germany.[166]

PLO cooperation and training of international terrorists and regional guerrilla movements range across the ideological spectrum. For example, Abu Iyad, one of Arafat's key lieutenants, asserted in a 1981 interview that the PLO was willing to establish connections with such groups as the West German neo-Nazis led by Karl-Heinz Hoffman.[167] In addition, excerpts from a pamphlet published on the seventh anniversary of the Lod Airport massacre outline the Japanese Red Army's (JRA) connection with the PLO. The relationship has resulted from mutual devotion to "simultaneous world revolution." The symbol of JRA-PLO cooperation, according to the pamphlet, is Comrade Okamoto, who was captured at Lod and released in 1985.[168] The following excerpts from a PLO office diary, captured in Tyre in June 1982, disclose the training of an array of terrorist and guerrilla groups.

- February 26—Final exams for the Salvadoran course

- April 6—The course for the comrades from Haiti began today

- May 16—The comrades from South Africa left today

- June 4—A group of five persons arrived from Turkey

- June 8—The course started for the comrades from Turkey

- June 11—A group arrived from Africa, ten people from Malawi

- June 23—The training started for the comrades from Malawi[169]

In addition to providing the kinds of assistance described here, PLO bases in Lebanon served as sanctuaries for personnel from these various factions and movements.

The relationship between the PLO and Central American insurgents reveals the geostrategic degree of its collaborative activities. As early as 1970 the Sandinista Front of National Liberation (FSLN) was involved operationally in terrorist actions with its Palestinian counterparts. Specifically, Sandinista cadres took part in the Black September Organization hijacking of five airplanes to Dawson's field in Jordan in 1970. One FSLN member, Patrick Arguello, was killed during the crisis, which was one of the factors that provoked King Hussein to oust the PLO from Jordan. During 1979, as the FSLN prepared for the final offensive against the Anastasio Somoza regime, the PLO sent assistance.[170] The link between the FSLN and PLO was confirmed by Arafat in 1981 when he stated that "the link between us is not new. Your comrades did not come to our country just to train, but also to fight. Your enemies are our enemies."[171] On other occasions Arafat has asserted that the PLO "has connections with all revolutionary movements throughout the world, in El Salvador, in Nicaragua."[172] In Nicaragua these connections have been translated into the PLO providing pilots for the Sandinistas, a fact confirmed in an interview with a former Sandinista counterintelligence officer[173] and in comments by Arafat in January 1982. Arafat also confirmed that the PLO was providing military assistance and advisory support to the Salvadoran guerrillas.[174]

The PLO likewise has been involved, on a smaller scale but in a similar manner, in Africa and particularly in Angola. Before the overthrow of Mohammad Reza Pahlavi, the Shah of Iran, the PLO also trained and supplied arms to several hundred Iranians. Consequently, upon seizing power the Ayatollah Khomeini converted the former Israeli embassy building into a PLO office. Furthermore, during the Iranian hostage crisis, it has been reported that PLO representatives provided advice and technical assistance.[175]

The PLO has also given assistance to various West European terrorist groups, most notably the Italian Red Brigade and the West German Baader Meinhoff group. In the case of the former, the PLO provided training and supplied arms, which was confirmed in testimony by members of the Red Brigade at the Aldo Moro trial.[176] In a related case, three Red Brigade defectors testified in statements to Judge Carlo Mastelloni, the investigating magistrate at the High Court of Venice, that at a meeting in Paris in the autumn of 1978 a formal agreement to cooperate was reached between representatives of the PLO and the Red Brigade. Arafat's deputy and the security chief of the PLO, Abu Iyad, allegedly was the PLO spokesman at the meeting. Material evidence of this cooperation was provided with the discovery of an arms cache near Venice in February 1982. As a result, the High Court of Venice issued arrest warrants for both Yasser Arafat and Abu Iyad.[177] Connections between West German terrorists and the PLO go back to the early 1970s.[178] In addition to providing arms and training personnel in Lebanon, the PLO joined the Baader Meinhoff gang in joint operations including the Munich Olympic Games and the Entebbe hijacking. There is evidence of PLO assistance and cooperation with other West European terrorist groups, but the Red Brigade and the Baader Meinhoff gang are the most prominent examples.

Conclusion

This chapter began with the assertion that over the last two decades the Soviet Union and the PLO have developed an increasingly close association. The evidence presented in this chapter provides substantial support for this hypothesis. The PLO has suffered setbacks and there are limitations to Moscow's commitment; nevertheless, the course of this relationship has been marked by a steady intensification of cooperation, especially following the 1973 war. As a result, Soviet political and paramilitary assistance increased significantly during this period, augmented by Moscow's East European and Cuban surrogates.

During the past fifteen years the PLO has emerged in the Middle East and on the international scene as one of the predominant practitioners of the art of protracted warfare. As a result, the PLO became both a recipient and a supplier of the kinds of assistance it received from the Warsaw Pact, bringing it into contact with terrorist and insurgent movements from many regions of the world. As its base expanded in Lebanon, so did the provision of arms and training to these groups.

The Israeli intervention in 1982 and the subsequent Syrian-PLO rift led to the destruction of the Lebanese base. It was also at this time that the PLO came face-to-face with the limits of Moscow's support. When presented with a choice between a state or a movement, the Kremlin is most likely to choose the former. Recent developments, however, disclose that this order of priorities did not cause the PLO and Yasser Arafat to distance themselves from the Soviet Union. It is highly likely that this connection will remain basically unaltered because it has been forged over two decades and is the long-term outgrowth of shared interests.

FIVE

Conflict in Southern Africa

SWAPO
AND THE
USSR

In the early 1970s, as Soviet involvement in Third World conflicts began to expand, the national liberation zone was extended into southern
Africa. In this chapter, I will examine Soviet policy as it relates to support for
the South-West Africa People's Organization (SWAPO) by asking the following
questions: Why and how did Soviet policy in southern Africa change during the
early 1970s and how did this change affect the Soviets' relations with SWAPO?
How were the political and paramilitary instruments of Soviet strategy, including
surrogate assets, employed in the case of SWAPO? What are the future prospects
for the Soviet-SWAPO relationship?

Soviet Policy
in Southern Africa

Soviet objectives in southern Africa in the 1980s reflect, in
general, Soviet goals in other regions of the Third World. Consonant with its
perception of its global role, Moscow seeks political influence in and access to
African states as well as the Organization of African Unity. Consequently, the
Soviets hope, first and foremost, is to weaken Western influence in Africa. Since
the mid-1960s, to improve its global power position, the Kremlin has sought
access, basing arrangements, and, where feasible, the establishment and main-

tenance of pro-Soviet and Marxist-Leninist governments. A corollary to extending Soviet influence is countering and isolating the People's Republic of China.

Although Soviet and African specialists might ascribe to these broad objectives of the Kremlin, they do not agree over which strategy Moscow has pursued in Africa over the last decade. One group of specialists believe that Moscow's policy has followed a clear-cut and expansive plan. Moscow's support for Marxist-Leninist governments and liberation movements; cooperation with such unlikely allies as Moammar Khadafy and, formerly, Idi Amin; and efforts to secure air and naval privileges in Africa support this assertion.[1] Others contend that, rather than following a preconceived plan, Soviet policy is selective, reacting to targets of opportunity.[2] The situation in Angola during the mid-1970s is a case in point.

Each side presents persuasive arguments, but the evidence in this study suggests that Soviet strategy in southern Africa since the mid-1970s cannot be described simply as a reaction to targets of opportunity. Before this time, caution and restraint were apparent in the Soviets' policy as they realized that the southern African situation was evolving and that they had neither the political access nor the military capabilities to project power into the region on a large scale. It was not until the 1970s that the situation became more receptive to an expanding Soviet role. Furthermore, only then did Moscow develop the power projection capabilities required to increase its activities.

A brief review of Soviet African policy since the early 1960s supports these assertions. The Kremlin began to recognize the importance of Africa in the early 1960s, but many leaders of these new states approached Soviet overtures cautiously. According to Colin Legum, this caution was the result of the following factors: African anti-imperialism was directed against all foreign governments; very few African nationalist movements at that time were revolutionary; many nationalists drew their inspiration from Western democracy and from Gandhi and Jawaharlal Nehru, not from Marxism; African nationalism was imbued with black consciousness and Pan-Africanism, limiting the impact of non-African concepts; nonalignment influenced nationalists' thinking; and nationalist leaders, even radicals like Kwame Nkrumah, Ahmed Sekou-Toure, and Julius K. Nyerere, denied the necessity for class struggle.[3] Also, Moscow hurt itself in the first half of the 1960s through heavy-handed and bungled operations (for example, the Congo, Guinea, Kenya).

By the early 1970s the Kremlin appeared to have learned from its experience in the 1960s and established diplomatic relations with a number of black African states, in part, by means of military and economic assistance. Especially as a result of arms transfers, Soviet access widened. Increasingly, Moscow exploited local rivalries, secessionist impulses, and national liberation movements by assuming a major role as supplier of arms and advisers. Arms transfers were important in helping establish closer relations with Guinea, Ghana, Nigeria, Mali, Benin, Upper Volta, and Uganda.

Changing attitudes among African elites, due to internal political developments, also contributed to growing Soviet access. According to Legum, in the "post-independence period, nationalist forces . . . ceased to be mass movements." Governments had come "under the control of particular power groups concerned with preserving their dominant positions." Consequently, anxious to buttress their own weak position, they "enlisted the support of major extracontinental powers."[4]

In sum, while African doubts and dissatisfaction with Moscow remained, Soviet readiness to assist both struggling governments and liberation movements increased Soviet opportunities in and access to southern Africa in the early 1970s. The events in Angola of 1974–1975, from Moscow's perspective, further accelerated these political opportunities.[5]

The Impact of Events in Angola

There are several reasons why southern Africa was not a high-priority region for the Soviet Union before 1974. To begin with, the area was dominated by Portugal, South Africa, and Rhodesia, and regional independent black states and insurgent movements were relatively ineffectual. Moscow did provide, on a relatively small scale, the following movements with weapons and training: Popular Movement for the Liberation of Angola (MPLA), Front for the Liberation of Mozambique (Frelimo), Zimbabwe African People's Union (ZAPU), African National Congress (ANC), and South-West Africa People's Organization (SWAPO).

In the case of the MPLA the Soviet ties, although limited, extend back at least to the early 1960s. For instance, during that time the MPLA chief, António Agostinho Neto, visited Moscow several times, and Soviet propaganda concentrated its commentary on this faction of the insurgent movement.[6] Nevertheless, this support was marginal, especially when compared with the influx of Cuban arms and advisers during the mid-1960s, including Ernesto ("Che") Guevara's tour of Africa to establish a new Third World revolutionary union under Cuban and Algerian sponsorship. Cuba initially focused on the Belgian Congo, where the pro-American General Joseph Mobutu was competing with Moise-Kapenda Tshombe. Also at this time Fidel Castro began to provide assistance to the MPLA in the form of arms and training of cadres in camps in the Congo. Unlike a decade later, however, Cuban involvement was not in support of Soviet policy but in competition with it. In fact, the Moscow-Havana rift resulted in a shutoff of Soviet oil supplies to Cuba. The Kremlin's position toward the MPLA at this time remained constrained.

During the late 1960s Soviet policy toward insurgent movements in southern Africa began to change within the context of an evolving Soviet policy in the Third World. By the end of 1968 this resulted in a more improved relationship with Neto and the MPLA. In the early 1970s Soviet support included both arms and military training, as well as international political efforts to enhance the cause and reputation of the MPLA including the use of international front political action. For instance, in January 1969 the World Peace Council (WPC) and the Afro-Asian People's Solidarity Organization cosponsored a conference aimed at fostering support for six African liberation movements: the MPLA, Party for Independence of Guinea-Bissau and Cape Verde, Frelimo, ANC, ZAPU, and SWAPO.[7] A WPC conference in Rome in June 1970 focused on mobilizing international opposition to the Portuguese among the governments, parties, and organizations of Western Europe.[8] The Twenty-fourth CPSU Congress in March 1971 reiterated Soviet support for insurgent movements in southern Africa.

Political changes in Portugal in 1974 presented both superpowers with the opportunity to influence the course of events in Angola, but only the USSR was able to react in a meaningful way. During the latter half of 1974, Soviet foreign propaganda escalated its positive commentary about the MPLA, and large amounts of Soviet military hardware began to be transferred to the MPLA via the port of Brazzaville. This all followed, according to Christopher Stevens, an August 1974 meeting in Lusaka between Neto and KGB officials that marked, in his estimation, the point at which the Kremlin decided to escalate its commitment to the MPLA.[9] By the end of 1974, enough arms were transferred to equip a force well in excess of 5,000. Additionally, larger numbers of MPLA cadres began to go to the USSR for military and political education. The Soviets likewise utilized their surrogate network in these efforts; thus, MPLA cadres were trained in other Warsaw Pact states as well as in Cuba. These proxies also sent advisers to assist the MPLA in Angola and were involved in the infrastructure for transporting and delivering weapons.

During 1975–1976 the intervention of the USSR and its surrogates increased dramatically. The introduction of 20,000 Cuban troops and Soviet aid on a vast scale settled the conflict in Angola in favor of the MPLA—at least for the remainder of the 1970s. The specifics of these actions are beyond the scope of this chapter, but note that the initial success of the MPLA signaled an important shift in Soviet policy in southern Africa.[10] The massive influx of Soviet arms and Cuban surrogates in mid-1975 and 1976 played a major role in the MPLA victory and demonstrated the Kremlin's readiness to project power to achieve policy objectives.

It is also important to recognize that, as Stephen Hosmer and Thomas Wolfe explain, the Angola situation had "some unique attributes" and "advantageous factors that facilitated the successful communist intervention."[11] This included the fact that in 1975 there was a political vacuum in Angola and no unity among the guerrilla factions. Consequently, an outside force—in this case the Soviet Union and its Cuban surrogate—that was willing to provide sufficient support to one faction could directly assist in the seizure and consolidation of power. The MPLA also benefited from the support of local Portuguese military personnel. External support for the National Front for the Liberation of Angola (FNLA) and the National Union for the Total Independence of Angola (UNITA) also existed; however, the United States did not sustain this effort. Furthermore, initial U.S. aid to the FNLA did not include weapons. In August 1975, the first increment of $32 million in covert military aid to the FNLA and UNITA began to arrive, but in December of that year, the U.S. Senate voted to prohibit further assistance. The increased prospect of external assistance for these guerrilla factions from Zaire and South Africa threatened to swing the balance against the MPLA; in July 1975, Zaire committed troops to help the FNLA, and later in the summer a small South African force entered Angola. Thus, by October 1975, a joint FNLA-UNITA effort threatened to turn the situation against the Cuban-MPLA forces. Against this backdrop the Soviets undertook to transport large amounts of military assistance to the MPLA by sea and air.

These events transformed the political context in southern Africa. Arthur Klinghoffer summarizes the situation and its implications for Soviet foreign policy in the following terms:

> In a regional context the Soviets saw Angola as a test case that would determine the future of black majority rule throughout southern Africa. They believed the Western states were trying to retard the liberation process and that they had secured the support of South Africa, Zaire, and Zambia in their effort to combat the MPLA . . . Soviet spokesmen maintained that an MPLA triumph in Angola would pave the way for the elimination of white minority rule in Rhodesia, Namibia, and South Africa. They later described the MPLA victory as a stimulus to southern African liberation movements and as a major contribution to the positive change in the region's military balance of forces.[12]

As a result, Moscow was able to strengthen ties with other insurgent movements in southern Africa. Angola provided the Soviets with a base for conducting operations throughout the region. In the period following 1976, Moscow took advantage of the opportunity and rapidly increased military assistance to ZAPU, SWAPO, and the ANC. According to Hosmer and Wolfe, Soviet and Cuban training and equipping of southern African liberation movements expanded, "particularly to the SWAPO forces operating in Namibia."[13]

SWAPO and the Soviet Union

The conflict in Namibia has two distinct elements: an international law debate about South Africa's continuing mandate over the area and a violent conflict between a white ruling government and a black majority in this sparsely populated but mineral-rich territory. The origins of these disputes and their present-day continuation have been documented and need not be reiterated here.[14]

Black nationalism began to develop in Namibia, as it did throughout Africa, during the 1950s. The South-West Africa People's Organization (SWAPO) originated during this time as a discussion group and political organization that actively opposed South African rule of Namibia. This changed, however, in the 1960s, when SWAPO turned to guerrilla tactics and began accepting assistance from China, the Soviet Union, Ghana, Algeria, and Tanzania.

South Africa's refusal to grant Namibia independence caused many SWAPO activists to depart for other parts of Africa and for Europe and the United States, from where they promoted Namibian independence. In 1974, as the political situation in Namibia underwent significant change, several thousand members of the Ovambo tribe relocated to Angola and Zambia, many in SWAPO bases. According to one specialist, during this time it became "clear . . . that violent action [was] considered by SWAPO to be the only means of toppling the white regime."[15] Not everyone in SWAPO (let alone other Namibian groups) agreed with its militant approach, but by the mid-1970s SWAPO had become the only Namibian political organization recognized and supported by the U.N. and the Organization of African Unity (OAU).[16] SWAPO's political and ideological perspective was ambiguous. During the 1970s, a rift developed in the organization resulting in 20 percent of the organization forming a splinter party called SWAPO-Democrats (SWAPO-D). According to Andreas Shipanga, president of SWAPO-D, following the split SWAPO became openly Marxist-Leninist in orientation.[17] This was reflected in the political program adopted at the July–August 1976 meeting of SWAPO's central committee in Lusaka.[18] Also at that time, Sam Nujoma, head of SWAPO, was able to convince the Zambian government to arrest the leaders and between one and two thousand members of SWAPO-D.[19]

In sum, by 1976 SWAPO had adopted a pronounced Marxist-Leninist position, a fact reflected in their publications as well as in the public statements of Nujoma and other leaders. This development was followed by an intensification of armed struggle through SWAPO's military arm, the People's Liberation Army of Namibia, and the more moderate elements within SWAPO were ousted from the organization. In conjunction with these developments and following the events in Angola, Moscow began to markedly increase its international political support and military assistance to SWAPO. According to Walter Hahn and Alvin Cottrell,

> The experience of the Angolan and Mozambican revolutionary struggles confirmed the Soviets' appreciation of the radicalizing effect of armed struggle on national liberation movements, and of the political benefits to Moscow in being able to demonstrate that Soviet support made the crucial difference in the particular movements' achievement of victory. Soviet preference for armed conquest of power in the remaining "unliberated" areas of southern Africa, emerges clearly . . . The Soviets urged intensification of the armed struggle on the Namibian national liberation movement, SWAPO.[20]

The remainder of this chapter will examine how the Soviets have employed their various political and military instruments, as well as those of their surrogates, to promote and assist SWAPO since 1976.

Soviet Political-Military
Support for SWAPO Since 1976

The emergence of Angola as a pro-Soviet state was an important contributing factor to the intensification of Moscow's involvement in southern Africa. Of equal consequence was SWAPO's adoption of a pronounced Marxist-Leninist stance and its escalation of armed struggle against the Republic of South Africa. The growing crisis within South Africa also likely influenced the Soviet calculus. Before these developments the Kremlin treated SWAPO as a minor actor; however, in 1976 the political and military elements of Soviet strategy were mobilized to bolster the insurgents.

Foreign Propaganda

Before 1976, the conflict in Namibia was of secondary consequence in Soviet propaganda, but as Moscow's policy shifted, so did the degree and complexity of its coverage. Before I examine the major themes, targets, and objectives of this campaign, we need an overview of the Soviet propaganda effort since 1976.

The picture the Soviets present is one of an irreconcilable struggle between the forces of imperialism and those of genuine national liberation. Conveyed in a number of thematic variations, this message is articulated consistently through multiple Soviet propaganda channels. South Africa is a major target, but so are its "Western patrons." The United States, to protect its geostrategic and economic interests, is said to use any and all means to keep the South African regime in power. South Africa is characterized as an illegal or pariah state that the international community should isolate and bring the harshest sanctions against. SWAPO, in contrast, is presented as a progressive vanguard and the sole legitimate representative of the Namibian people.

Namibia, important because of its mineral wealth, is not the only concern in the region for the West, which also seeks to weaken and/or overthrow other independent states in southern Africa, according to Soviet commentary. The West cannot tolerate independent regimes because they will deny it access to critical resources and markets. The most frequent excuse the United States and its allies use to impede African nationalism is the "Soviet threat."

These are the central messages Soviet propaganda has amplified since 1976, using a number of thematic variations related to the issues and events of the day. The major themes and subthemes are that the West supports without reservation the Republic of South Africa, genuine liberation (SWAPO) is far preferable to neocolonial solutions of the conflict in Namibia, the Republic of South Africa is an illegitimate regime, the West and Israel have provided South Africa with nuclear weapons, the Soviet Union is the natural ally of black African states and insurgent movements, and SWAPO recognizes the vital importance of Soviet support.

Soviet commentary asserts that Western support for South Africa is based on economic and geostrategic needs as well as on the "fear of communism." Strategic minerals and investment potential are recurring themes related to Western interests in Namibia. For instance, TASS declared in August 1978 that "the Western monopolies are continuing their ruthless exploitation of the natural resources of Namibia. Their actions in this territory, unlawfully occupied by the racialist Republic of South Africa, are outright pillage."[21] Soviet foreign propaganda frequently cites Nujoma and other SWAPO leaders to reinforce this point.[22]

Western strategic and military requirements also receive significant coverage:

> In the eyes of the imperialists—particularly of North American imperialists—South Africa's strategic significance is increasing at present in connection with the U.S. ruling circles' global plan of becoming a hegemonic force in the international arena. In their view, South Africa is an important link in the plans to set up a network of military bases in the Indian Ocean basin and to couple together "quick reaction forces" . . . The United States plans to use the continent's southern tip to control sea and air communications between the Atlantic and Indian oceans.[23]

In 1981 Moscow asserted that the Republic of South Africa had become an unofficial member of NATO.[24] To protect these geostrategic and economic interests, the West was said to be attempting to subvert independent African states and liberation movements through the use of the Central Intelligence Agency. Thus, a March 1, 1979, *Radio Peace and Progress* broadcast asserted

American imperialism is frightened by the changes taking place now on that continent. After the downfall of Portuguese colonial empire the borders of the independent nations shoved right up to Rhodesia and South Africa, the last bulwarks of international imperialism in Africa. The growth of the National Liberation Movement in the South African Republic, in Namibia and Zimbabwe as well as the strengthening of the African solidarity limit the imperialist circles of the United States in their possibilities of preserving the last racist and colonial hotbeds on the continent. That's why Washington is stepping up its secret war with the national liberation movement and progressive regimes of Africa.[25]

The real intentions of the United States and its allies, as described above, are masked by their fallacious charge that their involvement is necessary to check the Soviet threat to the region.[26] According to *Pravda* of September 24, 1981, the Contact Group (five Western members of the U.N. Security Council— the United States, the United Kingdom, France, West Germany, and Canada) "share Pretoria's opinion of the so-called communist threat to Africa for it is precisely this malicious fabrication that the racists use to justify their attempts to install their own puppet regime in Africa."[27] Moscow constantly belittles Western efforts to negotiate a settlement in which SWAPO would have to share power. This is a brazen attempt "to save" Pretoria "by inducing them [SWAPO] to make concessions."[28] The Soviets also note that, to achieve these objectives and keep the South African regime in power, the West has supported Pretoria economically, militarily (including mercenaries), and diplomatically to prevent implementation of U.N. resolutions.[29]

Soviet foreign propaganda seeks to denigrate and isolate South Africa and its real and alleged Western allies while attempting to enhance the legitimacy of SWAPO. "Liberation" under SWAPO will be "genuine" because it is the legal and sole representative of the Namibian people and is recognized as such by the U.N., the OAU, and the Nonaligned Movement.[30] Soviet propaganda consistently associates the Soviet Union with these developments.[31]

The SWAPO forces represent "genuine liberation" because of their commitment to complete independence from foreign interference. SWAPO has rejected Western solutions and intends to install a "socialist" regime in Namibia aligned with the socialist bloc, as described by the SWAPO leadership in *Pravda* in December 1978: "[I]n this struggle we rely on solidarity of the progressive forces of the socialist countries and fraternal African people."[32] Although SWAPO would like to come to power through a peaceful transition, it will not be coerced into an agreement. Thus, explains *Pravda*, "SWAPO does not object to a peaceful path . . . but decisively rejects the racist conditions to the settlement of the Namibia problem."[33]

For its own part, Moscow is extremely pessimistic about any solution short of armed revolutionary struggle because of the purported Western commitment to a neocolonial solution.[34] "It would appear to be no mere chance that the United States, the FRG, France, Britain, and Canada, whose close ties to the Republic of South Africa are well known, tried to create the illusion . . . that a 'settlement' of the Namibian problem was possible but along different lines suiting Pretoria."[35] In addition to the themes discussed above are associated charges that South Africa is an illegitimate regime, that the West and Israel have assisted Pretoria in developing nuclear weapons, that the Soviet Union is the natural ally of black African states and insurgent movements, and that SWAPO recognizes the vital nature of Soviet support.

The assertion that South Africa is an illegitimate and brutal regime permeates Soviet commentary and needs no further examination here.[36] Western assistance in developing nuclear weapons has also received extensive coverage since the late 1970s. Moscow employs this theme to demonstrate how far the West will go to keep Pretoria in power.[37] Thus, on August 13, 1980, *Radio Moscow* observed that "South Africa is already in a position to produce its own atomic bombs . . . and it seems the greatest role in encouraging the nuclear ambitions of the South African racists has been played by the United States."[38] The uses to which Pretoria will put these weapons are obvious to Moscow: "to threaten and blackmail independent, free Africa, and terrorize the oppressed nonwhite population of South Africa."[39]

Israel is also implicated in the acquisition of nuclear weapons by South Africa. According to Moscow, there began in 1979 "more active cooperation between Zionist Israel and the racist South African regime in the military field, especially in the development of nuclear weapons." Both Pretoria and Tel Aviv's nuclear capabilities are the result of U.S. and NATO assistance. Both can be expected to employ these weapons to "blackmail independent states in the Middle East and Africa."[40]

Moscow presents its own policy in southern Africa as selfless—seeking peace, national liberation, an end to the arms race in southern Africa—and identifies itself as the natural ally of black African states and movements like SWAPO.[41] The Soviets assert that peace and the elimination of tensions are the objectives, but they explain that these can be accomplished only through the elimination of unacceptable regimes.[42] The theme of recognition by SWAPO's leadership of the importance of Moscow's assistance is continually replayed in Soviet propaganda.[43]

An analysis of Soviet foreign propaganda provides insight into Moscow's foreign-policy objectives. An escalation in the coverage of SWAPO signaled that southern Africa had become a more significant policy issue for the Kremlin and triggered the beginning of a broader political warfare campaign, with other instruments brought into play. Soviet foreign propaganda set the thematic pattern that, as we shall see in the following sections, served as a guide for front-group political operations conducted in international organizations.

International Front Organizations

The major fronts advancing Soviet objectives in southern Africa are the World Peace Council (WPC) and the Afro-Asian People's Solidarity Organization (AAPSO). As the most important Soviet front, the WPC takes the lead in almost all major front campaigns. Through collaboration with SWAPO and other insurgent movements, it actively promotes their programs on a regional and international basis. To this end, the WPC has either sponsored or cosponsored a number of international and regional conferences as well as used their own organizational meetings (WPC Council, WPC Presidential Committee, WPC Bureau of the Presidential Committee) as forums for this purpose. The WPC also utilizes its various publications and information centers in Helsinki, Havana, Addis Ababa, and New York to promote the cause of SWAPO and other insurgent movements in southern Africa.[44] The WPC also cooperates with other fronts, U.N. bodies, the OAU, and the Nonaligned Movement on issues related to southern Africa.

Directed by the Soviet Afro-Asian Committee, AAPSO also focuses part of its activities on southern Africa and on insurgent movements active in the region. These activities involve either sponsoring or cosponsoring (frequently with the WPC) regional and international conferences. For example, in June 1977 AAPSO helped establish the Continuation Committee of the World Conference Against Apartheid, Racism and Colonialism, renamed the International Committee Against Apartheid, Racism and Colonialism in South Africa. The committee has held international conferences in London, Paris, and Stockholm. The AAPSO forces also use their own organizational meetings (AAPSO Council, AAPSO Executive Committee, AAPSO Permanent Secretariat) as forums for promoting the Kremlin's policy in southern Africa. In a manner similar to the WPC, AAPSO's various publications advance the same themes as those found in Soviet propaganda.[45]

The WPC and AAPSO are the key international fronts focused on southern Africa, but a number of others are also involved to a lesser degree. These include the World Federation of Trade Unions, the International Union of Students, and the World Federation of Democratic Youth.[46]

International front propaganda. In almost every respect, WPC and AAPSO propaganda reflect the Soviet thematic pattern described previously. The only significant differences are that the fronts focus more on South African domestic repression and that their commentary is generally harsher in tone and advocates more extreme measures. As with Moscow, WPC and AAPSO propaganda did not begin to concentrate on Namibia and SWAPO until 1976. Previously, coverage of these subjects was combined with that on other insurgent movements in Africa. Also, the degree of coverage was minor when contrasted with that occurring since 1976.[47]

An indicator of the secondary importance of SWAPO before 1976 is its conspicuous absence from AAPSO's Programme of Action for 1974 and 1975, even though Sam Nujoma, the head of SWAPO, was listed as a member of the AAPSO Presidium (and WPC Presidential Committee). Thus, although ties between the fronts and SWAPO existed, the issue was not a consequential one for Moscow nor for the fronts.

With the change in Soviet policy, the WPC and AAPSO expanded and focused their propaganda efforts. For example, beginning in 1976, the periodicals *New Perspectives* (WPC) and *Solidarity* (AAPSO) began to assert that the "struggle in southern Africa" had entered a "new phase," and that the "liberation of Namibia and Zimbabwe" were "now Africa's first priority."[48] Both called for immediate international action to accelerate the "liberation" of the region.[49] This call was reflected in the WPC's 1976 program:

- WPC-U.N.-OAU-SWAPO seminar to discuss ways to intensify actions in solidarity with Namibia
- World Conference Against Apartheid and publication of a series of pamphlets in cooperation with the U.N.
- U.N. Security Council to make the arms embargo against South Africa mandatory and without qualification
- Full support to the U.N. Special Committee Against Apartheid, Special Committee of 24, Council for Namibia and Commission for Namibia[50]

At the same time, front propaganda criticized South Africa for real and alleged domestic repression and asserted that the United States, Western Europe, and Israel were in complicity with Pretoria's actions.[51] Here the congruence of front and Soviet propaganda is virtually complete. The United States was charged with initiating a diplomatic offensive against the "liberation struggle" in southern Africa to protect its economic investments. The U.S. objective was to co-opt the "liberation movement" into believing a compromise settlement was possible, while providing Pretoria with all necessary military assistance to maintain control.[52] As early as spring 1976, *New Perspectives* stated that "South Africa is now virtually an incipient nuclear power" thanks to Western assistance.[53] Additionally, the "twin sister" of the apartheid regime, "Zionist Israel," is also said to have assisted in this matter.[54]

During 1977 the WPC and AAPSO expanded and developed themes established the previous year. They continued to call for the "final assault for South Africa's liberation" in various international forums, most important, the U.N.[55] Pretoria continued to receive harsh criticism for its "illegal occupation" of Namibia, as did the United States and Western Europe for their unrestrained bolstering of South Africa.[56] Each of these themes received expanded coverage in front publications. Thus, 1977 was marked by increased attention to SWAPO's program and strategy, apparently to enhance its reputation as the sole legitimate representative of the Namibian people.[57]

Since 1978 there has been no significant change in the pattern described above, as fronts have followed the Soviet position on all major issues concerning southern Africa. The tone of front propaganda, however, has become more harsh and strident, especially in its recommendations for dealing with southern Africa. For instance, in a *New Perspectives* article entitled "Apartheid Must Be Totally Destroyed," it is made clear that the international community can and should support any and all means to accomplish this:

> The international community must fully recognize that Apartheid cannot be reformed but must be totally destroyed. The international community must fully respect the right of oppressed people and their national liberation movement to choose their means of struggle, including armed struggle, and lend all assistance needed by them . . . It must denounce collaboration with Apartheid as an offense against the international community and take firm measures to stop collaboration.[58]

The theme of armed struggle as the only solution has been increasingly advanced by the WPC and AAPSO in conjunction with calls for the international community to impose harsh and mandatory sanctions against South Africa.[59] For example, WPC head, Romesh Chandra, in an address to the U.N. Special Committee Against Apartheid in November 1981, declared that it is necessary for the international community to back all "concrete steps to ensure sanctions, to ensure in all fields a complete boycott of the South African apartheid regime." To this end, Chandra announced publication of a new WPC bulletin entitled *International Mobilization for the Liberation of Southern Africa and Against Apartheid*. Initiated in cooperation with the U.N. Centre Against Apartheid, the bulletin was designed to help "carry on the struggle" and mobilize support for the "liberation movements," the top leaders of which, Chandra noted, were "members of the Presidential Committee on the World Peace Council."[60]

Since the late 1970s, the charges of Western complicity with Pretoria have become equally strident. According to the WPC, "the United States is the heartland of imperialism, a racist nation . . . There is no doubt that without the full support of the United States . . . the oppressive, racist, apartheid establishment could not survive for a single year."[61] On the diplomatic front, the United States has been consistently charged with "obstructing the implementation of international agreements for the independence of Namibia," and this obstruction has been characterized as only part of a larger "conspiracy by imperialist countries for protecting the South African regime."[62] With regard to military assistance, the NATO powers continue to be charged with having "helped South Africa to become a nuclear power," as well as providing other forms of military assistance.[63] This charge of Western militarization of South Africa and the danger it causes for the entire region is authoritatively presented in an article by Anatoli Gromyko, director of the Institute of Africa, USSR Academy of Sciences. Western multinational corporations remain targets for increasingly virulent attacks.[64] The "real objective" of this Western conspiracy—"to keep the apartheid regime in their exclusive club, to preserve it . . . to enable it to become even more of a menace to Africa"—is repeated without pause.[65]

One final aspect of front propaganda focused on southern Africa is the continual effort by fronts to associate their own efforts with those of the U.N. and the Nonaligned Movement to increase the credibility of their own position, as well as the status of SWAPO. Thus, it is not just the WPC and SWAPO but the U.N. and the Nonaligned Movement that support the program and the call to action put forth by the fronts.

International conference diplomacy. Since the late 1970s the number of international conferences and meetings the WPC and AAPSO sponsored or took part in that either directly or indirectly focused on Namibia and South Africa is not easily determined. Nevertheless, the evidence suggests that both fronts increased their conference activities on the South Africa–Namibia question.

The actual changes in front activity began to appear during the latter half of 1976. The following are some of the conferences, directly involving the WPC and AAPSO, that focused, either directly or indirectly, on the South Africa–Namibia question.[66] (These issues are often combined with related subjects, the most prevalent being the liberation of all of southern Africa.)

- *Emergency Solidarity Conference with the People of South Africa— Addis Ababa (October 30–31, 1976)*

  This meeting was cosponsored by AAPSO and the African National Congress (ANC).

  The conference adopted a 27-point Programme of Action that included calls for the intensification of the boycott of South African goods, the mobilization of international support for a world conference against apartheid in Europe, the exposure of the economic cooperation of the imperialist states with South Africa, closer contacts with the U.N. Special Committee Against Apartheid and with the OAU, and concrete measures to strengthen the political, moral, and material support to the ANC and SWAPO.

Members of 90 national and international organizations took part in the conference, including the assistant secretary general of the OAU; the U.N. secretary general, Kurt Waldheim, sent a message supporting the meeting.

- *U.N. Conference Against Apartheid—Lagos (August 22–26, 1977)*

  Attended by more than 1,000 participants from 102 countries, the conference adopted two documents: a Declaration and an Action Programme. The conference called for universally applied economic and other measures to secure the elimination of apartheid and proclaimed 1978 as the International Antiapartheid Year.

  The WPC took part in the conference and called for all governments and intergovernmental organizations to aid the armed struggle of the liberation movements in southern Africa.

- *World Conference Against Apartheid, Racism, and Colonialism in Southern Africa—Lisbon (June 16–19, 1977)*

  Sponsored by AAPSO, the conference was attended by 200 U.N., national, and international organizations.

  The conference Program of Action called for all governments, international organizations, and nongoverning organizations to strongly condemn the policy of apartheid, to boycott racist regimes, to assist liberation movements (including ANC, the Patriotic Front, and SWAPO), and to disseminate information.

- *International Conference for the Liberation of South Africa—New Delhi (September 28–October 2, 1978)*

  Cosponsored by the WPC, AAPSO, and the All-India Peace and Solidarity Committee in cooperation with the U.N. Special Committee Against Apartheid, the conference was held in conjunction with the U.N. Antiapartheid Year.

  Delegates from 70 countries and 15 international organizations and leaders from the ANC, the Patriotic Front, and SWAPO attended.

  The conference concentrated on four issues: imperialist conspiracies in southern Africa, South Africa and the arms race, southern Africa and the struggle for economic liberation, and violation of human rights in southern Africa.

- *Nongoverning Organizations Conference for Action Against Apartheid—Geneva (August 28–31, 1978)*

  This conference was a follow-up to the U.N. World Conference to Combat Racism and Racial Discrimination (held a week earlier).

  WPC president Romesh Chandra addressed both meetings and urged the U.N. and all governments to carry out a list of nine specific actions against South Africa.

  Chandra also reported on the WPC World Conference for the Eradication of Racism held in Basel, Switzerland, the previous May 1978 and its contribution to the U.N. world conference.

- *International Conference of Solidarity with the Struggle of the African and Arab Peoples Against Imperialism and Reaction—Addis Ababa (September 14–17, 1978)*

  Cosponsored by AAPSO and the WPC, the conference was attended by 130 political parties, national and international organizations, and liberation movements.

  The political commission of the conference produced 22 resolutions and messages of support on various Arab and African issues, including assistance to liberation movements in southern Africa (SWAPO, the ANC, and the Patriotic Front).

- *Continuation Committee of the World Conference Against Apartheid, Racism, and Colonialism—Paris (December 13–14, 1978)*

  The continuation committee was established in 1977 by the WPC and AAPSO.

  The conference included special reports by southern African liberation movements (the ANC, SWAPO, and the Patriotic Front).

During the late 1970s AAPSO also sponsored the following conferences that either directly or indirectly focused on the Namibia–South Africa issue: Colombo International Conference (Colombo, June 27–28, 1978), International Conference in Support of the Struggles of the Peoples of Southern Africa and in Solidarity with the Frontline States (Lusaka, April 1979), and the International Conference for Independence, Solidarity and Security (Colombo, May 1980). Similar WPC-sponsored conferences, as well as front cooperative involvement in U.N. conferences (covered in the next section), concerned with southern Africa also took place. Furthermore, these activities continued into the 1980s, as the WPC, AAPSO, and other fronts combined propaganda and political action in support of SWAPO.

Perhaps one of the most important developments since the late 1970s has been the extent to which the fronts have attempted to legitimize their conference activities through interaction with the U.N., the OAU, and the Nonaligned Movement. Particularly through U.N. recognition, the fronts have been able to portray themselves as an independent part of the mainstream of world public opinion.

Political Activities Within the U.N.

During the 1970s, various national liberation movements, including SWAPO, were granted permanent observer status both in the U.N. General Assembly and in specialized committees. These insurgent movements also received other forms of political support and financial assistance. In large part these developments were the result of the joint efforts of the more radical Afro-Asian states and Soviet-bloc and surrogate countries.

One key U.N. body in which these states have been active is the Special Committee on the Situation with Regard to the Implementation of the Declaration on the Granting of Independence to Colonial Countries and Peoples (hereafter, the Committee of 24). Since its inception in 1961, the Committee of 24 has consistently espoused anticolonial and anti-Western positions, even though this has resulted in the promotion of principles that conflict both with conventional international practice and with the founding tenets of the U.N. itself. These include recognizing specific "liberation" movements as the sole representatives of the people they claim to defend, granting these movements matériel as well as moral support, and bestowing them with official observer status in the General Assembly and with compensation from U.N. funds to maintain a mission at the U.N. headquarters and cover expenses during regular sessions.

The Soviet Union has played an active role in the activities of the Committee of 24 since it was established in 1961.[67] During its first decade, the Soviet Union sought to intensify and widen the scope of the committee's activities. The extent of this effort is reflected in General Assembly Resolution 2521, which presents as "principles of law" the objectives of the Committee of 24. The wording of 2521 appears intended to require binding legal compliance.[68]

By the early 1970s, committee activities began to reflect its radical stance, which resulted in the withdrawal of the United States and Great Britain. The composition of the committee and its activities explain this development. Over the years resolutions and recommendations have been worked out by a coalition of communist and anti-Western Afro-Asian states. This coalition has come to dominate the committee's twelve-member Afro-Asian caucus. The combination of the caucus with the committee's communist members leaves little room for compromise in deliberations and decisions.

Seymour Finger, the last U.S. representative to the Committee of 24, described its activities during the late 1960s and early 1970s in the following terms: "[W]ith the twelve Afro-Asian and four communist members . . . there is little . . . negotiation with the committee. Decisions are presented on a take-it-or-leave-it basis . . . This has led to lopsided votes and the lack of serious consultation." Finger goes on to explain that the lack of meaningful consultation and negotiation on the Committee of 24's program of action in 1970 resulted in the U.S. decision to withdraw.[69]

In sum, during the 1960s, the Soviet bloc and its surrogates formed an alliance with radical Afro-Asian countries to move the Committee of 24 in a more militant direction. According to one specialist, during this period "in conjunction with the Africans and Asians, the Eastern European members [used] the Committee of 24 to expose and condemn western colonialism . . . Their calls for vigorous measures often [exceeded] the exuberance of the Third World delegates."[70] By the 1970s, however, these unworkable activities and resolutions began to be implemented.

Following the lead of the Committee of 24, the General Assembly began in the early 1970s to recognize various national liberation movements as the sole authentic representatives of the people they claimed to fight for. These movements included the MPLA, Frelimo, SWAPO, and the PLO. Beyond official recognition, the Committee of 24 and the General Assembly began directly and indirectly to fund some of these guerrilla movements and to treat them in a manner normally reserved for states. Additionally, Article 58 of the U.N. Charter opened another avenue for the Committee of 24 by stating that the "Organization shall make recommendations for the coordination of the policies and activities of the specialized agencies." The Committee of 24 interprets this article to mean that once the General Assembly adopts its recommendations, the committee has the authority to request that other U.N. agencies assist in the implementation of its objectives. Such assistance includes financial aid, as well as propaganda and conference diplomacy, in support of these national liberation movements.

The Committee of 24 activities on behalf of SWAPO in the latter half of the 1970s can be grouped into the two general categories: publicity and procurement of financial assistance. The coalition of Afro-Asian and Soviet bloc and surrogate states discussed above continued to direct the committee's activities during the period. By 1980 the coalition included the USSR, Czechoslovakia, Bulgaria, Cuba, Afghanistan, and Ethiopia. Generally aligned with them were the Congo, Iraq, Syria, Mali, Tanzania, and Sierra Leone. Additionally, a communist-bloc member often holds one of the committee's leadership positions.[71]

Over the last decade the Committee of 24 has promoted and assisted SWAPO through the following activities: cooperation with the OAU, coordination with other U.N. committees concerned with Namibia and South Africa (for example, the council on Namibia and the Special Committee against Apartheid), direct cooperation with SWAPO, dissemination of information and conference diplomacy, and material assistance through various U.N. committees. A brief examination of each of these will demonstrate how the communist–Afro-Asian coalition influences the output of the committee.[72] The objective of these activities is to help fashion a broad base of international support for SWAPO.

Cooperation between the Committee of 24 and the OAU is an important aspect of this process. The OAU involvement with U.N. committees concerned with decolonization is documented each year in a report entitled *Cooperation Between the United Nations and the Organization of African Unity*. An examination of these documents reveals continuing coordination between the OAU and the Committee of 24 on the Namibia question.[73] An example of this coordination can be seen in the following excerpts from the 1977 report by a Committee of 24 representative who participated in the activities of the OAU's Coordinating Committee for the Liberation of Africa (Luanda, June 1977).

> The significance of holding the . . . session in Luanda is self-evident . . . The significant contribution of the People's Republic of Angola in support of the struggle of the Namibian people under the leadership of their national liberation movement, SWAPO, is a matter of common knowledge. It was therefore to be expected that the session . . . would devote considerable time to discussing practical ways of intensifying the struggle in that territory. In this respect, the participation of very high level SWAPO delegation . . . served to enrich immensely the committee's deliberations. Availing myself of the presence in Luanda of various leaders and officials of the liberation movements, I took the opportunity to hold an exchange of views with them on matters of common and vital interest concerning the question of decolonization. I was able to hold extensive discussions with the President of SWAPO, Comrade Sam Nujoma.[74]

Inside the U.N., committee cooperation with SWAPO is extensive and takes a number of forms. This is evident in U.N. General Assembly resolutions extending recognition and support to SWAPO, beginning in the mid-1970s with U.N. Resolution 3111, which recognized SWAPO as the sole representative of the Namibian people. Resolution 3295 reiterated recognition of SWAPO and directed agencies and committees within the U.N. to render all possible assistance to the people of Namibia. The Committee of 24 frequently employs this resolution to exact assistance for SWAPO from other U.N. agencies and committees. In 1977, the General Assembly stipulated that any independence talks under U.N. auspices can only take place between SWAPO and South Africa.[75] This stand was reiterated by the General Assembly in 1978 and 1979.

In addition to its activities on behalf of SWAPO in the General Assembly, the Committee of 24 cooperates with the council on Namibia and the Special

Committee against Apartheid. The former was established to serve as the legal administering authority for Namibia until independence and to assist SWAPO through two special programs it coordinates—the Nationhood Programme for Namibia and the U.N. Institute for Namibia. An examination of the activities of the institute denotes the interaction and cooperation between the council for Namibia and the Committee of 24.

The U.N. Institute for Namibia was established in Lusaka in 1976 to assist in providing trained midlevel administrators to staff the civil service of a future independent Namibia. The following summary of meetings between the Committee of 24, SWAPO, and the institute demonstrates the degree of cooperative interaction between them.

> The SWAPO role in the work of the institute was spelled out by Mr. Garoeb, the SWAPO representative at the session: "the political impetus for the liberation of Namibia and for its future administration will, of course, be provided independently by SWAPO. The head of the Council on Namibia agreed and observed that the U.N. has "supported the armed struggle of the Namibian people led by SWAPO to achieve self-determination . . . [This] reflects the Organization's solid political endorsement for a united Namibia under SWAPO." The chairman of the Committee of 24 then commented on the committee's close cooperation with the Council on Namibia. This was followed by a recounting by another SWAPO representative, Mr. Muyongo, of the role of the Committee of 24 and Council on Namibia in providing political and material support for SWAPO.[76]

The dissemination of information and international publicity is one of the formal responsibilities of the Committee of 24, as stipulated to the committee by the General Assembly in 1979 (Resolution 34/39). According to paragraph 12(e) of the resolution, the assembly requested the committee "to take all necessary steps to enlist worldwide support . . . in the implementation of the relevant resolutions of the United Nations, particularly as concerns the oppressed peoples of Namibia."[77] To this end, the Committee of 24 is involved in both international conference diplomacy and dissemination of materials through the U.N. Department of Public Information.

Committee of 24 international conference diplomacy often is coordinated with other U.N. committees and nongoverning organizations (NGOs) that promote SWAPO and other liberation movements in Africa. In a 1974 report of the committee, special emphasis was placed on the contribution of the NGOs. Among those singled out were the WPC, AAPSO, and the World Council of Churches.[78] A brief examination of these activities will disclose the degree of interaction between the Committee of 24, other U.N. bodies, and NGOs.

During May 1977, for example, the committee took part in the WPC-sponsored World Assembly of Peace Builders. Held in Warsaw, the assembly focused, in part, on the struggle against colonialism and apartheid and passed resolutions of solidarity with SWAPO and the ANC and against South Africa. The Committee of 24 representative at the assembly, Mr. Meytchev of Bulgaria, addressed the participants on the work of the U.N. against colonialism and in support of national liberation movements.[79] Earlier in 1977, the Committee of 24; U.N. Special Committee Against Apartheid; U.N. Council for Namibia; U.N. Educational, Scientific, and Cultural Organization; U.N. Children's Fund; and U.N. Industrial Development Organization sent representatives to participate in a seminar organized by the Revolutionary Union of Guinean Women and the Women's International Democratic Federation. The meeting was held to review the role of women in the struggle for liberation in Africa and to promote solidarity and support for these movements.[80] Additionally, the Committee of 24 participated in two major U.N.-sponsored conferences in Maputo and Lagos, both of which focused on southern Africa. The World Conference for Action Against Apartheid, held in Lagos during August 1977, was organized by the U.N. in cooperation with the OAU and the Federal Government of Nigeria. The conference included representatives from 112 governments, twelve intergovernmental organizations, five liberation movements, and 51 NGOs. It passed a 32-point action program condemning South Africa and its Western allies, demanding punishment of the crime of apartheid, recognizing the inalienable right of national liberation movements to employ all means available, and proclaiming that the U.N. and the international community had a special responsibility to support and assist southern African liberation movements.[81]

An examination of other years during the period under investigation shows a similar pattern. For instance, during 1980 the following international conference agenda was described in the committee's annual report.[82]

- *NGO Subcommittee on Racism, Racial Discrimination, Apartheid, and Decolonization.* The committee accepted an invitation by the NGO subcommittee to participate in an International Conference on Women and Apartheid to be held in Helsinki. It also accepted an invitation by the NGO subcommittee to attend an International NGO Action Conference for Sanctions Against South Africa in Geneva.

- *Afro-Asian People's Solidarity Organization/World Peace Council.* The committee accepted an invitation from AAPSO and WPC to participate in the World Parliament of Peoples for Peace in Sofia.

- *Council of European National Youth Committees and the Pan-African Youth Movement.* The committee accepted an invitation to be represented at the Second Solidarity Conference on the Struggle of the Peoples of Southern Africa in Bonn.

- *International Committee Against Apartheid, Racism, and Colonialism.* The committee accepted invitations to attend a special session of the international committee against apartheid in Stockholm and its International Conference in Solidarity with the Struggle of the People of Namibia in Paris.

The Committee of 24 has promoted SWAPO and other "liberation movements" through the dissemination of written and oral propaganda on a worldwide scale. As a result of General Assembly Resolutions 43/41, 43/92, and 43/95, the Department of Public Information (DPI) of the secretariat has the responsibility of assisting the Committee of 24 to carry out these activities. A review of the committee's 1980 report details its role in promoting the cause of SWAPO through the DPI's international communications program, whose activities can be divided into press and publications, external relations, and radio and visual services.

The press and publications section of the DPI covers the activities of the Committee of 24, as well as those of other U.N. bodies concerned with southern Africa (for example, the U.N. Council on Namibia and the U.N. Special Committee Against Apartheid). Detailed reports from international conferences, resolutions, and other relevant materials are disseminated at the U.N. to the media and also are circulated through the worldwide U.N. network of 62 information centers that serves 132 countries.[83]

The activities of the Committee of 24 also receive regular coverage in two U.N. periodicals: *Objective Justice* and the *United Nations Monthly Chronicle.* The Namibian issue and SWAPO are the exclusive subjects of the U.N.'s *Namibia Bulletin.* Items in this publication include SWAPO war communiqués. For example, the third issue of 1980 provides a detailed description of all "significant military operations" carried out by SWAPO during the period August 1– September 22, 1980, including accounts of ambushes and sabotage.[84] The DPI also reprints and circulates SWAPO's own publications. For instance, a special folder of material produced by the DPI entitled *For Self-Determination and Genuine National Independence for Namibia* contains a copy of SWAPO's political program and constitution, a poster of SWAPO head Sam Nujoma, and various publications of those U.N. committees concerned with Namibia.[85] These are but a few examples of the many publications circulated by the DPI on a worldwide basis.[86]

With respect to external relations, the materials described above are circulated by the DPI's Information Support Section through the 62 U.N. information centers. According to the DPI's report of 1980, this section "continues to instruct the information centers to intensify publicity efforts . . . particularly on special observances such as the Week of Solidarity with the Colonial Peoples of Southern Africa Fighting for Freedom, Independence, and Equal Rights." These activities include screening of films on the struggle for independence in southern Africa, distribution to national radio and television networks of radio and audio-visual materials, exhibitions of photographs and literature, briefings for NGOs, and assisting member governments in these respective areas.[87]

Finally, the DPI's radio and visual services make available films on the Namibia–South Africa issue, including *Generations of Resistance* (focusing on the development of black nationalism in southern Africa), *Free Namibia* (describing the growth of SWAPO and its unswerving determination to fight for freedom), and *Namibia: A Trust Betrayed* (tracing the history of colonialism in the region).[88] The photograph and exhibits division prepared a special exhibit for the International Year of Solidarity with the People of Namibia "to be used as a semipermanent exhibit at U.N. headquarters in New York and in Geneva and Vienna." All 62 U.N. information centers also received the exhibit.[89] The radio services also assist in the work of the Committee of 24. According to its 1980 report, the committee's work "will be covered intensively" in the regular news-casts and news programs of the radio service in sixteen languages.[90] Programs were prepared and broadcast to southern Africa and included commentary by members of SWAPO and other liberation movements. The report goes on to note:

- On the occasion of special observances, such as . . . the Day of Solidarity with the People of Namibia and their Liberation Movement (SWAPO) . . . broadcasting organizations in all parts of the world will be provided with relevant radio material.

- Throughout 1980, the Service will continue to produce daily radio programs in six languages spoken in southern Africa, devoted exclusively to U.N. efforts against apartheid and in support of . . . the peoples of southern Africa . . . Radio Service will produce a special series of radio programs on Namibia.[91]

This division also produces television spots on Namibia and South Africa, which are made available to the media, and provides special radio coverage of the two General Assembly sessions on Namibia (at a cost of $600,000).

Another way in which the Committee of 24 assists SWAPO is materially. As noted previously, the committee has the authority to request that other U.N. agencies assist in the implementation of its objectives. A brief and selective overview of this assistance, directly or indirectly channeled to SWAPO during 1980, follows.

- *International Labor Organization (ILO).* The ILO provides assistance to SWAPO and other liberation movements in the field of technical and vocational training. SWAPO nominates candidates for this training. Funding for these programs is not always listed. However, one of the larger projects—a pilot vocational training center for Namibian refugees in Angola—received $3,150,000.[92]

- *Food and Agriculture Organization (FAO)*. The FAO provides assistance to refugees from colonial territories, including Namibia, and plays a major role in the U.N. nationhood program for Namibia. According to its 1980 report, these activities are carried out in direct cooperation with SWAPO. In cooperation with the World Food Program, FAO provided an emergency food assistance project for 30,000 refugees in SWAPO-controlled camps in Angola at a cost of $951,000. The total cost for food assistance since 1977 is $4,947,000.[93]

- *World Health Organization (WHO)*. According to the report, in 1979 WHO continued to strengthen its collaboration with SWAPO. This consisted of assistance in the fields of technical manpower and provision of drugs and medical equipment as well as personnel training. The cost of this is difficult to determine. However, in 1980 $830,000 was earmarked for a WHO collaborative program with OAU-recognized liberation movements.[94]

- *U.N. Industrial Development Organization (UNIDO)*. The UNIDO group developed a training project for Namibia in industrial management and administration. The cost of the project was $44,500, and SWAPO was requested to select the candidates.[95]

- *U.N. International Children's Emergency Fund (UNICEF)*. Since 1974, UNICEF has provided assistance to refugee women and children under the auspices of various liberation movements, including SWAPO. This amounted to $3.4 million for 1974–1978 and $1.37 million in 1979.[96]

- *U.N. Educational, Scientific, and Cultural Organization (UNESCO)*. This group is involved in aiding refugees and national liberation movements through various projects and programs (regular programs cost $456,000 in 1979–1980); UNESCO also administers programs funded by the U.N. Development Program.[97]

- *U.N. Development Program (UNDP)*. The UNDP is involved in assisting OAU-recognized liberation movements. For the 1977–1981 period, SWAPO received $7.75 million in assistance.[98]

- *Office of the U.N. High Commission for Refugees (UNHCR)*. The UNCHR committed, during 1979–1981, $10 million to Namibia refugee camps under the direction of SWAPO.[99]

- *U.N. Council for Namibia.* Through the council for Namibia, SWAPO receives funds for its international activities. According to its 1979 budget, the council provided SWAPO with $182,500 in direct aid.[100]

It is difficult to estimate the total amount of humanitarian aid channeled through U.N. organizations to SWAPO. One analyst estimates that, for the 1977–1981 period, U.N. agencies allocated $40 million in aid.[101] The review of appropriate U.N. documents presented above suggests that this estimate is not exaggerated. The documents, however, are frequently vague and may not give an accurate picture; the amount could be higher. We can hardly quarrel with the concept of humanitarian aid in and of itself, but when allocated for distribution through a guerrilla movement, such aid becomes a political tool that can be used to mobilize and recruit individuals to the insurgents' cause. This assistance is possibly as important as the military equipment SWAPO receives from the Soviet bloc.

Arms Transfers

As Soviet involvement in southern Africa grew during the mid-1970s, military assistance to insurgent factions fighting for power likewise expanded. Following the seizure of power in Angola, the flow of arms increased to pro-Moscow elements to ensure that they could consolidate power and remain dependent on the USSR as the guarantor of their security. Arms transfers is one measure employed by the Kremlin to solidify the dependency relationship and thus retain influence in newly established pro-Moscow states. These allies, in turn, provide base areas from which other insurgent movements in the region can receive Soviet-bloc assistance. This pattern unfolded in Angola during the latter half of the 1970s.

Increased Soviet transfers of weapons, military supplies, and equipment to southern Africa have been documented in statistical records compiled by the U.S. Arms Control and Disarmament Agency (ACDA), Central Intelligence Agency (CIA), Stockholm International Peace Research Institute, and International Institute for Strategic Studies. One CIA report notes that for the 1975–1979 period Soviet–East European arms agreements with sub-Sahara Africa totaled $4.3 billion. This was a dramatic increase over the $760 million allotted during 1959–1974.[102] The trend continued after 1979 and, as figures from ACDA demonstrate, during the 1978–1982 period Angola was the major recipient. Of the $1.15 billion in arms received by Angola, $1.02 billion was supplied by the Soviets or East European–bloc states. Other recipients during 1978–1982 included Mozambique ($250 million), Zambia ($220 million), and Botswana ($140 million).[103]

The amount of military assistance transferred to insurgent movements in sub-Sahara Africa is missing from the data compiled by ACDA, CIA, and others because of Soviet attempts to conceal this activity. Nevertheless, a number of sources provide some evidence of Soviet arms transfers to insurgent movements since the mid-1970s. The Bulgarians, according to Trong Gilberg, have openly acknowledged that they furnish various kinds of military assistance to "liberation movements" in southern Africa, including SWAPO. Similar arrangements exist with East Germany and Czechoslovakia.[104] Roger Kanet explains that, in addition to provision by East European states, the Kremlin has given military support to SWAPO. In fact, he asserts that SWAPO forces receive "most of their military supplies from the Soviets and their allies."[105] This fact has been corroborated by former members of SWAPO and other political factions in southern Africa. In his testimony before the Senate Committee on the Judiciary, Jariretundu Kozonguizi, former head of the South-West African National Union and executive member of AAPSO, presented evidence of large amounts of Soviet equipment and weaponry placed at the disposal of SWAPO.[106] Andreas Shipanga, one of the original founders of SWAPO in 1958, presented similar testimony to the committee concerning Soviet, East German, and Cuban involvement with SWAPO.[107]

In sum, the quantity of weapons transferred to SWAPO by the USSR and its surrogates is difficult to estimate, but it is clear that arms are channeled from the Soviet Union, Eastern Europe, and Cuba to Angola and then to SWAPO base camps. According to Chester Crocker, assistant secretary of state for African affairs, SWAPO receives 90 percent of its military support through these routes.[108]

Although the exact quantity of arms transferred is difficult to estimate, more is known about the kinds of military equipment provided. By the early 1980s a number of advanced Soviet heavy weapons were identified such as T-55 tanks, armored cars and troop carriers, medium-range artillery, and MiG-17s, MiG-19s, and MiG-21s.[109] According to one source, during the 1977–1980 period the Soviets delivered the following heavy weapons to sub-Sahara African states: 1,060 tanks and self-propelled guns, 2,150 artillery, 1,520 armored personnel carriers and armored cars, 210 supersonic combat aircraft, 90 subsonic aircraft, 100 helicopters, and 1,360 surface-to-air missiles.[110]

In terms of surface-to-air missiles, the Soviets have provided the SA-3s and SA-6s, along with early-warning radar systems.[111] These have been deployed, in part, to defend Angolan-Cuban military bases and SWAPO sanctuaries in southern Angola. Their primary purpose, however, would appear to be the consolidation of power by the Popular Movement for the Liberation of Angola (MPLA). Installation of these systems signals a significant commitment by Moscow to Angola and, to a lesser extent, SWAPO.

Soviet and Eastern-bloc light weapons are likewise transferred to southern Africa through the same channels. Probably the most common of these weapons is the Kalashnikov AK-47 assault rifle, which is an extremely reliable weapon and especially adaptable to SWAPO's unconventional warfare strategy. Other Soviet-bloc weapons that appear frequently include a wide range of light and small arms.[112]

There is no evidence that SWAPO is acquiring a conventional capability for the purposes of confronting the South African security forces. Therefore, the heavy arms appear to be employed principally by Angola to consolidate power and defend SWAPO base areas. Thus, although SWAPO does employ heavy weapons, lighter weapons are of primary importance to its current unconventional warfare strategy. Available evidence suggests that SWAPO receives more than enough arms to conduct these operations.

Training SWAPO Forces

Soviet training of SWAPO personnel is not confined to military matters but includes preparation in both political warfare techniques and procedures for establishing an insurgent organizational infrastructure. The political-military training of SWAPO is carried out in the USSR, Soviet surrogate states, and base camps in locations contiguous to Namibia.

As described earlier, the Kremlin maintains a number of facilities within the USSR for training terrorists and insurgents. According to Igor Glagolev, a former senior member of the Institute of World Economy and International Relations of the USSR Academy of Sciences, one of these facilities, "the Lumumba University, plays an active role in the Soviet infiltration of African countries. The majority of its students are Africans who study at the expense of the Soviet government."[113] After finishing the course of instruction at Lumumba, those who are to receive training in unconventional warfare are taken to specialized training centers. Evidence of specialized military instruction for members of SWAPO's People's Liberation Army of Namibia (PLAN) can be found in recent congressional hearings on Soviet involvement in southern Africa. Published in the hearings were PLAN documents that identify one group of 150 members who received training in various military skills including reconnaissance and sabotage.[114] A smaller number of PLAN officers identified in the documents were "to be trained in 'Political Commissarship' in the Soviet Union."[115]

Since the latter half of the 1970s, the influx of students into Soviet and East European academic institutions grew "to record heights." During 1979 there were "more than 50,000 [students] studying in communist countries. About 40 percent were from sub-Sahara Africa."[116] These figures identify students only from less-developed countries, but presumably the academic training of officials from SWAPO and similar movements also increased. It is known that Namibians being educated under the auspices of UNESCO, ILO, and UNIDO receive training in the USSR and Eastern Europe.

Training of PLAN cadres also takes place in the Eastern-bloc states. East Germany has played an active role in promoting guerrilla movements throughout the African continent, and a number of them, including SWAPO, have official standing in East Berlin.[117] In 1977 a SWAPO delegation visited East Germany, and since then PLAN cadres have received training there. Hungary and Poland likewise have provided training of SWAPO cadres.[118] As we will detail in the next section, Soviet, Eastern-bloc, and Cuban advisers provide training in military, political, and administrative skills in Angolan and Zambian base camps.

Soviet training of insurgent cadres encompasses generally all aspects—military, political, organizational—of protracted insurgent warfare. This certainly is true in the case of SWAPO. Military training was discussed previously and need not be reiterated here; however, a closer look at the other elements of training is instructive, including the establishment within PLAN of a special command structure. The position of political commissar is entrenched in PLAN's organizational framework, as well as within SWAPO itself. These cadres, selected on the basis of their educational level and ideological commitment, are trained at special CPSU schools in the USSR, East Germany, and Cuba.

General ideological instruction is given to all who are recruited for, or pressed into, the service of SWAPO and PLAN. The political manual and political program of SWAPO, as well as other publications and documents, are infused with Marxist-Leninist language.[119] For example,

> The ideas of socialist orientation, as stated in the revised political program of SWAPO, have become our way of life, and we have now to grasp this great truth, that the first step in the revolution currently waged by the Namibian proletariat and the working peasants is to raise the two friendly classes in our society to the position of the ruling class which, at the time, is the first step to winning the battle of a people's democracy.
>
> Only in this way, shall we Namibian participants in the current liberation struggle (which we are waging on behalf of the general masses of all our people) be able to use the political supremacy of people's power to wrest state power from the colonial bourgeoisie, for the purpose of centralizing all the means of production and distribution in the hands of the worker and peasant masses.[120]

Since 1976, when SWAPO's political program was altered, Marxist-Leninist principles have been an integral element of the Soviet training program. The relationship between SWAPO's actions in Namibia and the "international struggle" against imperialism underlies this preparation and is also articulated in SWAPO publications.[121]

Former members of SWAPO report specialized training in underground tactics: Dickson Namolo claims that during 1978 he spent six months in the Soviet Union studying "underground work and intelligence." He explains that "in our training on underground work, we were taught how to work with the civilians, how to organize people, get their cooperation and recruit them as informers." [122] This training continued when Namolo returned to Angola.

The SWAPO cadres employ tactics, closely akin to those of the Viet Cong during the 1960s, to weaken the influence of village chiefs in Namibia. For example, former SWAPO member Emanuel Hashiko has testified about the intimidation and execution of headmen and the abduction of other officials. [123] Another report asserts that PLAN cadres killed 94 civilians, including eleven local chiefs, four deputy chiefs, and a member of the Ovambo legislative assembly. [124] The objective is to intimidate headmen and the population so as to prevent their cooperation with the South African government and possibly mobilize them to support SWAPO. Sabotage, kidnapping, threats, and execution are basic insurgent tactics that are employed in conjunction with various positive measures. The SWAPO cadres are schooled in these procedures by the Soviet Union and its surrogates.

Advisory Assistance

In addition to the provision of arms and training of SWAPO cadres in the USSR and Eastern-bloc states, beginning in the mid-1970s Moscow and its surrogates maintained a large number of advisers in southern Africa. Their role in the region appears to be twofold. In Angola, and to a lesser extent Mozambique, Soviet policy seeks to assist in the consolidation of power during the period following a revolution. In Angola this includes supervision of the establishment of the internal security and military forces. Soviet and surrogate personnel also train and provide advisory support to insurgent movements active in the region. Angola serves as a springboard for Soviet initiatives in southern Africa and hosts the largest number of Soviet, Cuban, and East German personnel in the region.

Initially the deployment of advisers was designed to assist the MPLA against FNLA-UNITA forces who were receiving some assistance from Zambia, South Africa, and the United States. By the end of February 1976, the Soviet air- and sealift brought the number of Cuban troops to 20,000. In December 1979, Castro put the figure at 36,000. [125] During this period, Havana also sent approximately 6,500 economic technicians to Angola. Soviet and Eastern-bloc personnel figures for 1975–1979 number 1,400 military and 2,700 economic advisers. [126] Among the East European states, East Germany sent the largest contingent. One source estimates that by 1980 there were 1,000 East German advisers in Angola, and in 1982, approximately 2,500. [127]

In addition to assisting the MPLA to consolidate power, these advisers apparently helped Neto put down an attempted coup in May 1977. Having provided the Angolans with this level of assistance, it is not surprising that Moscow officially solidified its relationship with Luanda through a Treaty of Friendship and Cooperation. Signed on October 8, 1976 (predating the abortive coup by half a year), the treaty committed both countries to "further broaden and deepen their cooperation" in a number of unspecified areas "corresponding [to] agreements in the military sphere."

One area of cooperation that can be identified is the use of Angola as a base for training and equipping other southern African liberation movements, particularly SWAPO forces operating in Namibia. Since 1975 SWAPO has established training and support bases in Angola with the help of the USSR, Cuba, East Germany, and the MPLA government. These bases include regional headquarters for the direction of operations across the Namibian border. Angola is divided into three zones—western, central, eastern—each of which contains security and military personnel from the Soviet Union and its surrogates. Most of the guerrilla training now takes place in the central zone because SWAPO bases closer to the border were destroyed by South African forces during 1983.

In addition, a much smaller number of SWAPO bases were established in Zambia. According to Hosmer and Wolfe, beginning in the late 1970s military aid was channeled to SWAPO through Zambia and other frontline states.[128] The number of Soviet and surrogate advisers is, however, much smaller than in Angola. For instance, there were approximately 100 Cuban military and paramilitary advisers in Zambia by the early 1980s.[129] In total, military advisers numbered fewer than 300,[130] with East Germany providing approximately 150.[131]

What role do these security and military advisers play in Angola? With respect to the MPLA army, it has been reported that more than 1,000 Soviet officers occupy key positions in the military command and control structure.[132] East Germans are in similar positions within Angolan intelligence and internal security police.[133] Cuban advisers and technicians are found at all levels of the Angolan infrastructure, while Cuban troops support MPLA forces. In effect, Soviet and surrogate advisers are involved at the ground level with all aspects of Angolan internal security and military affairs. In terms of the army, Soviet advisers were observed at the platoon level in southern Angola in 1981.[134]

The picture in terms of SWAPO is not as clear. It is known that large-scale training of SWAPO members by Soviet, East German, and Cuban personnel is taking place inside Angola. These advisers are also involved in planning SWAPO operations and in the development of base areas.[135] (The extent of this involvement, however, is difficult to determine.) Peter Vanneman and Martin James assert that the Soviets are providing air defense weaponry for SWAPO sanctuaries in Angola:

> Before the South African raids into Angola in the last half of 1981, the Soviets had installed a formidable modern surface-to-air missile

defense system. The missiles were the radar-homing missiles intended for low-flying aircraft. There were four missile sites around each of the major stopping points used by SWAPO.[136]

This has apparently continued in the period following the 1981 South African incursion into Angola. Cuban and Soviet personnel have gone into the field to observe (and presumably evaluate) operations by SWAPO forces.

Conclusion

This case study examined the ways in which Moscow has employed its political and military instruments since the mid-1970s to assist SWAPO. In terms of political measures, the escalation of Soviet propaganda coverage of SWAPO not only signaled that the insurgency had become an important policy issue but also triggered the initiation of a broader political warfare campaign. This activated the international front organizations, who expanded their use of propaganda and international conference diplomacy to promote the themes of Soviet overt propaganda. The cause of SWAPO was also advanced through political action within international organizations. Almost simultaneously the paramilitary assistance to SWAPO increased in conjunction with these political measures.

Nevertheless, despite these developments SWAPO remains weak, and there appears to be no real possibility of a military victory over South Africa in the near future. A SWAPO political victory through a negotiated settlement is likewise uncertain. A brief examination of negotiations over the last decade lends support to this assertion. To begin with, Namibia is multiethnic in composition. Its black community, which makes up 78 percent of the total population (of the remaining 22 percent, 12 percent are white and 10 percent are of mixed Afro-European ancestry), is divided into eleven ethnic groups of which the Ovambo (consisting of seven major tribes) make up nearly half. SWAPO's base of support lies mainly in the northern half of Namibia, an area heavily populated by Ovambo. However, the degree of actual support for SWAPO is not easy to gauge, and opposition does exist to SWAPO's violent approach and Marxist-Leninist ideology.[137]

Beyond tribal divisiveness, SWAPO has been opposed by other Namibian political parties, including the Ovamboland Independent Party (OIP) and the Democratic Cooperative Development Party (DEMCOP). The OIP represents an Ovamboland-oriented perspective, and its program is focused on development within the existing political situation. As a result, according to one expert, "its impact must remain limited, and its survival and the implementation of its program depend on the South African government."[138]

In the center between SWAPO and OIP stands DEMCOP. Its original program called for cooperation with South Africa to promote prosperity and development in Namibia. Opposing communism, DEMCOP asserts that "under democracy every member of the people has a say in the affairs of its government."[139] Starting in 1970, DEMCOP sought recognition from South Africa but has been unsuccessful, partly because of South Africa's policy of separate development for Namibia. DEMCOP leaders subsequently expressed a willingness to work with SWAPO to attain common objectives. Nevertheless, some observers believe that had Pretoria recognized DEMCOP, SWAPO's influence among Namibians would have been weakened.

In 1975 the Turnhalle constitutional talks were launched, resulting in the Democratic Turnhalle Alliance (DTA). The DTA, however, is very controversial because of its composition. As Kenneth Adelman notes, Pretoria failed to usher moderate black elites into the process. The South Africans denied participation to multiethnic political parties, insisted on ethnic representation, and, thus, found themselves dealing largely with uneducated blacks and unsophisticated chiefs.[140] L. H. Gann and Peter Duignan, in contrast, argue that this was an important step toward Namibian independence.[141] Although the significance of the DTA remains an open question, especially in light of recent developments, it is another obstacle to a political settlement with SWAPO.

As noted earlier in this study, an internal rift split SWAPO during the latter 1970s. About 20 percent of the organization formed SWAPO-Democrats (SWAPO-D). Ignored by the OAU, U.N., and front-line states, they have been dealt with harshly by Sam Nujoma and the SWAPO leadership, who persuaded Zambia to incarcerate the leaders and between one and two thousand members of SWAPO-D.

In sum, SWAPO does not appear to possess the unanimous political support it claims. It is neither a unified party nor the only political organization in Namibia. Nevertheless, since the mid-1970s, the Nujoma-led elements of SWAPO have been the only Namibians to receive the support of the U.N., the OAU, individual Third World states, and the Soviet Union and its surrogates. This support creates a further obstacle to a negotiated political settlement. Agencies of the U.N., for instance, contribute millions annually to SWAPO-run institutions, including the U.N. Institute for Namibia in Lusaka. Its executive director is a key member of SWAPO, and the Namibians it has educated over the years have been "heavily if not totally made up of SWAPO members."[142]

This united front in support of SWAPO has given Pretoria great pause in negotiating, and thus Pretoria has consistently blocked any settlement that would install SWAPO as the dominant force in a Namibian coalition government. A settlement on these grounds, Pretoria reasons, is potentially dangerous to its security, as it seems likely that Moscow and its surrogates would continue to assist and build up SWAPO during the initial coalition period toward eventual

SWAPO consolidation of control. The lessons of Nicaragua and elsewhere are understood by Pretoria. The possibility of a postsettlement coup is likewise understood by SWAPO-D and other Namibian political organizations.

In light of the above, what course will the Soviet Union follow in the coming years? Since the mid-1970s the Kremlin has implemented a policy of protracted warfare and designed its long-term policy effort to foster the efforts of SWAPO, while isolating South Africa in the international arena. Through the strategy outlined above, Moscow has contributed to the gradual escalation of instability. It would seem, therefore, important to the USSR that the conflict situation in Namibia be continued and expanded and that all peace initiatives be postponed as long as possible.

Soviet support for SWAPO should be understood within the context of its broader policy in southern Africa. The Kremlin's indirect pattern, established over the last decade, will most likely continue for the foreseeable future, unless the current crisis in South Africa reaches the point of political climax and revolution. This pattern includes military assistance to factions in the region that cannot seize or maintain power without it. Efforts to isolate South Africa internationally in all possible spheres and by all possible means will continue. Likewise, opposition to all peace initiatives and discrediting Western involvement in the process can be expected.[143] Furthermore, a large number of Soviet and surrogate personnel will remain in the region playing the multiple roles described in this study.

SIX

Revolutionary Insurgency in Central America and Soviet-Cuban Involvement

During the latter half of the 1970s, conflict and political instability in Central America reached a crisis level. The seriousness of the situation by the mid-1980s led to the following conclusion by the National Bipartisan Commission on Central America (Kissinger Commission):

> The tortured history of Central America is such that neither the military nor the political nor the economic nor the social aspects of the crisis can be considered independently of the others. Unless rapid progress can be made on the political, economic and social fronts, peace on the military front will be elusive and would be fragile. But unless the externally supported insurgencies are checked and the violence curbed, progress on those other fronts [also] will be elusive and would be fragile.[1]

In effect, according to the commission, instability in Central America was the result of both indigenous conditions and external encouragement and support. There can be little disagreement that domestic discontent in various Central American countries is, in part, the result of economic and social inequalities that invite internal strife and revolution. The Kissinger Commission places the current instability in the region in a historical perspective and describes the factors contributing to the intensification of indigenous splits in the nations of Central America.[2] These have been described in detail in other related reports and studies.[3] What is not always addressed in the literature is the extent to which these indigenous disagreements and inequalities are exploited by other states and their surrogates. In Central America the Cuban regime of Fidel Castro, supported by the USSR, has played an important role in promoting and supporting insurgency and terrorism in the region. Increasingly, Nicaragua has followed Cuba and initiated a similar policy. It now appears that Managua has emerged, in many respects, as a Cuban surrogate. Although the USSR and its Cuban and Nicaraguan allies did not create the problems that increase the likelihood of revolution in El Salvador, Guatemala, and elsewhere, they have developed an integrated strategy and infrastructure of capabilities for exacerbating these situations. On these developments the Kissinger Commission concluded:

> Whatever the social and economic conditions that invite insurgency in the region, outside intervention is what gives the conflict its present character. Of course, uprisings occur without outside support, but protracted guerrilla insurgencies require external assistance. Indeed, if wretched conditions were themselves enough to create such insurgencies, we would see them in many more countries of the world. Propaganda support, money, sanctuary, arms supplies, training, communications, intelligence, logistics, all are important in both morale and operational terms. Without such support from Cuba, Nicaragua, and the Soviet Union, neither in El Salvador nor elsewhere . . . would such an insurgency pose as severe a threat.[4]

However, Soviet foreign policy as it relates to Latin America did not always encourage and/or indirectly assist regional insurgent groups. During the 1960s and well into the 1970s, Moscow chose not to support factions advocating protracted armed struggle.

Soviet Policy Toward Latin America: 1956–1976

During the late 1970s the Soviet view of armed struggle in Latin America underwent an important change. Before this Moscow's foreign policy in the region was set within the context of what it termed "the peaceful road to socialism." According to Robert Leiken, this "line represented a reversal . . . Armed revolution was now discouraged in favor of 'peaceful liberation from foreign oppression.'"[5] This earlier Soviet policy in Latin America, Leiken observes, should be understood as part of Khrushchev's strategy of peaceful coexistence, which was "designed to shelter the Soviet Union from challenges to its spheres of influence, to reduce the possibility of distracting overseas adventures, to promote trade with the West for the acquisition of technology . . .

to stimulate trade with the Third World for needed raw materials, foodstuffs, and markets for foreign exchange for purchases from the West."[6]

This policy signaled a significant change in the original political line of the Comintern as the Kremlin leadership apparently discerned a new stage in the liberation struggle. Economic consolidation became the central task and "basic link in the further development of the revolution."[7] In effect, Moscow hoped to employ diplomacy and economic assistance to draw the nations of the developing world into the socialist camp. The Soviet Union, since the early days of the Bolshevik regime, had symbolically linked itself to the anti-imperialist struggle in the Third World, so this new policy was an important tactical variation. The traditional Leninist alliance between socialism and the armed struggle for national liberation was de-emphasized, while Soviet economic assistance was touted as the way to enable emerging nations to achieve independence. In the words of Nikita Khrushchev, the USSR would provide the means by which to "avoid the dangers of a new enslavement."[8]

Ironically, as the new Soviet policy unfolded, Latin America experienced a successful culmination of the kind of armed insurrection Moscow asserted was outmoded. The seizure of power by Fidel Castro in Cuba appears to have taken the Kremlin by surprise. This may have been due, in part, to the strategy employed by the insurgents. Their approach, largely articulated by Ernesto ("Che") Guevara, argued that the introduction of small bands of guerrillas (*foco* "insurrectionary guerrilla nucleus") into a given country could result in the successful overthrow of an existing government without a mass base of support in the population. Once it became apparent that Castro would successfully consolidate power, Moscow sought to establish what promised to be a strategically valuable relationship with Cuba. The Cuban revolution signaled the possibility of a wave of revolutionary upheavals throughout the region and, followed by Castro's declaration that the revolution was socialist in character, offered the prospect of the spread of Marxism-Leninism to an area noncontiguous with the USSR and not as the result of a cataclysmal war.[9] This reinforced the assertion of the global nature of the inevitable triumph of communism.

By the early 1960s, Khrushchev began at least rhetorically to support "wars of national liberation."[10] In certain regions of the world, as noted in earlier chapters, this was not simply rhetoric. Beginning in 1965, as demonstrated in Chapter 3, the USSR increased its support and assistance to the Vietnamese. Following the 1967 Arab-Israeli war, a number of guerrilla factions, as noted in Chapter 4, likewise began to receive support. Soviet policy in Latin America, however, remained basically unchanged, as seen in the tensions that arose between Havana and Moscow at that time. The Kremlin leadership rejected as adventuristic Cuban attempts to extend the *foco* strategy throughout the region and felt that Havana ignored the "objective conditions" in the target states. An examination of the "concrete conditions and the actual correlation of forces" revealed the flaws in the *foco* strategy and, therefore, its inapplicability for Latin American revolutionaries.[11] Soviet policy remained committed to traditional communist parties playing the lead role in a peaceful struggle.[12]

The nontransferability of the Cuban model was, from the Soviet perspective, borne out by a number of revolutionary setbacks in Latin America during the mid-1960s. Guerrillas who took to the hills following the strategy outlined by Che Guevara were still there in the late 1960s but had advanced no farther. In some cases they controlled remote rural areas; elsewhere they were eliminated by successful counterguerrilla operations. The most important setback for the *foco* strategists was the death of Che Guevara in Bolivia in 1967; there had been no victories since Cuba, and his death symbolized the limits of this approach.[13] Consequently, for Latin American revolutionaries, going to the mountains lost much of its appeal. Those who continued to advocate armed struggle shifted the battlefield to the cities.[14] The Tupamaros in Uruguay were the prototype of this transition from rural to urban guerrilla warfare and terrorism. Although exceedingly violent, this strategy (and its variations) brought forth no victories.[15]

Consequently, Moscow appeared to be vindicated in its adherence to a policy that instructed Latin American communist parties to join broad electoral front coalitions. Soviet theoretical writing continued to argue that communists in Latin America should "collaborate with and support representatives" of other parties "if they are in power and carrying out anti-imperialist reforms."[16] By the late 1960s the Soviets had established diplomatic relations with Brazil, Chile, Colombia, Peru, Ecuador, and Bolivia. Leon Goure and Morris Rothenberg note that the presence of more than 300 Soviet diplomatic personnel and the large Soviet diplomatic, economic, cultural, and scientific missions throughout Latin America greatly expanded Moscow's contacts with governments and social, economic, and political elites.[17]

The trends that unfolded at the end of the 1960s continued into the early 1970s. Guerrilla factions following either the urban or the rural model of armed insurrection failed to make any real headway toward the seizure of power. Traditional communist parties, however, appeared to be advancing and active in reformist and/or nationalist movements in Bolivia, Chile, Ecuador, Peru, and Uruguay. More important, the Popular Unity government in Chile, which took office in 1970 as the result of an electoral victory by a coalition of communist, socialist, and other radical and leftist elements, signified the "objective correctness" of Moscow's peaceful transition policy.

Yet another coalition partner for Latin American communist parties, in Moscow's view, was a "progressive" military. During the late 1960s and early 1970s, military coups in Panama, Ecuador, Bolivia, and Peru brought to power military governments that promulgated social reform, nationalized the property of U.S. multinationals, and often welcomed Soviet diplomatic and economic overtures. Soviet analysts came to believe that Latin America was experiencing a new generation of military officers that would initiate "a radical anti-imperialist trend, brought about by their awareness of the fact that under conditions of imperialist dependence it is impossible to achieve national progress."[18] In effect, an enlightened military could play a "progressive" role and implement a peaceful transition to socialism. This acknowledgment was accompanied by efforts to foster pro-Soviet factions in Latin American armed forces.

The September 1973 military coup in Chile was a serious setback both for the Soviet policy of peaceful transition and for the identification of the military as a progressive force. The latter argument was further undermined by the decision of Peru's military leadership, a progressive element singled out by Moscow for economic and military assistance, to permit large U.S. investment in that country. Similar developments elsewhere in the region revealed serious flaws in Kremlin policy. By the mid-1970s it must have appeared to Moscow that the opportunity to extend its influence in Latin America had diminished.

Moscow backed armed coups, invasions, occupations, and guerrilla movements in Angola, South Yemen, Sudan, Ethiopia, Kampuchea, Laos, Afghanistan, and elsewhere, but no Latin American revolutionary movement appeared capable of seriously challenging an existing government through armed struggle. Consequently, bringing Latin America within the framework of escalating Soviet support for insurgent movements in other regions of the Third World would have, from the perspective of the USSR, paid little dividend. Ironically, crucial to Soviet success in other parts of the Third World was Cuba, its Latin American surrogate, especially in Africa where Cuban advisers and troops were deployed. The ability of the USSR to employ Cuban forces in this way was, in my view, its major success in Latin America during the late 1960s and early 1970s.

New Trends in Armed Insurrection

The Case of Nicaragua

Opposition to the rule of Anastasio Somoza in Nicaragua grew dramatically during the late 1970s.[19] On May 29, 1979, the Sandinista Front of National Liberation (FSLN) initiated its final offensive against the Somoza regime. Shortly thereafter, units of the Sandinista Army entered Managua, which was a remarkable turnabout for a movement that had, on more than one occasion, suffered crippling defeats.

The origins of the FSLN date back to 1961, when it was formally established.[20] Several of its founders identified with Castro and the Cuban revolution. In 1962 the Cuban government provided arms for FSLN guerrilla units entering

Nicaragua. The 1960s were, however, not successful years for the FSLN, as they suffered repeated defeats.

From the point of view of strategy, Che Guevara's defeat in Bolivia was an important lesson for elements of the FSLN. Recognizing the consequences for a guerrilla movement with no base of support within the rural population or infrastructure in the cities, the FSLN devoted the years 1967–1977 to organizing in both areas.[21] This period was marked by the split of the FSLN into three feuding factions. The leaders and their cliques were Tomás Borge, Prolonged Popular War (GPP); Humberto and Daniel Ortega, Insurrectional Tendency (TI); and Jaime Wheelock, Proletarian Tendency (TP).

Each of these factions or tendencies was Marxist-Leninist in orientation, but the factions differed sharply over strategy and tactics. Consequently, disagreements over how, when, and where to seize power, as well as the size and composition of the social base from which the movement would emerge, weakened the ability of the Sandinistas to challenge Somoza and influenced the degree to which Cuba was willing to lend support. Thus, until the latter half of 1977, Cuban aid to Nicaragua was confined to safe haven, propaganda, small amounts of arms, and limited training of cadres.

An examination of the different approaches taken by the FSLN factions discloses the seriousness of the problem. The GPP argued that the revolution could only come about through a rural guerrilla strategy patterned after the Chinese and Vietnamese models. First articulated in 1969, this strategy was adopted after a futile attempt to implement the Cuban *foco*.[22] The GPP program was anticapitalist, anti-United States, and internationalist in outlook.[23] The road to power was a long and protracted one, involving years of struggle before a direct military challenge could take place. The leaders of the GPP—Borge, Henry Ruiz, and Bayardo Arce—were ideological purists who also maintained international linkages. Borge traveled to Cuba in 1960 to seek support and has maintained close ties with Havana ever since. Ruiz attended Patrice Lumumba University in Moscow, trained with the PLO, and had ties to the North Vietnamese in the 1960s.[24]

The TP took a more orthodox Marxist-Leninist approach, arguing that the seizure of power would take place only after the successful establishment of an urban mass organization of workers. The struggle would be prolonged, with the FSLN serving as the vanguard element of the revolution. The TP criticized the GPP for lapsing into rural guerrilla adventurism. The leaders of the TP likewise maintained international ties with Wheelock studying in Chile in the early 1970s and traveling widely in Eastern Europe. A leading theoretician, in 1975 he advanced a stinging critique of GPP strategy.[25] For this insubordination he was purged (along with his followers) from the GPP-dominated FSLN National Directorate.[26]

The third faction—the TI—sought to steer a middle course between the GPP-TP debate using the strategic concept of insurrectionalism, which asserted that before a Marxist-Leninist state could be established the revolution had to pass through a democratic-popular stage. The TI called for the FSLN to form a broad alliance with the alienated elements from the middle class—professionals, the small self-employed, students, the church, the business community, and various political parties (especially the Social Democrats).[27] The chief spokesmen for the TI—Daniel and Humberto Ortega—were closely aligned with Cuba. In many ways the TI represented the volunteerism of Che Guevara's *foco* approach; rather than waiting for the "objective conditions" the vanguard would help create or facilitate them. However, unlike *foco*, the TI was not restricted to rural areas. The TP and the GPP objected to TI insurrectionalism.[28] The TI defended the broad alliance concept as tactical and temporary and asserted that at no time did it suggest such a compromise would carry into the postrevolutionary stage.[29]

Thus, as the Somoza regime began to come apart in 1977, the Sandinistas found themselves splintered. The strategy adopted by the FSLN National Directorate in May 1977 to overcome these differences consisted of the following tenets:

- Build up intermediate mass organizations around day-to-day issues while maintaining coordination . . . and FSLN control.
- Create a broad anti-Somoza front . . . that includes bourgeois/democratic opposition groups, but preserves the hegemony of FSLN power.
- Unify the tendencies of the FSLN into a single, ideologically pure vanguard.
- Mobilize everyone for insurrection through agitation in the mass organizations, radicalization of the broad opposition front, and exemplary military action by the FSLN.
- Construct a strong Sandinista Army . . . Engage in a policy of active accumulation of forces . . . Develop a military doctrine of an uninterrupted offensive designed to put the enemy on the strategic defensive.[30]

This strategy of alliance with non-Marxist elements inside Nicaragua, as well as with noncommunist states and organizations outside its borders, began to take root following the unsuccessful campaign in October 1977. Although small FSLN offensive military actions achieved a margin of success, there was little public response and no mass insurrection.

Events in 1978 opened the way for the FSLN to establish alliances with moderate and democratic elements. The assassination of Pedro Joaquin Chamorro, the editor of *La Prensa* and a leading critic of Somoza, resulted in mass demonstrations.[31] These led to street fighting in many locations and on February 21, 1978, to a spontaneous insurrection in the Indian barrio of Monimbo in Masaya, which took elite troops to bring under control. Throughout 1978 Nicaraguan business, religious, moderate political, and civic leaders moved to irrevocably oppose Somoza. This included the Group of Twelve—prominent Nicaraguans who aligned themselves with the TI in 1977. At this time the Broad Opposition Front, composed of various moderate political elements and headed by Alfonso Robelo, was also formed.

In August 1978 Eden Pastora and a 25-person TI commando unit seized the Nicaraguan Chamber of Deputies, after which the commandos flew out of the country with the deputies. In exchange for the deputies some 60 prisoners were released (including Tomás Borge), the government paid a half million dollars in ransom, and the FSLN was permitted to broadcast its call for insurrection. The assault on the Chamber of Deputies resulted in nationwide strikes, rioting, and a Sandinista call for an urban offensive, during which FSLN squads struck unsuccessfully at several national guard garrisons. Although the FSLN could claim no victories as a result of this insurrection, Humberto Ortega believed that these events favorably shifted the long-term balance of forces, allowed the guerrillas to gain battlefield experience, demonstrated the viability of urban warfare, and permitted the FSLN to identify major government weaknesses.[32]

Not all the FSLN factions agreed with this assessment. The head of the TP, Jaime Wheelock, criticized the TI's habit of calling for premature insurrections that caused high civilian losses due to National Guard bombardment and cleanup operations in urban areas. Wheelock believed this would undermine popular support for the FSLN.[33] Thus, as late as the fall of 1978, factionalism continued to plague the FSLN.

At this point Cuba played a key role in the Nicaraguan revolution. Throughout 1978 a high-ranking member of the Americas Department of the Cuban Communist Party, Armando Ulises Estrada, made a number of secret trips to attempt to unify the three factions.[34] Apparently, Castro required unity as a prerequisite for increased military assistance. The shortage of military supplies, as well as recognition that the situation was rapidly reaching the final stage, brought the tendencies together. On March 7, 1979, the leaders of the GPP, TP, and TI announced the formation of a nine-man Combined National Directorate (DNC).[35] The Pastora wing of the TI was excluded, as were other elements of the revolutionary coalition. The insurrectional strategy became the military doctrine of the FSLN.

Following unification of the FSLN factions, Cuba increased the supply of weapons, training, and advisory personnel. A network for channeling arms and supplies was set up that ran from Cuba to Costa Rica. The following excerpt from an interview with Pastora outlines how this unfolded.

> During preparations for the final offensive, the Cubans set up an operations center in San José under Julian Lopez Diaz . . . The operation was set up in May 1979. They operated right through the San José international airport. In fact, they unloaded the arms right in front of the OAS observers.[36]

These supply and support operations helped neutralize Somoza's National Guard, culminating in the collapse of the Nicaraguan government on July 11, 1979.

Within a short period following Somoza's defeat, the DNC of the FSLN began to consolidate control. Utilizing ties with Cuba, the USSR, and the East European bloc, it rapidly began to convert Nicaragua into a state modeled after Cuba. Consequently, during the first few years after the revolution, many non-communist coalition members found themselves in either marginal positions or isolated. Testimony by former Sandinista intelligence and military officers, as well as captured documents, reveals the degree to which Moscow and its surrogates (mainly Cuba) were involved in these activities.[37]

The testimony of a former counterintelligence officer, Miguel Bolanos Hunter, describes the role of Soviet, Cuban, East German, and Bulgarian intelligence in establishing and advising the Nicaraguan General Directorate of State Security (DGSE) apparatus.[38] State security is a principal means of consolidating power and maintaining control in communist regimes. Bolanos pointed out that immediately following the revolution a large number of FSLN cadres were sent to Cuba for training in intelligence and counterintelligence techniques. In addition to Nicaraguans, he noted that Grenadians and Angolans were receiving the same instruction. At the intelligence school in Cuba the instructors were General Directorate of Intelligence officers, while KGB officials served in an observer capacity. Within the DGSE, Cuban advisers were assigned to all levels of the geographic and functional departments of intelligence and counterintelligence. East German intelligence provided technical support to the DGSE, while the Bulgarians assisted in counterintelligence matters.

In addition to intelligence, Bolanos' testimony outlined Soviet surrogate involvement in other parts of the Nicaraguan government. Members of the Cuban Americas Department advised the FSLN's Department of International Relations on international political and psychological operations,[39] while the Department of Special Operations (DOE) helped establish bases from which to train Salvadoran and other guerrillas. The DOE also helps monitor and direct the Salvadoran operations (discussed in greater detail later in this chapter).[40]

Pastora described Cuban and Soviet assistance in other power consolidation measures, the most important being the establishment of the armed forces.[41] As with the DGSE, Pastora observed that Cuban advisers are found at the various levels of the Nicaraguan Army, where they not only instruct and advise but also select Nicaraguans for training in Cuba and other Soviet surrogate states. The degree of Kremlin involvement can be seen in Pastora's meetings with Soviet defense minister Marshal Dmitrii Ustinov. Pastora also explained that other Soviet allies were involved with the Nicaraguan armed forces, including the PLO.

Bolanos outlined how quickly the FSLN permitted the Soviets and Cubans to use its territory as a base for training and advising the Salvadoran guerrillas. In effect, Nicaragua almost immediately became part of the regional infrastructure for promoting insurgency and terrorism in Latin America. In addition to Cuban, East European, PLO, and Nicaraguan personnel serving as instructors and advisers, there are "internationalist" elements (MIR of Chile, Montoneros of Argentina, M–19 of Colombia, and Tupamaros of Uruguay).[42]

The Nicaraguans also became directly involved in political and propaganda efforts, both regionally and internationally, on behalf of the Salvadoran guerrillas. These activities are disclosed in documents captured in both Central America and Grenada.[43]

In the aftermath of the FSLN victory in Nicaragua, El Salvador's fragmented guerrilla factions assumed a new strategy that closely resembled that of the Sandinistas.

The Lessons of Nicaragua Applied to El Salvador

Guerrilla and insurrectionary factions existed in El Salvador long before the Sandinista revolution. However, similar to the tendencies within the FSLN, the guerrilla and revolutionary factions in El Salvador were sharply fragmented. Following the FSLN victory, the Cubans and the Soviets, in conjunction with the Sandinistas, began to focus more attention on developments in El Salvador.

As in Nicaragua the fragmentation of the left into competing factions received prompt attention and culminated in a unification agreement in December 1979. A meeting in Havana led to a trilateral coordinating body composed of the Communist Party of El Salvador (PCES), the Armed Forces of National Resistance (FARN), and the Popular Liberation Forces (FPL). During 1980 they were joined by the People's Revolutionary Workers Party. These factions formed the Farabundo Marti National Liberation Front (FMLN) that, in conjunction with its political arm, the Democratic Revolutionary Front, has served as the umbrella organization for the Salvadoran guerrillas.

It appears, on the basis of captured documents, that Cuba played an important part in the unification process. During May 1980, following discussions in Cuba, the coalition took the title of the Unified Revolutionary Directorate (DRU). In letters addressed to Manuel Pineiro, the head of the Americas Department of the Cuban Communist Party (CCP), the DRU thanked the CCP for its "valuable ideas and suggestions . . . relative to the process of political, organic, and functional consolidation attained by the DRU." The letters contained additional information on operational details concerning the Salvadoran insurgency, revealing the close cooperative relationship at the highest levels between Cuba and the Salvadoran revolutionaries.[44] In another letter addressed to Fidel Castro dated December 16, 1979, the PCES, FARN, and FPL thank him for help in forging the earlier unification agreement among themselves.[45]

Following the creation of the DRU, Cuba began to supply arms to the Salvadoran guerrillas. During the second half of 1980, Nicaragua became the center of a network for transferring arms into El Salvador, and base areas were established in Nicaragua for training and advising guerrilla cadres. Finally, the FSLN directorate offered the DRU a headquarters in Nicaragua.

The arrangements between the Salvadoran guerrillas, members of the Warsaw Pact, and other Soviet clients to transfer arms, as well as the routes and infrastructure, will be discussed later in this chapter. The point is that by the end of 1980 the FMLN was employing weapons never before introduced in El Salvador. As a result of this buildup, the DRU announced its "final offensive," which followed, in many respects, the Sandinista revolutionary approach. Ernest Evans observes that "the combined effect of their own learning experiences plus the victory of the Sandinistas have led the revolutionary movements in El Salvador and Guatemala to adopt a strategy of revolution that is broadly similar to that of the FSLN."[46] Thus, the final offensive that the FMLN launched in 1981 was modeled on the FSLN final offensive of 1979.[47]

Beginning with countrywide armed actions to create the impression that El Salvador was "under siege," the guerrillas hoped to instigate a popular insurrection and disintegrate the army. Neither of these developments transpired. The Salvadoran population did not follow DRU appeals, and the army remained intact and fought back. Although the guerrillas caused considerable damage, they were unable to topple the Christian Democratic–armed forces junta of El Salvador.

The FMLN suffered not only a tactical setback with the failure of the final offensive but also losses and damage to the infrastructure. Drawing again on the Sandinista experience, the decision was taken to follow the prolonged war strategy of the Tomás Borge–led GPP, which called for a war of attrition and economic sabotage to be carried out in conjunction with the rebuilding of guerrilla strength both in El Salvador and in base camps in Nicaragua. The number of guerrillas did increase, and they were armed with more sophisticated equipment acquired from various Soviet surrogates. The prolonged war approach has had a damaging impact on the economy, as the FMLN set out to disrupt the government's ability to provide food, water, transportation, electricity, sanitation, and employment. The political process has not been similarly destabilized, as the March 1982 election demonstrated.

Over the last few years the guerrillas have operated in somewhat larger numbers in the countryside utilizing more sophisticated communications equipment and weaponry (by 1985 increasing losses changed this). As we shall describe later in the chapter, the FMLN has been able to acquire this assistance with continued Nicaraguan backing, whose sources can be traced to members of the Warsaw Pact, Cuba, and other states aligned with the USSR. This assistance has included arms and logistic supplies, training, and advisory support (command and control). Nevertheless, the insurgency strategy remains, at least for the time being, focused on protracted and indirect tactics, the result of improvements in the ability of the Salvadoran armed forces to conduct operations against the guerrillas, as well as to a loss of popular support by the FMLN. The latter is, in part, the result of political reform on the part of the Napoleón Duarte government. Additionally, the U.S. government has sought to affect the supply network through which the FMLN receives arms in two ways. First, public diplomacy has focused attention on the role of the Warsaw Pact countries, Cuba, and Nicaragua in the Salvadoran conflict. Second, Washington has provided assistance to the Nicaraguan Democratic Resistance (contras) in their struggle against the FSLN.

The USSR and
Revolution in Latin America

By the end of the 1970s, a changing and politically volatile environment in Latin America (particularly in the central region) contributed to a marked shift in Soviet policy. Revolutionary developments in Central America presented the USSR with an opportunity to extend its strategy of promoting and assisting national liberation movements. The events in Nicaragua were, in retrospect, a precipitant that led Moscow to begin a reassessment of the probability for successful revolution in the region.

With the triumph of the FSLN in 1979, the Soviet Union's objectives and policy changed. The peaceful road to socialism, discredited in the first half of the decade, gave way to new policy. According to Moscow, "the armed road . . . is the most promising in the specific conditions of most of the Latin American countries . . . there is no single example of victorious revolution in the continent that has pursued the peaceful road . . . only the armed road has led to victory in Latin America."[48] The head of the International Department of the CPSU, Boris Ponomarev, began to include insurgent movements in Latin America among those capable of carrying out revolutionary change through armed struggle.[49] According to Daniel Papp, "the Soviets count the geographic widening of the revolutionary process as one of the most important features of the late twentieth century. Soviet commentary on national liberation in Latin America illustrates this point."[50]

This new emphasis can be found in the more theoretical literature of specialists from the International Department and institutes of the Academy of Sciences, as well as in the official media organs of the CPSU. In the case of the latter, the early 1980s saw frequent reference to the escalating revolutionary process in Latin America. For example, *Izvestiya* observed that "the revolutionary process in Latin America is developing exceptionally rapidly . . . Central America is on the move."[51] Likewise, *Pravda* asserted that "the early eighties showed that the flame of the liberation struggle had been kindled on the very threshold of the imperialist citadel."[52]

While these and other party organs were enthusiastic about the revolutionary potential in the region, they likewise recognized that the resurgent U.S. interest in assisting governments like El Salvador could affect the course of these developments. This concern has taken the form of a harsh assessment of U.S. policy and its implications. Washington is said to be planning either a coup or an invasion of El Salvador. *Radio Moscow* in August 1983 broadcast that "the U.S. administration is planning to carry out a military coup in El Salvador, as a result of which a government made up of representatives of rightist forces . . . would be brought to power."[53] A year later TASS reported that Washington "is preparing for an outright military invasion."[54] This planned intervention in El Salvador, according to Soviet commentary, was part of a global strategy to defeat national liberation movements. In an article concerned with U.S. Special Forces, *Pravda* stated "the formation of the new U.S. subversive-international corps . . . is yet another link in the chain of attempts by U.S. imperialism to crush national liberation movements by crude military force."[55]

During the period following Salvador Allende's overthrow in Chile, Academy of Sciences and International Department specialists examined the question of the revolutionary prospects in Latin America. Jerry Hough notes that "Soviet testimony is universal that officials and established scholars did not expect a Sandinista victory in Nicaragua and gave the movement no significant support."[56] This was true through early 1978, but Soviet surrogate support escalated after that time. By the end of the decade, we find a new trend among specialists as Hough notes "In the first discussion of Nicaragua in the journal *Latin America* after the Sandinista revolt" one scholar "firmly asserted that the need to support new left forces was an important lesson of [this] revolution."[57] Hough is referring to Kiva Maidanik, a leading Latin American specialist at the Institute of the World Economy and International Relations. Nevertheless, Hough continues to find a debate among Soviet scholars over these new developments in Latin America:

> While a radical claimed that "the victory of the Nicaraguan revolution forced many not only to reject approaches and stereotypes that existed earlier, but essentially to reexamine their relationship to [guerrilla] movements, their theoretical opinions, strategy, and methods," schol-

ars who had been associated with the thesis of the Europeanization of Latin America still seemed skeptical about Central America, although they expressed the point only in asides or by implication. [In other words, broad coalitions could still result in peaceful liberation].[58]

While Hough may have found an ongoing debate among Soviet scholars, the official CPSU position following the FSLN victory viewed national liberation movements employing strategies of armed struggle as an important feature of Latin American politics. Writing in *Kommunist,* the CPSU theoretical journal, the head of the Communist Party of El Salvador, Shafik Jorge Handal, stated that victory will come "by the armed struggle . . . there is no other way."[59] It is significant that Handal was selected to articulate this position, for it signaled to the nonruling communist parties in Latin America that the old line of political compromise, collaboration, and alliance, if not completely eclipsed, had undergone an important modification. This new line was also articulated in *World Marxist Review,* the English-language edition of *Problems of Peace and Socialism.* This publication is used by the CPSU's International Department to communicate instructions to nonruling communist parties and revolutionary movements. Paralleling *Kommunist,* this new line was endorsed in *World Marxist Review* by the leaders of various Latin American communist parties.[60]

Soviet Political-Military Support of Insurgency in Latin America

By mid-1978 support for the FSLN increased, supplied chiefly through Cuba, which serves, in part, as a regional surrogate for the USSR. Following the FSLN victory in Nicaragua, Soviet pronouncements observed that armed revolutionary struggle in the region was on the rise. Although Western observers may still find evidence of a debate among Soviet scholars over the issue of armed struggle versus strategies of coalition and reform as the path to power, the official CPSU position appears to have shifted to armed struggle.

In the remainder of this chapter we will examine how this new policy was translated into political and paramilitary assistance by the USSR and its surrogates for insurgent movements in Nicaragua and El Salvador.

Foreign Propaganda

Soviet overt propaganda responded slowly to the revolutionary events unfolding in Nicaragua in late 1977 and early 1978. During 1977, coverage of these developments was nominal and increased only marginally in the early part of 1978. During the latter half of that year, however, Soviet commentary escalated, whereas Cuban propaganda coverage of Nicaragua was intensive from the latter half of 1977 on. Since mid-1978, Soviet and Cuban propaganda directed toward Central America generally have paralleled and reinforced one another. Cuba maintains significant propaganda capabilities including *Prensa Latina,* the press agency of the Cuban government, which has 35 field offices and combines news-gathering and propaganda dissemination with intelligence operations. Additionally, *Radio Havana* transmits extensively throughout Latin America. An examination of the thematic patterns found in *Gramma Weekly Review* and *Radio Havana* discloses a strong similarity with those promoted in Soviet coverage of the events first in Nicaragua and then El Salvador.[61]

Before examining these patterns, the following observations are necessary. Growing Soviet interest in the region, as described previously, is reflected in the scope and extent of their propaganda commentary. As Central America became more important in Soviet foreign policy, events first in Nicaragua and then in El Salvador were discussed in greater detail and in relationship to U.S. policy in the region. Soviet propaganda set the tone and thematic framework for the general political offensive and also provided guidelines for the propaganda and political action of the international front organizations and their local affiliates.

Athough the Soviet propaganda campaign does not differ appreciably from other cases examined in this study, there are unique situational factors. Perhaps the most interesting development is the Soviet attempt to portray U.S. policy in El Salvador as a replay of the Vietnam experience. This analogy is actively promoted both in Soviet international propaganda and through the political action of the international front apparatus. Although nothing has developed akin to the previously discussed Stockholm conference campaign on Vietnam, there is an attempt by the fronts to reach those groups in the United States that oppose the Reagan administration's Central American policy.

Soviet media coverage of the crisis in Nicaragua expanded only as the likelihood of Somoza's overthrow approached reality. This parallels, with a time lag, growing paramilitary assistance provided mainly through Cuba. The general thematic patterns are similar to those described in previous case studies—U.S. foreign policy, motivated by regional, imperialist, and hegemonic interests, now faced a serious threat from the Sandinista national liberation movement.

Throughout Central America the United States was described as desperately seeking to retain its interests in the region. According to TASS of September 14, 1978, "the U.S. would now like to bring down the wave of liberation movements in Central America while preserving firm its position in the area."[62] During 1978 developments in Nicaragua likewise received expanded remarks. This was true both of U.S. relations with Somoza and of Washington's willingness to take any steps, including military intervention according to *Izvestiya,* to keep Somoza's government in power:

About 1,000 specially trained U.S. paratroopers have abruptly transferred from the United States to the Panama Canal Zone. The local
press reports that a large proportion of these "special" troops is made
up of veterans of the dirty war in Vietnam and military police specializing in the suppression of demonstrations by the people . . . The
opinion is also being voiced that the Americans want to use the Panama Canal Zone to transfer troops to Nicaragua to render military aid
to dictator Somoza's corrupt regime.[63]

The U.S. rationale for "expanding its role in Nicaragua," according to Soviet propaganda, was to employ the "dictatorial regime in Nicaragua . . . not
only to suppress the liberation movement, but also as a loyal watchdog of the
interests of foreign monopolies, mainly North American, in this region of the
world."[64] The Somoza government was described as a "dictatorial regime" which
remained "in power due to brute force."[65] The Carter administration claimed it
was embarrassed by "Somoza and his ilk" and criticized Nicaragua for the hypo-
critical nature of its human rights policy. However, as *Radio Moscow* observed,
"it so happens that Washington's words do not match up in any way with their
actions. While moralizing on the necessity for respecting civil rights, the United
States has at the same time resumed military aid to Anastasio Somoza, one of
the vilest tyrants not only in Central America, but in all Latin America."[66]

At this point, Moscow began to observe that international opposition to the
Somoza regime and U.S. assistance were both rapidly expanding. The assertion
of growing international opposition is both a central theme and an objective of
Soviet propaganda campaigns. It plays a key part in efforts by the USSR and
their surrogates and fronts to mobilize opinion and opposition worldwide. According to *Pravda* of September 8, 1978, "[T]he struggle of the Nicaraguans
. . . is meeting with broad support from the world public. Venezuela has urged
the United Nations to help ensure conditions for expression of the Nicaraguan
people's will."[67] On September 14, 1978, TASS reported that the "influential
political figure . . . Senator Frank Church demanded an end to all U.S. aid to
Nicaragua."[68] In other words, this opposition was growing both internationally
and within influential circles in the United States.

The extent of Moscow's international commentary reached a new plateau in
1979. The revolution in Nicaragua and U.S. policy were the major issues covered. Themes prior to Somoza's departure included U.S. maneuvers to maintain
Somoza in power, the inevitability of the Sandinista victory, and growing international solidarity and support for the insurgent victory.

As the events unfolded in Nicaragua, the United States was charged with
planning a major intervention "in the domestic affairs of Nicaragua . . . The
United States not only continues but also increases military support to the So-

moza regime."[69] Washington also allegedly utilized "the latest methods of ideo-logical sabotage" as a "means of misinforming the Latin Americans with the communist threat."[70] The real objective of this ideological offensive was to "im-plant in the hemisphere bloody, repressive and fascist regimes and support them."[71] In the case of Somoza, during 1979 the United States was said to be undertaking all measures necessary to prop up his regime, including preparing to intervene.[72]

The Sandinistas, as might be expected, were characterized in quite positive terms. Successful military operations were frequently reported and placed within the context of the inevitability of victory.[73] In conjunction with this, the justness of the Sandinista movement was said to have engendered international support and solidarity.[74]

Following the FSLN victory, Soviet propaganda presented a picture of Moscow-Managua solidarity. Leonid Brezhnev stated that "the Soviet Union ex-presses readiness to normalize diplomatic relations and to develop multifaceted ties with Nicaragua."[75] The FSLN leadership was receptive, as Daniel Ortega observed, "The Nicaraguan government is striving to consolidate relations with the USSR . . . Soviet-Nicaraguan relations will strengthen and will become a stronger bulwark for our revolution."[76]

In the months following the revolution, Soviet propaganda warned of an impending U.S. counterrevolution.[77] For example, TASS of November 10, 1979, reported that the "U.S. spy agency is working out plans to subvert the revolution in Nicaragua." It is "preparing various . . . plans of interference . . . with the aim of splitting the revolutionary forces and destabilizing the situa-tion."[78] This appears to have anticipated events by two years.

By the end of 1979, coverage of Central American politics expanded to include growing commentary about El Salvador. It would be "the next Central American country to be gripped by . . . antidictatorial struggle."[79] Since then it has remained at the center of Soviet propaganda focused on the region. Between 1980 and 1982 these efforts intensified and included the following themes: the revolutionary insurgency was reaching its final stages, U.S. interference was continuing to escalate, El Salvador and Vietnam were analogous, the United States bears responsibility for atrocities, and opposition was growing to U.S. policy.

As previously demonstrated, Soviet propaganda attempts to present the in-surgent cause as just and success as inevitable.[80] According to *Izvestiya* of Jan-uary 8, 1981, the "U.S. cannot halt the Central American revolutionary tide,"[81] and on January 11, 1981, TASS provided extensive coverage as the FMLN "launched a decisive offensive against the reactionary junta."[82] As the "final offensive" unfolded, Soviet propaganda continued to expand. However, when it failed, there was little commentary.

The political program of the insurgents was also covered. For instance, it is not uncommon to find TASS or *Pravda* carrying a communiqué or segments of the political program of the FMLN. On January 12, 1981, for instance, TASS published a communiqué by the FMLN outlining the program to be implemented after the revolution.[83]

The U.S. involvement in El Salvador received extensive and negative commentary. As in the Vietnam case study, U.S. policy was described as "convulsively trying to preserve its dominance in this country . . . the military-civilian junta in El Salvador is kept in power only by American support." The Reagan administration policy was "feverishly arming the regime in El Salvador" and "muscle-flexing . . . in the Caribbean."[84] Administration defense of its policy was rejected out of hand, as a TASS report of Secretary of State Alexander Haig's remarks to the Senate Appropriations Committee demonstrates:

> In an attempt to justify actions that smack of interventionism Haig reverted to his pet theme and again groundlessly spoke about interference by Cuba and other "East bloc countries" in the affairs of El Salvador, tried to convince his listeners that this invention of his— the "subversive activity" of socialist countries was "threatening stability and international peace." But it is universally known that a real but not mythical threat to El Salvador just as to other Central American countries is posed exactly by the United States.[85]

At another point the administration was criticized for sending "cutthroats from among the American Green Berets corps" to El Salvador. The report went on to explain that the "Green Berets became notoriously known for the atrocities they perpetrated during the Vietnam War." In El Salvador they "instruct . . . terrorists and criminals in fighting their own people."[86]

Attempts by the Reagan administration to seek a negotiated solution were described as maneuvers and not as a reflection of policy. Legitimate peace proposals, like that of José Lopez Portillo of Mexico, had been sidestepped by Washington, revealing its willingness to continue "threatening the security of the Central American and Caribbean nations."[87] The electoral process in El Salvador had been manipulated by Washington. The U.S. objective in the 1982 election, according to Moscow, was to "install in El Salvador a government that would be responsive to Washington's plans."[88] Additionally, the Reagan administration policy in El Salvador was straightforwardly and often portrayed as analogous to the U.S. experience in Vietnam. For example, on January 6, 1981, *Radio Moscow* stated,

> The demagoguery about "human rights" has been drowned out by the notorious "domino theory," all but forgotten since the American aggressors' defeat in Vietnam. The Washington "Hawks" began loudly intimidating people with the idea that the flames of the revolution in

Nicaragua would spread to neighboring countries and that this chain reaction could spread even further across the area south of the Rio Grande.[89]

During 1982 the Vietnam analogy was amplified further. "If we assess the new U.S. policy in this region, we will see several well known methods and trends . . . similar to the escalation of U.S. interference in Vietnam in the 1960s. This interference began . . . with a small group of military advisers that grew . . . to more than 500,000 officers and men."[90] As the U.S. and the West European press began to "refer to El Salvador as the Second Vietnam," Soviet propaganda channels were quick to replay their commentary.[91] As with U.S. policy in Vietnam, the Reagan administration's policy in El Salvador was alleged to cause great suffering and world public opinion was rapidly mobilizing against it.

Although the United States was not directly committing atrocities in El Salvador, it was charged with "training, equipping, and directing those who were." In El Salvador, Washington was operating through the "ruling junta, which has become an obedient tool in its hands . . . the genocide policy has already meant that 10,000 people have died and 3,000 disappeared without a trace," stated *Izvestiya* on January 6, 1981.[92] *Radio Moscow* labeled this intervention "by proxy" and observed that U.S. "advisers are playing a big role in the punitive operations which junta troops carry out against patriotic forces and civilians."[93] Throughout 1981–1982, the United States was identified as the source of all real and alleged excesses in El Salvador.[94]

Soviet commentary likewise stressed growing domestic and international opposition to U.S. policy in El Salvador. In terms of the former, opposition voices in the Congress received special notice. The following examples are characteristic of how these statements were replayed. On March 25, 1981, TASS noted that the Reagan administration plan of "stepping up support of the military junta in El Salvador" had "come under growing criticism in Congress . . . Clarence Long (Democrat-Maryland), who recently returned from a trip to El Salvador, came out against U.S. involvement."[95] On April 13, 1981, it was reported that "Congressman Michael Barnes has strongly criticized the U.S. administration's policy of all-around support to the Salvadoran junta which launched bloody terror against the people."[96] Similarly, on May 3, 1981, *Pravda* observed that the "House of Representatives Foreign Affairs Committee had voted by an overwhelming majority against granting military aid to the Salvadoran junta. The committee vote . . . reflects the mounting opposition to the Reagan administration's shortsighted policy on El Salvador."[97] The objective was not only to suggest "mounting opposition" but also to imply that it was approaching the level of overwhelming resistance both at home and in the international arena.[98]

The pattern during 1980–1982 is remarkably consistent with what was described in the Vietnam case study. The specific themes parallel one another with marked congruence. Although there are important differences between Vietnam and El Salvador, Soviet propaganda did not take these into account. The objective was to discredit the Salvadoran government as a brutal and illegitimate tool of the United States. Washington had embarked on another Vietnam adventure. The U.S. attempts to defend its Central American policy as necessary to prevent Soviet-Cuban subversion were maligned. Growing opposition in the United States revealed that the Reagan administration had been unable to amass domestic support. Opposition was also growing internationally as support for the cause of the insurgents mounted, and the FMLN, in a manner resembling the strategy of the Sandinistas, was now entering the final stage of the insurrection.

I have previously outlined the failure of the FMLN final offensive. As a result, the guerrillas reverted to a prolonged war strategy of attrition and economic sabotage, while drawing on assistance from Nicaragua, Cuba, and other Soviet surrogates to increase military strength. Soviet propaganda, in the aftermath of the failure of the final offensive, has generally reiterated the themes described above but with the recognition that the conflict will be protracted and prolonged because of the Reagan administration's policy in El Salvador and Nicaragua. Although this may be the case, Moscow's description of the measures taken by the United States is presented in the following familiar terms.

Broadly, this is part of growing U.S. aggressiveness concentrated on the Third World. According to Moscow, the intervention by the administration in El Salvador "is yet another link in the chain of attempts by U.S. imperialism to crush national liberation movements by crude military force."[99] To accomplish this, new interventionist military commands have been established and the CIA assigned a central role. With respect to the former, Soviet propaganda has concentrated on the Joint Special Operations Command (JSOC) and the Rapid Deployment Force. The JSOC, which includes the Special Forces (Green Berets), received the harshest verbal attack. According to TASS, the reason for establishing this new command by "U.S. ruling circles" is "to suppress guerrilla movements—i.e., the peoples' national liberation struggle." The United States had "made international terrorism an instrument of state policy."[100] Within this context, the Special Forces have been described as "murderers and goons who left their bloody mark on Indochina" and "gangs of sophisticated killers."[101] Additionally, TASS has charged that "the CIA's role in executing the policy . . . has grown and keeps growing even further."[102]

During this period, the charge that the United States is planning either direct or indirect military intervention has received extensive coverage. Within the region, both El Salvador and Nicaragua have been identified as the principal targets. In the case of the Sandinistas, this has especially increased as U.S. support to the contras has grown.

In addition to conducting a propaganda campaign on behalf of the FMLN, the Soviet Union and its surrogates provided the guerrillas with the means to carry out their own propaganda efforts. Since December of 1980, the Salvadoran insurgents have been broadcasting from Nicaragua to El Salvador using a new radio station, *Radio Liberacion*. The U.S. State Department claims that this is heavily subsidized by the Sandinista regime.[103]

International Front Organizations

The themes identified in the Soviet Central American propaganda campaign were advanced through the Kremlin's major international front organizations. As in the previously examined cases, the fronts utilized the instruments of propaganda and conference diplomacy, which resulted in a number of international and regional conferences on Central American issues. The overall campaign, however, has not approached the level of sophistication and intensity found in the previous examples, and nothing resembling the Stockholm conference campaign on Vietnam has evolved. Front conference activity has escalated since 1978, but these efforts have been dispersed among several fronts. Although of growing importance, Central American issues do not appear to be a "major priority" for any of the principal front organizations. Nevertheless, since 1978 they have focused considerable attention on these subjects.

Reflecting growing Kremlin interest and involvement in the region, Soviet front group propaganda and political action expanded during the final stages of the revolution in Nicaragua. The World Peace Council (WPC) and other fronts utilized their publications to promote many of the same themes found in Soviet foreign propaganda and coordinated their conference activities on these subjects. In the case of the WPC, its local affiliates in the United States focused their activities, in part, on the issue of revolution in Central America and U.S. policy.

As with Soviet commentary, front propaganda was slow to respond to events in Nicaragua during late 1977 and early 1978. During 1977, for instance, developments in Latin America received only general treatment in *New Perspectives*, the major propaganda journal of the WPC. Furthermore, a comparison with coverage of other issues reveals that these developments were of secondary importance, which was also true of the World Federation of Trade Union's (WFTU's) *World Trade Union Movement* and other front organization publications.

Furthermore, even when Latin America was the main subject of examination, Nicaragua was overlooked. For instance, 1977 issues of *New Perspectives* contain a series of articles on fascism and dictatorships in Chile, Brazil, Paraguay, Uruguay, Bolivia, and Haiti.[104] Ironically, although the authors foresaw the eventual success of revolutionary forces in each of these places, Nicaragua, the place where a Marxist-Leninist movement eventually came to power, was not covered. During 1977 only one brief essay on this subject appeared in *New Perspectives*, and a special issue devoted to the WPC's 1977 World Assembly of the Builders of Peace did not mention Nicaragua in the Latin American and Caribbean report from the conference.[105] A similar trend can be found in the publications of other major front organizations.

Only in 1979 did the FSLN receive serious support in Soviet front-group propaganda. Once under way, three themes were stressed: the necessity of armed struggle in support of the just cause of the insurgents,[106] the repressive nature of the Somoza regime,[107] and U.S. support for the Nicaraguan government and its commitment to intervene to maintain Somoza in power.[108] The overt propaganda campaign of the fronts, belated though it was, carried a basically simple message that was played back through international and regional conference activities. Nevertheless, it is apparent that the WPC, the WFTU, and other fronts were playing "catch up" in 1979, reacting to rapidly moving developments in Nicaragua.

Following the seizure of power in Nicaragua, Soviet front organization propaganda took a more active (as opposed to reactive) stance in its coverage of the insurgency in El Salvador. Since 1980, U.S. policy in the region, specifically in El Salvador, became the primary target, which mirrored developments in Soviet commentary. The U.S. policy in El Salvador was cast within the broader charge of repression and imperialism. According to the May 1981 issue of WFTU's *World Trade Union Movement:*

> [T]he Reagan administration in the U.S.A. continues to defy world public opinion. In close alliance with such executioners of human rights as Pinochet's junta in Chile, the Reagan administration is pouring arms and military "advisers" into El Salvador to back up the repression of the popular forces. In order to justify this open support of terror and repression in El Salvador, a campaign of misinformation and lies has been launched by the Reagan administration accusing the victims of terror of being "terrorists." All this is painfully reminiscent of the Pentagon's invention of the Gulf of Tonkin incident, which was the prelude to naked aggression in Vietnam.[109]

This passage, which reflects the Soviet campaign, is indicative of the line taken by the fronts. A major part of their regional commentary was refocused to excoriate U.S. policy; combined with this theme was the assertion that El Salvador is analogous to Vietnam: "U.S. imperialism is trying to repeat in El Salvador the adventurist warmongering policy put into effect in Vietnam, thus jeopardizing the stability and peace of Central America."[110]

The other major themes of this campaign—the legitimacy of the Salvadoran insurgents and their impending victory—were replayed frequently as the FMLN initiated the "final offensive." During that time, *New Perspectives, World Trade Union Movement,* and similar front publications concentrated on these topics.

Following the defeat of the FMLN's attempt to seize power, front propaganda became less intensive and the campaign broadened to encompass a wider range of issues in the region.

This effort appears, in retrospect, to have been an example of concentrating assets on a target of opportunity. Consequently, when El Salvador seemed to be approaching the brink, limited assets were stretched to respond to a crisis situation. The major targets appear to be within the Central American region. Front propaganda and political action focused on elites, political parties, unions, and related organizations. Perhaps this explains the articulation of a few major themes, as opposed to Soviet commentary, which was directed at the broader international community.

In conjunction with this propaganda campaign, during 1979 the number of regional and international conference activities of the fronts began to increase. Unlike the previous cases, however, these conferences and meetings were small (in size and scope) and regionally focused. Few programs approached the efforts described in earlier chapters. In terms of scope, Nicaragua and El Salvador are sometimes treated separately or combined into larger undertakings.

Although preceded by earlier activities, the first major front conference occurred July 13–15, 1979, in Caracas.[111] Sponsored by the WPC, this World Conference of Solidarity with Nicaragua was attended by 300 representatives from 60 countries, with many participants from Latin America. The objective was to build support and recognition for Nicaragua and its provisional government. The conference called for international support for FSLN admission into the Nonaligned Movement, the U.N. Conference on Trade and Development, the Group of 77 (developing countries), and the General Assembly of the U.N.[112] In late September 1979, the WPC Presidential Committee meeting, which was held in Panama, amplified the same message and presented "testimony" on human rights violations in El Salvador.[113]

During 1980–1981 a number of the fronts utilized their own organizational meetings, as well as regional and international conferences, to build support for the themes described above. For instance, the World Federation of Democratic Youth (WFDY) sponsored a Caribbean Youth Anti-Imperialism seminar during the summer of 1980. Held in Jamaica, the seminar focused on U.S. imperialism and its efforts to destabilize El Salvador and other states in the region.[114] On a much broader plane, the WPC devoted part of its World Parliament of Peoples for Peace to Central American issues. Attended by delegates from 137 countries, 326 political parties, and 100 international organizations (including U.N. committees), the conference included a commission on national liberation movements in Central America and human rights hearings focused partially on El Salvador.[115]

During 1981, the WFDY, the International Organization of Journalists (IOJ), the WPC, and other fronts took part in the Central American effort. The

IOJ, in conjunction with its regional affiliate, the Federation of Latin American Journalists, convened a world meeting of journalists in Managua. The session was used, in part, to express solidarity with "the revolutionary process in Nicaragua" and "struggle against imperialism in Central America and the Caribbean."[116] Note how quickly the Sandinistas involved Nicaragua in Soviet front political actions. As we shall see below, Nicaragua was the site for other front-sponsored conferences focused on Central American issues. For instance, the Latin American and Caribbean youth meeting was held in Managua and promoted the same message sponsored by the WFDY, condemning U.S. military maneuvers against Nicaragua and El Salvador. The WPC Presidential Committee meeting, convened in Havana, followed the same script.[117]

Even though the failure of the FMLN "final offensive" was a setback, Soviet front political action continued but at a more deliberate pace. Furthermore, in addition to those already mentioned, other front organizations became involved. For instance, WFTU's tenth congress, which met in Havana during February 1982, devoted considerable attention to El Salvador and other Central American issues.[118] During the summer of the same year, the International Union of Students (IUS) sponsored a tribunal on U.S. imperialism that focused on the "struggle of the Central American peoples."[119]

This general pattern has continued since 1982, as a number of fronts periodically initiate various political actions focused on El Salvador and Nicaragua. During the spring of 1983, the WPC and its Nicaraguan affiliate convened a conference on peace and sovereignty in Central America. During the summer the WPC issued a booklet entitled *Against Imperialist Aggression and Intervention in Central America and the Caribbean.*[120] The United States and eastern Caribbean states intervened in Grenada during the fall of 1983, which was followed by an escalation of front political action. The WPC sponsored an emergency peace meeting in Mexico City November 2–4, 1983, to discuss peace in Central America in view of developments in Grenada. The meeting adopted a declaration on Grenada, a resolution on Central America, and a program for action against U.S. policy.

During the spring of 1984 the WPC, in conjunction with the Afro-Asian People's Solidarity Organization, the International Association of Democratic Lawyers, the IUS, the WFDY, and the Women's International Democratic Federation, formed an international preparatory committee for an international conference of solidarity with Nicaragua and Central America under the auspices of the nongoverning organizations.[121] The Latin American affiliates of the WPC also convened a regional meeting on this and related issues.[122] Similar events were held during the remainder of 1984.

The conference activities described above provide a means to observe how the fronts take the themes amplified in their publications and employ them in political action campaigns. Unlike the previous cases, however, this one proceeded in a somewhat divergent fashion. To begin with, rather than one front playing the predominant role, a number of them mobilized to take part. Evidently, the decision appears to have been made to offset the problem of limited assets by combining the efforts of several organizations rather than assigning the Central American "account" to any one front. The sample of conference activities confirms this multiorganizational approach. A second difference is the emphasis on regional rather than international actions. In the case of Central America, targeting appears to have been on elites, parties, unions, and other groupings in this region.

At the national level Soviet international fronts use their affiliates to conduct propaganda and political action. With respect to Central American issues, the activities of the U.S. Peace Council (USPC) are noteworthy. Founded in 1979, the USPC, an affiliate of the WPC, has been active in the United States since 1980.

The USPC leadership is staffed in large part by members of the U.S. Communist Party (CPUSA).[123] The USPC, since its inception, has focused on the nuclear freeze and the revolution in Central America and been active in the protest movement in the United States that opposes the Reagan administration policy in El Salvador and Nicaragua. During 1980, the USPC played a role in the establishment of the Committee in Solidarity with the People of El Salvador (CISPES), one of the most active organizations seeking to end U.S. support for El Salvador.[124] The CISPES steering committee includes members of the USPC.

An early CISPES action was to circulate a forgery labeled *Dissent Paper on El Salvador and Central America*. The document claimed to represent the views of the intelligence community and the Departments of State and Defense. The unsigned article warned of U.S. policy in El Salvador "leading to increased military engagement with far-reaching implications for our strategic interests." The authors went on to state that the purpose of "this dissenting paper" was to "promote open discussion (in the Carter and Reagan administrations) of realistic alternatives to our potential escalated military involvement in Central America and the Caribbean."[125] The fabrication was used as the basis for a *New York Times* article on March 6, 1981. The *Times* subsequently admitted on March 9, 1981, that it had been misled.

Additionally, CISPES publishes the *El Salvador Alert,* which supports the insurgents while condemning U.S. policy in Central America. A major theme of CISPES propaganda has been the Vietnam–El Salvador analogy. One finds similar themes in the literature of the USPC. Additionally, in its 1981 program for action this U.S. affiliate of the WPC set the following objectives: "building support movements, in cooperation with existing solidarity organizations, and through . . . teach-ins and demonstrations for the Salvadoran people fighting to defeat the ruling fascist junta."[126] In the spring of 1982, before the elections in El Salvador, CISPES and the USPC organized one such demonstration in Washington. Also at this time representatives of the USPC and CISPES helped form the World Front in Solidarity with the People of El Salvador (FMSPS).[127] The principal objective of the FMSPS is to build international support for the FMLN. Since its inception the FMSPS has established ties with national-level groups in the United States, Canada, Mexico, Colombia, Puerto Rico, Jamaica, and the Dominican Republic, as well as in a number of West European states.[128]

Finally, the solidarity coordinator for the USPC and other CPUSA members assisted Farid Handal, brother of the chief of the El Salvador Communist Party, during his February 1980 visit to the United States. According to his report, he visited the United States to solicit support for the revolution in El Salvador. During his trip to Washington, D.C., Handal noted that members of the CPUSA played an important role in the arrangements for meetings with members of the U.S. Congress. Other parts of the report discuss his visits to New York, Chicago, San Francisco, Los Angeles, and San Jose and meetings with other elements of the movement opposing U.S. policy in El Salvador.[129]

Political Activities in International Organizations

In the case of the South-West Africa People's Organization and the PLO, the Soviet bloc worked closely with radical Afro-Asian states to use the U.N. as a forum to promote the cause and enhance the legitimacy of these insurgent movements. In each instance, this was carried out through specialized U.N. committees. As the Kremlin began to focus on insurgency movements in Central America, however, there was no U.N. committee through which to pursue a related course of political action. As a result, Moscow appears to have refocused its efforts on the Nonaligned Movement and the Socialist International. In each instance, overtly or clandestinely, Cuba played an important role.

During the 1960s and 1970s, the Nonaligned Movement supported the cause of guerrilla movements in Africa and the Middle East, including an active role on their behalf in the U.N. The Soviets seek to utilize all avenues to raise the international credibility of the national liberation movements they back, and they apparently view the Nonaligned Movement as one such avenue. To understand this, a brief review of the history of the Nonaligned Movement is necessary, as well as an understanding of how Cuba came to play an important role in this aspect of Soviet policy.

When the nonaligned nations gathered in Havana in September 1979 for their sixth summit, the 94 delegations in attendance included representatives from virtually the entire Third World. The Nonaligned Movement had come a long way from the 1960s; by the mid-1970s it had taken on many of the characteristics of an international organization. It had developed an institutional structure that included an office of chairman and convened summits at three-year intervals, including a foreign ministers' conference in the year before each summit. In 1973 a coordinating bureau was established to implement nonaligned policy at the U.N. and to organize annual ministerial meetings. Since the mid-1970s, the deliberations of the nonaligned have had an impact on both the annual agenda of the U.N. General Assembly (in which they constitute an overwhelming majority) and the continuing north-south dialogue.

The selection of Cuba as host for the sixth summit and therefore as chairman of the nonaligned nations symbolized a potentially important shift in the movement's political orientation. When the world's leading neutralists organized in 1961, their primary aim was to ease international tensions and stand clear of the bipolarism that characterized the international system.[130] By 1979, the priorities of the movement and the means by which they were to be pursued had undergone considerable change.[131] Thus, the nonaligned have become increasingly radical at the expense of internal tensions and strains.

The roots of the Nonaligned Movement can be traced to the 1955 Bandung Conference of Afro-Asian States, the first major gathering of Third World countries.[132] In 1961, the Nonaligned Movement convened its first major international conference, focusing on the themes of anticolonialism, economic development, and peaceful coexistence. Held in Belgrade and attended by 25 nations, the tone of the conference was conciliatory. As long as the nonaligned focused on ameliorating international tension as a first priority, they maintained a position equidistant between East and West. However, as the issues of colonialism, imperialism, national liberation, and international economics came to the fore, nonalignment took on an increasingly anti-Western hue.

Cuba was a founding member of the Nonaligned Movement and, during the 1960s, the only Latin America affiliate. At that time Cuban foreign policy was at odds with the majority position of the Nonaligned Movement.[133] As one of the radical members, Havana emphasized the issues of imperialism, anticolonialism, and underdevelopment and rejected the position of neutrality between East and West as irrational, arguing that the Third World and the socialist camp shared many concerns. Cuba likewise found itself at odds with the prevailing consensus in the U.N. during the 1960s but benefited from membership in the organization. On certain issues, although not the radical ones, Cuba enjoyed the support of nonaligned members. Additionally, membership in the Nonaligned Movement tended to soften the image of Cuba as a "Soviet proxy" in Latin America.

Early in the Nonaligned Movement's second decade, moderation gave way to radicalism over the question of the international economic order. The 1973 nonaligned summit in Algiers declared that "imperialism is still the greatest obstacle on the road toward emancipation and progress of the developing countries . . . Imperialism does not only oppose the economic progress of the developing countries, but also adopts a more aggressive attitude toward those who oppose its intentions."[134] However, the conference split over who constituted the imperialists. Algeria proposed a theory of "two imperialisms," one capitalist, the other communist. Cuba asserted that the socialist countries were the "natural allies" of the nonaligned. In the end, the communist bloc was not labeled as imperialist, and Castro emerged as one of the movement's leading spokesmen.

As the nonaligned moved left, the Cuban role expanded and its foreign policy became increasingly pro-Soviet in orientation and action.[135] Anticolonialism, national liberation, imperialism, and economic development dominated the agenda of the nonaligned. Castro also continued to promote the position that the nonaligned should ally with the socialist countries. During the early 1970s, the Nonaligned Movement focused attention on national liberation movements. For example, the 1973 summit took a strong position in favor of the PLO and passed a Declaration on the Struggle for National Liberation.[136] The nonaligned actively promoted this issue in the U.N. in the early 1970s, influencing its agenda. Active support for national liberation movements actually began in 1970 when the nonaligned accepted as a member the South Vietnam provisional revolutionary government (Viet Cong). The fifth nonaligned conference placed even greater emphasis on its responsibility to national liberation movements and implicitly praised the communist bloc's support of them.[137] Sri Lanka praised Cuba for its role in Angola.[138] During the latter half of the 1970s, support for national liberation became a central theme of the nonaligned, focusing on movements in Africa and the Middle East.

Cuba emerged as a prominent member of the nonaligned, but tension continued to exist over its contention that the communist bloc was a natural ally of the Third World. Tito went so far as to imply that Cuba represented a new form of colonialism in Africa. Cuba replied that its policy in Angola and Ethiopia was consistent with nonaligned support of the principles of self-determination and nonintervention. The importance of Cuba in the Nonaligned Movement was signaled by its selection as the site of the sixth summit in 1979. Apparently, Havana (and Moscow) saw the 1979 meeting as an opportunity to consolidate gains and shift the movement further left. Additionally, the summit was used to introduce new issues, including national liberation and colonialism in Latin America.

Although there were disagreements at Havana in 1979, the summit was unanimous in its condemnation of U.S. imperialism, especially in Latin America. Cuba also hoped to take the nonaligned states in a direction more in harmony with Soviet interests, which included acceptance of the communist bloc as a "natural ally" of the nonaligned.

In terms of this study the focusing of nonaligned attention on the issues of imperialism and national liberation in Latin America was an important development.[139] Castro stressed the need to actively support armed struggle in Latin America and Africa and to oppose the imperial and neocolonial nature of U.S. foreign policy. These themes were articulated in the documents adopted by the summit. For example, the political declaration on Latin American issues began by condemning U.S. policy in the region:

> Latin America is one of the regions of the world that historically has suffered greatly from the aggression of the United States imperialism, colonialism, and neocolonialism . . . The Conference condemned the presence of foreign military bases in Latin America and the Caribbean . . . as a threat to peace and security in the region, and again demanded that the United States restore to those countries . . . their territories occupied against their will.[140]

The summit documents "greeted with satisfaction the victory of the Nicaraguan people and their vanguard, the Sandinista Liberation Front, over the Somoza dictatorship, the product of imperialist intervention."[141] The FSLN was officially welcomed as a member of the Nonaligned Movement, as was the Maurice Bishop government in Grenada.[142] The summit's economic resolution called for "aid and solidarity for reconstructing Nicaragua" and urged "all member countries of the movement to give their support to the International Solidarity Fund for the Reconstruction of Nicaragua."[143] The political declaration also called on the U.N. to "carry out emergency projects of aid to Nicaragua" and "warned of the need to maintain international vigilance over machinations directed against the long-suffering and heroic Nicaraguan people." Finally, Nicaragua was to serve as the model for revolution throughout Central America and the Caribbean.[144]

In sum, the Havana conference widened the scope of nonaligned support for national liberation movements to include those in Latin America. Although this may prove to be an important long-term development, it did not receive the coverage of three other controversial issues: Who should represent Kampuchea? Would Egypt be suspended from the nonaligned ranks? Should the communist bloc be recognized as a natural ally? Excessive Cuban pressure on the third issue resulted in unexpected opposition to Havana. The final declaration of the summit omitted virtually all references to cooperation with the communist bloc.[145]

Both radicals and moderates scored some notable successes at the Havana summit, and other issues were settled through compromise. On balance, parts of the Cuban agenda were achieved, reflected by subsequent developments. Although the movement seems to have reached an uneasy equilibrium after the 1979 summit, nonaligned support for the theme of national liberation in Latin America has not diminished. Placing this theme on the nonaligned agenda broadened it from a regional to an international issue. In the years following the Havana summit, the dual issues of U.S. imperialism and national liberation in Latin America remained important agenda items. In this respect, it appears that Cuba took an issue that was a "natural one" for the nonaligned (national liberation) and promoted it successfully within the movement. This, more than likely, was seen by Moscow as another way of rallying international opinion in support of insurgent movements like the Sandinistas and the FMLN. Thus can shared interests be maneuvered to serve the policy objectives of the Soviet Union and its Cuban surrogate.

In the aftermath of the Havana summit, Nicaragua was welcomed into the U.N., while within the U.N., Third World and communist bloc countries publicly supported insurgency in El Salvador and elsewhere in Central America. Because no specialized committee structure exists similar to that of the Committee of 24 or the Committee on the Exercise of the Inalienable Rights of the Palestinian People, it does not appear that the U.N. provides the same opportunities, except as a public forum, for the USSR on the issue of insurgency in El Salvador and elsewhere in Central America. Nevertheless, the importance of the Nonaligned Movement cannot be discounted.

On a smaller and more clandestine scale the Cubans also attempted to influence the position of the Socialist International (SI) on Central American issues. Documents captured in Grenada not only confirm Havana's attempt to influence the organization but also reveal the surrogate role played by the New Jewel Movement (the ruling party in Grenada headed by Maurice Bishop) on behalf of the USSR and Cuba. The most interesting of these documents identifies a "secret regional caucus" of "progressive forces" from Central America and the Caribbean that apparently had been formed and operated in cooperation with the Cuban Communist Party (CCP).[146] The inclusion of the CCP in the list of participants at a meeting of the secret caucus is significant because the SI officially bars membership by communist states. A review of the documents reveals that Cuba was operationally involved in a secret attempt to influence the SI; meanwhile, members of the SI were debating whether or not to establish relations with Cuba. The issue was debated on the pages of the SI publication *Socialist Affairs*. For example, Jean Ziegler, a Social Democratic member of the Swiss Federal Parliament, argued:

> In that ocean of suffering which constitutes Latin America, Cuba is today an island of light. Thus, the Cuban revolution has become the cause of all free men on earth . . . What is the state of relations, in mid-1981, between the Socialist International and Cuba? They are at a standstill . . . The SI must establish clear and durable relations with Cuba.[147]

Other members of the SI disagreed. The international secretary of the Portuguese Socialist Party asserted that Cuba did not comply with the SI's basic principles approved in Frankfurt in 1951: "International communism is the instrument of a new imperialism which falsely claims a share in the socialist tradition."[148]

The Bishop government in Grenada sought to use its affiliation in the SI to conduct active measures on behalf of its Cuban and Soviet patrons. The New Jewel Movement and other members of the secret caucus were to focus on promoting "progressive and revolutionary forces" from the region, including the FSLN government of Nicaragua and the FMLN guerrillas in El Salvador.[149] Grenada's report on the SI's fifteenth congress documents this operation.

> In making a comparative analysis of this Congress' section on Latin America and the Caribbean with the previous Congress, one clearly observes important progress . . . The way the Congress dealt with Nicaragua is truly illustrative . . . The establishment of an International Committee for the Defense of the Nicaraguan Revolution and the support of the SI to the Sandinista Front is unmistakable proof.[150]

This operation exemplifies how the USSR can take advantage of shared interests to maneuver an international organization to take steps that serve Soviet foreign policy goals and how Soviet regional clients can play a central role in these political actions.

Arms Transfers

Earlier we described Cuba's role in unifying the three factions of the FSLN. Negotiations occurred throughout 1978, and a formal alliance was established in March 1979. Before these developments, the shortage of arms had been a serious problem. The FSLN initiated an urban offensive in August and rural combat in November of 1978, but its ability to maintain military pressure on the Somoza government was constrained by equipment shortfalls. According to Nolan, "the continuing arms shortage made the retrieval of weapons and munitions the major tactical objective of any engagement."[151]

During 1977–1978 as the FSLN began to re-emerge in Nicaragua, arms were provided by various Latin American countries, including Venezuela, Panama, and Costa Rica. Cuba also provided small amounts of assistance. Once the factions were unified, however, Havana increased military support operations and concentrated on establishing a logistic network for channeling military assistance to the FSLN, using a network set up near the northern Costa Rican city of Liberia.[152] Cuban aircraft flew directly to the airport in Liberia with arms that allowed the Sandinistas to offset the conventional military superiority of the Nicaraguan National Guard. This logistic support was important in the FSLN "final offensive." According to Eden Pastora, Cuban assistance first came through Panama and then Costa Rica. In the case of the former, he believes Omar Torrijos, the head of Panama and then Costa Rica, sought to prevent the Sandinistas from becoming too closely aligned with Havana.

Omar Torrijos made what I consider was a very intelligent maneuver. He asked Fidel for arms for himself, which he then gave to us. Torrijos wanted to insulate us from Cuba . . . In this way we began to receive thousands of rifles, machine guns, bazookas and other types of military equipment through Panama from Cuba . . . Cuba was able to jump over the obstacle that had been erected by Panama. An airlift was started in June and July 1979 between Havana and Liberia . . . Cuban help was now more obvious and the moral commitment to Cuba was now out in the open.[153]

Following the seizure of power, the transformation of the guerrilla force into a regular army became a first priority. By the mid-1980s the number of soldiers on active duty has been estimated at 62,850.[154] In addition, the militia has expanded. Under a nationwide universal military service law, the armed strength of Nicaragua (regulars and reserve) currently numbers more than 100,000.[155] With respect to the conventional arms buildup, the material is almost exclusively from the Soviet bloc, which includes 120 T-54/55 medium tanks and 30 PT-76 light amphibious tanks. With respect to artillery, Nicaragua now has approximately 50 152-mm and 122-mm howitzers as well as 24 122-mm multiple rocket launchers. The Soviets have also supplied various antiaircraft guns and SA-7 surface-to-air missiles. The Sandinista air capabilities include six Mi-24, twelve Mi-8, and six Mi-2 helicopters; a few light transport aircraft; and four tactical support aircraft.[156] The delivery of Soviet MiGs remains a possibility. If this does not occur for political reasons, other substitutes might be acquired. In sum, the Soviet Union and its surrogates have been instrumental in arming the Sandinista military, whose force is unmatched by any other state in the region.

Captured documents and Nicaraguan defectors have described Salvadoran guerrilla bases in Nicaragua, which serve as central command and control, training, and communications facilities. Following the unification of the guerrilla factions in El Salvador (again as the result of Cuban influence), arms shipments through Nicaragua escalated. Communist governments and other suppliers began to send weapons through Cuba and Nicaragua for covert distribution to the guerrillas in El Salvador. The USSR has abstained from acting as a direct supplier, relying instead on such allies and proxies as East European states, Vietnam, and Ethiopia.

By the end of 1980, Nicaragua had become the center for clandestine arms transfers to the FMLN. The origins of some of the arms, however, can be traced back to Warsaw Pact members and other Soviet surrogates. A report by Shafik Handal, head of the Communist Party of El Salvador, on his 1980 trip to Soviet surrogate countries in search of arms, provides a window into this network for acquiring and transporting assistance to insurgent movements. Handal arranged for arms to be smuggled to El Salvador from Bulgaria, Czechoslovakia, East Germany, Hungary, Vietnam, and Ethiopia. The report also discloses the concerted efforts by the USSR and its allies to obscure their involvement. For instance, U.S.-made weapons were to be transferred from Vietnam and Ethiopia. The Czechs were to provide rebuilt World War II weapons and other Czech weapons that are readily available on the world market. Soviet-produced arms, however, were not to be made available, at least at that time. During the trip Handal often met with high-level government officials including Vietnam's Lê Duân, Ethiopia's Haile Mariam Mengistu, and leading officials from the CPSU's International Department.[157] These arms were to be shipped first to Cuba, then airlifted to Nicaragua for subsequent shipment to the FMLN in El Salvador.

The composition of the arms flow to the guerrillas and the collaboration of Nicaragua with Cuba in transshipping these military supplies have been described by former Sandinista and FMLN officials. For example, Alejandro Montenegro, a Salvadoran guerrilla field commander captured in mid-1982, has stated that the arms he received "came from Vietnam to Havana. Havana to Managua. Managua to El Salvador."[158] In addition to Vietnam, he identified Ethiopia, the Soviet bloc, Cuba, and Nicaragua as arms suppliers.[159] Eden Pastora corroborated these observations during an oral history interview:

> As far as what Managua gives the Salvadorans, what I can tell you is the following: I wish that the United States had given me half of what Managua is giving the Salvadorans. The FAL rifles that Castro gave us went to the Salvadorans. [The network that was established in Costa Rica in 1979 for the Sandinistas evidently was redirected and arms still in Costa Rica were infiltrated into El Salvador for the FMLN]. So did the M-16s from Vietnam. Also M1s, M60 machine guns, and light antitank rockets. While air is the most common route used, they also take the arms across the Gulf of Fonseca in small boats. Another route is by land through Honduras.[160]

There is evidence that the PLO has helped transport arms to the FMLN and has also provided other assistance. Yasser Arafat has publicly stated that his organization maintains relations with the FMLN: "We have connections with all revolutionary movements throughout the world, in El Salvador, Nicaragua—and I reiterate Salvador."[161] He has also observed that the PLO has sent pilots to Nicaragua and guerrilla fighters to El Salvador.[162] The relationship between the PLO and the Nicaraguan FSLN was described in an interview with Miguel Bolanos Hunter, a former counterintelligence officer with Nicaraguan State Security.

> The PLO opened an office in Managua within a month of the Revolution, but PLO members had already been involved in fighting . . .

they also train Salvadoran guerrillas at three camps in Nicaragua. One is at Ostional in the southern province of Rivas. I heard this from a Chilean who is also an instructor there. FSLN-PLO relations have existed for quite a long time. They go back to the 1960s. The first links were arranged through Cuba.[163]

As Pastora noted above, the supply network between Nicaragua and El Salvador consists of air, sea, and land routes. Weapons arrive in Nicaragua from Cuba; overland arms shipments reach El Salvador through Honduras from Nicaragua and Costa Rica.[164] According to former guerrilla commander Montenegro, he received shipments mostly by overland routes through Honduras in specially designed trucks.[165] The Honduran military has from time to time intercepted arms moving from Nicaragua to El Salvador. For instance, a group of Salvadoran guerrillas were caught by Honduran security forces in March 1983 with arms and a map tracing a route from Nicaragua through Honduras to El Salvador. In January 1981, the Hondurans captured a truck that contained weapons in a false compartment.

Arms are also transported by small boats from Nicaraguan Pacific ports across the Gulf of Fonseca to El Salvador. One of these transshipment points, La Concha, was visited by the Western media following an attack by contra forces in the fall of 1983. The disguised facilities served as centers for arms transfers to Salvadoran guerrillas.[166] Apparently, other vessels also leave from the Nicaraguan northwestern coast to ship arms and supplies through bays and inlets that dot the coast of El Salvador.[167] Once these small shipments arrive, they are transported along trails to guerrilla redoubts.[168]

Light aircraft have also been used to move arms to the FMLN. Many of these flights originate at Papalonal, a former sugar plantation north of Managua, and drop the supplies into guerrilla-controlled areas in northeastern El Salvador. According to Bolanos, "these planes drop thirty to forty rifles at a time, along with logistic supplies. Because of radar intervention, the Sandinistas use parachute drops to deliver their supplies when it is difficult to make a landing."[169]

The amount of military equipment and logistical support transferred to the FMLN has varied. Situational factors appear to affect the degree of the buildup. For instance, during the rapid preparation for the "final offensive" of 1981, the flow of arms and supplies increased. In the aftermath of the failed offensive, however, the guerrillas reverted to a prolonged-protracted war approach, which demanded a smaller but steadier flow of arms, ammunition, explosives, and related supplies. The improvements in the Salvadoran army since 1982 have kept the FMLN at this stage of insurgent strategy. In light of the FMLN's reliance on attrition, terrorism, and economic sabotage, the guerrillas have required somewhat less support, and their ranks have declined since 1983. Nevertheless, the supply network described above remains intact.

Training Sandinista and FMLN Forces

Political-military training of Sandinista cadres by Cuba and members of the Warsaw Pact and other states dates back to the early 1960s. For instance, Daniel and Humberto Ortega, among others, received guerrilla and command-level military training in Cuba during this early period.[170] At the Tricontinental Congress of 1966, the Cuban government pledged support for revolutionary movements around the world.[171] By the end of the decade, FSLN cadres benefited from this pledge.

In the first half of the 1970s, Sandinista cadres could be found in PLO bases in the Middle East.[172] Earlier in this study I noted that the FSLN took part in terrorist operations with the PLO. During the multiairplane hijacking by the Popular Front for the Liberation of Palestine in Jordan in 1970, a Sandinista died in the operation. Douglas Payne reports that

> [The] first FSLN group traveled in 1969 through Europe to a camp outside Amman, Jordan, where it was joined by a group of FSLN students from Patrice Lumumba University in Moscow led by Henry Ruiz. There they received guerrilla training under the direction of George Habash's Popular Front for the Liberation of Palestine . . . A second group came through Europe in 1970 and was trained at a PLO camp outside Beirut.[173]

During this period FSLN members reportedly also received training in North Korea. In 1971–1972, a group led by Humberto Ortega went to "Czechoslovakia for a first round of training. Subsequently, after being joined by the last students in Moscow, the combined group proceeded to North Korea for six months of military instruction."[174]

During 1976, the FSLN was in serious disarray. Key leaders were either dead, in prison, or outside the country, and factional disagreements had split the movement. During this time, training of cadres in Cuba declined. However, Pastora observed that beginning in mid-1978 special military training resumed.[175] This coincided with the increase of arms transfers and the establishment of a logistics center in northern Costa Rica, as described in the previous section. Apparently, several camps in Cuba are used specifically for training Latin American revolutionaries. Training normally lasts for three to six months and includes instruction in the use of weapons and paramilitary tactics. FSLN cadres going to Cuba during 1978 used Panama as a transit point, and, at this same time, an operational center was set up with Cuban assistance in Costa Rica. By the end of the year Cuban advisers were sent to train FSLN forces in northern Costa Rica. This location, which is contiguous to the zone of conflict, cut down on clandestine transport problems.

Following the seizure of power, the USSR and its surrogates provided the Sandinistas with training and advisory support to help the National Directorate consolidate power during the immediate postrevolutionary period. This was achieved through the development of an internal security infrastructure that could quell internal opposition, mobilize the population, and insulate the leadership cadres. Additionally, to protect against a new form of internal threat—resistance movements employing insurgent strategies—that might challenge these regimes, military and counterinsurgency training and advisory support was required.

Former Sandinista counterintelligence officer Miguel Bolanos Hunter has provided firsthand insight into the Soviet, Cuban, East German, and Bulgarian roles that established the Nicaraguan General Directorate of State Security (DGSE). He notes that within the DGSE apparatus officers from the Cuban intelligence occupy key administrative positions. In fact, the head of the intelligence directorate is a Cuban who has served as a link between the FSLN and Cuba for a number of years. Following the revolution, FSLN cadres were sent to Cuba for intelligence and counterintelligence training. In addition to Cubans, there were Soviet KGB instructors at the intelligence school in Cuba. Bolanos noted that Grenadians and Angolans were receiving similar training; thus, they, as well as the Nicaraguans, were being educated in the art of power consolidation and control. In addition to basic training in counterintelligence skills, Bolanos received special instruction on how to manipulate and manage the foreign media in Nicaragua. Those Nicaraguan cadres who were considered both politically reliable and capable were selected to attend the five-year course at the higher KGB school in Moscow.[176]

In addition to intelligence, Soviet-bloc and Cuban advisers provided training in other power consolidation techniques. Pastora explained that Soviet surrogate military advisers were "in place" almost immediately following Somoza's fall and that they provided training as part of the rapid buildup of the Nicaraguan armed forces. "The first thing that the Cubans did when they arrived was to select who was to be sent for training in Cuba and other Soviet-bloc countries. They chose people for tanks, artillery, and aviation . . . They were chosen on the basis of two criteria—ideological commitment and physical ability."[177]

The Americas Department of the CCP and the Department of Special Operations (DOE) have also been involved in training activities, especially the promotion of guerrilla insurgency in the region. DOE and other Soviet surrogate personnel assist in the training of Salvadoran guerrilla forces. Along with various USSR clients, the FSLN also employs international propaganda assistance to national liberation movements. In cooperation with the CCP's Americas Department, the FSLN established a Department of International Relations to conduct more effective political warfare campaigns in the region. As noted earlier, the objective of these tactics is to assist in legitimizing the cause and actions of the guerrilla movements in the international arena, while discrediting U.S. policy. In sum, one finds coordination between the FSLN's Department of International Relations, the CCP's Americas Department, and the CPSU's International Department, indicating important institutional and operational arrangements.[178] Training of Salvadoran guerrillas increased sharply in 1980 following the unification of the different insurgent factions. Cuba concentrated on helping prepare the FMLN for the 1981 "final offensive." It has been reported that between 250 to 500 guerrillas received instruction at this time.[179] The Sandinistas also provided training to Salvadoran guerrillas and used Nicaragua as a transit point for sending cadres to other external training locations. Captured guerrilla documents reveal that Cuba and Nicaragua continued to coordinate the bulk of FMLN cadre military training following the failure of the "final offensive."[180]

Military training camps for FMLN guerrillas have been identified in various parts of Nicaragua, including bases in the southern province of Rivas, in northwestern Nicaragua near the Tamarindo River, and outside Managua, where Cuban and Nicaraguan personnel serve as instructors, according to Bolanos.[181] Former FMLN commander Montenegro has noted that his forces were trained in base camps both in northwest Nicaragua and in Cuba.[182]

Advisory Support

For analysis purposes, this study has separated training from advisory support. The latter includes the provision of advice on a number of related operational matters, including command and control, irregular combat direction, tactical intelligence, and logistic coordination. Unlike training that can occur in either the surrogate state or the base camps contiguous to the area of conflict, advisory support is generally confined to the latter.

During the final stage of the conflict in Nicaragua, the Cubans apparently provided advisory support to the FSLN. According to Pastora, "during the preparation for the final offensive the Cubans set up an operations center in San José under Julian Lopez Diaz."[183] A member of the Americas Department, Diaz later became the Cuban ambassador to Nicaragua. One of his subordinates in the San José base was Andres Barahona, also known as Renan Montero, apparently a Cuban intelligence officer, now in charge of the intelligence section of the Nicaraguan DGSE. The U.S. State Department has charged that "Cuban military advisers from the Department of Special Operations . . . were with FSLN columns and maintained direct radio communications to Havana."[184]

Cuba also appears to have encouraged other Central American communist parties to support the Sandinistas, including sending cadres to take part in the final stages of the revolution. Nolan has identified internationalist units that were involved during 1979, including groups from Colombia and Panama.[185] Bolanos, during an oral history interview, described an international brigade that fought in northern Nicaragua during the final offensive. In addition to Latin Americans, he noted that PLO members served as combatants.[186] The use of international brigades is not a new development; during the Spanish Civil War such units fought on the side of the republican forces.

In the previous section military camps in Nicaragua for training Salvadoran guerrillas were identified. In addition to instructors, Cuban DOE officials have provided advisory support to the FMLN. Former guerrilla commanders have noted that command, control, communications, and other support activities were established and maintained for the Salvadoran guerrillas by the Sandinistas and the Cubans.[187] Bolanos noted, however, that the Soviets are not involved in training or advisory support of the FMLN in Nicaragua. "We got the impression that the Soviets do not want to go into something if they can do it through a surrogate. Also, because of the possible East-West confrontation, they had to be careful."[188] He also pointed out that Cuban and Nicaraguan advisory assistance extends only to the border of El Salvador. Internationalist elements, however, including Chileans and Montoneros (Argentinian terrorists), do cross over. "They [Cuban and Nicaraguan advisers] sent in Chileans in groups of 10 and 15."[189]

Conclusion

During the 1970s, instability, conflict, terrorism, and guerrilla insurgency expanded in Latin America, thanks, in part, to a host of internal problems and divisions. By the end of the decade, however, outside powers were attempting to exacerbate these conflicts. Soviet foreign policy was slow to recognize the revolutionary potential in the region. During the 1960–1975 period, the Kremlin position on change in Latin America rejected revolutionary insurgent warfare. Moscow proposed a "peaceful road to socialism" approach and directed Latin American communist parties to join broad electoral front coalitions and support parties and even military officers that came to power advocating anti-imperial reforms. The Allende government in Chile symbolized the correctness of the Soviet position; his overthrow in 1973 signaled the flaws.

During the late 1970s, events in Nicaragua led to an important shift in the Kremlin's view of revolutionary potential in Central America. This new position, which recognized that "the armed road . . . is the most promising in the specific conditions of most of the Latin American countries," was stated officially in CPSU comments and publications. However, there is still a debate among Soviet specialists from the institutes of the Academy of Sciences over whether peaceful or armed strategy is appropriate for facilitating social change in Latin America.

The change in policy led to an escalation in Soviet political and military assistance for guerrilla movements, which, in the case of Nicaragua, came only in the final stages of the conflict. With respect to arms, training, and advisory support, the Cubans played a central role. The international propaganda and political action campaign involved the USSR and a number of its surrogates and fronts. Following the FSLN seizure of power, these political and military assets were focused on El Salvador. It appears that the Soviet bloc and Cuba believed that the probability of the FMLN "final offensive" achieving the same results as the FSLN was quite high. The military buildup of the guerrillas, accomplished through Cuban and Nicaraguan arms shipments, training, and advisory assistance, supports this proposition. The escalation in propaganda and political action by the USSR and its surrogates and fronts in support of the Salvadoran guerrillas in 1980–1981 is a second indicator of this policy decision. The evidence suggests that front assets and tactics were stretched at this time to mobilize regional opposition to U.S. policy.

Following the defeat of the FMLN offensive, the guerrillas reverted to a more protracted strategy. Although political and paramilitary assistance continued, Soviet-bloc, Cuban, and Nicaraguan efforts were more modulated. At least three developments seemed to contribute to this decision. First, the correlation of political and military forces between the FMLN and the Salvadoran government had shifted in favor of the latter. Since then improvements in the Salvadoran armed forces have forced the FMLN to protract the conflict, and political reform has cut into its popular support. Second, the United States has demonstrated its resolve to assist the Duarte government and, to a lesser extent, to back the contras in their conflict with the FSLN. Third, Soviet Third World policy over the last five to ten years has taken on a new responsibility. In Afghanistan, Nicaragua, Angola, and Ethiopia, the regimes backed by the USSR have been challenged by noncommunist insurgent movements, which has resulted in Moscow and its surrogates diverting resources and assets to meet these challenges. If it were not for this new threat, these resources could have been used elsewhere. All of the above seem to contribute to the approach now taken by the Soviet bloc, Cuba, and Nicaragua toward the FMLN and other insurgent movements in the region.

SEVEN

Conclusion: Soviet Strategy and Revolutionary Warfare

A
Comparative
Analysis

This study has focused on those aspects of Soviet Third World policy concerned with providing political and military assistance to revolutionary movements conducting insurgent warfare. According to a recent study prepared by the Congressional Research Service for the House Armed Services Committee, this assistance is one element in a range of "special operations" employed by the USSR "to outflank rivals at global, theater, and local levels across the politico-military spectrum." In addition to insurgencies, the study notes that the Soviets focus "particular attention" on "transnational terrorism and psychological operations." Furthermore, "de facto proxies augment Moscow's capabilities, when direct Soviet involvement might be imprudent or too expensive."[1]

What follows is a comparative assessment, on the basis of the four cases in this study, of how the USSR has implemented its political-military strategy for aiding revolutionary insurgent movements. Assessing the findings from the examples, I identify common patterns and differences in Soviet behavior and discuss possible future trends in this aspect of Soviet foreign policy. Will Kremlin leaders continue to respond to protracted revolutionary insurgency in a manner similar to that of the late 1960s through the early 1980s or will the reduced rhetoric of the Twenty-seventh CPSU Congress result in curtailed assistance? I conclude with a postscript that addresses the implications and significance of these developments for U.S. foreign policy.

Trends in Soviet Policy

Since the early years of CPSU rule, the Kremlin leadership has employed various indirect or protracted conflict tactics as part of a policy that aims to shift the correlation of forces to its favor, including support for national liberation or revolutionary insurgent movements. Soviet responsibility for providing this assistance is stipulated in Article 28 of the Soviet Constitution.[2] During the 1970s, however, Soviet involvement in protracted wars in the Third World grew significantly. The Twenty-fourth CPSU Congress in 1971 officially announced this growth, although its implementation in the field was already under way. Successive congresses in 1977, 1981, and 1986 reiterated this policy, although successively less rhetorically.

Among the factors contributing to Soviet activism was the achievement of parity with the United States in nuclear and conventional capabilities, which seemed to make Moscow more inclined to project power and influence in the Third World. Another contributing factor was growth in the requisite political and military capabilities, thereby enhancing the Soviet capacity to assist insurgent forces. A rapidly declining U.S. willingness to use force and maintain commitments, exemplified by the withdrawal from Vietnam, likewise influenced Soviet policy. Consequently, what the USSR terms the national liberation zone expanded to encompass areas such as southern Africa, the southern part of the Arabian peninsula, and Latin America.

To implement Soviet policy, an integrated political and military strategy has been employed, augmented by an array of surrogate assets. A comparative analysis of the elements of Soviet strategy, as delineated in the four case studies, reveals several common patterns. Nevertheless, divergences do exist. Before summarizing these similarities and differences, we must address a perennial question about Moscow's policy in the Third World.

Students of Soviet involvement in Third World conflicts frequently disagree over whether this policy is one of "taking advantage of targets of opportunity" or one of "creating an opportunity by instigating instability and revolution." The findings of this study suggest that both arguments are valid. On the one hand, instability in the Third World is the result, in part, of regional and indigenous political, social, and economic differences. The USSR cannot create such conditions, but it can exploit them as "targets of opportunity." On the other hand, many insurgent movements fail to grow regardless of the extent of socioeconomic deprivation or oppressive domestic or foreign control. Soviet encouragement and assistance can help these movements mature. Each case study illustrates varying degrees of both propositions.

During 1965 Soviet involvement in the Vietnam conflict changed dramatically as the Kremlin began to display a greater readiness to support insurgent conflicts in the Third World. This change served as the prototype of Moscow's strategy of political-military support for movements conducting revolutionary warfare in the 1970s and 1980s. Although the conflict in Vietnam predated Soviet involvement, Soviet assistance contributed to the Democratic Republic of Vietnam (DRVN) and the Viet Cong's (VC's) ability to sustain their momentum and expand their efforts. Arms transfers in the form of air defense systems were a major contribution to the North Vietnamese war effort, and the quality and quantity of weapons transferred by 1970 permitted the North Vietnamese Army to modernize and develop into a conventional force. The Soviet political warfare campaign helped ensnare the United States in the Vietnam quagmire. Withdrawal of the United States from Vietnam and the impact of the war on the U.S. body politic apparently contributed to the Kremlin's decision to escalate support for other insurgent movements during the 1970s, as did changing regional and indigenous political conditions.

Soviet support for the Palestine Liberation Organization (PLO) is a manifestation of this policy decision. In the wake of the 1967 war, the Kremlin began to view the PLO as a new force that might affect the Middle East scene. Although various developments contributed to this perception, only after the 1973 war did the USSR grant the PLO full recognition; during 1974, the PLO was permitted to open an office in Moscow. By the end of the decade the PLO-Soviet relationship had become increasingly close, as seen in the growth of political and military assistance provided by Warsaw Pact members. As the PLO developed a territorial base in Lebanon, it evolved into a supplier of arms and training to other guerrilla and terrorist organizations. Although political developments in the region had a significant impact on escalating Soviet support, there are apparent limits to how far the Kremlin will go, as became evident during the Syrian-PLO crisis following the Israeli intervention in Lebanon in 1982.

The events in Angola during the first half of the 1970s helped extend the new Soviet policy into southern Africa. Until 1974, the region appears to have been relatively unimportant when compared with other parts of the Third World; the conditions for political instability and insurgency were present, but the region was dominated by South Africa, Portugal, and Rhodesia. Although Moscow had not ignored existing guerrilla movements, its assistance was relatively small in scale. Political changes in Portugal in 1974 presented both superpowers with new opportunities in southern Africa. As the political situation in the region changed, the Kremlin intensified its backing of insurgent movements, particularly the Popular Movement for the Liberation of Angola (MPLA). The subsequent consolidation of power by the MPLA, due in part to extensive Soviet and Cuban assistance, further altered the regional political landscape. Angola became a base area from which to assist other insurgents, resulting in a significant increase in Soviet-bloc paramilitary assistance and international political support for the South-West Africa People's Organization (SWAPO), the Namibian guerrilla organization challenging South Africa.

During the late 1970s, political violence in Central America caused a marked change in Kremlin policy toward the region, with events in Nicaragua providing the impetus. The USSR, principally through its Cuban surrogate, stepped up military support to the Sandinista Front of National Liberation (FSLN) during 1978. In 1979, Havana helped organize, arm, and transport an international brigade to fight alongside Sandinista forces and also provided sophisticated weaponry. In conjunction with this, Moscow expanded its international political activities to promote the FSLN. The FSLN victory in Nicaragua led to a general increase in Soviet-bloc support for other guerrillas in the region, particularly those in El Salvador.

What follows is a comparative assessment of how the USSR employed political and paramilitary strategy instruments (as well as those of its surrogates) to promote insurgency and revolution in these four cases.

Foreign Propaganda

For the USSR, international or foreign propaganda is a consequential instrument of statecraft. In conjunction with other political warfare techniques, propaganda seeks to influence the policies of other governments, undermine confidence in their leaders and institutions, disrupt relations between nations, and discredit and weaken major opponents. It also promotes and supports friendly states and movements.

An analysis of Soviet foreign propaganda that promotes revolutionary insurgency, as used in the four cases examined in this study, reveals the following patterns:

- Soviet foreign propaganda provides insight into Moscow's foreign-policy agenda. In each case an increase in propaganda coverage signaled that an insurgency had become an important policy issue for the Kremlin, which resulted in an expansion of other kinds of political and military assistance for the guerrillas.

- The initiation of a Soviet propaganda campaign signaled the beginning of a broader political warfare operation in which other political action instruments would be brought into play. In each case, as foreign propaganda coverage grew and began to promote the cause of the insurgents, international front groups became active. Soviet-bloc and surrogate political action also began in various international and/or regional organizations.

- In each case, Soviet overt propaganda set the thematic pattern for the international front organizations to follow and guided and established the parameters for political action within international and regional organizations. Although not perfectly congruent, I conclude that overt propaganda established the framework from which the other instruments took their cues. It is important to note that international fronts did not concentrate on as many themes as Soviet propaganda did and that their treatment of issues was generally more crude, more simplistic in approach, and more vitriolic in tone than the Soviets, perhaps because of the target audience and the instrument itself. Soviet overt propaganda is focused worldwide and is the official voice of the USSR, which may account for its somewhat less strident tone. Multiple targets may explain its thematic complexity.

- Of the three political warfare instruments examined, foreign propaganda reflected the most sophisticated use of the Soviet technique of *kombinatsia,* "the combining and interrelating of multiple issues in support of a central set of themes." Worldwide campaigns are broader and more complex as a result of the multiple and diverse audiences. A typical Soviet foreign propaganda campaign communicates to the Third World that the Soviets are aligned with and actively supporting the cause of national liberation and opposed to the neocolonial policy of the United States. To the Western allies of the United States, the Soviet objective is to characterize the United States as warlike, recklessly aggressive, and capable of plunging Europe into a global confrontation.

- Specifically targeted propaganda channels narrow the thematic emphasis. For instance, radio broadcasts aimed at regional audiences may not reflect the complex number of themes in Soviet worldwide communications but concentrate instead on issues more germane to the region.

- The overall objectives of Soviet propaganda (as well as the instruments of political warfare) are to promote the insurgent program and discredit the government against which the insurgency is directed. Nevertheless, in each case the United States was also a major target, receiving, at minimum, as much attention as the government under attack. This occurred whether or not the United States was significantly involved in the conflict. It appears that propaganda campaigns conducted in support of insurgency in the Third World are combined with the long-term Soviet assertion that U.S. policies are incompatible with those of the developing nations. Consequently, the actual degree of U.S. involvement in the conflict has no apparent impact on how Soviet propaganda covers the issue. Whether Vietnam, Namibia, Nicaragua, or El Salvador, we find little variance in this pattern, even though U.S. involvement actually varied dramatically.

- We also find a high degree of continuity in these campaigns. For instance, the insurgent movements are presented as the sole legitimate representatives of the people, to the exclusion of other political parties. The insurgent political program is praised and military actions justified on the grounds that the policy of the United States and its clients permit no alternative. The USSR and the socialist bloc are characterized as the natural allies of revolutionary insurgent movements. There is nothing surprising about these thematic patterns, but, once under way, each campaign reflects the ability of Soviet propagandists to intensify and concentrate their efforts.

- The propaganda of Moscow's surrogates follows the thematic efforts of the USSR, as noted in the Central American case study. Soviet and Cuban propaganda coverage of Nicaragua and El Salvador closely paralleled and reinforced each other.

International Front Organizations

The themes of Soviet overt propaganda and the policy objectives they advance are amplified through the Kremlin's major international front organizations. The methods employed by the fronts are twofold. Reflecting the Kremlin's approach to political warfare, they combine words (propaganda) and deeds (political action). For the latter the fronts use a technique we have labeled *international conference diplomacy.*

Front involvement in conference diplomacy can support Soviet foreign-policy objectives in several ways. First, the front conferences are frequently attended by the educated elite of Third World and, depending on the issue, Western countries. If the USSR can fashion the agenda of the meeting (and its recommendations), it may influence the attitudes of these participants. Beyond influence, the second objective is to persuade conference participants to initiate specific political actions. Third, the proceedings and documents of the conference are generally reproduced in a format that can be used regionally and internationally for propaganda purposes.

On the basis of an assessment of front propaganda and conference diplomacy, the following trends can be derived:

- The USSR maintains a number of international front groups, but in the cases examined in this study, the World Peace Council (WPC) played a key role in every campaign. This is not surprising in that since its inception the WPC has taken the lead in almost every major front action.

- Although the WPC took the lead in each campaign, there were divergences in the overall pattern. In the case of both Vietnam and the PLO, the WPC played the central role, with other fronts providing secondary support. In the Namibian example, the Afro-Asian People's Solidarity Organization (AAPSO) was as involved as the WPC in terms of central responsibility. With respect to Central America, a wider coalition of fronts was mobilized to carry out propaganda and conference activities, including the WPC. In sum, the four case studies reveal the following general patterns: (1) one or two major fronts take individual or joint responsibility for directing the campaign and conducting the majority of conference operations or (2) the campaign is decentralized, with a number of front organizations brought into play but no particular one conducting the majority of operations.

- In almost every respect, the general thematic pattern of front propaganda efforts mirrored Soviet commentary, with an increase in the timing of front coverage coinciding with its Soviet counterpart. The two differed in tone (front propaganda is harsher), and the fronts tended to concentrate their efforts on fewer themes. Front propaganda campaigns were not as broad in scope or targeted to as many audiences as those of their Soviet patron.

- A smaller number of themes, a more simplistic approach, and a more vitriolic tone—the factors differentiating front propaganda from Soviet propaganda—are found in three of the four insurgencies studied. In the case of Vietnam, although WPC propaganda followed the Soviet line and focused on condemning U.S. policy as criminal and praising that of the DRVN-VC, the major focus was the "rapidly growing" worldwide opposition to the U.S. role in Vietnam. (This was, of course, also a Soviet theme.) Proportionally, however, anti–Vietnam War sentiments received much wider coverage in WPC propaganda. The same pattern held true for front propaganda focused on insurgencies in Central America and the Middle East. With respect to Namibia, however, WPC and AAPSO commentary was as broad in scope as that of the USSR.

- International propaganda is only one method of an international front organization. Equally if not more important is the tactic of international conference diplomacy. International conferences may be divided into the following categories: meetings of the front organizations, international and regional conferences or meetings sponsored by one or more of the fronts, and international conferences sponsored by other international organizations in which the fronts play an active role.

- The particular conference activity differed from case to case. For instance, the WPC and AAPSO used all three approaches in their campaign to support SWAPO, including major programs in cooperation with various U.N. committees. The same is true of WPC activities in support of the PLO. However, we find a different pattern in the other two cases. For example, the WPC had sole responsibility for the ongoing Stockholm conference during the Vietnam War. Conference diplomacy in support of insurgency in Central America reveals still another pattern, where, unlike the other cases, the conferences and meetings were smaller in size and scope and regionally focused. Perhaps the most interesting development in the Nicaraguan and Salvadoran examples was the number of fronts involved in the campaign. Evidently, given the limited resources of the fronts, the decision was made to mobilize several fronts to devote a portion of their time to the effort rather than assign the Central American account to a single organization.

- In three of the four cases, the WPC or AAPSO created special international commissions or committees focused specifically on the issues surrounding the insurgent conflict. Their task was to coordinate activities during the intervals between major conference events and to implement the actions proposed at such meetings. For example, the WPC Stockholm Conference on Vietnam, which met annually, established a Continuing Committee and an International Liaison Committee that would coordinate activities to implement policy and programs. Likewise, the WPC established the International Commission of Inquiry into Israeli Crimes Against the Lebanese and Palestinian Peoples and the International Committee of Solidarity with the Palestinian People to focus on the PLO and the Middle East conflict. Finally, AAPSO created the International Committee Against Apartheid, Racism and Colonialism in South Africa. As of yet, no such organizational arrangement has emerged to coordinate activities on an ongoing basis for insurgency in Central America.

- The fronts attempt to link their international political activities with those of the U.N. and/or other international and regional organizations. For instance, beginning in the late 1970s, the WPC and AAPSO increasingly sought to interact with the U.N. and the Organization of African Unity on the Namibian issue. The same was true of WPC interaction with the U.N. on the Palestinian question. The objectives are to legitimize the activities and gain credibility for the fronts.

- The political action campaigns in the international arena are introduced at the state level by the front's national-level affiliates, as seen in the Central American case. During the first half of the 1980s, the U.S. Peace Council (USPC) was increasingly active in the movement opposing the Reagan administration's policies in Central America. The USPC, whose leadership is drawn from the U.S. Communist Party, was instrumental in establishing the Committee in Solidarity with the People of El Salvador, which has been involved since 1981 in conducting or taking part in actions against U.S. policies in El Salvador. These include the May 3, 1981, march on the Pentagon, the distribution of a forged State Department document on El Salvador, civil disobedience actions in 1983 and 1984 in a number of cities, and the planning and organizing of major annual demonstrations in Washington, D.C., in 1983–1985.

- A review of front activities reveals that Eastern Europeans and other Soviet surrogates and allies play prominent roles. The councils, presidential committees, bureaus, and other leadership bodies that direct the fronts are staffed, in part, by individuals from these states. Their integration into the campaigns and programs of the fronts is readily apparent in our review of the various international conferences and propaganda activities of the WPC, AAPSO, and other fronts. It appears that as soon as a state moves into the Soviet sphere it becomes involved in front activities. The documents captured in Grenada support this assertion. Interestingly, it was a role the New Jewel Movement welcomed and pursued.

Political Activities Within International Organizations

During the 1960s, Moscow changed from a defensive to an offensive strategy in its approach to international organizations. For instance, in the U.N. it aggressively staked out a position that placed it firmly on the side of anticolonialism and newly established Third World states. As many of these new states became increasingly radical and anti-Western, Moscow maneuvered to take political advantage of these developments. Since the late 1960s, either in the General Assembly or in specialized U.N. committees, the USSR has cooperated with and supported the activities of the radical Afro-Asian bloc.

The Kremlin thus approaches the U.N. and other international organizations as arenas in which to conduct political warfare, including rallying support for Third World insurgency movements.

- In all four cases, the USSR sought to use international organizations as forums for promoting the cause and enhancing the reputation and credibility of insurgent movements. These political actions were integrated into larger political warfare campaigns. Compared with its foreign propaganda and front activities, however, Moscow uses more variation in employing this technique.
- During the latter half of the 1960s, the USSR sought to maneuver the U.N. to take up the issue of U.S. involvement in Vietnam. At that time,

however, the power balance in the U.N. was not as anti-Western as it would become in the 1970s and 1980s, and there was no specialized committee through which the Soviets could advance their objectives in the General Assembly. Consequently, although Moscow could use the U.N. as a public forum from which to criticize U.S. policy in Vietnam, it was unable to move beyond propaganda to political action or to mobilize the General Assembly against the United States.

- The examples of the PLO and SWAPO underscore the change effected by the USSR to carry out political warfare activities in the U.N. In the case of SWAPO, a specialized committee—the Committee of 24—existed, and Moscow was (and is) actively involved in its day-to-day deliberations. Along with its surrogates, the Soviet Union has played an active part in the committee's work since the very early days of its existence. As the committee became increasingly militant and anti-Western, the power balance shifted, and it proceeded to play an important role in the General Assembly's recognition of SWAPO and in the U.N.'s continuing support of and interaction with SWAPO.

- A similar pattern exists with respect to the PLO. Specialized committees concerned with the Palestinian issue existed, and the USSR and its surrogates became involved in their activities. As with the Committee of 24, the Committee on the Exercise of the Inalienable Rights of the Palestinian People consists primarily of radical Afro-Asian states, members of the Warsaw Pact, and Cuba, Afghanistan, and Laos. The committee has played a central role not only in the General Assembly's recognition of the PLO but also in a host of other U.N. activities that promote and assist the PLO, especially the U.N. Department of Public Information.

- The Central American case study demonstrates that the U.N. is not the only international organization against which this technique is directed. As the Kremlin began to concentrate on insurgent movements in Nicaragua and El Salvador, it faced the problem of having no specialized committee structure in the U.N. through which to promote the cause of the guerrillas. Consequently, it appears to have decided to work through its Cuban surrogate to maneuver the Nonaligned Movement to promote the cause and program of national liberation movements in Central America. Cuban ascendancy in the organization during the latter half of the 1970s provided the opportunity for placing this theme on the nonaligned agenda in 1979. Because the members of the Nonaligned Movement help fashion the U.N. agenda, there was an indirect payoff to this operation, however Cuban heavy-handedness prevented a successful follow-up to this initial success with the Nonaligned Movement.

- Documents captured in Grenada after October 1983 depict an attempt on the part of Moscow's surrogates to intervene directly in the Socialist International (SI) to influence the course of debate and the position of the SI on Central American questions. The documents describe Grenada and Nicaragua's roles in a secret faction of the SI. This faction was under the guidance of Cuba, which as a communist regime is not eligible for SI membership.

Arms Transfers

Although international propaganda and political action aim to enhance the legitimacy of revolutionary insurgent movements on the world scene, the objective of paramilitary and military aid is to improve the capacity and skill of the guerrillas to carry out protracted combat operations against government forces and officials. Consequently, arms and related logistic assistance are of central importance.

- In each case study, an increase in arms transfers and other forms of military assistance coincided with the initiation of a propaganda and political warfare campaign.

- The procedure for transferring arms differed from situation to situation. In certain instances there was little doubt where and how the arms arrived; in the case of the DRVN-VC, the Soviets openly acknowledged their role. In other situations, Moscow used covert and indirect channels; for instance SWAPO, where arms have been transferred through front-line states. The emergence of Angola as a surrogate has added to Soviet flexibility in this instance. Some of the arms transferred through these channels came not from the USSR but from the Eastern-bloc states.

- In other instances, indirect and clandestine channels have been replaced by overt ones. Before the early 1970s, arms provided to the PLO came indirectly through Arab governments, but this changed as the PLO gained international legitimacy in the aftermath of the 1973 war. Thus, the process became direct, and there was no longer any need for plausible deniability.

- In the case of Nicaragua, Cuba played the central role in the 1978 arms buildup for the FSLN by becoming the conduit through which Eastern-bloc arms flowed. An analogous situation now exists in El Salvador. Arms acquired clandestinely from members of the Warsaw Pact, Vietnam, and Ethiopia are funneled through Cuba and Nicaragua.

- The kinds of arms transferred by the USSR and its surrogates also differed from case to case, depending on the stage of the conflict and the needs of the recipient. The DRVN received a sophisticated air defense system, and the USSR also helped equip the North Vietnamese Army as it evolved into a modern conventional army (this became apparent during the Easter offensive of 1972). SWAPO, however, generally received weapons appropriate for the irregular and protracted combat that it employs, which is also true of the guerrillas in El Salvador, particularly since the failure of their final offensive in 1981. As the PLO became a state within a state in Lebanon during the latter half of the 1970s, the kinds of arms it required changed. Although the PLO continued to employ irregular operations against Israel (requiring light weapons), inside Lebanon more conventional capabilities were needed to hold territory and/or take new ground. The change in the kinds of Soviet-bloc arms transferred reflected this new requirement.

Training Insurgent Forces

Soviet-bloc and surrogate training of insurgent forces involves both political and military instruction and can take place in a number of locations, including Soviet-bloc states or base areas contiguous to the conflict location. The kinds of training provided also depend on the stage of the conflict. Each of these variations can be observed in this study.

- In the case of the PLO, as the USSR drew closer during the period surrounding the 1973 war, facilities in various Warsaw Pact states were opened to the Palestinians. The Soviet political warfare campaign in support of the PLO centered on Fatah, but other factions also received training. As the base in Lebanon developed, the Soviets provided training in both conventional and unconventional combat. Once established in Lebanon, the PLO became more than a recipient of military assistance, passing expertise on to the cadres of other insurgent and terrorist groups from various regions of the globe. PLO cadres who traveled to the Eastern bloc also received instruction in political warfare techniques and insurgent organizational development.

- From the example of the PLO, we can see the diverse nature of the training available. In the case of the DRVN, it was confined mainly to assisting the North Vietnamese Army learn to operate the air defense system and MiG aircraft, as they did not require the kind of political-military training assistance provided to the PLO, SWAPO, and other movements.

- In the case of the insurgent movements from southern Africa and Central America, surrogate states in each region served as the location for a portion of the training assistance provided, specifically Cuba, Nicaragua, and Angola. In these states, political-military training was undertaken by both indigenous and Warsaw Pact personnel, and insurgent cadres traveled to the Soviet Union and Eastern Europe for this assistance.

Advisory Assistance

Although the same personnel may serve both as training instructors and as advisers, I have divided them into separate categories. Advisory assistance involves providing various kinds of operational consultation to insurgent forces. Unlike training, which can take place either in the Soviet bloc or areas contiguous to the location of the conflict, advisory support is generally confined to the latter.

- Of the cases investigated, it was in southern Africa and Central America that this form of assistance was most prominent. In Angola, Soviet-bloc and Cuban personnel provide advisory assistance to SWAPO. Similarly, during the final stages of the Nicaraguan revolution, Cuban advisers assisted the FSLN through an operations center established in San José. Cuban officers from the Department of Special Operations, along with their Nicaraguan counterparts, assist the FMLN insurgents in the same way.

- In two instances Soviet surrogates have gone beyond advisory support by introducing armed forces. In southern Africa, Cuban troops were deployed in the Angolan conflict in the mid-1970s to ensure victory for the MPLA. Cuba also appears to have helped to introduce an international brigade into the Nicaraguan conflict during the 1979 final offensive.

Coordination and Integration

Since the late 1960s, Soviet strategy for assisting movements conducting revolutionary warfare has evolved in a number of important ways. To begin with, the Soviets have expanded and refined their political-military instruments. Also, the capabilities of a number of Soviet surrogates and allies augment those of the USSR. Finally, in some cases, surrogates played multiple roles, while others confined their involvement to one activity.

What is equally interesting about Soviet strategy, as it has evolved over the past fifteen years, is the degree of coordination and integration among the political and military instruments. On the basis of the case studies, we can see how these techniques are expanded and implemented concurrently, once the decision is taken to either begin or increase support and assistance. Integration and coordination include not only Soviet instruments but those of its allies and proxies.

Although not suggesting or implying that the systematic implementation of a coordinated strategy is unique to the Soviet Union, the evidence presented does demonstrate that the Kremlin has developed a strategic approach to achieve policy objectives. This does not in and of itself guarantee success, but it can be argued that it contributed to Soviet achievements in the Third World during the 1970s and early 1980s. Of course, there are residual costs to expansion.

Internal Security and the Consolidation of Power

The USSR has traditionally been involved in promoting revolutionary insurgent warfare, but during the 1980s the Kremlin found itself giving aid to newly established Marxist-Leninist regimes facing similar internal security challenges. The objective of this aid is to ensure that regimes that come to power through Leninist means and with Soviet-bloc assistance remain in power. This may be accomplished through the development of an internal security infrastructure that can quell internal opposition, mobilize the population, and insulate the leadership cadres. To protect against a new form of internal threat—resistance movements employing insurgent strategies—the Soviet Union provides military and paramilitary advice and support.

Primary source materials disclose that the USSR and its surrogates have been involved in power consolidation activities in Nicaragua and Angola. Following the overthrow of the Somoza government, the FSLN began to consolidate control in Nicaragua and moved rapidly to create a political system based on the Cuban model. Cuban, Soviet, and other Eastern-bloc assistance was introduced to help achieve this objective, which focused on two institutions—the internal security services and the armed forces. With respect to the former, Soviet, Cuban, East German, and Bulgarian intelligence officers played important roles in establishing and advising the Nicaraguan state security apparatus. Soviet-bloc and Cuban assistance also contributed significantly to the organization and equipping of Nicaragua's armed forces. The establishment of these institutions provides communist governments with the principal means through which to maintain power. Thus far, they appear to have served the FSLN well, as it has dealt with growing internal political opposition from church, press, union, and other domestic groups and the paramilitary challenge of the contra forces.

A similar pattern can be seen in Angola. Following the seizure of power in 1976, in large part as a result of the introduction of Cuban troops and Soviet-bloc arms, the MPLA sought to expand and professionalize its internal security service and armed forces. In conjunction with this, personnel from each institution received training in the USSR and/or surrogate states. Arms transfers also expanded as the MPLA forces changed from a guerrilla into a conventional army, reflected in the types of arms sent to Angola. In light of the growing seriousness of the anticommunist insurgent threat, Cuban forces remained in Angola to help maintain the MPLA in power.

Although not an official government, the PLO received similar assistance during the latter half of the 1970s and early 1980s. At that time the PLO was a de facto government in southern Lebanon. As a result, its cadres received training by Soviet, East European, Cuban, and Vietnamese personnel in conventional military tactics, also reflected in the types of arms transferred to the PLO and captured by Israel during its 1982 intervention in southern Lebanon.

This study did not examine developments in Afghanistan, Mozambique, Ethiopia, or South Yemen, but it appears that these regimes have received varying amounts of the same kinds of assistance.

Future Prospects
for Soviet Policy

Will the Soviet Union continue to employ the policies described above under the new CPSU leadership? Despite the de-emphasis and reassessment of these policies that appeared in the new CPSU program published in 1985, Moscow has, over the last decade and a half, made heavy political and financial investments in its active support of insurgent movements conducting revolutionary warfare.[3] To draw back now could rescind the political message that Moscow has been sending to friends and foes since the late 1960s. Also, an institutional constituency for these policies has developed in various parts of the party and state apparatus, which may well remain committed to their implementation. There have been costs involved; nevertheless, over the past fifteen years a number of Soviet-backed Marxist-Leninist insurgent movements and political factions have come to power. A map of the regions of the Third World in the 1980s shows that the number of self-professed Marxist-Leninist states aligned with Moscow has increased dramatically since the late 1960s. Not only has this enhanced the international reputation of the USSR in the Third World, but it has contributed to the geostrategic position of the Soviet Union. For example, it has gained access to new facilities in Vietnam, Angola, Ethiopia, and South Yemen.

In spite of these gains, perhaps the ensuing costs have become prohibitive. It has been argued that the rhetorical shift of senior party officials and documents away from the Third World—demonstrated by the contrast between Brezhnev's enthusiasm at the Twenty-fourth, Twenty-fifth, and, to a lesser extent, Twenty-sixth CPSU Congresses and the 1985 party program and Gorbachev's report to the Twenty-seventh CPSU Congress—may be evidence of this. Some Soviet observers believe this rhetorical shift signals a radical change in policy. Certainly there is no denying that there is a price to be paid for expansion. From a financial perspective, Cuba alone costs the Kremlin an estimated $4–$5 billion a year. According to Charles Wolf and his Rand associates, the cost of Soviet Third World policy has more than doubled during the decade of the 1970s; by 1980 it had reached between $35 and $46 billion.[4]

A second and related expense has to do with maintaining these regimes in power in the face of indigenous insurgent challenges. In Afghanistan, this has necessitated the deployment of more than 100,000 Soviet troops to check the *mujahedin*. Similarly, Cuba intervened militarily in Angola and Ethiopia, and Vietnam invaded and occupied Cambodia. In other instances, while not providing troops, the Soviet Union and/or its surrogates have provided internal security and counterinsurgency measures.

Additionally, the political and economic performance of a number of new pro-Soviet and Marxist-Leninist regimes has been disastrous. Economically, South Yemen, Mozambique, and particularly Ethiopia have managed to destroy what ranged from adequate to healthy agricultural production. Politically, narrow bases of support engendered not only indigenous guerrillas but also serious factionalism within vanguard parties which resulted in the Mafia-style shootout that took place in the Politburo of the Yemen Socialist Party in 1986.

The U.S. policy toward Third World conflicts has undergone important although limited change in the 1980s. In Central America, Washington has shown a willingness to assist friendly governments threatened by revolutionary insurgent movements. Although there are real constraints on this policy, in El Salvador this assistance has made a difference. The Reagan administration has also given limited aid to insurgent movements threatening four Marxist-Leninist states (Afghanistan, Nicaragua, Angola, Cambodia), which has further complicated Soviet policy.

Although recent Soviet policy assessments have not been sanguine, early indications suggest that the current Soviet leadership will stake out a position between an unaltered continuation of the policy of the 1970s and a radical shift in emphasis due to disillusionment with the activism of Brezhnev. In real terms this means continuing internal security and military assistance to regimes like Angola, Afghanistan, Ethiopia, Nicaragua, and South Yemen. To withdraw support could result in the victory of an anticommunist insurgency. It appears that the current leadership does not want and cannot afford the image of being unable to live up to its commitments. This is evidenced by the fact that the Soviets, under Mikhail Gorbachev (who publicly indicated he wishes to withdraw), have initiated major offensives against the insurgents in Angola and Afghanistan and that Nicaragua has received increased arms transfers. If the United States chose to significantly raise the costs to the USSR by giving more aid to one or more resistance movements, Moscow would be faced with the specter of escalation. (As I discuss below, the probability of the United States intensifying any one of these conflicts to the point where the Kremlin faces hard choices is not high.)

With respect to revolutionary insurgent movements, it is likely that Moscow will maintain the status quo—those organizations already receiving either direct or indirect assistance will continue to do so. However, if an attractive opportunity presented itself, it is not unlikely that the Kremlin would seriously consider increasing assistance. For instance, if the crisis in South Africa dramatically escalates, then Moscow would certainly be tempted to increase aid to SWAPO and the African National Congress. Similarly, following the 1988 U.S. presidential election, a new administration might reduce commitments in Central America. It is plausible that through its Cuban surrogate the USSR would attempt to exploit this situation. Barring developments along these lines, however, it is probable that the Soviets will continue to support selected revolutionary insurgent movements at existing levels.

EIGHT

Postscript: Implications for U.S. Foreign Policy

Many national security specialists suggest that today and in the years to come the most likely types of conflict that will threaten U.S. interests and in which force may have to be employed are those that lie at the lower end of the conflict spectrum.[1] Various studies have demonstrated that over the last fifteen years what the U.S. national security community refers to as low-intensity challenges have increased markedly throughout the international arena.[2] These have taken a variety of forms, including revolutionary insurgency and international and state-sponsored terrorism.

What measures have been taken by the United States to respond to these low-intensity challenges to U.S. interests? Following the U.S. withdrawal from Vietnam in 1973, the commitment and, hence, the strategy, organization, and capabilities for responding to revolutionary insurgency and other low-intensity threats were greatly reduced. Administrations in the period between the U.S. exit from Vietnam and the election of Ronald Reagan paid little attention to this form of conflict, reflected by drastic cuts in low-intensity conflict (LIC) capabilities. In terms of appropriations, the Special Operations Forces (SOF) budget (including Special Forces and Rangers) was more than $1 billion in the late 1960s. By 1975, spending declined to under $100 million. Even in the first years of the Reagan administration the SOF budget grew slowly through 1982, increasing in 1983 to well over $200 million.[3] The 1970s saw marked reductions in CIA paramilitary assets, which play an important role in counterinsurgency and related activities.[4] According to one former specialist, by the end of the

1970s the ability of the United States to conduct LIC operations had "withered into virtual uselessness."[5]

During the 1970s deep-seated opposition developed in and out of government to U.S. involvement in this form of conflict. In addition to the budget constraints and reduction in forces noted above, the Congress passed the Clark and Hughes-Ryan Amendments, which constrained executive policy in Third World conflicts. In the midst of these developments, revolution toppled governments in Iran and Nicaragua, guerrilla activities increased in Latin America and elsewhere, and, as this study documents, the USSR became increasingly involved in promoting revolutionary insurgency in different regions of the developing world.

The rhetoric of senior officials and the increased appropriations for SOF imply that the Reagan administration reversed the policy trends of the 1970s. Nevertheless, there has been confusion both inside and outside the administration over what constitutes major LIC threats and opportunities. Furthermore, increased spending on SOF has not necessarily improved the United States' ability to conduct LIC activities. Bureaucratic resistance and organizational impediments have significantly affected strategy formulation and policy implementation. A brief comment on each of these points demonstrates that this period of renewed interest has not resulted in a clearly articulated policy and requisite strategy.

An examination of the public rhetoric of the Reagan administration reflects the difficulties that persist within both the executive branch and the national security bureaucracy in defining the parameters of LIC.[6] At different times LIC has been described as counterinsurgency, assisting anticommunist resistance movements, counterterrorism, or, more broadly, "limited politico-military struggle."[7] In effect, after six years of "concern" over LIC threats, there are still members of the Reagan administration, as well as senior military officers, asserting that defining the parameters of this form of conflict remains an ambiguous and vexing problem.

Nevertheless, under a revitalization plan scheduled for completion in 1990, active-duty SOF will increase from the current level of 14,900 (a significant increase from the late 1970s) to 20,900. Spending has also risen dramatically. In 1984 the budget was $350 million; the 1987 proposed appropriation rose to $1.6 billion.[8]

Despite these developments some observers have noted that although the United States is spending considerably more on SOF, these forces still do not have the capabilities necessary to respond effectively to the primary low-intensity challenges.[9] While it is correct that the United States is spending more on SOF, the money is not concentrated on LIC missions. SOF revitalization has been focused on force readiness and equipment to meet the regional commander-in-chief's (CINC's) plans and the services' responsibilities for conventional wartime preparation. Thus, the SOF are being equipped to fight behind enemy lines in a general conventional war. Although important, especially in terms of new NATO doctrines, this appears to be the least likely mission that SOF will be required to carry out in the future. A conventional wartime emphasis for SOF means that LIC missions are accorded a secondary priority, resulting in shortfalls of doctrine, strategy, and equipment.

Military command and control and interagency coordination have been perennial problems in developing policy to respond to threats below the conventional war level. This was true during the Kennedy administration, in many ways the high point of post–World War II executive concern with LIC, and remains the case today. In 1981, the Reagan administration began to develop the organization and capabilities to respond effectively to LIC threats. As the administration approaches the latter stage of its second term, however, the word *develop* must still be emphasized, as it remains very difficult for many at the top level of the military services and relevant government agencies to construe planning a response to LIC as either necessary or viable.

Within the military, throughout the post–World War II period, a conventional mindset resting on conventional perceptions of war has made it difficult to develop the capabilities and organization required. To remedy this situation the Reagan administration initiated a number of organizational steps that, due to existing attitudes within the command system and services, have proven ineffective. Thus, while the Reagan administration has emphasized the LIC challenge and increased both appropriations and forces, there remains a strong impetus within the armed services to subsume these missions within the existing command structure. The services view conventional war as the major contingency they must prepare to address, and they task the SOF to support this mission. An important portion of SOF revitalization, consequently, has been directed toward force readiness and equipment to meet the CINC's plans and the services' responsibilities for fighting behind Soviet and East European lines in a conventional war in Europe. This perspective is held by senior service officers, including General John Chain, former Air Force deputy chief of staff for operations and director of politico-military affairs of the State Department, who stated before Congress that while he "fully supports the existence of Special Forces," they "should be used only as traditional, behind-the-lines commandos who organize guerrillas and engage in sabotage to support the U.S. military during war."[10]

In addition to the military, there is opposition within those civilian agencies that theoretically have a role in LIC missions, including the intelligence community, where there is strong resistance to paramilitary operations. During the congressional investigations of U.S. intelligence during the latter half of the 1970s, the paramilitary mission of the CIA was greatly downgraded.[11] The impact of this has been spelled out by one former practitioner: "Under Admiral Stansfield Turner's stewardship" there were "drastic personnel reductions and maintained equipment inventories were at levels below what are necessary to sustain the third option [paramilitary operations], if it were selected for implementation."[12] When the Reagan administration chose to employ this capability, it found, in addition to these shortfalls, an institutional opposition to the paramilitary function.[13] Similar attitudes exist in other civilian agencies. There has also been the erratic behavior of Congress, which has fluctuated from cutting off aid to the Nicaraguan contras (and then restoring it) and limiting the number of military advisers in El Salvador to repealing the Clark Amendment and voting funds to the noncommunist insurgents in Cambodia.

What has been the impact of these developments? Many argue that the United States cannot afford to approach LIC in an ad hoc or disjointed manner, especially in light of Soviet activism in these conflicts over the last decade and a half, but it appears that the Reagan administration has not advanced very far since 1980. Therefore, the U.S. response to what appear to be the primary LIC missions—counterinsurgency, anticommunist resistance, counterterrorism—remains disjointed and ad hoc. Evidence of this, summarized below, becomes even more vivid when considered against the backdrop of the findings of this study:

■ Counterinsurgency

Recent studies conclude that the United States is not, as yet, fully prepared to work with Third World military and internal security forces facing a political-military insurgency.[14]

The SOF forces do not have as a first priority civic action, nation building, psychological operations, security assistance, or advisory support missions related to counterinsurgency.[15] In many instances, the army continues to train Third World forces facing insurgency to fight a U.S.-style conventional war (much like it prepared the army of Vietnam) and to rely on U.S. equipment and support (for example, El Salvador).[16]

Six years of the Reagan administration have not resulted in a significant improvement in the SOF's ability to accomplish political-military counterinsurgency tasks in the LIC environment. Shortfalls in equipment, language skills, area and cultural orientation, human intelligence collection, and strategy continue to exist.[17]

The reasons for these developments are many and varied and have plagued administrations since President Kennedy attempted to initiate a counterinsurgency revolution in the U.S. armed forces. Bureaucratic and organizational commitment to conventional warfare defeated that revolution and continues to hamper developments today.[18]

■ Anticommunist Resistance

Many of the problems that plague counterinsurgency preparation also affect the U.S. ability to support anticommunist resistance movements. The United States has not developed the means to assist these movements in creating political and military structures and strategies that can effectively prosecute a protracted political-military struggle.[19]

The United States presently does not have a corps of experts on resistance strategies who know the local cultural and physical environment in which current resistance activities are being conducted. Such a corps of experts would develop doctrine, strategy, and assistance programs that would provide political-military training and advice.[20]

Even in those cases where the United States is providing military support, it is reported that the equipment arrives in a sporadic fashion, is often inappropriate for this kind of conflict, and is siphoned off by governments where the resistance is based. The fact that the United States has not progressed very far past the military side of resistance support and training raises the follow-on question about the state of political training being provided. The previous points appear to answer this question.

■ Counterterrorism

Most of the recent SOF revitalization for LIC has gone into building up counterterrorist (CT) assets. However, even in the CT realm it is argued that the United States still needs to address and overcome shortfalls.[21]

It has been reported that when the White House wanted to send Navy SEALS to free the *Achille Lauro* hostages, the mission encountered serious problems. The plane assigned to carry them was not in shape to make the trip. After trying three planes the SEALS finally took off; however, they arrived too late.[22] Serious airlift problems reportedly also limited the U.S. SOF-CT response during the TWA crisis in 1985.

As a result of the evidence summarized above (as well as additional corroborating facts), both houses of Congress conducted investigations on SOF and LIC during 1986. The consensus of the committee members is summed up in the words of Senator William Cohen: "[W]e are not well prepared for unconventional conflict and it shows . . . A new form of warfare has emerged, a form of warfare that we have not properly understood, and that we have not effectively deterred."[23] The investigations led to legislation mandating organizational reforms within the military and civilian agencies responsible for LIC.[24]

In light of the lack of progress through one and a half terms of the Reagan administration and given Soviet policy and strategy as described here, a case can be made to support these legislative measures. Passing legislation is one thing, implementing it quite another. Changing the "wiring diagram" or organizational chart will not necessarily solve the problem.

Low-intensity conflict is part of the U.S.-Soviet security equation. The Kremlin has frequently made this clear, regardless of whether superpower relations were in a state of détente or tension and confrontation. Evidence of this abounds in Soviet commentary and, as noted above, the USSR's self-assigned responsibility to support "national liberation" movements is stipulated in Article 28 of the *Constitution (Fundamental Law) of the Union of Soviet Socialist Republics.* This study documents that not only has the Kremlin developed the requisite strategy and capabilities, but it also has implemented the policy, as can be seen in the cases examined here. Although I focused on a limited sample, one recent study of Soviet and/or surrogate support for revolutionary insurgency identifies more than twenty instances since the late 1960s.[25]

This brief review suggests that, even during the period of renewed U.S. concern with LIC, integrated strategies, organizations, and capabilities have yet to be developed. Until these requirements are met, the United States is likely to continue to respond to LIC challenges in a fragmented manner. The same cannot be said for the Soviet Union.

Notes

Chapter 1

1. Harry Eckstein, "On the Etiology of Internal Wars," in Ivo Feierabend, Rosalind Feierabend, and Ted Robert Gurr, eds., *Anger, Violence, and Politics* (Englewood Cliffs, N.J.: Prentice-Hall, 1972), pp. 9–10.

2. Ibid.

3. For a review of the different terminology employed over the period since the early 1950s, see Richard Shultz and Gregory Kozicz, "Unconventional War, Counterinsurgency, and Low Intensity Conflict: The American Experience," unpublished manuscript (1986).

4. Joint Low-Intensity Project Final Report, *Volume I—Analytical Review of Low-Intensity Conflict* (Fort Monroe, Va.: U.S. Army Training and Doctrine Command, August 1, 1986).

5. Shultz and Kozicz, "Unconventional War"; David Dean, ed., *Low Intensity Conflict and Modern Technology* (Maxwell Air Force Base, Ala.; Air University Press, 1986); Sam Sarkesian and William Scully, *U.S. Policy and Low-Intensity Conflict* (New Brunswick, N.J.: Transaction Books, 1981).

6. Robert Asprey, *War in the Shadows: The Guerilla in History,* 2 vols. (Garden City, N.Y.: Doubleday, 1975).

7. See Mao Tse-tung, *Selected Works of Mao Tse-tung,* 4 vols. (Peking: Foreign Language Press, 1965). For a Western interpretation, see Samuel Griffith, *Peking and People's War* (New York: Praeger, 1966).

8. For an important summary statement on the Chinese approach, see Lin Piao, *Long Live the Victory of People's War!* (Peking: Foreign Language Press, 1965).

9. Roger Trinquier, *Modern Warfare* (New York: Praeger, 1964), preface.

10. Ibid.

11. Cited in Peter Paret, *French Revolutionary Warfare from Indochina to Algeria* (New York: Praeger, 1964), p. 16.

12. Colonel Lacheroy et al., "La Guerre du Viet-Minh," *Revue Militaire d'Information* (February–March 1957): 25–41; J. Hogard, "Guerre Revolutionnaire et Pacification," *Revue Militaire d'Information* (January 1957): 7–24; Ximenes, "La Guerre Revolution-

naire," *Revue Militaire d'Information* (February–March 1957): 9–22; L. M. Chassin, "Guerre en Indochine," *Revue de Defense Nationale* (July 1953): 11–22.

13. Robert Thompson, *Revolutionary War in World Strategy* (New York: Taplinger, 1970), pp. 5, 16.

14. See Dennis Duncanson, *Government and Revolution in Vietnam* (London: Oxford University Press, 1968); Richard Clutterbuck, *The Long, Long War: Counterinsurgency in Malaya and Vietnam* (New York: Praeger, 1966); Frank Kitson, *Low Intensity Operations* (Harrisburg, Penn.: Stackpole Press, 1971).

15. George Tanham, *Communist Revolutionary Warfare: From Vietminh to Viet Cong* (New York: Praeger, 1968); Edward Lansdale, *In the Midst of War* (New York: Harper & Row, 1972); Edward Lansdale, "Vietnam: Do We Understand Revolution," *Foreign Affairs* 43 (October 1964): 75–86; Douglas Pike, *Viet Cong* (Cambridge, Mass.: MIT Press, 1966); Douglas Pike, *War, Peace, and the Viet Cong* (Cambridge, Mass.: MIT Press, 1970); Bernard Fall, *The Two Vietnams* (New York: Praeger, 1967); Bernard Fall, *Vietnam Witness 1953–1966* (New York: Praeger, 1966); Lt. Gen. William Yarborough, "Needed—A New Approach to Counterinsurgency," unpublished manuscript (1968); Gen. Richard Stilwell, *The Army's Role in Counterinsurgency,* declassified report (1961).

16. This appears to be the case in a number of recent examples, including Vietnam and Nicaragua. See Doan Van Toai and David Chanoff, *The Vietnamese Gulag* (New York: Simon & Schuster, 1986), and Shirley Christian, *Nicaragua: Revolution in the Family* (New York: Random House, 1985).

17. Ekkart Zimmermann, *Political Violence, Crises, and Revolution* (Cambridge, Mass.: Schenkman, 1983), p. 416.

18. Michael Nacht, "Internal Change and Regime Stability," *Adelphia Papers,* no. 167 (Summer 1981): 54.

19. Mostafa Rejai, *The Comparative Study of Revolutionary Strategy* (New York: David McKay, 1977), chap. 3.

20. For a useful discussion of social behavior theory and its adaption to the study of international relations, see James Dougherty and Robert Pfaltzgraff, *Contending Theories of International Relations* (New York: Harper & Row, 1981).

21. Zimmermann, *Political Violence.* This provides the most comprehensive, recent categorization of these explanations and findings.

22. Ted Robert Gurr, *Why Men Rebel* (Princeton, N.J.: Princeton University Press, 1970).

23. Ivo Feierabend and Rosalind Feierabend, "Aggressive Behavior Within Politics, 1948–1962: A Cross-National Study," *Journal of Conflict Resolution* 10 (September 1966); Feierabend, Feierabend, and Gurr, *Anger, Violence, and Politics.*

24. Raymond Tanter and Manus Midlarsky, "A Theory of Revolution," *Journal of Conflict Resolution* 11 (September 1967): 172.

25. Manus Midlarsky and Raymond Tanter, "Toward a Theory of Political Instability in Latin America," *Journal of Peace Research* 4, no. 3 (1967): 209–27.

26. James Davies, "The J-Curve of Rising and Declining Satisfaction as a Cause of Some Great Revolutions and a Contained Rebellion," in Hugh Graham and Ted Robert Gurr, eds., *Violence in America* (New York: Praeger, 1969).

27. Gurr, *Why Men Rebel*.

28. Samuel Huntington, *Political Order in Changing Societies* (New Haven, Conn.: Yale University Press, 1968), p. 265.

29. Charles Tilly, "Revolutions and Collective Violence," in Fred I. Greenstein and Nelson W. Polsby, eds., *Handbook of Political Science: International Politics,* vol. 8 (Reading, Mass.: Addison-Wesley, 1975), pp. 546–47.

30. Bard O'Neill, "Insurgency: A Framework for Analysis," in Bard O'Neill, William Heaton, and Donald Alberts, eds., *Insurgency in the Modern World* (Boulder, Colo.: Westview Press, 1980), pp. 1–3.

31. Chalmers Johnson, *Revolutionary Change* (Boston: Little, Brown, 1966); Neil Smelser, *Theory of Collective Behavior* (New York: The Free Press, 1963); Robert Jessop, *Social Order, Reform and Revolution* (New York: Macmillan, 1972); Mark Hagopian, *The Phenomenon of Revolution* (New York: Dodd, Mead, 1974).

32. Hagopian, *Phenomenon of Revolution,* pp. 134–86.

33. Eric Wolf, *Peasant Wars of the Twentieth Century* (London: Faber and Faber, 1973).

34. Eric Wolf, "Peasant Rebellion and Revolution," in Norman Miller and Roderick Aya, eds., *National Liberation: Revolution in the Third World* (New York: The Free Press, 1971), pp. 268–69.

35. Jeffrey Paige, *Agrarian Revolution* (Riverside, N.J.: The Free Press, 1975), p. 70.

36. Thomas Greene, *Comparative Revolutionary Movements* (Englewood Cliffs, N.J.: Prentice-Hall, 1974).

37. Hagopian, *Phenomenon of Revolution,* pp. 184–86.

38. O'Neill, "Insurgency: A Framework for Analysis," pp. 14–16.

39. Rejai, *Comparative Study of Revolutionary Strategy;* Greene, *Comparative Revolutionary Movements.*

40. T. S. Kuhn, *The Structure of Scientific Revolutions* (Chicago: University of Chicago Press, 1970); Dougherty and Pfaltzgraff, *Contending Theories of International Relations.*

41. Alexander George and Richard Smoke, *Deterrence in American Foreign Policy* (New York: Columbia University Press, 1974), chap. 4 and appendixes. The use of the case-study approach in social science research has been employed extensively, especially as it relates to decisionmaking and public administration. With respect to the latter see Edwin A. Bock, ed., *Essays on the Case Method in Public Administration* (Chicago: Public Administration Service, 1965). For a discussion of the use of this approach by political scientists, see Harry Eckstein, "Case Study and Theory in Political Science," in Fred I. Greenstein and Nelson W. Polsby, eds., *Handbook of Political Science: Strategies of Inquiry,* vol. 7 (Reading, Mass.: Addison-Wesley, 1975). See also G. David Garson, *Political Science Methods* (Boston: Holbrook Press, 1976), and Sidney Verba, "Some

Dilemmas in Comparative Research," *World Politics* 20 (October 1967): 111–27. The focused-comparison approach (or variations of it) has been utilized extensively in the study of international conflict and crisis management. Among the standard works, see Alexander George, David Hall, and William Simons, *The Limits of Coercive Diplomacy* (Boston: Little, Brown, 1971); Richard Smoke, *War: Controlling Escalation* (Cambridge, Mass.: Harvard University Press, 1977); Glenn H. Snyder and Paul Diesing, *Conflict Among Nations* (Princeton, N.J.: Princeton University Press, 1977); Michael Brecher, ed., *Studies in Crisis Behavior* (New Brunswick, N.J.: Transaction Books, 1978); Richard Ned Lebow, *Between Peace and War* (Baltimore, Md.: Johns Hopkins University Press, 1981); Barry Blechman and Stephen Kaplan, eds., *Force Without War* (Washington, D.C.: The Brookings Institution, 1978); and Stephen S. Kaplan, ed., *Diplomacy of Power: Soviet Armed Forces as a Political Instrument* (Washington, D.C.: The Brookings Institution, 1981).

Chapter 2

1. Among the standard and more recent works, I would recommend W. Raymond Duncan, ed., *Soviet Policy in Developing Countries* (Waltham, Mass.: Ginn-Blaisdell, 1970); W. Raymond Duncan, ed., *Soviet Policy in the Third World* (New York: Pergamon, 1980); Roger Kanet, ed., *The Soviet Union and the Developing Nations* (Baltimore, Md.: Johns Hopkins University Press, 1974); Robert Donaldson, ed., *The Soviet Union in the Third World: Successes and Failures* (Boulder, Colo.: Westview Press, 1981); Stephen Hosmer and Thomas Wolfe, *Soviet Policy and Practice Toward Third World Conflicts* (Lexington, Mass.: Lexington Books, 1983); Elizabeth Valkenier, *The Soviet Union and the Third World, An Economic Bind* (New York: Praeger, 1983); Richard Lowenthal, *Model or Ally? The Communist Powers and the Developing Countries* (New York: Oxford University Press, 1977); Walter Laqueur, ed., *The Patterns of Soviet Conduct in the Third World* (New York: Praeger, 1983); Daniel Papp, *Soviet Perceptions of the Developing World in the 1980s* (Lexington, Mass.: Lexington Books, 1985); Bruce Porter, *The USSR in the Third World Conflicts* (London: Cambridge University Press, 1984); Carol Saivetz and Sylvia Woodby, *Soviet–Third World Relations* (Boulder, Colo.: Westview Press, 1985); Rajan Menon, *Soviet Power and the Third World* (New Haven, Conn.: Yale University Press, 1986); Joseph Whelan and Michael Dixon, *The Soviet Union in the Third World: Threat to World Peace?* (New York: Pergamon-Brassey, 1986); Jerry Hough, *The Struggle for the Third World* (Washington, D.C.: The Brookings Institution, 1986); S. Neil MacFarlane, *Superpower Rivalry and Third World Radicalism: The Idea of National Liberation* (Baltimore, Md.: Johns Hopkins University Press, 1985).

2. Whelan and Dixon, *Soviet Union in the Third World,* p. 3.

3. Alvin Rubinstein, *Soviet Foreign Policy Since World War II: Imperial and Global* (Cambridge, Mass.: Winthrop, 1981), p. 214.

4. Hosmer and Wolfe, *Soviet Policy and Practice,* chaps. 1–6.

5. Papp, *Soviet Perceptions,* pp. 24–25.

6. For instance, contrast Hough, *Struggle for the Third World,* with Papp, *Soviet Perceptions.*

7. For a general discussion, see Whelan and Dixon, *Soviet Union in the Third World,* pp. 7–13. See also Robert Donaldson, "The Soviet Union and the Third World," *Current History* 81 (October 1982): 313–17.

8. Saivetz and Woodby, *Soviet–Third World Relations,* chap. 7; Menon, *Soviet Power and the Third World,* pp. 33–60.

9. Porter, *USSR in Third World Conflicts.*

10. Steven David, "Soviet Involvement in Third World Coups," *International Security* 11 (Summer 1986): 3–36; Steven David, *Third World Coups and International Security* (Baltimore, Md.: Johns Hopkins University Press, 1987).

11. *Program of the Communist Party of the Soviet Union—1961* (New York: Crosscurrents Press, 1961), p. 43.

12. Ibid., pp. 43–44.

13. Bard O'Neill, William Heaton, and Donald Alberts, eds., *Insurgency in the Modern World* (Boulder, Colo.: Westview Press, 1980); Sam Sarkesian and William Scully, *U.S. Policy and Low-Intensity Conflict* (New Brunswick, N.J.: Transaction Books, 1981); Robert Osgood, *Limited War Revisited* (Boulder, Colo.: Westview Press, 1979); Frank Barnett, B. Hugh Tovar, and Richard Shultz, *Special Operations in U.S. Strategy* (Washington, D.C.: National Defense University Press, 1984); Douglas Blaufarb, *The Counterinsurgency Era* (New York: The Free Press, 1977); Richard Shultz, "Psychological Operations in Revolutionary Warfare: Threats, Opportunities and U.S. Policy," in Carnes Lord, ed., *Psychological Operations and Political Warfare in U.S. Strategy* (Washington, D.C.: National Defense University Press, 1988).

14. Rubinstein, *Soviet Foreign Policy Since World War II,* p. 215.

15. Papp, *Soviet Perceptions* p. 4.

16. V. I. Lenin, "Imperialism—The Highest Stage of Capitalism," in *Selected Works,* vol. 1 (Moscow: Progress Publishers, 1970).

17. Rubinstein, *Soviet Foreign Policy Since World War II,* p. 215.

18. *Second Congress of the Communist International* (London: New Park, 1977), pp. 110–11.

19. Adam Ulam, *The Bolsheviks* (New York: Macmillan, 1965), p. 215. Among the best general works on the Comintern, see Gunther Nollau, *International Communism and World Revolution, History and Methods* (London: Hollis & Carter, 1961); Franz Borkenau, *World Communism* (Ann Arbor; University of Michigan Press, 1962); E. H. Carr, *Twilight of the Comintern, 1930–1935* (New York: Pantheon, 1983).

20. *Second Congress of the Communist International,* pp. 117–18.

21. Papp, *Soviet Perceptions,* p. 6.

22. Adam Ulam, *Expansion and Coexistence: Soviet Foreign Policy 1917–1973* (New York: Praeger, 1974), p. 137.

23. Conrad Brandt, *Stalin's Failure in China* (New York: Norton, 1958); Edmond Chubb, *China and Russia* (New York: Columbia University Press, 1971); James Harrison, *The Long March to Power* (New York: Praeger, 1972).

24. Menon, *Soviet Power and the Third World*, p. 2.

25. Andry Zhdanov, "The International Situation," in *For a Lasting Peace, For a People's Democracy* (November 10, 1947), p. 2.

26. Melvin Gurtov, *The First Vietnam Crisis* (New York: Columbia University Press, 1967), pp. 6–15.

27. Gavriel D. Ra'anan, *International Policy Formation in the USSR* (Hamden, Conn.: Archon Books, 1983), chap. 10.

28. Hosmer and Wolfe, *Soviet Policy and Practice*, p. 4.

29. Rubinstein, *Soviet Foreign Policy Since World War II*, p. 217.

30. Nikita Khrushchev, *Report of the Central Committee of the CPSU to the Twentieth Party Congress* (Moscow: Foreign Language Publishing House, 1956).

31. Papp, *Soviet Perceptions*, pp. 10–11.

32. *Program of the Communist Party of the Soviet Union—1961*, p. 49.

33. Hosmer and Wolfe, *Soviet Policy and Practice*, chaps. 3, 4; Saivetz and Woodby, *Soviet–Third World Relations*, chap. 2.

34. Wynfred Joshua and Stephen Gibert, *Arms for the Third World: Soviet Military Aid Diplomacy* (Baltimore, Md.: Johns Hopkins University Press, 1969), chaps. 1, 2.

35. Central Intelligence Agency, *Communist Aid to Less Developed Countries* (Washington, D.C.: CIA, 1976).

36. Ibid.

37. Uri Ra'anan, "Moscow and the 'Third World,'" *Problems of Communism* 14 (January–February 1965): 22–31.

38. Hosmer and Wolfe, *Soviet Policy and Practice*, p. 22.

39. Whelan and Dixon, *Soviet Union in the Third World*, p. 15.

40. U.S. Congress, House Committee on Foreign Relations. *The Soviet Union and the Third World: A Watershed in Great Power Policy?* 95th Congress, 1st Session (Washington, D.C.: GPO, 1981), pp. 21–35.

41. Hosmer and Wolfe, *Soviet Policy and Practice*, p. 28.

42. Leonid Brezhnev, *Report of the CPSU Central Committee to the 24th Congress of the Communist Party of the Soviet Union* (Moscow: Novosti Press Agency, 1971). For the complete congress materials, see *Foreign Broadcast Information Service Daily Report—Soviet Union*, April 5–9, 1971 (hereafter cited as *FBIS—Soviet Union*).

43. *FBIS—Soviet Union*, April 6, 1971, supplement, pp. 76–83.

44. Vernon Aspaturian, "Soviet Global Power and the Correlation of Forces," *Problems of Communism* 24 (May–June 1980): 1–18.

45. For a discussion of the decision to expand the use of disinformation as an instrument of Soviet strategy, see Richard Shultz and Roy Godson, *Dezinformatsia: Active Measures in Soviet Strategy* (New York: Pergamon-Brassey, 1984); Ladislav Bittman,

The KGB and Soviet Disinformation (New York: Pergamon-Brassey, 1985); Brian D. Dailey and Patrick J. Parker, eds., *Soviet Strategic Deception* (Lexington, Mass.: Lexington Books, 1987). This has been corroborated in oral history interviews conducted with several former Soviet and East European intelligence officers. This project is under the auspices of the International Security Studies Program of the Fletcher School of Law and Diplomacy, Tufts University.

46. On Soviet views concerning splits in NATO see Shultz and Godson, *Dezinformatsia;* Clive Rose, *Campaigns Against Western Defense* (London: Macmillan, 1985). With respect to the impact of the U.S. withdrawal from Vietnam, see Boris Ponomarev, "Invincibility of the Liberation Movement," *Kommunist* (January 1980), trans. in *JPRS/ USSR Report* (March 1980): 11–32.

47. Leonard Schapiro, "The International Department of the CPSU: Key to Soviet Policy," *International Journal* 32 (Winter 1976/77): 41–55; Elizabeth Teague, "The Foreign Department of the Central Committee of the CPSU," *Radio Liberty Research Bulletin,* October 27, 1980, pp. 1–47. See also Robert W. Kitrinos, "International Department of the CPSU," *Problems of Communism* 33 (September–October 1984): 47–75. For the perspective of former Soviet officials on this question, see Arkady Shevchenko, *Breaking with Moscow* (New York: Knopf, 1985), and the interview with Stanislav Levchenko in Shultz and Godson, *Dezinformatsia,* chap. 5.

48. Boris Ponomarev, *Some Problems of the Revolutionary Movement* (Moscow: Progress Publishers, 1975) and *Lenin and the World Revolutionary Process* (Moscow: Progress Publishers, 1980).

49. Boris Ponomarev, "Universal-Historical Significance of the Great October Socialist Revolution," *Kommunist* (November 1977), trans. in *JPRS/USSR Report* (January 1978): 42, 46.

50. Boris Ponomarev, "Great Vital Force of Leninism," *Kommunist* (May 1980), trans. in *JPRS/USSR Report* (July 1980): 11.

51. Ibid., pp. 11–12.

52. Ponomarev, "Invincibility of the Liberation Movement," pp. 29–30.

53. Ibid., pp. 14–15.

54. See *Appearance of Soviet Leaders* (Washington, D.C.: CIA/National Foreign Assessment Center, 1978, 1979, 1980).

55. For the complete text of the meeting, see "Protocol of Talks Between PLO and Soviet Delegations in Moscow," in Ray Cline and Yonah Alexander, *Terrorism: The Soviet Connection* (New York: Crane, Russak, 1984), pp. 83–106.

56. Rostislav Ulyanovsky, *National Liberation* (Moscow: Progress Publishers, 1977).

57. Karen Brutents, *National Liberation Revolutions Today,* vol. 1 (Moscow: Progress Publishers, 1977), p. 16.

58. Petr Manchka, *In the Vanguard of the Revolutionary Struggle in Africa* (Moscow: Political Literature Publishers, 1975).

59. Harriet Fast Scott and William Scott, *The Soviet Art of War* (Boulder, Colo.: Westview Press, 1982), p. 291.

60. V. D. Sokolovskiy, *Soviet Military Strategy,* ed. and trans. by Harriet Fast Scott (New York: Crane, Russak, 1975), pp. 180–84.

61. A. A. Grechko, "The Leading Role of the CPSU in Building the Army of a Developed Socialist Society," *Voprosy Istorii KSPP* [Problems of History of the CPSU], trans. in *FBIS—Soviet Union,* May 1974. Also contained in Scott and Scott, *Soviet Art of War,* p. 243.

62. N. V. Ogarkov, "Military Strategy," *Sovetskaya Voyennaya Entsiklopedia* [Soviet Military Encyclopedia], vol. 7 (Moscow: Voyenizdat, 1979), p. 564.

63. "Documents and Materials: Long-Range Subjects for Military-Historical Research in 1981–1990," *Voyenno-Istoicheskiy Zhurnal* (June 1981), trans. in *JPRS/USSR Report—Military Affairs* (September 1981): 65–66.

64. For instance, in a 1981 article, Capt. N. Chikhachev underscores Brezhnev's report to the Twenty-sixth CPSU Congress, stressing the Soviet role in "guarding the progressive conquests" that have occurred "in a number of Afro-Asian and Latin American nations." See "Guarding the Progressive Conquests," *Kommunist Vooruzhennykh Sil* (July 1981), trans. in *JPRS/USSR Reports—Military Affairs* (December 1981). In an article in the same periodical, Maj. Gen. V. Khalipov concentrates on those documents from the Twenty-sixth congress concerned with the "national liberation struggles" and Soviet policy. See "Irreversible Process of Revolutionary Renewal of the World," *Kommunist Voorushennykh Sil* (May 1981), trans. in *JPRS/USSR Report—Military Affairs* (August 1981).

65. Mark Katz, *The Third World in Soviet Military Thought* (Baltimore, Md.: Johns Hopkins University Press, 1982), pp. 123–25.

66. Henry Trofimenko, "America, Russia, and the Third World," *Foreign Affairs* 59 (Summer 1981): 1021–40.

67. Francis Fukuyama, "A New Soviet Strategy," *Commentary* 68 (October 1979): 52–58.

68. "Proceedings of the 26th CPSU Congress," *FBIS—Soviet Union,* February 24, 1981, supplement 1, pp. 5–54.

69. *Documents and Resolutions,* Communist Party of the Soviet Union, Twenty-fifth Congress (Moscow: Novosti, 1976).

70. Charles Wolf et al., *The Costs of the Soviet Empire* (Santa Monica, Calif.: The Rand Corporation, 1983).

71. *Wall Street Journal,* January 30, 1984, p. 32.

72. *FBIS—Soviet Union,* February 25–March 14, 1986.

73. See Stephen Sestanovich, "Do the Soviets Feel Pinched by Third World Adventures," *Washington Post,* May 20, 1984, p. B1; Sweryn Bialer, "A Wounded Russian Bear Is Dangerous," *Washington Post,* January 22, 1984, pp. C1–C2; Robert Kaiser, "The USSR: The Generation That Failed," *Washington Post,* September 23–25, 1984, p. A1; Hough, *Struggle for the Third World,* chaps. 8–9.

74. Francis Miko, "The 27th Soviet Party Congress and the West," *Survival* 28 (July/August 1986): 302. See also Dimitri Simes, "Gorbachev: A New Foreign Policy," *Foreign Affairs: America and the World—1986* 65 (1987): 477–500.

75. Frederick Barghoorn, *Soviet Foreign Propaganda* (Princeton, N.J.: Princeton University Press, 1964), pp. 4–5. See also Peter Kenez, *The Birth of the Propaganda State* (Cambridge, Eng.: Cambridge University Press, 1985).

76. Shultz and Godson, *Dezinformatsia,* chaps. 2–3.

77. Ibid, chap. 3. See also Baruch Hazan, *Soviet Impregnational Propaganda* (Ann Arbor, Mich.: Ardis, 1982); Martin Ebon, *The Soviet Propaganda Machine* (New York: McGraw-Hill, 1987).

78. Shultz and Godson, *Dezinformatsia,* pp. 25–31.

79. The general purposes of the front organizations appear to be as follows. They enable Moscow to promote its policy under the camouflage of peace, racial equality, and national liberation to a much wider audience. They also provide a means for criticizing and isolating its main enemies strategically, politically, and morally. Fronts offer a way to improve the image of the Soviet Union internationally by distracting attention from repressive and aggressive Soviet policies. The fronts focus on the real and alleged shortcomings of Soviet enemies, while remaining silent on Soviet problems. They also defend aggressive Soviet foreign policy like the invasion of Afghanistan, and they may assist the KGB in spotting targets for recruitment. For background on the fronts, see Witold Sworakowski, *The Communist International and Its Front Organizations: A Research Guide and Checklist of Holdings in American and European Libraries* (Stanford: Hoover Institution Press, 1965); James Atkinson, *The Politics of Struggle* (Chicago: Henry Regnery Company, 1966); John Roche, *The History and Impact of Marxist-Leninist Organizational Theory* (Cambridge, Mass.: Institute for Foreign Policy Analysis, 1984); Roy Godson, *Labor in Soviet Global Strategy* (New York: National Strategy Information Center, 1984); Rose, *Campaigns Against Western Defense.* Each year the U.S. journal *Problems of Communism* publishes an annual checklist and discussion of the activities of Moscow's international fronts.

80. See Nollau, *International Communism;* Borkenau, *World Communism;* Carr, *Twilight of the Comintern.*

81. This concept—conference diplomacy—is borrowed from Arieh Eilan, "Conference Diplomacy," *The Washington Quarterly* 4 (Autumn 1981): 24–29.

82. John J. Dziak, *Soviet Perception of Military Power: The Interaction of Theory and Practice* (New York: National Strategy Information Center, 1981), p. 40.

83. Schapiro, "The International Department of the CPSU," p. 44. See also Jerry Hough, "Soviet Policymaking Toward Foreign Communists," *Studies in Comparative Communism* 15 (Autumn 1982): 167–83.

84. Dziak, *Soviet Perception of Military Power,* pp. 40, 41.

85. Vladimir Sakharov and Umberto Tosi, *High Treason* (New York: G. P. Putnam's Sons, 1980). For a background sketch on Boris Ponomarev, see "The Foreign Departments of the Central Committee of the CPSU," *Radio Liberty Research Bulletin,* October 27, 1980, pp. 14–18, 21–24.

86. Shultz and Godson, *Dezinformatsia,* chap. 5. This was reconfirmed in an oral history interview with Levchenko conducted under the auspices of the International Security Studies Program of the Fletcher School of Law and Diplomacy, Tufts University.

87. Arieh Eilan, "Soviet Diplomacy in the Third World," in Laqueur, *Patterns of Soviet Conduct,* chap. 2; Rubinstein, *Soviet Foreign Policy Since World War II,* chaps. 9–10.

88. Rubinstein, *Soviet Foreign Policy Since World War II,* p. 196.

89. Ibid., pp. 210, 212.

90. In the case of SWAPO, the key U.N. body Moscow has concentrated on is the Committee of 24 or Special Committee on the Situation with Regard to the Implementation of the Declaration on the Granting of Independence to Colonial Countries and Peoples. In the case of the PLO, two U.N. bodies are involved in a similar capacity. Each of these cases is examined in detail in Chapters 4 and 5.

91. U.S. Congress, Senate Select Committee on Intelligence, *Soviet Presence in the U.N. Secretariat* 99th Congress, 1st Session (Washington, D.C.: GPO, 1985).

92. See 1983 Appropriation Request of the FBI Before the House Subcommittee on Appropriations, 1 April 1982. Also cited in Juliana Pilon, "The UN and the USSR," *Survey* 27 (Autumn–Winter 1983): 95–96.

93. Pilon, "The UN and the USSR," p. 96. See also Shevchenko, *Breaking with Moscow.*

94. These points were made in an interview with former KGB officer Stanislav Levchenko; see oral history interviews, International Security Studies Program of the Fletcher School of Law and Diplomacy, Tufts University.

95. Shultz and Godson, *Dezinformatsia,* pp.31–33.

96. Sokolovskiy, *Soviet Military Strategy,* pp.180–83.

97. Large amounts of arms become especially important as the insurgency reaches its more advanced or what Theodore Shackley terms the *operational* phase of conflict. At this point, the opposition is able to "surface to confront security forces in open combat. Their tactics are now more hit than run." During earlier phases, few arms are required because violent tactics are confined to sabotage and terrorism. Theodore Shackley, *The Third Option* (New York: Reader's Digest Press, 1981), p. 87.

98. Daniel Papp, "The Soviet Union and Southern Africa," in Robert Donaldson, ed., *The Soviet Union and the Third World* (Boulder, Colo.: Westview Press, 1981), p. 79. See also Peter Vanneman and Martin James, *Soviet Foreign Policy in Southern Africa* (Pretoria: Africa Institute of South Africa, 1982).

99. For a discussion of the development of Soviet power projection capabilities in the 1970s, see W. Scott Thompson, *Power Projection* (New York: National Strategy Information Center, 1978); more recent developments are described in Hosmer and Wolfe, *Soviet Policy and Practice.*

100. Oral history interview with Michael Voslensky conducted under the auspices of the International Security Studies Program of the Fletcher School of Law and Diplomacy, Tufts University.

101. Neil Livingstone, "Terrorism: The International Connection," *Army,* December 1980, p. 16.

102. John Barron, *KGB Today* (New York: Reader's Digest Press, 1983), p. 21.

103. Harriet Fast Scott and William Scott, *The Armed Forces of the USSR* (Boulder, Colo.: Westview Press, 1978) chap. 11. See also the statements by KGB officer Vladimir Kuzichkin in *Time,* November 22, 1982, pp. 33–34, where he specifically identifies a terrorist training school at Balashikha.

104. John Collins, *Green Berets, SEALS and Spetsnaz: U.S. and Soviet Special Military Operations* (New York: Pergamon-Brassey, 1987).

105. See John Dziak, "Soviet Intelligence and Security Services in the 1980s: The Paramilitary Dimension," in Roy Godson, ed., *Intelligence Requirements for the 1980s: Counterintelligence* (New York: National Strategy Information Center, 1981), chap. 4.

106. Ibid., pp. 96, 110. Dziak notes that Yuri Andropov served with the partisans during World War II. Although Andropov is recognized for expanding the KGB's role in political active measures campaigns directed against the West, this suggests that he was also inclined toward the paramilitary techniques under discussion.

107. Dziak, "Soviet Intelligence and Security Services in the 1980s," pp. 96, 99–100. See also Collins, *Green Berets, SEALS, and Spetsnaz.*

108. See John Barron, *KGB: Secret World of Secret Agents* (New York: Reader's Digest Press, 1974); Leonard Schapiro, "The Soviet Union and the PLO," *Survey* 23 (Summer 1977): 193–207; Claire Sterling, *The Terror Network* (New York: Holt, Rinehart & Winston, 1981); U.S. Congress, Senate Subcommittee on Security and Terrorism of the Committee on the Judiciary, *Terrorism: The Role of Moscow and Its Subcontractors,* 97th Congress, 1st Session (Washington, D.C.: GPO, 1981).

109. Brian Crozier, *The Surrogate Forces of the Soviet Union,* Conflict Studies no. 92 (London: Institute for the Study of Conflict, 1978).

110. See Barron, *KGB Today,* appendix B: "Organization of the KGB."

111. Dziak, "Soviet Intelligence and Security Services in the 1980s."

112. Richard Shultz, "Soviet Use of Surrogates to Project Power into the Third World," *Parameters* 16 (Autumn 1986): 32–42.

113. Trong Gilberg, "East European Military Assistance to the Third World," in John Copper and Daniel Papp, ed., *Communist Nations' Military Assistance* (Boulder, Colo.: Westview Press, 1983), p. 74.

114. Ibid., p. 75.

115. See Rose Gottemoeller, "The Potential for Conflict Between Soviet and Cuban Policies in the Third World," *Conflict* 3, no. 4 (1982): 245–65, for a discussion of competing arguments.

116. Edward Gonzalez, "Complexities of Cuban Foreign Policy," *Problems of Communism* 26 (November–December 1977): 3–9.

117. Gavriel Ra'anan, "Surrogate Forces and Power Projection," in Uri Ra'anan, Robert L. Pfaltzgraff, Jr., and Geoffrey Kemp, eds., *Projection of Power* (Hamden, Conn.: Archon Books, 1982), p. 298.

118. Ibid., pp. 298–99.

119. Barron, KGB; Crozier, *Surrogate Forces of the Soviet Union;* Robert Leiken, *Soviet Strategy in Latin America* (Washington Papers: No. 93) (New York: Praeger, 1982).

120. W. Raymond Duncan, *The Soviet Union and Cuba* (New York: Praeger, 1985).

121. Laqueur, *Patterns of Soviet Conduct,* p. 15.

122. U.S. Congress, Senate Subcommittee on Security and Terrorism of the Committee on the Judiciary, *The Role of the Soviet Union, Cuba, and East Germany in Fomenting Terrorism in Southern Africa,* vol. 2, 97th Congress, 2d Session (Washington, D.C.: GPO, 1982), p. 26.

123. Vanneman and James, *Soviet Foreign Policy in Southern Africa,* pp. 38–39.

124. Ibid.; Ra'anan, "Surrogate Forces and Power Projection."

125. Gilberg, "East European Military Assistance to the Third World," p. 81.

126. Ibid., p. 82.

127. For the text, see *The African Communist* (London), no. 75 (Fourth Quarter 1978).

Chapter 3

1. Joseph Buttinger, *Vietnam: A Political History* (New York: Praeger, 1972); Bernard Fall, *Vietnam Witness 1953–1966* (New York: Praeger, 1966); Douglas Pike, *Viet Cong* (Cambridge, Mass.: The MIT Press, 1966); Frank Trager, ed., *Marxism in Southeast Asia* (Stanford: Stanford University Press, 1959); George Tanham, *Communist Revolutionary Warfare: From Vietminh to Viet Cong* (New York: Praeger, 1968); John McAlister, *Vietnam: The Origins of Revolution* (Garden City, N.J.: Doubleday, 1971); Paul Mus, *VietNam: Sociologie d'une guerre* (Paris: Editions du Seuil, 1952); Jean Lacouture, *Vietnam: Between Two Truces* (New York: Vintage, 1966); Ellen Hammer, *The Struggle for Indochina* (Stanford: Stanford University Press, 1954); William Duiker, *The Rise of Nationalism in Vietnam* (Ithaca, N.Y.: Cornell University Press, 1976); William Duiker, *Vietnam: Nation in Revolution* (Boulder, Colo.: Westview Press, 1983); James Harrison, *The Endless War: Fifty Years of Struggle in Vietnam* (New York: The Free Press, 1983); Huynh Kim Khanh, *Vietnamese Communism, 1925–1945* (Ithaca, N.Y.: Cornell University Press, 1982).

2. Donald Zagoria, *Vietnam Triangle* (New York: Pegasus, 1967), p. 36.

3. Hammer, *Struggle for Indochina,* pp. 297–98. See also Charles McLane, *Soviet Strategies in Southeast Asia* (Princeton, N.J.: Princeton University Press, 1966); Geoffrey Jukes, *The Soviet Union in Asia* (Berkeley: University of California Press, 1973).

4. Adam Ulam, *Expansion and Coexistence: Soviet Foreign Policy, 1917–1973* (New York: Praeger, 1974), p. 533.

5. Bernard Brodie, *War and Politics* (New York: Macmillan, 1973), chap. 3.

6. Ulam, *Expansion and Coexistence,* p. 533.

7. Ibid., pp. 533–34.

8. Fall, *Vietnam Witness,* p. 75.

9. Buttinger, *Vietnam,* p. 362.

10. P. J. Honey, *Communism in North Vietnam* (Cambridge, Mass.: The MIT Press, 1966), p. 75.

11. William Zimmerman, "The Korean and Vietnam Wars," in Stephen S. Kaplan, ed., *Diplomacy of Power: Soviet Armed Forces as a Political Instrument* (Washington, D.C.: The Brookings Institution, 1981), p. 336.

12. Ulam, *Expansion and Coexistence*, p. 669.

13. Arthur Dommen, *Conflict in Laos*, (New York: Praeger, 1964), p. 178.

14. Richard Rosser, "The Soviets and Vietnam: A Tragic Miscalculation?" *South Atlantic Quarterly* 72 (Summer 1973): 392.

15. Ibid., p. 393.

16. Zagoria, *Vietnam Triangle*, p. 43.

17. Ibid.

18. For accounts of these developments see *The Pentagon Papers: The Defense Department History of United States Decisionmaking on Vietnam* (Boston: Beacon Press, 1971), vol. 2; Buttinger, *Vietnam;* Guenter Lewy, *America in Vietnam* (New York: Oxford University Press, 1968); Frances Fitzgerald, *Fire in the Lake: The Vietnamese and the Americans in Vietnam* (Boston: Little, Brown, 1972).

19. Richard Shultz, "Strategy Lessons From an Unconventional War: The U.S. Experience in Vietnam," in Sam C. Sarkesian, ed., *Nonnuclear Conflicts in the Nuclear Age* (New York: Praeger, 1980), pp. 140–45.

20. *The Pentagon Papers*, vol. 3, p. 42.

21. Ibid., p. 82.

22. James C. Thompson, *Rolling Thunder* (Chapel Hill: University of North Carolina Press, 1980).

23. "Soviet Aid to North Vietnam" (Board of Studies for Southeast Asia, December 1971). Mimeo.

24. Zimmerman, "Korean and Vietnam Wars," p. 343.

25. Ulam, *Expansion and Coexistence*, p. 701.

26. V. D. Sokolovskiy, *Soviet Military Strategy*, edited and translated by Harriet Fast Scott (New York: Crane, Russak 1968), p. 184.

27. Ibid., p. 181.

28. Ibid., p. 184.

29. Lt. Col. N. Zagorodnikov, "The Military Might of the Socialist System and the World Revolutionary Process," *Kommunist Vooruzhennykh Sil,* no. 16 (August 1966). The author notes that new historical conditions exist in which Soviet military power has become a direct factor in safeguarding the world revolutionary process.

30. Mohamed Heikal, *The Sphinx and the Commissar: The Rise and Fall of Soviet Influence in the Middle East* (New York: Harper & Row, 1978), p. 162.

31. Zagoria, *Vietnam Triangle*, p. 43.

32. William E. Griffith, ed., *Sino-Soviet Relations 1964–1965* (Cambridge, Mass.: The MIT Press, 1967), p. 73.

33. Richard Shultz and Roy Godson, *Dezinformatsia: Active Measures in Soviet Strategy* (New York: Pergamon-Brassey, 1984), chap 3.

34. *Foreign Broadcast Information Service Daily Report—Soviet Union,* June 24, 1966, pp. BB 15–16, (hereafter cited as *FBIS—Soviet Union).*

35. Ibid., May 13, 1966, pp. BB 3–4.

36. Ibid., March 25, 1966, pp. BB 3–4.

37. Ibid., December 9, 1966, pp. BB 10–11.

38. Shultz and Godson, *Dezinformatsia,* chap. 3.

39. *FBIS—Soviet Union,* January 21, 1966, p. BB 4.

40. Ibid., December 23, 1966, pp. BB 8–9.

41. Ibid., August 12, 1966, p. BB 4.

42. Ibid., October 10, 1968, pp. BB 2–3.

43. Ibid., August 12, 1966, p. BB 3.

44. Ibid.

45. Ibid., February 25, 1966, pp. BB 2–3.

46. Ibid., May 13, 1966, p. BB 3.

47. Ibid., January 14, 1966, p. BB 2.

48. Ibid., March 18, 1966, p. BB 2.

49. Ibid., January 14, 1966, p. BB 2; March 18, 1966, p. BB 2; February 25, 1966, p. BB 3; February 11, 1966, p. BB 6.

50. Ibid., November 18, 1966, p. BB 1.

51. Ibid., January 21, 1966, p. BB 4.

52. Ibid., July 8, 1966, pp. BB 1–2.

53. "Vietnam in Flames," *New Times,* no. 6 (1968): 1–2.

54. *FBIS—Soviet Union,* April 1, 1968, p. AA 2.

55. Ibid., March 4, 1968, p. AA 12.

56. Peter Braestrup, *Big Story* (Boulder, Colo.: Westview Press, 1983); Harry Summers, *On Strategy: The Vietnam War in Context* (Carlisle, Penn.: Strategic Studies Institute, U.S. Army War College, 1981); Andrew Krepinevich, *The Army and Vietnam* (Baltimore, Md.: Johns Hopkins University Press, 1986).

57. *FBIS—Soviet Union,* April 22, 1968, pp. A 3–4.

58. Ibid., August 2, 1968, p. A 9.

59. Ibid., December 6, 1968, p. A 4.

60. Ibid., February 9, 1968, pp. AA 5–6; February 12, 1968, pp. AA 4–5; March 4, 1968, pp. AA 11–12; April 5, 1968, pp. AA 2–3.

61. Ibid., May 17, 1968, pp. A 3–4; June 17, 1968, p. A. 5; November 1, 1968, pp. A 1–2; November 14, 1968, p. A 2.

62. Ibid., January 29, 1968, p. AA 31; February 12, 1968, pp. AA 4–5.

63. Ibid., Feburary 9, 1968, pp. AA 5–6; February 12, 1968, pp. AA 4–5; March 4, 1968, pp. AA 11–12; April 5, 1968, pp. AA 2–3.

64. Ibid., January 26, 1968, p. AA 35–36; January 29, 1968, p. AA 31; May 24, 1968, pp. AA 1–2. "Washington's Other War," *New Times,* no. 32 (1967): 1.

65. *FBIS—Soviet Union,* January 12, 1970, pp. A 7–8.

66. Ibid., January 14, 1972, p. C 1.

67. "Vietnam and Nuremberg," *New Times,* no. 13 (1969): 29–30.

68. *FBIS—Soviet Union,* July 3, 1972, pp. AA 6–7.

69. Ibid., January 3, 1972, pp. C 1–2.

70. Ibid., November 3, 1972, p. AA 5.

71. Ibid., November 6, 1972, p. AA 1.

72. Ibid., January 3, 1972, pp. C 1–2.

73. *Bulletin of Peace* (February 1965): 1–4.

74. "American Women Telephone the White House," *Perspectives,* no. 2 (1966): 8–9.

75. "An Appeal for Peace in Vietnam by the American Friends, *Perspectives,* no. 2 (1967): 10–11.

76. "21 October—Biggest World Day of Action for Peace in Vietnam" *Perspectives,* nos. 11–12 (1967): 8–10.

77. *World Peace Council Bulletin,* no. 6 (1967): 1–8.

78. *World Peace Council Bulletin,* nos. 3,6,7–8, and 9–12 (1967); *Perspectives,* nos. 3, 6, 11–12 (1967), nos. 6, 11–12 (1968).

79. "Stockholm Was the Spark," *Perspectives,* no. 11–12 (1967): 6.

80. "To Bring the Atrocities into the Open," *New Perspectives,* (May 1971): 19–21.

81. "Ecocide, Biocide, and Genocide in Vietnam," *New Perspectives* (July–August 1972); 44–45.

82. "To Bring the Atrocities into the Open," pp. 19–21.

83. "Ecocide, Biocide, and Genocide in Vietnam," pp. 44–45. For a comprehensive statement on this subject see *The World Accuses* (Printed in the German Democratic Republic, 1973).

84. "Bodies—I Want More Bodies," *New Perspectives* (August 1971): 18.

85. "The Living and the Dead Accuse," *New Perspectives* (August 1971): 24–26.

86. "Humanism in Contrast to Barbarism," *New Perspectives* (August 1971): 19–20.

87. "The Hoax of Nixon's Troop Withdrawals"; and "Wiring the War: Electronic Deaths," *New Perspectives* (December 1971): 12.

88. "Nixon's Doctrine of Vietnamization," *New Perspectives* (January–February 1972): 8–10.

89. The 1970–1972 issues of *Peace Courier* contain numerous examples.

90. "Stockholm Was the Spark," p. 6.

91. Ibid.

92. *World Conference on Vietnam—Documents* (Stockholm: World Peace Council, 1967), pp. 1–14.

93. Ibid., pp. 4–5.

94. Ibid., p. 3.

95. Information Letter no. 2 (International Liaison Committee), (June 1968): 1.

96. Ibid., pp. 4–5.

97. Information Letter no. 1 (International Liaison Committee), (March 1969): 1–2.

98. *Stockholm Conference on Vietnam* (Stockholm: World Peace Council, 1969), pp. 1–2/list of participants.

99. U.S. Congress, House Hearings Before the Committee on Internal Security. *National Peace Action Coalition (NPAC) and Peoples Coalition for Peace and Justice (PCPJ) Part 2*, 92nd Congress, 1st Session (Washington, D.C.: GPO, 1971).

100. Ibid., p. 1862.

101. For example, see *World Conference on Vietnam, Laos, and Cambodia* (Stockholm: World Peace Council, 1970).

102. Information Letter no. 5 (International Liaison Committee) (October 1969): 1.

103. This was contained in a special notice sent by the International Liaison Committee to all organizations planning for the fall offensive. It was sent out in October 1969.

104. Uri Ra'anan et al., eds., *Hydra of Carnage: International Linkages of Terrorism. The Witnesses Speak.* (Lexington, Mass.: Lexington Books, 1985), p. 511.

105. *Yearbook of the United Nations* (New York: U.N., 1965), p. 85.

106. Ibid., p. 88.

107. Ibid.

108. Ibid., pp. 88–89.

109. Seymour Finger, *Your Man at the UN* (New York: New York University Press, 1980), p. 126.

110. *U.N. Document S/10134* (New York: U.N. 1972), p. 2.

111. *The Pentagon Papers*, vol. 4, p. 137.

112. U.S. Arms Control and Disarmament Agency, *World Military Expenditures and Arms Transfers 1965–1974* (Washington, D.C., 1976), p. 74.

113. *The Pentagon Papers*, vol. 4, p. 137.

114. Ibid., p. 223.

115. Ibid., p. 226.

116. Ibid., p. 231.

117. *The Military Balance, 1964–1965* (London: International Institute for Strategic Studies, 1964), pp. 11–12.

118. For a discussion of these restrictions see William C. Westmoreland, *A Soldier's Report* (Garden City, N.Y.: Doubleday, 1976), p. 76.

119. *The Military Balance 1966–1967* (London: International Institute for Strategic Studies, 1966), p. 11.

120. William W. Momyer, *Air Power in Three Wars* (Washington, D.C.: Department of the Air Force, 1978), p. 118.

121. *The Military Balance, 1966–1967*, p. 11.

122. Cited in Momyer, *Air Power in Three Wars*, p. 119.

123. *The Military Balance, 1966–1967,* p. 12.

124. *The Military Balance, 1968–1969* (London: International Institute for Strategic Studies, 1968), p. 14.

125. Momyer, *Air Power in Three Wars,* p. 138.

126. *The Military Balance, 1968–1969,* p. 13.

127. Momyer, *Air Power in Three Wars,* p. 123.

128. Cited in Paul Burbage et al., *The Battle for the Skies Over North Vietnam, 1964–1972* (Southeast Asia Monograph Series) (Washington, D.C.: Office of U.S. Air Force History, 1976), p. 145.

129. *The Military Balance, 1972–1973* (London: International Institute for Strategic Studies, 1972), p. 55.

130. *SIPRI Yearbook 1973* (Stockholm: Stockholm International Peace Research Institute, 1973), p. 301.

131. Ibid., p. 302.

132. *The Military Balance, 1972–1973,* p. 55.

133. *The Pentagon Papers,* vol. 4, pp. 489–90.

134. Momyer, *Air Power in Three Wars;* Burbage, *Battle for the Skies Over North Vietnam;* Paul Burbage et al., *The Air Force in Southeast Asia: Toward a Bombing Halt* (Southeast Asia Monograph Series) (Washington, D.C.: Office of U.S. Air Force History, 1970); George Eckhardt, *Command and Control, 1950–1969* (U.S. Army Vietnam Studies) (Washington, D.C.: GPO, 1974); John Tolson, *Airmobility* (U.S. Army Vietnam Studies) (Washington, D.C.: GPO, 1973).

135. Momyer, *Air Power in Three Wars,* p. 119.

136. Ibid., pp. 119–120.

137. Burbage et al., *Battle for the Skies Over North Vietnam,* p. 135.

138. Momyer, *Air Power in Three Wars,* p. 123.

139. Comments by Henry Kissinger contained in State Department *Bulletins,* LXVIII, no. 750 (January 8, 1973): 33–41. See also Henry Kissinger, *White House Years* (Boston: Little, Brown 1979), chap. 27, pp. 31–33.

140. U.S.G. Sharp and William Westmoreland, *Report on the War in Vietnam* (Washington, D.C.: GPO, 1968); Westmoreland, *Soldier's Report;* U.S.G. Sharp, *Strategy for Defeat: Vietnam in Retrospect* (San Rafael, Calif.: Presidio Press, 1979).

141. *The Military Balance, 1968–1969,* pp. 68–69.

142. *The Military Balance, 1965–1966* (London: International Institute for Strategic Studies, 1965), p. 11.

143. *The Military Balance, 1967–1968* (London: International Institute for Stragetic Studies, 1967), p. 13.

144. *The Military Balance, 1972–1973,* p. 55. The history of the People's Army of Vietnam is contained in Douglas Pike, *PAVN: People's Army of Vietnam* (San Francisco, Calif.: Presidio Press, 1986).

145. George C. Herring, *America's Longest War* (New York: John Wiley & Sons, 1979), p. 240.

146. Kissinger, *White House Years,* chap. 25.

147. John Doglione et al., *Airpower and the 1972 Spring Invasion* (Southeast Asia Monograph Series) (Washington, D.C.: Office of U.S. Air Force History, 1976), p. 4.

148. Momyer, *Air Power in Three Wars,* p. 326.

149. Douglas Pike, *Viet Cong;* Michael Conley, *The Communist Insurgent Infrastructure in South Vietnam: A Study of Organization and Strategy* (Washington, D.C.: Center for Research in Social Systems, The American University, 1966).

150. *New York Times,* December 15, 1968.

151. *New York Times,* October 4, 1966.

152. *New York Times,* August 12, 1965.

153. Zimmerman, "Korean and Vietnam Wars," p. 348.

154. *New York Times,* August 29 and 30, 1966.

155. Momyer, *Air Power in Three Wars,* p. 142.

156. Cited in Zimmerman, "Korean and Vietnam Wars," p. 346.

157. Stephen Hosmer and Thomas Wolfe, *Soviet Policy and Practice Toward Third World Conflicts* (Lexington, Mass.: Lexington Books, 1983), p. 247.

158. Richard Nixon, *The Memoirs of Richard Nixon* (New York: Grosset & Dunlap, 1978), p. 391.

Chapter 4

1. Uri Ra'anan et al., *Hydra of Carnage: International Linkages of Terrorism. The Witnesses Speak* (Lexington, Mass.: Lexington Books, 1985), pp. 492–513.

2. Galia Golan, "The Soviet Union and the PLO Since the War in Lebanon," *Middle East Journal* 40 (Spring 1986): 285–305.

3. *Contemporary Mideast Backgrounder,* December 29, 1981, pp. 3–4.

4. Arieh Y. Yodfat and Yuval Arnon-Ohanna, *PLO Strategy and Tactics* (New York: St. Martin's Press, 1981), pp. 84–85.

5. *Middle East Record* 3 (1967): 319.

6. Ra'anan et al., *Hydra of Carnage,* pp. 571–73.

7. Roberta Goren, *The Soviet Union and Terrorism* (London: Allen & Unwin, 1984), p. 7.

8. Bard O'Neill, "Toward a Typology of Political Terrorism," *Journal of International Affairs* 32 (Spring/Summer 1978): 17–42.

9. *Middle East Record* 3 (1967): 3.

10. V. Kadryavtsev, "Middle East: Military Solution," *New Times,* April 10, 1968; L. Zavyalov, "Tel Aviv Maneuvres," *New Times,* August 13, 1969; S. Astahov, "Israeli Expansionism and the Palestinian Refugees," *International Affairs* (July 1968).

11. *New York Times,* January 23, 1970.

12. Ra'anan et al., *Hydra of Carnage,* pp. 514–18.

13. Mohamed Heikal, *The Road to Ramadan* (New York: Quadrangle, 1975), p. 65.

14. Cited in Galia Golan, *The Soviet Union and the Palestine Liberation Organization* (New York: Praeger, 1980), p. 11.

15. *BBC Summary of World Broadcasts/Soviet Union,* June 9, 1970.

16. Ra'anan et al., *Hydra of Carnage,* pp. 514–18.

17. O'Neill, "Toward a Typology of Political Terrorism," p. 25. For a more detailed discussion, see his book *Armed Struggle in Palestine: A Political Military Analysis* (Boulder, Colo.: Westview Press, 1978).

18. For a useful breakdown of the principal Palestinian organizations and groups, see Yodfat and Arnon-Ohanna, *PLO Strategy and Tactics,* appendix 1. See also Helena Cobban, *The Palestinian Liberation Organization* (Cambridge, Eng.: Cambridge University Press, 1984), chap. 7.

19. Yodfat and Arnon-Ohanna, *PLO Strategy and Tactics,* p. 89.

20. *BBC Summary of World Broadcasts/Soviet Union,* December 19, 1970.

21. *Foreign Broadcast Information Service Daily Report—Soviet Union,* April 8, 1971, Supplement, p. 6 (hereafter cited as *FBIS—Soviet Union*).

22. Ibid., March 3, 1973, p. H 1.

23. The link between Fatah and the BSO is documented in O'Neill, *Armed Struggle in Palestine,* pp. 290–91n.

24. Goren, *Soviet Union and Terrorism,* p. 117.

25. Uri Ra'anan, Robert L. Pfaltzgraff, Jr., and Geoffrey Kemp, *Arms Transfers to the Third World* (Boulder, Colo.: Westview Press, 1978), chap. 7.

26. *FBIS—Soviet Union,* August 5, 1974, pp. F 3–4.

27. Cited in Golan, *Soviet Union and the Palestine Liberation Organization,* p. 233.

28. Yodfat and Arnon-Ohanna, *PLO Strategy and Tactics,* appendix 2—The Palestinian National Covenant.

29. Brezhnev report to Twenty-fifth Congress.

30. Yodfat and Arnon-Ohanna, *PLO Strategy and Tactics,* p. 100.

31. Ra'anan et al., *Hydra of Carnage,* pp. 499–513.

32. For a discussion of the stage strategy see Goren, *Soviet Union and Terrorism,* p. 119.

33. Ibrahim Abu Lughod, "Flexible Militancy: A Report on the Sixteenth Session of the Palestine National Council," *Journal of Palestine Studies* 12 (Summer 1983): 25–40; Rashid Khalidi, *Under Siege: PLO Decisionmaking During the 1982 War* (New York: Columbia University Press, 1985).

34. *New York Times,* May 11, 1983; Naomi Weinberger, *Syrian Intervention in Lebanon* (New York: Oxford University Press, 1986).

35. *Le Monde,* May 27, 1983; *International Herald Tribune,* May 17, 1983.

36. *The Economist—Foreign Report,* March 10, 1983.

37. Ra'anan et al., *Hydra of Carnage,* pp. 492–98; for a Palestinian/Marxist interpretation of these developments see B. J. Odeh, *Errors and Betrayal in Lebanon* (Totowa, N.J.: Biblio, 1985).

38. Golan, "Soviet Union and the PLO Since the War in Lebanon," p. 300.

39. Judith Perera, "Riding the Bear," *The Middle East* (June 1984): 15–16.

40. Golan, "Soviet Union and the PLO Since the War in Lebanon," pp. 301–2.

41. *FBIS—Soviet Union,* November 6, 1974, p. F 4.

42. Ibid., September 4, 1974, p. F 1.

43. Ibid., November 13, 1974, p. F 5.

44. Ibid., October 11, 1974, p. F 3.

45. Ibid., December 3, 1974, p. F 6.

46. Ibid., April 26, 1974, pp. F 1–2.

47. Ibid., July 17, 1975, p. F 1.

48. Ibid., September 3, 1975, p. F 3.

49. Ibid., September 15, 1975, p. F 2.

50. Ibid., August 19, 1975, p. F 5.

51. Ibid., April 15, 1975, p. F 6.

52. Ibid., November 18, 1975, p. F 1.

53. Ibid., July 15, 1976, p. F 2.

54. *Le Monde,* July 20, 1976, p. 6.

55. *FBIS—Soviet Union,* May 24, 1976, p. F 6.

56. Ibid., January 16, 1976, pp. F 5–6.

57. Ibid., January 28, 1976, pp. F 3–4.

58. Ibid., February 28, 1977, p. B 4.

59. Leonard Schapiro, "The Soviet Union and the PLO," *Survey* 23 (Summer 1977): 193–207.

60. *FBIS—Soviet Union,* November 23, 1977, pp. F 9–12.

61. Richard Shultz and Roy Godson, *Dezinformatsia: Active Measures in Soviet Strategy* (New York: Pergamon-Brassey, 1984), chap. 3.

62. *FBIS—Soviet Union,* November 25, 1977, pp. F 5–6.

63. Ibid., April 11, 1977, pp. F 7–8.

64. Ibid., August 8, 1979, p. H 6.

65. Ibid., p. H 1.

66. Ibid., pp. H 1–2.

67. Ibid., June 5, 1979, p. H 1.

68. Ibid., October 22, 1981, pp. H 1–2.

69. Ibid., September 6, 1979, pp. H 5–6.

70. Ibid., July 26, 1979, p. H 1.

71. Ibid., June 10, 1981, p. H 1.

72. Ibid.

73. Ibid., August 16, 1979, p. A 2.

74. Ibid., May 4, 1981, p. H 3.

75. Ibid., June 27, 1983, p. H 4.

76. Ibid., November 7, 1983, p. H 1.

77. Ibid., November 23, 1983, pp. H 1–2.

78. Ibid., July 23, 1983, pp. H 3–4.

79. Ibid., February 20, 1985, p. H 1.

80. Ibid., March 6, 1985, p. H 1.

81. Ibid., January 4, 1984, p. H 2.

82. Ibid., January 23, 1984, p. H 3.

83. Ibid., July 30, 1985, p. H 1.

84. Ibid., January 24, 1984, p. CC 17.

85. For a listing of all major Soviet fronts and their structure and national-level affiliates, see *Soviet International Fronts* (Washington, D.C.: U.S. Information Agency, 1985).

86. Leo Kohtala, "Israeli Atrocities on Palestinian People," *New Perspectives*, no. 1 (1975): 35–36.

87. Leo Kohtala, "Mass Deportation of Palestinians," *New Perspectives*, no. 1 (1975): 36.

88. "In Defense of Human Rights," *Peace Courier* (February–March 1975): 6.

89. Farouk Maassarany, "Israeli Aggression in South Lebanon," *New Perspectives*, no. 1 (1978): 17–18.

90. Farouk Maassarany, "Foreign Intervention in Lebanon Must End," *New Perspectives*, No. 1 (1977): 37–38.

91. "Resolution on the Middle East Crisis," *Peace Courier* (October 1977): 12.

92. Mohammad Bajbouj, "Camp David Conspiracy Against Arab People," *New Perspectives*, No. 1 (1981): 27.

93. Tawfig Toubi, "Murderous Israeli-U.S. War Against Lebanon and Palestinian Peoples," *New Perspectives*, No. 5 (1982): 14.

94. "Israeli Invasion Endangers World Peace," *Peace Courier* (October 1982): 2.

95. "Palestinian Problem at UN," *Peace Courier* (October 1974): 7.

96. "Ho Chi Minh Award to Arafat," *Peace Courier* (October 1980): 6. Earlier in 1975 he was awarded the WPC's highest award, the Joliot-Curie Medal. See *Peace Courier* (October 1975): 3.

97. Yasser Arafat, "Palestinian Liberation Struggle Bravely Facing Imperialist Hurricane," *New Perspectives*, No. 1 (1981): 25–26.

98. "PLO Stands Against Imperialist Arms Race—For Liberation and Peace," *Peace Courier* (June 1984): 4.

99. "Palestine Solidarity Week," *Peace Courier* (April 1975): 7.

100. "International Conference on Middle East," *Peace Courier* (April 1975): 7.

101. "International Day of Solidarity with Lebanon," *Peace Courier* (May–June 1979): 1, 11.

102. "Palestine Solidarity Body Formed," *Peace Courier* (March 1980): 5.

103. Ra'anan et al., *Hydra of Carnage*, p. 11. The development of the Stockholm conference that Ponomarev is referring to is discussed in Chapter 3 of the book.

104. "WPC at UN Observance of Human Rights Anniversary," *Peace Courier* (January 1979): 1.

105. "WPC Petitions UN Human Rights Body," *Peace Courier* (March 1979): 8.

106. Discussed in International Association of Democratic Lawyers' publication *Review of Contemporary Law*, no. 2 (1979).

107. *Democratic Journalist*, (November 11–12, 1979). Published monthly by the International Organization of Journalists.

108. "Massacre in Beirut," *Peace Courier* (August–September 1982): 12–13.

109. "WPC Declares Beirut a 'Hero City,'" *Peace Courier* (October 1982): 3.

110. "Solidarity with Syrian People," *Peace Courier* (October–November 1983): 10.

111. *CPC Information*, August 1984. Monthly publication of the Christian Peace Conference.

112. "WPC Stands Against Imperialist Arms Race," *CPC Information*, August 1984, p. 4.

113. Paul Johnson, "Barbarous Parliament," *The New Republic* 173 (December 20, 1975): 10–14.

114. Cobban, *Palestinian Liberation Organization*, p. 230.

115. Daniel P. Moynihan and Susanne Weaver, *A Dangerous Place* (New York: Berkeley, 1980), chap. 9.

116. Cited in Juliana Pilon, "The United Nations' Campaign Against Israel," *Backgrounder*, June 16, 1983, p. 7.

117. Ra'anan, et al., *Hydra of Carnage*, pp. 509–11.

118. Raphael Israeli, *PLO in Lebanon: Selected Documents* (London: Weidenfeld & Nicolson, 1983), p. 18.

119. This annual report is titled *Report of the Committee on the Exercise of the Inalienable Rights of the Palestinian People*. Hereafter we will use the U.N. document number in footnoting this annual report.

120. *U.N. Document A/35/35*, Supplement no. 35 (New York, 1980), p. 1.

121. Ibid., p. 3.

122. *U.N. Document A/38/35*, Supplement no. 35 (New York, 1983), p. 3.

123. Ibid., p. 4.

124. *U.N. Document A/35/35*, Supplement no. 35 (New York, 1980), p. 5.

125. Ibid.

126. Ibid., p. 10; *U.N. Document A/34/35,* Supplement no. 35 (New York, 1979), pp. 9–10.

127. *U.N. Document A/34/35,* Supplement no. 35 (New York, 1979), p. 10.

128. Ibid.

129. *U.N. Document A/38/35,* Supplement no. 35 (New York, 1983).

130. *United Nations—Division for Palestinian Rights* (September–October 1983), pp. 6–9.

131. *U.N. Document A/C.5/37/L.2.* (New York, 1977).

132. Julius Stone, *Israel and Palestine: Assault on the Law of Nations* (Baltimore, Md.: Johns Hopkins University Press, 1981), p. 124.

133. Juliana Pilon, "The United Nations: Shattered Illusions," *Survey* 27 (Autumn-Winter 1983): 104.

134. U.S. Congress, Senate Select Committee on Intelligence, *Soviet Presence in the U.N. Secretariat,* 99th Congress, 1st Session (Washington, D.C.: GPO, 1985).

135. *U.N. Document A/37/35,* Supplement no. 35 (New York, 1982), p. 45.

136. *United Nations—Special Unit on Palestinian Rights* (1981).

137. *U.N. Document A/G.5/37/4.* (New York, 1983).

138. The U.N. Educational, Scientific, and Cultural Organization, for instance, excluded Israel from participation in its regional activities in a resolution passed in 1974.

139. Goren, *Soviet Union and Terrorism,* p. 108.

140. Yodfat and Arnon-Ohanna, *PLO Strategy and Tactics,* p. 87.

141. Schapiro, "Soviet Union and the PLO," p. 193. Golan takes a similar position in *Soviet Union and the Palestine Liberation Organization,* p. 14.

142. U.S. Congress, Senate Committee on the Judiciary, *Hearings on Terrorist Activities,* 94th Congress, 1st Session (Washington, D.C.: GPO, 1975).

143. Israeli intelligence estimate reported in Ray Cline and Yonah Alexander, *Terrorism: The Soviet Connection* (New York: Crane, Russak, 1984). p. 51.

144. Jillian Becker, *The PLO* (New York: St. Martin's Press, 1984), p. 204.

145. Information provided by the Israeli Defense Forces official and reported in Cline and Alexander, *Terrorism* p. 52.

146. Ibid.

147. Ibid., p. 53.

148. Goren, *Soviet Union and Terrorism,* p. 137.

149. Stefan Possoney and Francis Bouchey, *International Terrorism—The Communist Connection* (Washington, D.C.: American Council on World Freedom, 1978), p. 47.

150. David J. Kopilow, *Castro, Israel, and the PLO* (Washington, D.C.: The Cuban-American National Foundation, 1984), pp. 6–7.

151. Reported in Cline and Alexander, *Terrorism,* p. 33.

152. Oriana Fallaci, "A Leader of the Fedayeen: We Want a War Like the Vietnam War," *Life,* June 12, 1970, pp. 32–34.

153. David Milbank, *International and Transnational Terrorism: Diagnosis and Prognosis* (Washington, D.C.: Central Intelligence Agency, 1976), p. 21.

154. Claire Sterling, *The Terror Network* (New York: Holt, Rinehart & Winston, 1981), p. 15.

155. See PLO documents contained in Ra'anan et al., *Hydra of Carnage*, pp. 551–53.

156. U.S. Congress, Senate Foreign Relations Committee, *Hearings on International Terrorism*, 95th Congress, 1st Session (Washington, D.C.: GPO, 1977).

157. Contained in a program on the PLO that aired on PBS September 25, 1979. Statements also quoted in Cline and Alexander, *Terrorism*, pp. 46–47.

158. Edward Rosental, *Mind Conditioning* (Moscow: Novosti Press, 1978).

159. Ra'anan et al., *Hydra of Carnage*, pp. 540–43.

160. Ibid., pp. 544–47.

161. Cline and Alexander, *Terrorism*, p. 45.

162. *Economist—Foreign Report*, March 8, 1978, pp. 4–7; March 15, 1978, pp. 5–6.

163. Cline and Alexander, *Terrorism*, p. 63.

164. Goren, *Soviet Union and Terrorism*, pp. 142–83.

165. Israeli, *PLO in Lebanon; Daily Telegraph*, December 1, 1980, p. 1; Ra'anan et al., *Hydra of Carnage*, part 2, chap. 5.

166. *L'Express*, January 13, 1981, p. 1.

167. Ra'anan et al., *Hydra of Carnage*, pp. 538–39.

168. Ibid., p. 533.

169. Ibid., p. 531.

170. *Washington Post*, May 29, 1982, p. A7.

171. Reported in Kopilow, *Castro, Israel, and the PLO*, p. 12.

172. *Associated Press*, April 14, 1981. Cited in Kopilow, *Castro, Israel, and the PLO*, p. 12.

173. Ra'anan et al., *Hydra of Carnage*, pp. 309–20.

174. *Washington Post*, May 29, 1982, p. A12.

175. *FBIS—Middle East*, December 13, 1979, Supp. 39, p. 10.

176. Reported in Goren, *Soviet Union and Terrorism*, p. 190.

177. Ra'anan et al., *Hydra of Carnage*, p. 584.

178. Goren, *Soviet Union and Terrorism*, pp. 166–68.

Chapter 5

1. David Rees, "Soviet Strategic Penetration of Africa," *Conflict Studies*, no. 77 (November 1977); Brian Crozier, "The Surrogate Forces of the Soviet Union," *Conflict Studies*, no. 92 (February 1978); Peter Vanneman and Martin James, "The Soviet Intervention in Angola: Intentions and Implications," *Strategic Review* 4 (Summer 1976): 92–103.

2. David Albright, "Moscow's African Policy of the 1970s," in David Albright, ed., *Communism in Africa* (Bloomington: Indiana University Press, 1980); Colin Legum, "The USSR in Africa: The African Environment," *Problems of Communism* 27 (January–February 1978): 1–19; Roger Kanet, ed., *The Soviet Union and the Developing Nations* (Baltimore, Md.: Johns Hopkins University Press, 1974).

3. Colin Legum, "African Outlook Toward the USSR," in Albright, *Communism in Africa*, p. 10.

4. Ibid., p. 13.

5. See Arthur J. Klinghoffer, *The Angola War: A Study in Soviet Policy in the Third World* (Boulder, Colo.: Westview Press, 1980); William LeoGrande et al., *Cuba in Africa* (Pittsburgh, Pa.: University of Pittsburgh Press, 1980); Milene Charles, *The Soviet Union in Africa: The History of Soviet Involvement* (Washington, D.C.: University Press of America, 1980); Morris Rothenberg, *The USSR in Africa: New Dimensions of Soviet Global Power* (Coral Gables, Fla.: Advanced International Studies Institute, University of Miami, 1980).

6. John Marcum, *The Angolan Revolution: Exile Politics and Guerrilla Warfare (1962–1976),* vol. 2 (Cambridge, Mass.: The MIT Press, 1978), pp. 171–72.

7. Ibid., p. 224.

8. Marcum, *The Angolan Revolution,* vol 2, p. 229.

9. Christopher Stevens, "The Soviet Union and Angola," *African Affairs* 75 (April 1976): 137–51.

10. Arthur J. Klinghoffer, "The Soviet Union and Angola," in Robert Donaldson, ed., *The Soviet Union in the Third World: Successes and Failures* (Boulder, Colo.: Westview Press, 1981).

11. Stephen Hosmer and Thomas Wolfe, *Soviet Policy and Practice Toward Third World Conflicts* (Lexington, Mass.: Lexington Books, 1983), p. 84.

12. Klinghoffer, "Soviet Union and Angola," p. 99.

13. Hosmer and Wolfe, *Soviet Policy and Practice,* p. 86.

14. See Gerhard Totemeyer, *Namibia: Old and New* (New York: St. Martin's Press, 1978); Gerhard Totemeyer, *South West Africa/Namibia: Attitudes, Assessments, and Prospects* (Randburg, South Africa: Fokus Suid Publishers, 1977); John Seiler, ed., *Southern Africa Since the Portuguese Coup* (Boulder, Colo.: Westview Press, 1980); John Dugard, ed., *The South West Africa/Namibia Dispute* (Berkeley: University of California Press, 1973); Kenneth Adelman, *African Realities* (New York: Crane, Russak, 1980); David Soggot, *Namibia: The Violent Heritage* (New York: St. Martin's Press, 1986); Geisa Maria Rocha, *In Search of Namibian Independence: The Limitations of the United Nations* (Boulder, Colo.: Westview Press, 1984).

15. Totemeyer, *Namibia: Old and New,* p. 199.

16. In addition to splits within SWAPO, other political organizations do exist in Namibia, although SWAPO appears to be the strongest. I will discuss this further in the concluding part of this chapter.

17. U.S. Congress, Senate Subcommittee on Security and Terrorism of the Committee on the Judiciary, *The Role of the Soviet Union, Cuba, and East Germany in Fomenting Terrorism in Southern Africa,* vol. 1, 97th Congress, 2d Session (Washington, D.C.: GPO, 1982), pp. 697–98.

18. Ibid., pp. 889–901.

19. Ibid., p. 698. These developments were described in the 1982 congressional testimony by Andreas Shipanga, then president of SWAPO-Democrats.

20. Walter Hahn and Alvin Cottrell, *Soviet Shadow Over Africa* (Coral Gables, Fla.: Advanced International Studies Institute, University of Miami, 1976), pp. 74–75.

21. *Foreign Broadcast Information Service Daily Reports—Soviet Union,* August 24, 1978, pp. H 1–2, (hereafter cited as *FBIS—Soviet Union*).

22. Ibid., January 25, 1980, p. J 3. (For example, TASS in January 1980 repeated the following statement by Sam Nujoma: "The Pretorian authorities continue imprudently disregarding numerous decisions of the U.N. demanding that the racialist troops be withdrawn. This is naturally done with the support of the Western countries, which have a stake in preserving South African rule in Namibia, or in creating there a neocolonial regime under their aegis in order to continue plundering our country's natural resources.")

23. *FBIS—Soviet Union,* September 18, 1980, pp. J 1–2.

24. Ibid., June 19, 1981, p. J 1.

25. Ibid., March 6, 1979, pp. H 2–3.

26. Ibid., April 18, 1977, p. B 6. (According to an April 13, 1977, report in *Pravda,* "the paranoid fear of communism is not only the habitual reflex of the forces of imperialism and cold war in the U.S. and other Western countries. It also is a business calculation, a means of consciously deceiving the public . . . and safe-guarding the capitalist investment of the multi-national corporations.")

27. *FBIS—Soviet Union,* September 30, 1981, p. J 1.

28. Cited in Rothenberg, *The USSR and Africa,* p. 199.

29. *FBIS—Soviet Union,* January 27, 1978, p. B 14; February 22, 1978, pp. B 5–7; February 8, 1979, pp. H 1–3; February 10, 1977, pp. H 2–3; July 5, 1978, p. H 3; August 10, 1978, p. H 5; December 4, 1979, p. J 1; June 3, 1980, p. J 1; July 8, 1980, p. J 3; March 9, 1979, p. J 2; March 12, 1981, pp. J 1–2; July 5, 1978, p. H 3.

30. *FBIS—Soviet Union,* January 26, 1977, p. H 2; March 4, 1977, p. H 4; July 5, 1977, p. B 3; October 5, 1978, p. A 6; May 29, 1979, pp. J 2–3; March 20, 1981, pp. A 4–5; April 20, 1981, p. CC 10.

31. Ibid., May 22, 1979, p. J 1. (For example, TASS asserted in May 1979 that "The Soviet Union again expressed solidarity with the struggle of the people of Namibia for their independence . . . On the Soviet side a resolute support was expressed for the people of Namibia, and the U.N. efforts, and in particular, the activities of the U.N. Council on Namibia aimed at ensuring the independence and territorial integrity of Namibia, at enlisting international efforts for the purposes of rendering all kinds of assistance to the Namibian People in their just struggle.")

32. *FBIS—Soviet Union,* May 22, 1979, p. J 2.

33. Ibid., March 29, 1979, pp. J 2–3.

34. Ibid., January 26, 1977, pp. H 2–3; August 26, 1977, pp. H 1–2; July 24, 1978, p. H 1; August 4, 1978, pp. H 1–2; September 25, 1978, p. H 1; December 15, 1978, pp. H 1–2; January 25, 1980, p. J 3; May 14, 1980, p. J 1.

35. Ibid., January 22, 1979, pp. H 2–3.

36. Ibid., February 3, 1977, p. H 2; February 10, 1977, pp. H 2–3; March 4, 1977, p. H 4; March 29, 1977, pp. H 11–12.

37. Ibid., August 26, 1977, pp. H 1–2; March 8, 1978, pp. H 1–2; February 8, 1979, pp. H 1–2; October 29, 1979, p. J 1; November 13, 1979, pp. J 4–5; December 4, 1979, p. J 1; March 21, 1980, p. J 3.

38. Ibid., August 14, 1980, p. J 1.

39. Ibid., October 29, 1979, p. J 1.

40. Ibid., November 13, 1979, pp. J 4–5.

41. Ibid., July 5, 1977, p. H 2.

42. Ibid., March 29, 1977, pp. H 11–12; July 5, 1977, p. H 2; March 16, 1978, pp. H 5–6; August 31, 1978, p. H 2; March 29, 1979, pp. J 1–2; April 26, 1979, p. J 4; January 25, 1980, pp. J 1–2; July 8, 1980, pp. J 3–4; April 20, 1981, p. CC 10; May 22, 1981, pp. CC 1–2; September 21, 1981, p. J 3.

43. Ibid., August 31, 1978, pp. H 1–2. (For example, Sam Nujoma stated in August 1978 that the USSR "has always sided with our People's just cause. It is giving the most effective moral, political, and other aid and support both to SWAPO and other national liberation movements." Nujoma goes on to state that without "the Soviet Union's aid and support . . . we would have been unable to achieve the results which we have today.")

44. Major publications of the World Peace Council (WPC) include *New Perspectives, Peace Courier, Development and Peace,* and *International Mobilization* (in cooperation with the U.N. Centre against Apartheid) as well as booklets and pamphlets, many of which recount the final report and recommendations of international and regional conferences.

45. Major Afro-Asian People's Solidarity Organization (AAPSO) publications include *Solidarity* and *Development and Socio-Economic Progress.* It also publishes various booklets, many of which report on its international conferences.

46. Information was collected on these fronts and their activities related to southern Africa. Although a secondary issue for these organizations, their propaganda activities mirror those of the WPC and AAPSO. Because of space constraints, this material is not reported here.

47. During 1974 and most of 1975 the major issues in southern Africa included Angola, Mozambique, Rhodesia, and the nature and policies of the South African government and, more broadly, the national liberation struggle against colonialism, neocolonialism, and racism.

48. "Liberation of Namibia and Zimbabwe: Now Africa's First Priority," *Solidarity* (March–April 1976): 24–25.

49. "WPC, UN, and Problems in Southern Africa," *New Perspectives*, no. 1 (1976): 18–19.

50. "WPC and Namibia," *New Perspectives*, no. 1 (1976): 22.

51. "Apartheid is a Grave Menace to World Peace," *New Perspectives*, no. 1 (1976): 23; "Racism and the Struggle Against Racial Discrimination," *Solidarity* (May 1976): 28–34.

52. "U.S. Diplomatic Offensive Against Liberation Struggles in Southern Africa," *New Perspectives*, no. 5 (1976): 26–27.

53. "Growing Links of South Africa with NATO," *New Perspectives*, no. 2 (1976): 37; "MNCs Support Racist South Africa Regime," *New Perspectives*, no. 3 (1976): 19–20.

54. See the June 1976 special issue of *Solidarity* on Zionism, especially the article "Relations Between Zionist Israel and Apartheid," pp. 19–21.

55. "Final Assault for South Africa's Liberation," *New Perspectives*, no. 2 (1977): 19–21.

56. "South Africa's Illegal Occupation of Namibia," *New Perspectives*, no. 1 (1977): 41–43; "Brutal Repression in South Africa," *New Perspectives*, no. 2 (1977): 47.

57. "Political Programme of SWAPO," *Solidarity* (November–December 1977): 26–35.

58. "Apartheid Must Be Totally Destroyed," *New Perspectives*, no. 1 (1979): 26.

59. "Isolate Totally South Africa's Apartheid Regime," *New Perspectives*, no. 6 (1980): 29–30.

60. "Mandatory Sanctions Against South Africa Must be Imposed," *New Perspectives*, no. 2 (1982): 26–27.

61. "Imperialist Power Structure in U.S.A. Protects Racist Regimes in Africa," *New Perspectives*, no. 1 (1979): 30.

62. "Mandatory Sanctions Against South Africa Must Be Imposed in 1982," *New Perspectives*, no. 2 (1982): 26–27; "Impose Sanctions Against Apartheid Regime," *New Perspectives*, no 4 (1982): 21.

63. "Mandatory Sanctions Against South Africa Must Be Imposed," *New Perspectives*, no. 1 (1980): 24–26.

64. "Transnationals Buttress Apartheid Regime in South Africa," *New Perspectives*, nos. 3–4 (1980): 31–33.

65. "Western Powers' Conspiracy to Use Apartheid Regime Against the Third World," *New Perspectives*, no. 4 (1979): 16.

66. Information on these conferences is drawn from *Peace Courier* for the years 1976–1980.

67. The starting point was 1960, when the General Assembly passed the Declaration on the Granting of Independence to Colonial Countries and Peoples (General Assembly Resolution 1514). The resolution became the definitive expression of anticolonialism and a formal recognition that colonialism could no longer be regarded as legitimate. Resolution 1514 was a modified version of a memorandum circulated by the USSR in 1960.

Thus, Moscow played an important role in Resolution 1514. In 1961, the General Assembly, following the Soviet initiative, created (Resolution 1654) a watchdog body—the Committee of 24—to oversee implementation of Resolution 1514. For a discussion of these early developments see Alvin Rubinstein and George Ginsburgs, eds., *Soviet and American Policies in the United Nations* (New York: New York University Press, 1971); Alexander Dallin, *The Soviet Union and the United Nations* (New York: Praeger, 1962); Norman Padelford and Leland Goodrich, eds., *The United Nations in the Balance* (New York: Praeger, 1965); Alvin Rubinstein, *Soviet Foreign Policy Since World War II: Imperial and Global* (Cambridge, Mass.: Winthrop, 1981); John Stoessinger, *The United Nations and the Superpowers* (New York: Random House, 1970); Alvin Rubinstein, *The Soviet Union in International Organizations: Changing Policy Toward Developing Countries, 1953–1963* (Princeton, N.J.: Princeton University Press, 1964); James Mittelman, "Collective Decolonization and the UN Committee of 24," *The Journal of Modern African Studies* 14, no. 1 (1976): 41–64.

    68. The following are excerpts from General Assembly Resolution 2521.

    1. By arousing world public opinion and promoting practical action on the speedy liquidation of colonialism in all its forms and manifestations, and Declaration has played and will play an important role . . . in decolonialization.

    2. All people have the right of self-determination.

    3. Subjugation to alien domination constitutes a serious impediment to the maintenance of international peace and security.

    4. The Assembly declares the further continuation of colonialism . . . a crime which constitutes a violation of the Charter of the United Nations . . . and the principles of international law.

    5. Member states shall render all necessary moral and material assistance to the peoples of colonial territories in their struggle to attain freedom and independence.

    6. The Assembly recommends to the Security Council the widening of the scope of sanctions against Rhodesia, and imposition of complete sanctions on Portugal and South Africa as penalty for their colonialism and racism.

    7. The specialized agencies and international institutions associated with the U.N. shall intensify their activities related to the implementation of . . . the 1960 Declaration.

    8. Representatives of Liberation movements shall be invited . . . to participate in the proceedings . . . of U.N. organs.

    9. The Committee of 24 is directed to continue to send visiting missions to the colonial territories. General Assembly Resolution 2521 (October 12, 1970).

    69. Seymour Finger, "A New Approach to Colonial Problems at the United Nations," *International Organization* 26 (Winter 1972): 143–53. See also his book, *Your Man at the UN* (New York: New York University Press, 1980), p. 145.

    70. Mittelman, "Collective Decolonization," p. 48.

    71. For example, in 1980 the Bulgarian representative to the committee held one of the three vice-chairman positions.

    72. Although we are concerned with the products or activities of the committee, a second avenue for examining the influence of this perspective on the committee's actions

would be to examine the deliberations that take place when it is in session. Actions speak louder than words, but an examination of the Committee of 24's deliberations reveals how the radical Afro-Asian communist bloc coalition's words shape the committee's actions.

73. See the 1980 edition for a detailed account. *U.N. Document A/35/446.*

74. *U.N. Document A/AC,* 109/PV., p. 1086.

75. *Namibia: A Unique Responsibility* (U.N. Department of Public Information/631), p. 23.

76. *U.N. Document A/AC,* 109/PV, p. 968.

77. *U.N. Document A/35/23,* Rev. I, p. 58.

78. *U.N. Document A/9623,* Rev. I, p. 60.

79. *U.N. Document A/AC,* 109PV., p. 1078.

80. *U.N. Document A/AC,* 109/PV., p. 1062.

81. See *The Lagos Declaration for Action Against Apartheid* (U.N. Department of Public Information, 1977).

82. *U.N. Document A/35/23,* Rev. I, pp. 35–36.

83. *U.N. Document A/36/504.*

84. "SWAPO War Communique," *Namibia Bulletin* (October 1980): 14–24.

85. *For Self-Determination and Genuine National Independence for Namibia* (Folder prepared by the U.N. Department of Public Information (DPI), 1982).

86. It is difficult to determine everything the DPI publishes annually. I could locate no inclusive listing of these activities.

87. *U.N. Document A/35/23,* Rev. I, p. 68.

88. See the *United Nations Film and Video Catalogue 1983.*

89. *U.N. Document A/35/23,* Rev. I, p. 70.

90. Ibid.

91. Ibid.

92. *U.N. Document A/C.5/36/75,* Add 27.

93. *U.N. Document A/35/178,* pp. 4–9.

94. *U.N. Document A/AC,* 109/PV. 1173, pp. 22–26.

95. Ibid., p. 37.

96. *U.N. Document A/35/178,* pp. 33–34.

97. Ibid., pp. 34–35.

98. *U.N. Document A/35/178,* Add. I, pp. 2–9.

99. Ibid., pp. 17–34.

100. *U.N. Document A/33/7,* Add. 2.

101. Thomas Gulick, "How the UN Aids Marxist Guerrilla Groups," *Backgrounder* (1982): 8–12.

102. Central Intelligence Agency, *Communist Aid Activities in Non-Communist Less Developed Countries, 1979 and 1954–1979* (Washington, D.C.: CIA, 1980), p. 38.

103. U.S. Arms Control and Disarmament Agency, *World Military Expenditures and Arms Transfers 1972–1982* (Washington, D.C.: GPO, 1984), p. 95.

104. Trong Gilberg, "East European Military Assistance to the Third World," in John F. Copper and Daniel S. Papp, eds., *Communist Nations' Military Assistance* (Boulder, Colo.: Westview Press 1983), pp. 81–84.

105. Roger Kanet, "Soviet Military Assistance to the Third World," in Copper and Papp, *Communist Nations' Military Assistance*, pp. 53–54.

106. U.S. Congress, *The Role of the Soviet Union, Cuba, and East Germany in Fomenting Terrorism*, vol. 1, pp. 660–65.

107. Ibid., pp. 690–706.

108. Ibid., p. 7.

109. Stewart Menaul, *The Border Wars: South Africa's Response* (London: Institute for the Study of Conflict, 1984), pp. 7–8.

110. Raymond W. Copson, "The Soviet Union in Africa: An Assessment," in Walter Laqueur, ed., *The Patterns of Soviet Conduct in the Third World* (New York: Praeger, 1983), p. 198.

111. Peter Vanneman and Martin James, *Soviet Foreign Policy in Southern Africa* (Pretoria: Africa Institute of South Africa, 1982), p. 48.

112. *Regional Risk Assessment: Sub-Saharan Africa* (Alexandria, Va.: Risk International, 1979); Christopher Dobson and Ronald Payne, *The Terrorists: Their Weapons, Leaders and Tactics* (New York: Facts on File, 1979); Samuel Francis, "The Soviet Strategy of Terror," in U.S. Congress, *The Role of the Soviet Union, Cuba, and East Germany in Fomenting Terrorism*, vol. 1.

113. *Congressional Record*, December 12, 1979, p. E6100.

114. U.S. Congress, *The Role of the Soviet Union, Cuba, and East Germany in Fomenting Terrorism*, vol. 1, pp. 55–58.

115. Ibid., p. 59.

116. Central Intelligence Agency, *Communist Aid Activities in Non-Communist Less Developed Countries*, p. 3.

117. George A. Glass, "East Germany in Black Africa," *The World Today* (August 1980); see also Michael Sodaro, "The GDR and the Third World: Supplicant and Surrogate," in Michael Radu, ed., *Eastern Europe and the Third World* (New York: Praeger, 1981).

118. Gilberg, "East European Military Assistance to the Third World," p. 85.

119. For these and related documents see U.S. Congress, *The Role of the Soviet Union, Cuba, and East Germany in Fomenting Terrorism*, vols. 1–2.

120. "Namibia: The Struggle for Final Liberation," *Political Manual of the Namibian Institute of Revolutionary Studies* (Office of the SWAPO Organizing Secretary, 1977).

121. Ibid.

122. U.S. Congress, *The Role of the Soviet Union, Cuba, and East Germany in Fomenting Terrorism*, vol. 1, p. 607.

123. Ibid., pp. 611–18.

124. U.S. Congress, Senate Subcommittee on Security and Terrorism of the Committee on the Judiciary, *Report of the Chairman of the Subcommittee,* 97th Congress, 2d session (Washington, D.C.: GPO, November 1982), pp. 26–27.

125. Cited in Hosmer and Wolfe, *Soviet Policy and Practice,* p. 83.

126. Central Intelligence Agency, *Communist Aid Activities in Non-Communist Less Developed Countries,* pp. 15, 21.

127. Vanneman and James, *Soviet Foreign Policy in Southern Africa,* pp. 38–40.

128. Hosmer and Wolfe, *Soviet Policy and Practice,* p. 71.

129. Ibid., p. 99.

130. Central Intelligence Agency, *Communist Aid Activities in Non-Communist Less Developed Countries,* p. 16.

131. John Starrels, *East Germany: Marxist Mission in Africa* (Washington, D.C.: Heritage Foundation, 1981), p. 28.

132. Central Intelligence Agency, *Communist Aid Activities in Non-Communist Less Developed Countries,* p. 39.

133. Vanneman and James, *Soviet Foreign Policy in Southern Africa,* p. 39.

134. Ibid., p. 48.

135. See Copper and Papp, *Communist Nations' Military Assistance;* Starrels, *East Germany: Marxist Mission in Africa;* U.S. Congress, *The Role of the Soviet Union, Cuba, and East Germany in Fomenting Terrorism;* Vanneman and James, *Soviet Foreign Policy in Southern Africa.*

136. Vanneman and James, *Soviet Foreign Policy in Southern Africa,* p. 47.

137. Totemeyer, *Namibia: Old and New,* p. 198. See also Soggot, *Namibia: The Violent Heritage.*

138. Totemeyer, *Namibia: Old and New,* p. 217.

139. Ibid., p. 208.

140. Adelman, *African Realities,* p. 76.

141. L. H. Gann and Peter Duignan, *Africa South of the Sahara* (Stanford: Hoover Institution Press, 1981), pp. 61–62.

142. *Washington Post,* May 6, 1984, p. A7.

143. Richard Leonard, *South Africa at War* (Westport, Conn.: Lawrence Hill, 1983); Robert S. Jaster, *South Africa in Namibia* (Cambridge, Mass.: Center for International Affairs, Harvard University, 1985); Gerald Bender, James Coleman, and Richard Sklar, *African Crisis Areas and U.S. Foreign Policy* (Berkeley: University of California Press, 1985); Robert Rotberg et al., *South Africa and Its Neighbors* (Lexington, Mass.: Lexington Books, 1985).

Chapter 6

1. *Report of the National Bipartisan Commission on Central America* (Washington, D.C.: U.S. Department of State, January 1984), p. 4.

2. Ibid., chaps. 2–4.

3. Howard J. Wiarda, ed., *Rift and Revolution* (Washington, D.C.: American Enterprise Institute, 1984); Mark Falcoff and Robert Royal, eds., *Crisis and Opportunity* (Washington, D.C.: Ethics and Public Policy Center, 1984); Walter LaFeber, *Inevitable Revolutions: The United States and Central America* (New York: W. W. Norton, 1983); R. Daniel McMichael and John D. Paulus, eds., *Western Hemisphere Stability—The Latin American Connection* (Pittsburgh, Pa.: World Affairs Council of Pittsburgh, 1983); Tom Buckley, *Violent Neighbors: El Salvador, Central America, and the United States* (New York: Time Books, 1984); Martin Siskin, ed., *Trouble in Our Backyard: Central America and the United States in the Eighties* (New York: Pantheon, 1984); Jeffrey Barrett, *Impulse to Revolution in Latin America* (New York: Praeger, 1985).

4. *Report of the National Bipartisan Commission on Central America*, p. 87. For a similar assessment see Jiri Valenta, "The Soviet-Cuban Alliance in Africa and the Caribbean," *The World Today* 37 (February 1981): 715–46; Jiri Valenta, "The USSR, Cuba, and the Crisis in Central America," *Orbis* (Fall 1981); Robert Leiken, "Eastern Winds in Latin America," *Foreign Policy* 42 (Spring 1981): 94–113. For an alternative point of view see William LeoGrande, "The Revolution in Nicaragua: Another Cuba," *Foreign Affairs* 58 (Fall 1979): 28–50; Carla Anne Robbins, *The Cuban Threat* (New York: McGraw-Hill, 1983).

5. Robert Leiken, *Soviet Strategy in Latin America* (Washington Papers) (New York: Praeger, 1982), p. 16.

6. Ibid., pp. 15–18.

7. "To the Detriment of the Struggle of the People," *Pravda*, September 17, 1963. Cited in Leiken, *Soviet Strategy in Latin America*, p. 16.

8. Nikita Khrushchev, "Vital Questions of the Development of the Socialist World System," *World Marxist Review* 61 (September 1962): 18–19.

9. Ernesto ("Che") Guevara, *Guerrilla Warfare* (New York: Vintage Books, 1961); Hugh Thomas, *The Cuban Revolution* (New York: Harper Torchbooks, 1977). For a discussion of attempts to duplicate the Cuban experience in several Latin American countries see Richard Gott, *Guerrilla Movements in Latin America* (Garden City, N.Y.: Doubleday, 1971).

10. Two weeks before John F. Kennedy's inauguration, Khrushchev propounded a theory of wars of national liberation that he asserted the USSR was prepared to sponsor and promote. This speech, which was published in the important theoretical journal, *World Marxist Review*, No. 1 (1961), was reprinted in *Selected Readings: Counter-Insurgency* (Carlisle Barracks, Pa.: U.S. Army War College, 1962).

11. G. Karstag, "Concerning the Development of the Revolutionary Process in Latin America," *Latinskaya Amerika* (Moscow, January–February 1972), trans. in *JPRS/USSR Report* (Latin America) (March 1972): 74.

12. V. Tkachenko, "Latin America: Problems of the Liberation Struggle," *International Affairs*, no. 5 (1972): 10.

13. For his own account of these shortcomings in Bolivia see Ernesto ("Che") Guevara, *The Diary of Che Guevara* (New York: Bantam Books, 1968).

14. See Carlos Marighella, "Minimanual of the Urban Guerrilla," in James Kohl and John Litt, eds., *Urban Guerrilla Warfare in Latin America* (Cambridge, Mass.: The MIT Press, 1974); Abraham Guillen, "Strategy of the Urban Guerrilla," in Walter Laqueur, ed., *The Guerrilla Reader* (New York: Meridian Books, 1977).

15. James Miller, "Urban Terrorism in Uruguay: The Tupamaros," in Bard O'Neill, William Heaton, and Donald Alberts, eds., *Insurgency in the Modern World* (Boulder, Colo.: Westview Press, 1980).

16. "Latin America: The Ideological Front," *World Marxist Review*, No. 4, (1972). The issue was devoted to this theme.

17. Leon Goure and Morris Rothenberg, *Soviet Penetration of Latin America* (Coral Gables, Fla.: University of Miami Press, 1975), p. 133.

18. V. Bushuyev "New Trends in Latin American Armed Forces," *Krasnaya zvezda*, October 3, 1972, trans. in *JPRS/USSR Report* (Latin America, October 1972): 4.

19. John Booth, *The End and the Beginning: The Nicaraguan Revolution* (Boulder, Colo.: Westview Press, 1982); Shirley Christian, *Nicaragua: Revolution in the Family* (New York: Random House, 1985); Thomas Walker, *Nicaragua: The Land of Sandino* (Boulder, Colo.: Westview Press, 1981); Donald Hodges, *Intellectual Foundations of the Nicaraguan Revolution* (Austin: University of Texas Press, 1987).

20. David Nolan, *FSLN* (Coral Gables, Fla.: Institute of Inter-American Studies, University of Miami Press, 1984). See also Hodges, *Intellectual Foundations of the Nicaraguan Revolution*.

21. Harry Vanden, "The Ideology of Insurrection," in Thomas Walker, ed., *Nicaragua in Revolution* (New York: Praeger, 1982).

22. Nolan, *FSLN*, p. 33.

23. FSLN, "Program of the Sandinista Front of National Liberation," *Tricontinental* (March–April 1970).

24. Nolan, *FSLN*, pp. 150–51.

25. "Interview with Jaime Wheelock Román," *Latin American Perspectives* (Winter 1979): 125–26.

26. Nolan, *FSLN*, chaps. 5–6.

27. Humberto Ortega, "The Strategy of Victory," in Tomás Borge et al., *Sandinistas Speak: Speeches and Writings of Nicaragua's Leaders* (New York: Pathfinder Press, 1982), p. 59; "Interview with Daniel Ortega," *Latin American Perspectives* (Winter 1979): 114–18.

28. They argued that broad front alliance amounted to a reversion to the popular front approach rejected in the 1960s. It lacked a class base and would hand the revolution over to bourgeois reformers. See Nolan, *FSLN*, pp. 75–76.

29. Ortega, "Strategy of Victory," p. 57.

30. Taken from FSLN Direccion Nacional, *Nicaragua: On the General Political-Military Platform of the Sandinista Front for the Triumph of the Sandinista Popular Revolution* (Oakland, Calif.: Resistance Publications, 1979).

31. It was widely believed that his assailants were associated with the Somoza regime.

32. Ortega, "Strategy of Victory," p. 68.

33. Various accounts of this period report that the civilian losses were high. See account in Booth, *End and the Beginning*, pp. 162–65.

34. Richard Millett, "Historical Setting," in James Randolph, ed., *Nicaragua: A Country Study* (Washington, D.C.: GPO, 1982), p. 51; Nolan, *FSLN*, pp. 97–98; William Ratliff, "The Future of Latin American Insurgencies," in Georges Fauriol, ed., *Latin American Insurgencies* (Washington, D.C.: Georgetown University Center for Strategic and International Studies and the National Defense University, 1985), pp. 175–77.

35. The Ortega brothers and Victor Tirado represented the TI. Tomás Borge, Bayardo Arce, and Henry Ruiz represented the GPP. The TP was represented by Jaime Wheelock, Luis Carrion, and Carlos Nunez.

36. Oral history interview with Eden Pastora contained in Uri Ra'anan et al., eds., *Hydra of Carnage: International Linkages of Terrorism. The Witnesses Speak* (Lexington, Mass.: Lexington Books, 1986), p. 324.

37. See "Surrogate Actors in the Caribbean: Central America," in Ra'anan et al., *Hydra of Carnage*, pp. 307–60. For an analysis of this and related materials see Richard Shultz, "Soviet Use of Surrogates to Project Power into the Third World," *Parameters* (Autumn 1986). See also Stephen Gorman, "Power and Consolidation in the Nicaraguan Revolution," *Journal of Latin American Studies* 13 (May 1981): 133–49.

38. Oral history interview with Miguel Bolanos Hunter in Ra'anan et al., *Hydra of Carnage*, pp. 309–20.

39. Ibid., pp. 316–17.

40. Ra'anan et al., *Hydra of Carnage*, pp. 314–15.

41. Ibid., pp. 326–28.

42. Ra'anan et al., *Hydra of Carnage*, pp. 314–16.

43. Ibid., pp. 345–58, 391–429.

44. Ra'anan et al., *Hydra of Carnage*, pp. 342–44.

45. Ibid., pp. 340–41.

46. Ernest Evans, "Revolutionary Movements in Central America: The Development of a New Strategy," in Wiarda, *Rift and Revolution*, p. 180.

47. Nolan, *FSLN*, chap. 4. See also Ratliff, "The Future of Latin American Insurgencies" and Georges Fauriol, "Insurgencies and the Latin American Environment," in Fauriol, *Latin American Insurgencies*.

48. Nicholai Leonov, "Nicaragua," *American Latina*, no. 3 (1980): 15.

49. Boris Ponomarev, "Invincibility of the Liberation Movement," *Kommunist* (January 1980), trans. in *JPRS/USSR Report* (March 1980).

50. Daniel Papp, *Soviet Perceptions of the Developing World in the 1980s* (Lexington, Mass.: Lexington Books, 1985), p. 29.

51. Ibid.

52. Ibid.

53. *Foreign Broadcast Information Service Daily Report—Soviet Union*, August 22, 1983, p. K 3. (hereafter cited as *FBIS—Soviet Union*).

54. Ibid., November 23, 1983, p. A 5.

55. Ibid., August 9, 1984, p. K 1.

56. Jerry Hough, *The Struggle for the Third World* (Washington, D.C.: The Brookings Institution, 1986), p. 175.

57. Ibid.

58. Ibid., pp. 175–76.

59. Shafik Jorge Handal, "Na Puti k Svobode," [On the Road to Freedom], *Kommunist* (November 1980): 103.

60. Carlos Gonzales, "Revolution. The Way to It," *World Marxist Review* 22 (October 1979): 10–16; Milton Rene Paredes, "Central America: The Masses Are Beginning to Act," *World Marxist Review* 23 (May 1980): 38–41.

61. Information was collected and analyzed from *Gramma Weekly Review* and *Radio Havana*. Because of space and time constraints, however, this material is not presented.

62. *FBIS—Soviet Union*, September 15, 1978, p. B 7.

63. Ibid., March 1, 1978, p. N 1.

64. Ibid., February 1, 1978, pp. N 1–2.

65. Ibid.

66. Ibid., February 8, 1978, pp. N 1–2.

67. Ibid., September 13, 1978, p. N 1.

68. Ibid., March 15, 1979, pp. N 2–3.

69. Ibid., August 3, 1979. pp. K 1–2.

70. Ibid., March 15, 1979, p. N 3.

71. Ibid., August 3, 1979, pp. K 1–2.

72. Ibid., June 14, 1979, pp. K 1–2.

73. Ibid., February 9, 1979, p. N 1; March 30, 1979, p. K 1.

74. Ibid., February 9, 1979, p. N 1.

75. Ibid., July 26, 1979, pp. K 2–3.

76. Ibid., August 23, 1979, p. K 1.

77. Ibid., July 26, 1979, p. K 1; August 14, 1979, pp. K 1–2; August 21, 1979, pp. K 1–2.

78. Ibid., November 15, 1979, p. A 3.

79. Ibid., October 31, 1979, p. K 1.

80. Ibid., January 9, 1981, p. K 1.

81. Ibid., January 9, 1981, p. K 2.

82. Ibid., January 12, 1981, p. K 1.

83. Ibid., January 13, 1981, pp. K 1–2.

84. Ibid., March 16, 1981, pp. CC 1–2.

85. Ibid., March 30, 1981, p. A 2.

86. Ibid., April 1, 1981, pp. A 8–9.

87. Ibid., March 4, 1982, pp. K 1–2.

88. Ibid., April 28, 1982, pp. K 5–6.

89. Ibid., January 9, 1981, p. K 2.

90. Ibid., February 18, 1982, p. K 1.

91. Ibid., p. K 2.

92. Ibid., January 9, 1981, p. K 2.

93. Ibid., January 16, 1981, p. A 1.

94. Ibid., April 9, 1981, p. K 1.

95. Ibid., March 26, 1981, p. A 10.

96. Ibid., April 13, 1981, p. A 4.

97. Ibid., May 21, 1981, p. A 6.

98. Ibid., March 26, 1981, pp. A 9–11; April 13, 1981, pp. A 4–5; May 8, 1981, p. A 1; May 21, 1981, pp. A 6–7; September 11, 1981, pp. K 1–2.

99. Ibid., November 23, 1983, p. A 5.

100. Ibid., December 26, 1984, p. A 5.

101. Ibid., September 5, 1984, pp. A 4–5.

102. Ibid., December 15, 1984, pp. A 3–4.

103. U.S. Department of State, "Communist Interference in El Salvador," special report no. 80, February 23, 1981, p. 7.

104. See *New Perspectives,* nos. 1–6 (1977).

105. "World Assembly of Builders of Peace," *New Perspectives,* special number (1977).

106. "Intensifying Liberation Struggle in Nicaragua," *New Perspectives,* no. 2 (1979): 39–40.

107. "Deepening Crises in Nicaragua," *New Perspectives,* no. 3 (1979): 44–45.

108. "Resisting Imperialist Intervention in Nicaragua," *New Perspectives,* no. 4 (1979): 24.

109. "El Salvador—Stop Repression," *World Trade Union Movement,* no. 5 (1981), p. 4.

110. Ibid.

111. *Flashes,* April 7, 1979.

112. *Peace Courier* (August 1979).

113. *Peace Courier* (October 1979).

114. *Daily News* (Kingston) June 16, 1980.

115. *Peace Courier* (October, 1980).

116. *International Organization of Journalists' Newsletter* (March 1980).

117. *Havana Radio*, April 15–21, 1981.

118. *World Trade Union Movement*, no. 4 (1982).

119. *World Student News*, no. 7 (1982).

120. *Against Imperialist Aggression and Intervention in Central America and the Caribbean* (Helsinki: World Peace Council, 1982).

121. *Flashes*, no. 12 (1984).

122. *Peace Courier* (May 1984).

123. U.S. Congress, House Permanent Select Committee on Intelligence, *Soviet Active Measures*, 97th Congress, 2d Session (Washington, D.C.: GPO, 1982), p. 203.

124. Ibid. See also John Barron, *KGB Today* (New York: Reader's Digest Press, 1983).

125. U.S. Congress, *Soviet Active Measures*, p. 302.

126. Ibid., p. 292.

127. Ra'anan et al., *Hydra of Carnage*, pp. 345–46.

128. Ibid., pp. 347–48.

129. Ra'anan et al., *Hydra of Carnage*, pp. 350–58.

130. Lars Nord, *Nonalignment and Socialism* (Stockholm: Rabén and Sjögren, 1974); Carlos Romulo, *The Meaning of Bandung* (Chapel Hill: University of North Carolina Press, 1956).

131. Fouad Ajami, "The Fate of Nonalignment," *Foreign Affairs* 59 (Winter 1980/81): 366–85; "Reporter at Large: Conference on Nonaligned," *New Yorker*, October 22, 1979 pp. 145–48; Brian Crozier, "On What Side," *National Review*, October 12, 1979, p. 1282.

132. Romulo, *Meaning of Bandung;* Asian-African Conference, *Selected Documents of the Bandung Conference* (1955).

133. Rozita Levi, "Cuba and the Nonaligned Movement," in Cole Blasier and Carmelo Mesa-Lago, eds., *Cuba in the World* (Pittsburgh, Pa.: University of Pittsburgh Press, 1979); William LeoGrande, "Evolution of the Nonaligned Movement," *Problems of Communism* 29 (January –February 1980): 35–52.

134. *Nonalignment: Fourth Summit* (Algiers, Belgrade, NIP, 1973), p. 37.

135. Jacques Levesque, *The USSR and the Cuban Revolution* (New York: Praeger, 1978); D. Bruce Jackson, *Castro, The Kremlin, and Communism in Latin America* (Baltimore, Md.: Johns Hopkins University Press, 1969); Robert Wesson, *Communism in Central America and the Caribbean* (Stanford: Hoover Institution Press, 1982): W. Raymond Duncan, "Moscow and Latin America: Objectives, Constraints, and Implications," in W. Raymond Duncan, ed., *Soviet Policy in the Third World* (New York: Pergamon Press, 1980).

136. Peter Willetts, *The Non-Aligned in Havana* (New York: St. Martin's Press, 1981), p. 4.

137. Ibid., pp. 9–10.

138. *FBIS—Middle East and North Africa,* August 23, 1976.

139. Willetts, *Non-Aligned in Havana,* pp. 9–10.

140. Ibid., pp. 109–10.

141. Willetts, *Non-Aligned in Havana,* p. 113.

142. Evidence of Grenada's desire for solidarity with the communist bloc and its desire to play a surrogate role on behalf of the USSR can be found in the documents found during the October 1983 intervention by the United States and its eastern Caribbean allies. See documents contained in Ra'anan et al., *Hydra of Carnage,* pp. 361–429.

143. Willetts, *Non-Aligned in Havana,* p. 199.

144. Ibid., p. 113.

145. "Summary of the Final Declaration (6th Summit)," *Journal of Contemporary Asia,* no. 4 (1979); "Havana Summit Shows Up Non-Aligned Divisions," *Roundtable* (January 1980); "Havana Bomb Fails to Explode," *Far East Economic Review,* September 14, 1979.

146. Contained in Ra'anan et al., *Hydra of Carnage,* pp. 418–22.

147. Jean Ziegler, "Cuba, Castro and the Socialist International," *Socialist Affairs,* no. 4 (1981): 134–35.

148. Rui Mateus, "Cuba No," *Socialist Affairs,* no. 1 (1982): 24.

149. Ra'anan et al., *Hydra of Carnage,* pp. 419–20.

150. Ibid., p. 420.

151. Nolan, *FSLN,* pp. 95–6.

152. Christian, *Nicaragua,* p. 95.

153. Ra'anan et al., *Hydra of Carnage,* pp. 323–24.

154. *The Military Balance, 1985–1986* (London: International Institute for Strategic Studies, 1985), p. 152.

155. Ibid.

156. *The Military Balance, 1985–1986* pp. 152–53.

157. Ra'anan et al., *Hydra of Carnage,* pp. 335–39.

158. *New York Times,* July 18, 1983, p. A–10.

159. Ibid.

160. Ra'anan et al., *Hydra of Carnage,* p. 329.

161. *Wall Street Journal,* January 14, 1982, p. 4.

162. *Houston Chronicle,* June 4, 1982, sec. 1, p. 12.

163. Ra'anan et al., *Hydra of Carnage,* pp. 315–16.

164. For Salvadoran guerrillas' description of the network for transferring arms and logistics, see the captured documents contained in the U.S. State Department's Special Report no. 80, "Communist Interference in El Salvador," February 23, 1981. Nineteen

documents were released with this report. Through the words of Unified Revolutionary Directorate and FMLN officials, the documents provide a window into the arms transfer process.

165. *New York Times,* July 12, 1984, p. A–10.

166. *Washington Post,* September 21, 1983, pp. A-29, A-31.

167. Ibid.

168. *Washington Post,* June 18, 1984, pp. A-1, A-19.

169. Miguel Bolanos Hunter, "Nicaragua: A View from Within," in Falcoff and Royal, *Crisis and Opportunity,* p. 394.

170. See Nolan, *FMLN;* Christian, *Nicaragua;* and Douglas Payne, "The 'Mantos' of Sandinista Deception," *Strategic Review* 13 (Spring 1985): 9–20.

171. Cited in Pamela Falk, *Cuban Foreign Policy* (Lexington, Mass.: Lexington Books, 1985), p. 28.

172. David J. Kopilow, *Castro, Israel, and the PLO* (Washington, D.C.: Cuban-American National Foundation, 1984), pp. 10–14; Roberta Goren, *The Soviet Union and Terrorism* (London: Allen & Unwin, 1984), p. 177.

173. Payne, "'Mantos' of Sandinista Deception," pp. 14–15.

174. Ibid., p. 15.

175. Ra'anan et al., *Hydra of Carnage,* p. 324.

176. Ibid., pp. 309–14.

177. Ra'anan et al., *Hydra of Carnage,* pp. 326–27.

178. Ibid., pp. 316–17.

179. *Der Spiegel,* September 28, 1981, p. 7.

180. *New York Times* (March 21, 1985) p. A 3.

181. Ra'anan et al., *Hydra of Carnage,* pp. 317–20.

182. *New York Times,* July 12, 1984, p. A–10.

183. Ra'anan et al., *Hydra of Carnage,* p. 324.

184. U.S. Department of State, "Cuba's Renewed Support for Violence in Latin America," Special Report no. 90, December 14, 1981.

185. Nolan, *FSLN,* pp. 130–31.

186. Ra'anan et al., *Hydra of Carnage,* pp. 315–16.

187. *New York Times,* July 28, 1983, p. A-10; April 11, 1984, pp. A-1–A-8; and July 12, 1984, p. A-10.

188. Ra'anan et al., *Hydra of Carnage,* pp. 319.

189. Ibid.

Chapter 7

1. John Collins, *Green Berets, SEALS and Spetsnaz: U.S. and Soviet Special Military Operations* (New York: Pergamon-Brassey, 1987), p.1.

2. *Constitution (Fundamental Law) of the Union of Soviet Socialist Republics* (Moscow: Novosti Press, 1977).

3. *The Programme of the Communist Party of the Soviet Union* (Moscow: Novosti Press, 1985).

4. Charles Wolf et al., *The Costs of the Soviet Empire* (Santa Monica, Calif.: The Rand Corporation, 1983), p. 19.

Chapter 8

1. David Dean, ed., *Low Intensity Conflict and Modern Technology* (Maxwell Air Force Base, Ala.: Air University Press, 1986); Frank Barnett et al., eds., *Special Operations in U.S. Strategy* (Washington, D.C.: National Defense University Press, 1984); U.S. Department of Defense, *Proceedings of the Low Intensity Warfare Conference* (Washington, D.C.: Department of Defense, January 14–15, 1986).

2. Richard Shultz, "Low Intensity Conflict and U.S. Policy: Regional Threats, Soviet Involvement, and the American Response," in Dean, *Low Intensity Conflict;* Sam Sarkesian, "American Policy on Revolution and Counterrevolution," *Conflict* 5, no. 2 (1984): 137–84; Robert Harkavy and Stephanie Newman, eds., *The Lessons of Recent Wars in the Third World* (Lexington, Mass.: Lexington Books, 1985); William Taylor, Steven Maaranen, and Gerrit Gong, *Strategic Responses to Conflict in the 1980s* (Lexington, Mass.: Lexington Books, 1984).

3. "America's Secret Soldiers: The Buildup of U.S. Special Operations Forces," *The Defense Monitor* 14, no. 2 (1985): 2.

4. Roy Godson, ed., *Intelligence Requirements for the 1980s: Covert Action* (New York: National Strategy Information Center, 1981), chaps. 5, 7.

5. Theodore Shackley, *The Third Option* (New York: Reader's Digest Press, 1981), p. 19.

6. Richard Shultz and Gregory Kozicz, "Unconventional War, Counterinsurgency, and Low Intensity Conflict: The American Experience," unpublished manuscript (1986), pp. 28–37.

7. U.S. Army, "U.S. Army Operational Concept for Low-Intensity Conflict, Army Training and Doctrine Command," U.S. Army Training and Doctrine Command Pamphlet 524-44 (Fort Monroe, Va.: February 10, 1986).

8. "America's Secret Soldiers: The Buildup of U.S. Special Operations Forces," statement of Admiral William J. Crowe, Jr., USN, Chairman of the Joint Chiefs of Staff on *The Reorganization of Special Operations Forces.* House Armed Services Committee Subcommittee on Readiness, July 16, 1986, pp. 1–2.

9. John Collins, *Green Berets, SEALS and Spetsnaz: U.S. and Soviet Special Military Operations* (New York: Pergamon-Brassey 1987).

10. *Los Angeles Times,* November 18, 1984. Cited in "America's Secret Soldiers: The Buildup of U.S. Special Operations Forces," *The Defense Monitor*, p. 3.

11. Godson, *Intelligence Requirements for the 1980s: Covert Action.*

12. Shackley, *Third Option,* pp. 19–20.

13. "Is Covert Action Necessary," *Newsweek,* November 8, 1982, p. 53; "Arguing About Means and Ends," *Time,* April 18, 1983, p. 20; Philip Geyelin, "Covert Action Means Last Resort," *Washington Post,* May 31, 1984, p. A21; "Black Ops. 1963–1983," *Harper's,* April 1984; Arthur Bair et al., "Unconventional Warfare: A Legitimate Tool of Foreign Policy," *Conflict* 4, no. 1 (1983): 59–81.

14. Stephen Hosmer and George Tanham, *Countering Covert Aggression* (Santa Monica, Calif.: The Rand Corporation, 1986); John Waghelstein, "Post-Vietnam Counterinsurgency Doctrine," *Military Review* 65 (May 1985): 42–50; Stephen Hosmer, *Constraints on U.S. Strategy in Third World Conflict* (Santa Monica, Calif.: The Rand Corporation, 1985).

15. Maj. David Decker et al., "U.S. Army Special Operations in Low Intensity Conflict: Today/Tomorrow," unpublished manuscript, 1984.

16. Waghelstein, "Post-Vietnam Counterinsurgency Doctrine"; Tammy Arbuckle, "Same Hardware, Same Tactics, Same Conclusion in El Salvador?," *Armed Forces Journal International* (December 1985): p. 46.; Edward Luttwak, "Notes on Low-Intensity Warfare," *Parameters* 14 (December 1984): 11–18.

17. Hosmer and Tanham, *Countering Covert Aggression;* Harry Summer, "On Joint Doctrine for Low Intensity Conflict" in Dean, *Low Intensity Conflict;* Sam Sarkesian, "Low Intensity Conflict: Concepts, Principles, and Policy Guidelines," *Air University Review* 36 (January–February 1985): 4–23.

18. Andrew Krepinevich, *The Army and Vietnam* (Baltimore, Md.: Johns Hopkins University Press, 1986); Douglas Blaufarb, *The Counterinsurgency Era* (New York: The Free Press, 1977).

19. Uri Ra'anan et al., *Third World Marxist-Leninist Regimes: Strengths, Vulnerabilities and U.S. Policy* (New York: Pergamon-Brassey, 1985).

20. Hosmer and Tanham, *Countering Covert Aggression;* Shirley Christian, *Nicaragua: Revolution in the Family* (New York: Random House, 1985); Stephen Rosenfeld, "The Guns of July," *Foreign Affairs* (Spring 1986).

21. James Russell, "SOF: They Can't Get There From Here," *Military Logistics Forum* (April 1986): 41–49; Neil Livingstone and Terrell Arnold, eds. *Fighting Back: Winning the War Against Terrorism* (Lexington, Mass.: Lexington Books, 1985); Richard Shultz, "Can Democratic Governments Use Military Force in the War Against Terrorism: The U.S. Confrontation with Libya," *World Affairs* 148 (Spring 1986): 205–15.

22. *Wall Street Journal,* June 10, 1986, p. 60.

23. *New York Times,* September 6, 1986, p. A-9; *The Times* (London) August 4, 1986, p. 8.

24. See Amendment to Section 106 of the Goldwater-Nichols Department of Defense Reorganization Act of 1986. This was a compromise of Senate Bill 1224 and House Bill 1011.

25. Collins, *Green Berets, SEALS and Spetsnaz,* p. 44.

Bibliography

Books

Adelman, Kenneth. *African Realities*. New York: Crane, Russak, 1980.

Albright, David, ed. *Communism in Africa*. Bloomington: Indiana University Press, 1980.

Asprey, Robert. *War in the Shadows: The Guerrilla in History*, 2 vols. Garden City, N.Y.: Doubleday, 1975.

Atkinson, James. *The Politics of Struggle*. Chicago: Henry Regnery, 1966.

Barghoorn, Frederick. *Soviet Foreign Propaganda*. Princeton, N.J.: Princeton University Press, 1964.

Barnett, Frank, B. Hugh Tovar, and Richard Shultz, eds. *Special Operations in U.S. Strategy*. Washington, D.C.: National Defense University Press, 1984.

Barrett, Jeffrey. *Impulse to Revolution in Latin America*. New York: Praeger, 1985.

Barron, John. *KGB: Secret World of Secret Agents*. New York: Reader's Digest Press, 1974.

————. *KGB Today*. New York: Reader's Digest Press, 1983.

Becker, Jillian. *The PLO*. New York: St. Martin's Press, 1984.

Bender, Gerald, James Coleman, and Richard Sklar. *African Crisis Areas and U.S. Foreign Policy*. Berkeley: University of California Press, 1985.

Bittman, Ladislav. *The KGB and Soviet Disinformation*. New York: Pergamon-Brassey, 1985.

Blasier, Cole, and Carmelo Mesa-Lago, eds. *Cuba in the World*. Pittsburgh, Pa.: University of Pittsburgh Press, 1979.

Blaufarb, Douglas. *The Counterinsurgency Era*. New York: The Free Press, 1977.

Blechman, Barry, and Stephen Kaplan, eds. *Force Without War*. Washington, D.C.: The Brookings Institution, 1978.

Bock, Edwin A., ed. *Essays on the Case Method in Public Administration*. Chicago: Public Administration Service, 1965.

Booth, John. *The End and the Beginning: The Nicaraguan Revolution*. Boulder, Colo.: Westview Press, 1982.

Borkenau, Franz. *World Communism*. Ann Arbor: University of Michigan Press, 1962.

Braestrup, Peter. *Big Story.* Boulder, Colo.: Westview Press, 1983.

Brandt, Conrad. *Stalin's Failure in China.* New York: Norton, 1958.

Brecher, Michael ed., *Studies in Crisis Behavior.* New Brunswick, N.J.: Transaction Books, 1978.

Brezhnev, Leonid. *Report of the CPSU Central Committee to the 24th Congress of the Communist Party of the Soviet Union.* Moscow: Novosti Press, 1971.

Brodie, Bernard. *War and Politics.* New York: Macmillan, 1973.

Brutents, Karen. *National Liberation Revolutions Today,* 2 vols. Moscow: Progress Publishers, 1977.

Buckley, Tom. *Violent Neighbors: El Salvador, Central America, and the United States.* New York: Time Books, 1984.

Burbage, Paul, et al. *The Air Force in Southeast Asia: Toward a Bombing Halt.* Washington, D.C.: Office of U.S. Air Force History, 1970.

———. *The Battle for the Skies Over North Vietnam, 1964–1972.* Southeast Asia monograph series. Washington, D.C.: Office of U.S. Air Force History, 1976.

Buttinger, Joseph. *Vietnam: A Political History.* New York: Praeger, 1972.

Carr, E. H. *Twilight of the Comintern, 1930–1935.* New York: Pantheon, 1983.

Central Intelligence Agency. *Communist Aid to Less Developed Countries.* Washington, D.C.: CIA, 1976.

———. *Communist Aid Activities in Non-Communist Less Developed Countries, 1979 and 1954–1979.* Washington, D.C.: CIA, 1980.

Charles, Milene. *The Soviet Union in Africa: The History of Soviet Involvement.* Washington, D.C.: University Press of America, 1980.

Christian, Shirley. *Nicaragua: Revolution in the Family.* New York: Random House, 1985.

Chubb, Edmond. *China and Russia.* New York: Columbia University Press, 1971.

Cline, Ray, and Yonah Alexander. *Terrorism: The Soviet Connection.* New York: Crane, Russak, 1984.

Clutterbuck, Richard. *The Long, Long War: Counterinsurgency in Malaya and Vietnam.* New York: Praeger, 1966.

Cobban, Helena. *The Palestinian Liberation Organization.* Cambridge, Eng.: Cambridge University Press, 1984.

Collins, John. *Green Berets, SEALS and Spetsnaz: U.S. and Soviet Special Military Operations.* New York: Pergamon-Brassey, 1987.

Conley, Michael. *The Communist Insurgent Infrastructure in South Vietnam: A Study of Organization and Strategy.* Washington, D.C.: Center for Research in Social Systems, The American University, 1966.

Copper, John F., and Daniel S. Papp, eds. *Communist Nations' Military Assistance.* Boulder, Colo.: Westview Press, 1983.

Crozier, Brian. *The Surrogate Forces of the Soviet Union.* Conflict Studies, no. 92. London: Institute for the Study of Conflict, 1978.

Dailey, Brian D., and Patrick J. Parker, eds., *Soviet Strategic Deception*. Lexington, Mass.: Lexington Books, 1987.

Dallin, Alexander. *The Soviet Union and the United Nations*. New York: Praeger, 1962.

David, Steven. *Third World Coups and International Security*. Baltimore, Md.: Johns Hopkins University Press, 1987.

Dean, David, ed. *Low Intensity Conflict and Modern Technology*. Maxwell Air Force Base, Ala.: Air University Press, 1986.

Doan Van Toai and David Chanoff. *The Vietnamese Gulag*. New York: Simon & Schuster, 1986.

Dobson, Christopher, and Ronald Payne. *The Terrorists: Their Weapons, Leaders and Tactics*. New York: Facts on File, 1979.

Doglione, John et al. *Airpower and the 1972 Spring Invasion*. Southeast Asia Monograph Series. Washington, D.C.: Office of U.S. Air Force History, 1976.

Dommen, Arthur. *Conflict in Laos*. New York: Praeger, 1964.

Donaldson, Robert, ed. *The Soviet Union in the Third World: Successes and Failures*. Boulder, Colo.: Westview Press, 1981.

Dougherty, James, and Robert Pfaltzgraff. *Contending Theories of International Relations*. New York: Harper & Row, 1981.

Dugard, John, ed. *The South West Africa / Namibia Dispute*. Berkeley: University of California Press, 1973.

Duiker, William. *The Rise of Nationalism in Vietnam*. Ithaca, N.Y.: Cornell University Press, 1976.

———. *Vietnam: Nation in Revolution*. Boulder, Colo.: Westview Press, 1983.

Duncan, W. Raymond. *The Soviet Union and Cuba*. New York: Praeger, 1985.

———, ed. *Soviet Policy in Developing Countries*. Waltham, Mass.: Ginn-Blaisdell, 1970.

———, ed. *Soviet Policy in the Third World*. New York: Pergamon, 1980.

Duncanson, Dennis. *Government and Revolution in Vietnam*. London: Oxford University Press, 1968.

Dziak, John J. *Soviet Perception of Military Power: The Interaction of Theory and Practice*. New York: National Strategy Information Center, 1981.

Ebon, Martin. *The Soviet Propaganda Machine*. New York: McGraw-Hill, 1987.

Eckhardt, George. *Command and Control, 1950–1969*. U.S. Army Vietnam Studies. Washington, D.C.: GPO, 1974.

Falcoff, Mark, and Robert Royal, eds. *Crisis and Opportunity*. Washington, D.C.: Ethics and Public Policy Center, 1984.

Falk, Pamela. *Cuban Foreign Policy*. Lexington, Mass.: Lexington Books, 1985.

Fall, Bernard. *The Two Vietnams*. New York: Praeger, 1967.

———. *Vietnam Witness 1953–1966*. New York: Praeger, 1966.

Fauriol, Georges, ed. *Latin American Insurgencies.* Washington, D.C.: The Georgetown University Center for Strategic and International Studies and the National Defense University, 1985.

Feierabend, Ivo, Rosalind Feierabend, and Ted Robert Gurr, eds. *Anger, Violence, and Politics.* Englewood Cliffs, N.J.: Prentice-Hall, 1972.

Finger, Seymour. *Your Man at the UN.* New York: New York University Press, 1980.

Fitzgerald, Frances. *Fire in the Lake: The Vietnamese and the Americans in Vietnam.* Boston: Little, Brown, 1972.

Gann, L. H., and Peter Duignan. *Africa South of the Sahara.* Stanford: Hoover Institution Press, 1981.

Garson, G. David. *Political Science Methods.* Boston: Holbrook Press, 1976.

George, Alexander, David Hall, and William Simons. *The Limits of Coercive Diplomacy.* Boston: Little, Brown, 1971.

George, Alexander, and Richard Smoke. *Deterrence in American Foreign Policy.* New York: Columbia University Press, 1974.

Godson, Roy. *Labor in Soviet Global Strategy.* New York: National Strategy Information Center, 1984.

————, ed. *Intelligence Requirements for the 1980s: Counterintelligence.* New York: National Strategy Information Center, 1981.

————, ed. *Intelligence Requirements for the 1980s: Covert Action.* New York: National Strategy Information Center, 1981.

Golan, Galia. *The Soviet Union and the Palestine Liberation Organization.* New York: Praeger, 1980.

Goren, Roberta. *The Soviet Union and Terrorism.* London: Allen & Unwin, 1984.

Gott, Richard. *Guerrilla Movements in Latin America.* Garden City, N.Y.: Doubleday, 1971.

Goure, Leon, and Morris Rothenberg. *Soviet Penetration of Latin America.* Coral Gables, Fla.: University of Miami Press, 1975.

Graham, Hugh, and Ted R. Gurr, eds. *Violence in America.* New York: Praeger, 1969.

Greene, Thomas. *Comparative Revolutionary Movements.* Englewood Cliffs, N.J.: Prentice-Hall, 1974.

Greenstein, Fred I., and Nelson W. Polsby, eds. *Handbook of Political Science,* vol. 7, *Strategies of Inquiry,* vol. 8, *International Politics.* Reading, Mass.: Addison-Wesley, 1975.

Griffith, Samuel. *Peking and People's War.* New York: Praeger, 1966.

Griffith, William E., ed. *Sino-Soviet Relations 1964–1965.* Cambridge, Mass.: The MIT Press, 1967.

Guevara, Ernesto ("Che"). *Guerrilla Warfare.* New York: Vintage Books, 1961.

————. *The Diary of Che Guevara.* New York: Bantam Books, 1968.

Gurr, Ted Robert. *Why Men Rebel.* Princeton, N.J.: Princeton University Press, 1970.

Gurtov, Melvin. *The First Vietnam Crisis.* New York: Columbia University Press, 1967.

Hagopian, Mark. *The Phenomenon of Revolution*. New York: Dodd, Mead, 1974.

Hahn, Walter, and Alvin Cottrell. *Soviet Shadow Over Africa*. Coral Gables, Fla.: Advanced International Studies Institute, University of Miami, 1976.

Hammer, Ellen. *The Struggle for Indochina*. Stanford: Stanford University Press, 1954.

Harkavy, Robert, and Stephanie Newman, eds. *The Lessons of Recent Wars in the Third World*. Lexington, Mass.: Lexington Books, 1985.

Harrison, James. *The Endless War: Fifty Years of Struggle in Vietnam*. New York: The Free Press, 1983.

————. *The Long March to Power*. New York: Praeger, 1972.

Hazan, Baruch. *Soviet Impregnational Propaganda*. Ann Arbor, Mich.: Ardis, 1982.

Heikal, Mohamed. *The Road to Ramadan*. New York: Quadrangle, 1975.

————. *The Sphinx and the Commissar: The Rise and Fall of Soviet Influence in the Middle East*. New York: Harper & Row, 1978.

Herring, George C. *America's Longest War*. New York: John Wiley & Sons, 1979.

Hodges, Donald. *Intellectual Foundations of the Nicaraguan Revolution*. Austin: University of Texas Press, 1987.

Honey, P. J. *Communism in North Vietnam*. Cambridge, Mass.: The MIT Press, 1966.

Hosmer, Stephen. *Constraints on U.S. Strategy in Third World Conflict*. Santa Monica, Calif.: The Rand Corporation, 1985.

Hosmer, Stephen and George Tanham. *Countering Covert Aggression*. Santa Monica, Calif.: The Rand Corporation, 1986.

Hosmer, Stephen, and Thomas Wolfe. *Soviet Policy and Practice Toward Third World Conflicts*. Lexington, Mass.: Lexington Books, 1983.

Hough, Jerry. *The Struggle for the Third World*. Washington, D.C.: The Brookings Institution, 1986.

Hunt, Richard, and Richard Shultz, eds. *Lessons From an Unconventional War*. New York: Pergamon, 1982.

Huntington, Samuel. *Political Order in Changing Societies*. New Haven, Conn.: Yale University Press, 1968.

Huynh Kim Khanh. *Vietnamese Communism, 1925–1945*. Ithaca, N.Y.: Cornell University Press, 1982.

Israeli, Raphael. *PLO in Lebanon: Selected Documents*. London: Weidenfeld & Nicolson, 1983.

Jackson, D. Bruce. *Castro, the Kremlin, and Communism in Latin America*. Baltimore, Md.: Johns Hopkins University Press, 1969.

Jaster, Robert S. *South Africa in Namibia*. Cambridge, Mass.: Center for International Affairs, Harvard University, 1985.

Jessop, Robert. *Social Order, Reform and Revolution*. New York: Macmillan, 1972.

Johnson, Chalmers. *Revolutionary Change*. Boston: Little, Brown, 1966.

Joint Low-Intensity Project Final Report. *Volume I—Analytical Review of Low-Intensity Conflict.* Fort Monroe, Va.: U.S. Army Training and Doctrine Command, August 1, 1986.

Joshua, Wynfred, and Stephen Gibert. *Arms for the Third World: Soviet Military Aid Diplomacy.* Baltimore, Md.: Johns Hopkins University Press, 1969.

Jukes, Geoffrey. *The Soviet Union in Asia.* Berkeley, Calif.: University of California Press, 1973.

Kanet, Roger, ed. *The Soviet Union and the Developing Nations.* Baltimore, Md.: Johns Hopkins University Press, 1974.

Kaplan, Stephen S., ed. *Diplomacy of Power: Soviet Armed Forces as a Political Instrument.* Washington, D.C.: The Brookings Institution, 1981.

Katz, Mark. *The Third World in Soviet Military Thought.* Baltimore, Md.: Johns Hopkins University Press, 1982.

Kenez, Peter. *The Birth of the Propaganda State.* Cambridge, Eng.: Cambridge University Press, 1985.

Khalidi, Rashid. *Under Siege: PLO Decisionmaking During the 1982 War.* New York: Columbia University Press, 1985.

Khrushchev, Nikita. *Report of the Central Committee of the CPSU to the Twentieth Party Congress.* Moscow: Foreign Language Publishing House, 1956.

Kissinger, Henry. *White House Years.* Boston: Little, Brown, 1979.

Kitson, Frank. *Low Intensity Operations.* Harrisburg, Penn.: Stackpole Press, 1971.

Klinghoffer, Arthur J. *The Angola War: A Study in Soviet Policy in the Third World.* Boulder, Colo.: Westview Press, 1980.

Kohl, James, and John Litt, eds. *Urban Guerrilla Warfare in Latin America.* Cambridge, Mass.: The MIT Press, 1974.

Kopilow, David J. *Castro, Israel, and the PLO.* Washington, D.C.: The Cuban-American National Foundation, 1984.

Krepinevich, Andrew. *The Army and Vietnam.* Baltimore, Md.: Johns Hopkins University Press, 1986.

Kuhn, T. S. *The Structure of Scientific Revolutions.* Chicago: University of Chicago Press, 1970.

Lacouture, Jean. *Vietnam: Between Two Truces.* New York: Vintage, 1966.

LaFeber, Walter. *Inevitable Revolutions: The United States and Central America.* New York: W. W. Norton, 1983.

Lansdale, Edward. *In the Midst of War.* New York: Harper & Row, 1972.

Laqueur, Walter, ed. *The Patterns of Soviet Conduct in the Third World.* New York: Praeger, 1983.

———. *The Guerrilla Reader.* New York: Meridian Books, 1977.

Lebow, Richard N., ed. *Between Peace and War.* Baltimore, Md.: Johns Hopkins University Press, 1981.

Leiken, Robert. *Soviet Strategy in Latin America.* New York: Praeger, Washington Papers, 1982.

Lenin, V. I. *Selected Works,* 3 vols. Moscow: Progress Publishers, 1970.

LeoGrande, William. *Cuba's Policy in Africa, 1959–1980.* Policy Papers in International Affairs: No. 13. Los Angeles, University of California, 1980.

LeoGrande, William, et al. *Cuba in Africa.* Pittsburgh, Pa.: University of Pittsburgh Press, 1980.

Leonard, Richard. *South Africa at War.* Westport, Conn.: Lawrence Hill, 1983.

Levesque, Jacques. *The USSR and the Cuban Revolution.* New York: Praeger, 1978.

Lewy, Guenter. *America in Vietnam.* New York: Oxford University Press, 1968.

Lin Piao. *Long Live the Victory of People's War!.* Peking: Foreign Languages Press, 1965.

Livingstone, Neil and Terrell Arnold, eds. *Fighting Back: Winning the War Against Terrorism.* Lexington, Mass.: Lexington Books, 1985.

Lowenthal, Richard. *Model or Ally? The Communist Powers and the Developing Countries.* New York: Oxford University Press, 1977.

MacFarlane, S. Neil. *Superpower Rivalry and Third World Radicalism: The Idea of National Liberation.* Baltimore, Md.: Johns Hopkins University Press, 1985.

Manchka, Petr. *In the Vanguard of the Revolutionary Struggle in Africa.* Moscow: Political Literature Publishers, 1975.

Mao Tse-tung. *Selected Works of Mao Tse-tung,* 4 vols. Peking: Foreign Language Press, 1965.

Marcum, John. *The Angolan Revolution: Exile Politics and Guerrilla Warfare, 1962–1976.* 2 vols. Cambridge, Mass.: The MIT Press, 1978.

McAlister, John. *Vietnam: The Origins of Revolution.* Garden City, N.J.: Doubleday, 1971.

McLane, Charles. *Soviet Strategies in Southeast Asia.* Princeton, N.J.: Princeton University Press, 1966.

McMichael, R. Daniel, and John D. Paulus, eds. *Western Hemisphere Stability—The Latin American Connection.* Pittsburgh, Pa.: World Affairs Council of Pittsburgh, 1983.

Menaul, Stewart. *The Border Wars: South Africa's Response.* London: Institute for the Study of Conflict, 1984.

Menon, Rajan. *Soviet Power and the Third World.* New Haven, Conn.: Yale University Press, 1986.

Milbank, David. *International and Transnational Terrorism: Diagnosis and Prognosis.* Washington, D.C.: Central Intelligence Agency, 1976.

Miller, Norman, and Roderick Aya, eds. *National Liberation: Revolution in the Third World.* New York: The Free Press, 1971.

Momyer, William W. *Air Power in Three Wars.* Washington, D.C.: Department of the Air Force, 1978.

Moynihan, Daniel P., and Susanne Weaver. *A Dangerous Place*. New York: Berkeley, 1980.

Nixon, Richard. *The Memoirs of Richard Nixon*. New York: Grosset & Dunlap, 1978.

Nolan, David. *FSLN*. Coral Gables, Fla.: Institute of Inter-American Studies, University of Miami Press, 1984.

Nollau, Gunther. *International Communism and World Revolution, History and Methods*. London: Hollis & Carter, 1961.

Nord, Lars. *Nonalignment and Socialism*. Stockholm: Rabén and Sjögren, 1974.

Odeh, B. J. *Errors and Betrayal in Lebanon*. Totowa, N.J.: Biblio, 1985.

O'Neill, Bard. *Armed Struggle in Palestine: A Political Military Analysis*. Boulder, Colo.: Westview Press, 1978.

O'Neill, Bard, William Heaton, and Donald Alberts, eds. *Insurgency in the Modern World*. Boulder, Colo.: Westview Press, 1980.

Osgood, Robert. *Limited War Revisited*. Boulder, Colo.: Westview Press, 1979.

Padelford, Norman, and Leland Goodrich, eds. *The United Nations in the Balance*. New York: Praeger, 1965.

Paige, Jeffrey. *Agrarian Revolution*. Riverside, N.J.: The Free Press, 1975.

Papp, Daniel. *Soviet Perceptions of the Developing World in the 1980s*. Lexington, Mass.: Lexington Books, 1985.

Paret, Peter. *French Revolutionary Warfare from Indochina to Algeria*. New York: Praeger, 1964.

The Pentagon Papers: The Defense Department History of United States Decisionmaking on Vietnam, 4 vols. Boston: Beacon Press, 1971.

Pike, Douglas. *PAVN: People's Army of Vietnam*. San Francisco, Calif.: Presidio Press, 1986.

———. *Viet Cong*. Cambridge, Mass.: The MIT Press, 1966.

———. *War, Peace, and the Viet Cong*. Cambridge, Mass.: The MIT Press, 1970.

Ponomarev, Boris. *Lenin and the World Revolutionary Process*. Moscow: Progress Publishers, 1980.

———. *Some Problems of the Revolutionary Movement*. Moscow: Progress Publishers, 1975.

Porter, Bruce. *The USSR in the Third World Conflicts*. London: Cambridge University Press, 1984.

Possoney, Stefan, and Francis Bouchey. *International Terrorism—The Communist Connection*. Washington, D.C.: American Council on World Freedom, 1978.

Ra'anan, Gavriel D. *International Policy Formation in the USSR*. Hamden, Conn.: Archon Books, 1983.

Ra'anan, Uri, Robert L. Pfaltzgraff, Jr., and Geoffrey Kemp, eds. *Arms Transfers to the Third World*. Boulder, Colo.: Westview Press, 1978.

———. *Projection of Power*. Hamden, Conn.: Archon Books, 1982.

Ra'anan, Uri, Robert L. Pfaltzgraff, Jr., Richard Shultz, Igor Lukes, and Ernst Halperin, eds. *Hydra of Carnage: International Linkages of Terrorism. The Witnesses Speak.* Lexington, Mass.: Lexington Books, 1985.

Ra'anan, Uri, Francis Fukuyama, Mark Falcoff, Sam Sarkesian, and Richard Shultz. *Third World Marxist-Leninist Regimes: Strengths, Vulnerabilities and U.S. Policy.* New York: Pergamon-Brassey, 1985.

Randolph, James, ed. *Nicaragua: A Country Study.* Washington, D.C.: GPO, 1982.

Rejai, Mostafa. *The Comparative Study of Revolutionary Strategy.* New York: David McKay, 1977.

Robbins, Carla Anne. *The Cuban Threat.* New York: McGraw-Hill, 1983.

Rocha, Geisa Maria. *In Search of Namibian Independence: The Limitations of the United Nations.* Boulder, Colo.: Westview Press, 1984.

Roche, John. *The History and Impact of Marxist-Leninist Organizational Theory.* Cambridge, Mass.: Institute for Foreign Policy Analysis, 1984.

Romulo, Carlos. *The Meaning of Bandung.* Chapel Hill: University of North Carolina Press, 1956.

Rose, Clive. *Campaigns Against Western Defense.* London: Macmillan, 1985.

Rosental, Edward. *Mind Conditioning.* Moscow: Novosti Press, 1978.

Rotberg, Robert, Robert Henry Bienen, Robert Legvold, and Gavin Maasdorp. *South Africa and Its Neighbors.* Lexington, Mass.: Lexington Books, 1985.

Rothenberg, Morris. *The USSR in Africa: New Dimensions of Soviet Global Power.* Coral Gables, Fla.: Advanced International Studies Institute, University of Miami, 1980.

Rubinstein, Alvin. *Soviet Foreign Policy Since World War II: Imperial and Global.* Cambridge, Mass.: Winthrop, 1981.

———. *The Soviet Union in International Organizations: Changing Policy Toward Developing Countries, 1953–1963.* Princeton, N.J.: Princeton University Press, 1964.

Rubinstein, Alvin, and George Ginsburgs, eds. *Soviet and American Policies in the United Nations.* New York: New York University Press, 1971.

Sakharov, Vladimir, and Umberto Tosi. *High Treason.* New York: G. P. Putnam's Sons, 1980.

Saivetz, Carol, and Sylvia Woodby. *Soviet–Third World Relations.* Boulder, Colo.: Westview Press, 1985.

Sarkesian, Sam C., ed. *Nonnuclear Conflicts in the Nuclear Age.* New York: Praeger, 1980.

Sarkesian, Sam, and William Scully, eds. *U.S. Policy and Low-Intensity Conflict.* New Brunswick, N.J.: Transaction Books, 1981.

Scott, Harriet Fast, and William Scott. *The Armed Forces of the USSR.* Boulder, Colo.: Westview Press, 1978.

———. *The Soviet Art of War.* Boulder, Colo.: Westview Press, 1982.

Seiler, John, ed. *Southern Africa Since the Portuguese Coup.* Boulder, Colo.: Westview Press, 1980.

Shackley, Theodore. *The Third Option*. New York: Reader's Digest Press, 1981.

Sharp, U.S.G. *Strategy for Defeat: Vietnam in Retrospect*. San Rafael, Calif.: Presidio Press, 1979.

Sharp, U.S.G., and William Westmoreland. *Report on the War in Vietnam*. Washington, D.C.: GPO, 1968.

Shevchenko, Arkady. *Breaking with Moscow*. New York: Knopf, 1985.

Shultz, Richard, and Roy Godson. *Dezinformatsia: Active Measures in Soviet Strategy*. New York: Pergamon-Brassey, 1984.

Shultz, Richard, and Gregory Kozicz. "Unconventional War, Counterinsurgency, and Low Intensity Conflict: The American Experience." Unpublished manuscript, 1986.

Siskin, Martin, ed. *Trouble in Our Backyard: Central America and the United States in the Eighties*. New York: Pantheon, 1984.

Smelser, Neil. *Theory of Collective Behavior*. New York: The Free Press, 1963.

Smoke, Richard. *War: Controlling Escalation*. Cambridge, Mass.: Harvard University Press, 1977.

Snyder, Glenn H., and Paul Diesing. *Conflict Among Nations*. Princeton, N.J.: Princeton University Press, 1977.

Soggot, David. *Namibia: The Violent Heritage*. New York: St. Martin's Press, 1986.

Sokolovskiy, V. D. *Soviet Military Strategy*. Edited and translated by Harriet Fast Scott. New York: Crane, Russak, 1975.

Starrels, John. *East Germany: Marxist Mission in Africa*. Washington, D.C.: Heritage Foundation, 1981.

Sterling, Claire. *The Terror Network*. New York: Holt, Rinehart & Winston, 1981.

Stilwell, Gen. Richard. *The Army's Role in Counterinsurgency*. Declassified report, 1961.

Stoessinger, John. *The United Nations and the Superpowers*. New York: Random House, 1970.

Stone, Julius. *Israel and Palestine: Assault on the Law of Nations*. Baltimore, Md.: Johns Hopkins University Press, 1981.

Summers, Harry. *On Strategy: The Vietnam War in Context*. Carlisle, Pa.: Strategic Studies Institute, U.S. Army War College, 1981.

Sworakowski, Witold. *The Communist International and Its Front Organizations: A Research Guide and Checklist of Holdings in American and European Libraries*. Stanford: Hoover Institution Press, 1965.

Tanham, George. *Communist Revolutionary Warfare: From Vietminh to Viet Cong*. New York: Praeger, 1968.

Taylor, William, Steven Maaranen, and Gerrit Gong. *Strategic Responses to Conflict in the 1980s*. Lexington, Mass.: Lexington Books, 1984.

Thomas, Hugh. *The Cuban Revolution*. New York: Harper Torchbooks, 1977.

Thompson, James C. *Rolling Thunder*. Chapel Hill: University of North Carolina Press, 1980.

Thompson, Robert. *Revolutionary War in World Strategy*. New York: Taplinger, 1970.

Thompson, W. Scott. *Power Projection*. New York: National Strategy Information Center, 1978.

Tolson, John. *Airmobility*. U.S. Army Vietnam Studies. Washington, D.C.: GPO, 1973.

Totemeyer, Gerhard. *Namibia: Old and New*. New York: St. Martin's Press, 1978.

————. *South West Africa / Namibia: Attitudes, Assessments, and Prospects*. Randburg, South Africa: Fokus Suid Publishers, 1977.

Trager, Frank, ed. *Marxism in Southeast Asia*. Stanford: Stanford University Press, 1959.

Trinquier, Roger. *Modern Warfare*. New York: Praeger, 1964.

Ulam, Adam. *The Bolsheviks*. New York: Macmillan 1965.

————. *Expansion and Coexistence: Soviet Foreign Policy 1917–1973*. New York: Praeger, 1974.

Ulyanovsky, Rostislav. *National Liberation*. Moscow: Progress Publishers, 1977.

U.S. Arms Control and Disarmament Agency. *World Military Expenditures and Arms Transfers 1972–1982*. Washington, D.C.: U.S. Arms Control and Disarmament Agency, 1984.

————. *World Military Expenditures and Arms Transfers 1965–1974*. Washington, D.C.: U.S. Arms Control and Disarmament Agency, 1976.

U.S. Congress. House Committee on Foreign Relations. *The Soviet Union and the Third World: A Watershed in Great Power Policy?* 95th Congress, 1st Session. Washington, D.C.: GPO, 1981.

————. House Permanent Select Committee on Intelligence. *Soviet Active Measures*. 97th Congress, 2d Session, Washington, D.C.: GPO, 1982.

————. Senate Foreign Relations Committee. *Hearings on International Terrorism*. 95th Congress, 1st Session. Washington, D.C.: GPO, 1977.

————. Senate Select Committee on Intelligence. *Soviet Presence in the U.N. Secretariat*. 99th Congress, 1st Session, Washington, D.C.: GPO, 1985.

————. Senate Subcommittee on Security and Terrorism of the Committee on the Judiciary. *The Role of the Soviet Union, Cuba, and East Germany, in Fomenting Terrorism in Southern Africa*. Vols. 1 and 2. 97th Congress, 2d Session. Washington, D.C.: GPO, 1982.

————. Senate Subcommittee on Security and Terrorism of the Committee on the Judiciary. *Terrorism: The Role of Moscow and Its Subcontractors*. 97th Congress, 1st Session. Washington, D.C.: GPO, 1981.

U.S. Department of Defense. *Proceedings of the Low Intensity Warfare Conference*. Washington, D.C.: Department of Defense, January 14–15, 1986.

Valkenier, Elizabeth. *The Soviet Union and the Third World, An Economic Bind*. New York: Praeger, 1983.

Vanneman, Peter, and Martin James. *Soviet Foreign Policy in Southern Africa*. Pretoria: Africa Institute of South Africa, 1982.

Walker, Thomas. *Nicaragua: The Land of Sandino.* Boulder, Colo.: Westview Press, 1981.

———, ed. *Nicaragua in Revolution.* New York: Praeger, 1982.

Weinberger, Naomi. *Syrian Intervention in Lebanon.* New York: Oxford University Press, 1986.

Wesson, Robert. *Communism in Central America and the Caribbean.* Stanford: Hoover Institution Press, 1982.

Westmoreland, William C. *A Soldier's Report.* Garden City, N.Y.: Doubleday, 1976.

Whelan, Joseph, and Michael Dixon. *The Soviet Union in the Third World: Threat to World Peace?* New York: Pergamon-Brassey, 1986.

Wiarda, Howard J., ed. *Rift and Revolution.* Washington, D.C.: American Enterprise Institute, 1984.

Willetts, Peter. *The Non-Aligned in Havana.* New York: St. Martin's Press, 1981.

Wolf, Charles, K. C. Yeh, Edmund Brunner, Aaron Gurwitz, and Marilee Lawrence. *The Costs of the Soviet Empire.* Santa Monica, Calif.: The Rand Corporation, 1983.

Wolf, Eric. *Peasant Wars of the Twentieth Century.* London: Faber and Faber, 1973.

Yarborough, Lt. Gen. William. "Needed—A New Approach to Counterinsurgency." Unpublished manuscript, 1968.

Yodfat, Arieh Y., and Yuval Arnon-Ohanna. *PLO Strategy and Tactics.* New York: St. Martin's Press, 1981.

Zagoria, Donald. *Vietnam Triangle.* New York: Pegasus, 1967.

Zimmerman, Ekkhart. *Political Violence, Crises and Revolution.* Cambridge, Mass.: Schenkman, 1983.

Articles

Abu Lughod, Ibrahim. "Flexible Militancy: A Report on the Sixteenth Session of the Palestine National Council." *Journal of Palestinian Studies* 12 (Summer 1983): 25–40.

Ajami, Fouad. "The Fate of Nonalignment." *Foreign Affairs* (Winter 1980 / 81): 366–85.

Albright, David. "Moscow's African Policy of the 1970s." In David Albright, ed., *Communism in Africa.* Bloomington: Indiana University Press, 1980.

Arbuckle, Tammy. "Same Hardware, Same Tactics, Same Conclusion in El Salvador?" *Armed Forces Journal International* (December 1985): 46.

Aspaturian, Vernon. "Soviet Global Power and the Correlation of Forces." *Problems of Communism* 24 (May–June 1980): 1–18.

Bair, Arthur, et al. "Unconventional Warfare: A Legitimate Tool of Foreign Policy." *Conflict* 4, no. 1 (1983): 59–81.

Bialer, Sweryn. "A Wounded Russian Bear Is Dangerous." *Washington Post,* January 22, 1984, pp. C1–C2.

Chassin, L. M. "Guerre en Indochine." *Revue de Defense Nationale* (July 1953): 11–22.

Copson, Raymond W. "The Soviet Union in Africa: An Assessment." In Walter Laqueur, ed., *The Patterns of Soviet Conduct in the Third World*. New York: Praeger, 1983.

Crozier, Brian. "The Surrogate Forces of the Soviet Union." *Conflict Studies,* no. 92 (February 1978).

David, Steven. "Soviet Involvement in Third World Coups." *International Security* 11 (Summer 1986): 3–36.

Davies, James. "The J-Curve of Rising and Declining Satisfaction as a Cause of Some Great Revolutions and a Contained Rebellion." In Hugh Graham and Ted Robert Gurr, eds., *Violence in America*. New York: Praeger, 1969.

Donaldson, Robert. "The Soviet Union and the Third World." *Current History* 81 (October 1982): 313–17.

Dziak, John. "Soviet Intelligence and Security Services in the 1980s: The Paramilitary Dimension." In Roy Godson, ed., *Intelligence Requirements for the 1980s: Counterintelligence*. New York: National Strategy Information Center, 1981.

Eckstein, Harry. "Case Study and Theory in Political Science." In Fred I. Greenstein and Nelson W. Polsby, eds., *Handbook of Political Science,* vol. 7. Reading, Mass.: Addison-Wesley, 1975.

———. "On the Etiology of Internal Wars." In Ivo Feierabend, Rosalind Feierabend, and Ted Robert Gurr, eds., *Anger, Violence, and Politics*. Englewood Cliffs, N.J.: Prentice-Hall, 1972.

Eilan, Arieh. "Conference Diplomacy." *The Washington Quarterly* 4 (Autumn 1981): 24–29.

———. "Soviet Diplomacy in the Third World." In Walter Laqueur, ed., *The Patterns of Soviet Conduct in the Third World*. New York: Praeger, 1983.

Evans, Ernest. "Revolutionary Movements in Central America: The Development of a New Strategy." In Howard Wiarda, Jr., ed., *Rift and Revolution*. Washington, D.C.: American Enterprise Institute, 1984.

Feierabend, Ivo, and Rosalind Feierabend. "Aggressive Behavior Within Politics, 1948–1962: A Cross-National Study." *Journal of Conflict Resolution* 10 (September 1966): 249–71.

Finger, Seymour. "A New Approach to Colonial Problems at the United Nations." *International Organization* 26 (Winter 1972): 143–53.

Fukuyama, Francis. "Gorbachev and the Third World." *Foreign Affairs* 64 (Spring 1986): 715–31.

———. "A New Soviet Strategy." *Commentary* 68 (October 1979): 52–58.

Gilberg, Trong. "East European Military Assistance to the Third World." In John F. Copper and Daniel S. Papp, eds., *Communist Nations' Military Assistance*. Boulder, Colo.: Westview Press, 1983.

Glass, George A. "East Germany in Black Africa." *The World Today* 36 (August 1980): 305–15.

Golan, Galia. "The Soviet Union and the PLO Since the War in Lebanon." *Middle East Journal* 40 (Spring 1986): 285–305.

Gonzalez, Edward. "Complexities of Cuban Foreign Policy." *Problems of Communism* 26 (November–December 1977): 3–9.

Gorman, Stephen. "Power and Consolidation in the Nicaraguan Revolution." *Journal of Latin American Studies* 13 (May 1981): 133–49.

Gottemoeller, Rose. "The Potential for Conflict Between Soviet and Cuban Policies in the Third World." *Conflict* 3, no. 4 (1982): 245–65.

Guillen, Abraham. "Strategy of the Urban Guerrilla." In Walter Laqueur, ed., *The Guerrilla Reader.* New York: Meridian Books, 1977.

Hogard, J. "Guerre Revolutionnaire et Pacification." *Revue Militaire d'Information* (January 1957): 7–24.

Hough, Jerry. "Soviet Policymaking Toward Foreign Communists." *Studies in Comparative Communism* 15 (Autumn 1982): 167–83.

Johnson, Paul. "Barbarous Parliament." *The New Republic,* December 20, 1975, pp. 10–14.

Kaiser, Robert. "The USSR: The Generation That Failed." *Washington Post,* September 23–25, 1984, p. A1.

Kanet, Roger. "Soviet Military Assistance to the Third World." In John F. Copper and Daniel S. Papp, eds., *Communist Nations' Military Assistance.* Boulder, Colo.: Westview Press, 1983.

Khrushchev, Nikita. "Vital Questions of the Development of the Socialist World System." *World Marxist Review* 6 (September 1962): 1–20.

Kitrinos, Robert W. "International Department of the CPSU." *Problems of Communism* 33 (September–October 1984): 47–75.

Klinghoffer, Arthur J. "The Soviet Union and Angola." In Robert Donaldson, ed., *The Soviet Union in the Third World: Successes and Failures.* Boulder, Colo.: Westview Press, 1981.

Lacheroy, Colonel, et al. "La Guerre du Viet-Minh." *Revue Militaire d'Information* (February–March 1957): 25–41.

Lansdale, Edward. "Vietnam: Do We Understand Revolution." *Foreign Affairs* 43 (October 1964): 75–86.

Legum, Colin. "African Outlook Toward the USSR." In David Albright, ed., *Communism in Africa.* Bloomington: Indiana University Press, 1980.

———. "The USSR in Africa: The African Environment." *Problems of Communism* 27 (January–February 1978): 1–19.

Leiken, Robert. "Eastern Winds in Latin America." *Foreign Policy* 42 (Spring 1981): 94–113.

LeoGrande, William. "Evolution of the Nonaligned Movement." *Problems of Communism* 29 (January–February 1980): 35–52.

———. "The Revolution in Nicaragua: Another Cuba." *Foreign Affairs* 58 (Fall 1979): 28–50.

Livingstone, Neil. "Terrorism: The International Connection." *Army* (December 1980): 14–21.

Luttwak, Edward. "Notes on Low-Intensity Warfare." *Parameters* 14 (December 1983): 11–18.

"Manifesto for the Freedom, Independence, National Revival, and Social Progress of the Peoples of Tropical and Southern Africa." *The African Communist*, no. 75 (Fourth Quarter 1978).

Marighella, Carlos. "Minimanual of the Urban Guerrilla." In James Kohl and John Litt, eds., *Urban Guerrilla Warfare in Latin America*. Cambridge, Mass.: The MIT Press, 1974.

Midlarsky, Manus, and Raymond Tanter. "Toward a Theory of Political Instability in Latin America." *Journal of Peace Research* 4, no. 3 (1967): 209–27.

Miko, Francis. "The 27th Soviet Party Congress and the West." *Survival* 28 (July/August 1986): 291–305.

Miller, James. "Urban Terrorism in Uruguay: The Tupamaros." In Bard O'Neill, William Heaton, and Donald Alberts, eds., *Insurgency in the Modern World*. Boulder, Colo.: Westview Press, 1980.

Millett, Richard. "Historical Setting." In James Randolph, ed., *Nicaragua: A Country Study*. Washington, D.C.: GPO, 1982.

Mittelman, James. "Collective Decolonization and the UN Committee of 24." *The Journal of Modern African Studies* 14, no. 1 (1976) 41–64.

Nacht, Michael. "Internal Change and Regime Stability." *Adelphia Papers*, no. 167 (Summer 1981).

O'Neill, Bard. "Insurgency: A Framework for Analysis." In Bard O'Neill, William Heaton, and Donald Alberts, eds., *Insurgency in the Modern World*. Boulder, Colo.: Westview Press, 1980.

———. "Toward a Typology of Political Terrorism." *Journal of International Affairs* 32 (Spring/Summer 1978): 17–42.

Ortega, Humberto. "The Strategy of Victory." In Tomás Borge et al., *Sandinistas Speak: Speeches and Writings of Nicaragua's Leaders*. New York: Pathfinder Press, 1982.

Paredes, Milton Rene. "Central America: The Masses Are Beginning to Act." *World Marxist Review* 23 (May 1980): 38–41.

Payne, Douglas. "The 'Mantos' of Sandinista Deception." *Strategic Review* 13 (Spring 1985): 9–20.

Perera, Judith. "Riding the Bear." *The Middle East* (June 1984): 15–16.

Pilon, Juliana. "The United Nations' Campaign Against Israel." *Backgrounder,* June 16, 1983, pp. 1–21.

———. "The United Nations: Shattered Illusions." *Survey* 27 (Autumn–Winter 1983): 90–111.

Ponomarev, Boris. "Great Vital Force of Leninism." *Kommunist* (May 1980). Translated in *JPRS / USSR Report* (July 1980) 1–19.

————. "Invincibility of the Liberation Movement." *Kommunist* (January 1980). Translated in *JPRS / USSR Report* (March 1980): 11–22.

————. "Universal-Historical Significance of the Great October Socialist Revolution." *Kommunist* (November 1977). Translated in *JPRS / USSR Report* (January 1978): 28–48.

Ra'anan, Gavriel. "Surrogate Forces and Power Projection." Uri Ra'anan, Robert L. Pfaltzgraff, Jr., and Geoffrey Kemp, eds., *Projection of Power.* Hamden, Conn: Archon Books, 1982.

Ra'anan, Uri. "Moscow and the 'Third World.'" *Problems of Communism* 14 (January–February 1965): 22–31.

Rees, David. "Soviet Strategic Penetration of Africa." *Conflict Studies,* no. 77 (November 1977).

Rosenfeld, Stephen. "The Guns of July." *Foreign Affairs* 64 (Spring 1986): 678–714.

Rosser, Richard. "The Soviets and Vietnam: A Tragic Miscalculation?" *South Atlantic Quarterly* 72 (Summer 1973): 385–98.

Russell, James. "SOF: They Can't Get There from Here." *Military Logistics Forum* (April 1986): 41–49.

Sarkesian, Sam. "American Policy on Revolution and Counterrevolution." *Conflict* 5, no. 2 (1984): 137–84.

Schapiro, Leonard. "The International Department of the CPSU: Key to Soviet Policy." *International Journal* 32 (Winter 1976 / 77): 41–55.

————. "The Soviet Union and the PLO." *Survey* 23 (Summer 1977): 193–207.

Sestanovich, Stephen. "Do the Soviets Feel Pinched by Third World Adventures." *Washington Post,* May 20, 1984, p. B1.

Shultz, Richard. "Can Democratic Governments Use Military Force in the War Against Terrorism: The U.S. Confrontation with Libya." *World Affairs* 148 (Spring 1986): 205–13.

————. "Low Intensity Conflict and U.S. Policy: Regional Threats, Soviet Involvement, and the American Response." In David Dean, ed., *Low Intensity Conflict and Modern Technology.* Maxwell Air Force Base, Ala.: Air University Press, 1986.

————. "Psychological Operations in Revolutionary Warfare: Threats, Opportunities and U.S. Policy." In Carnes Lord, ed., *Psychological Operations and Political Warfare in U.S. Strategy.* Washington, D.C.: National Defense University Press, 1988.

————. "The Role of External Forces in Third World Conflict." *Comparative Strategy* 4, no. 2 (1983): 79–111.

————. "Soviet Strategy and Organization: Active Measures and Insurgency." In Dennis Bark, ed., *The Red Orchestra.* Stanford: Hoover Institution Press, 1986.

————. "Soviet Use of Surrogates to Project Power into the Third World." *Parameters* 16 (Autumn 1986): 32–42.

————. "Strategy Lessons From an Unconventional War: The U.S. Experience in Vietnam." In Sam C. Sarkesian, ed., *Nonnuclear Conflicts in the Nuclear Age.* New York: Praeger, 1980.

Simes, Dimitri. "Gorbachev: A New Foreign Policy." *Foreign Affairs: America and the World—1986* 65 (1987): 477–500.

Sodaro, Michael. "The GDR and the Third World: Supplicant and Surrogate." In Michael Radu, ed., *Eastern Europe and the Third World.* New York: Praeger, 1981.

Stevens, Christopher. "The Soviet Union and Angola." *African Affairs* 75 (April 1976): 137–51.

Tanter, Raymond, and Manus Midlarksy. "A Theory of Revolution." *Journal of Conflict Resolution* 11 (September 1967): 154–75.

Teague, Elizabeth. "The Foreign Department of the Central Committee of the CPSU." *Radio Liberty Research Bulletin,* October 27, 1980, pp. 1–47.

Tilly, Charles. "Revolutions and Collective Violence." In Fred I. Greenstein and Nelson W. Polsby, eds., *Handbook of Political Science,* vol. 8. Reading, Mass.: Addison-Wesley, 1975.

Trofimenko, Henry. "America, Russia, and the Third World." *Foreign Affairs* 59 (Summer 1981): 1021–40.

Valenta, Jiri. "The Soviet-Cuban Alliance in Africa and the Caribbean." *The World Today* 37 (February 1981): 45–53.

————. "The USSR, Cuba, and the Crisis in Central America." *Orbis* 25 (Fall 1981): 715–46.

Vanden, Harry. "The Ideology of Insurrection." In Thomas Walker, ed., *Nicaragua in Revolution.* New York: Praeger, 1982.

Vanneman, Peter, and Martin James. "The Soviet Intervention in Angola: Intentions and Implications." *Strategic Review* 4 (Summer 1976): 92–103.

Verba, Sidney. "Some Dilemmas in Comparative Research." *World Politics* 20 (October 1967): 111–27.

Waghelstein, John. "Post-Vietnam Counterinsurgency Doctrine." *Military Review* 65 (May 1985): 42–50.

Wolf, Eric. "Peasant Rebellion and Revolution." In Norman Miller and Roderick Aya, eds., *National Liberation: Revolution in the Third World.* New York: The Free Press, 1971.

Ximenes. "La Guerre Revolutionnaire." *Revue Militaire d'Information* (February–March 1957): 9–22.

Zhdanov, Andry. "The International Situation." In *For a Lasting Peace, For a People's Democracy* (November 10, 1947).

Zimmerman, William. "The Korean and Vietnam Wars." In Stephen S. Kaplan, ed., *Diplomacy of Power: Soviet Armed Forces as a Political Instrument.* Washington, D.C.: The Brookings Institution, 1981.

Special Collections

Oral History Interviews

During 1984 the International Security Studies Program, Fletcher School of Law and Diplomacy, initiated a project to conduct in-depth oral history interviews on the subject of Soviet decisionmaking as it relates to the panoply of protracted and low-intensity operations, including arms transfers, training and advisory support, intelligence, psychological warfare, disinformation and active measures, and the use of surrogate forces. The primary objective is to determine, through information and insights provided by those directly or indirectly involved, how the Soviet Union's decisionmaking and operational apparatus plans these activities, integrates them with East European–bloc and other surrogate (Cuban, Nicaraguan, and so on) capabilities, and implements them in the field. The goal is to ascertain how policy and process proceed from Moscow, through the East European bloc, through the other surrogates to where they are finally implemented. These interviews were used throughout this study and are documented in the notes.

Soviet International Propaganda

In each case-study chapter of this book there is an analysis of Soviet international propaganda as it relates to the specific revolutionary insurgency movement under examination. The primary source material is drawn from Soviet foreign radio broadcasting, which plays a central role in the Soviet international propaganda efforts. External broadcasting greatly expanded during the 1960–1980 period: in 1960, weekly hours of Soviet international broadcasting totaled approximately 1,047; by 1970 this figure doubled, to 2,155; and by 1980 the total hours broadcast per week had reached 2,762. The data for this study are drawn from the *Foreign Broadcast Information Service (FBIS)*. To a lesser extent, I also drew on various other Soviet publications, including *New Times, International Affairs,* and *World Marxist Review.*

International Front Organization Materials

Soviet international front organizations produce a great volume of published materials, which they use for both propaganda and international political mobilization efforts. In the text I refer to the latter as international conference diplomacy. Front publications are the best primary sources with which to investigate these international political actions. In each case-study chapter I examine and analyze how major Soviet front groups employ propaganda, front publications, and international conference political actions to promote the cause of revolutionary insurgencies backed by the USSR. In the notes to each case-study chapter, the various publications of the World Peace Council, Afro-Asian People's Solidarity Organization, World Federation of Trade Unions, and other major fronts are cited (and will not be listed here).

U.N. Documents

Among the political warfare tactics utilized by the USSR to internationally promote the cause of revolutionary insurgent movements is political action within the U.N. and other international and regional organizations. Three of the four case studies in the volume examine this aspect of Soviet strategy as it relates to the U.N. I extensively analyzed a large number of U.N. documents to study this activity of the USSR and its allies and surrogates, including the annual records of such specialized U.N. bodies as the Special Committee on the Situation with Regard to the Implementation of the Declaration on the Granting of Independence to Colonial Countries and Peoples (Committee of 24), the Committee on the Exercise of the Inalienable Rights of the Palestinian People, and the Special Unit on Palestinian Rights. These materials are referenced in the relevant chapters.

Index